International Review of Studies on Emotion

VOLUME 1

Edited by

K. T. STRONGMAN

University of Canterbury,
Christchurch, New Zealand

JOHN WILEY & SONS

Chichester · New York · Brisbane · Toronto · Singapore

Copyright ©1991 by John Wiley & Sons Ltd,
        Baffins Lane, Chichester,
        West Sussex PO19 1UD, England

Other Wiley Editorial Offices

John Wiley & Sons, Inc., 605 Third Avenue,
New York, NY 10158–0012, USA

Jacaranda Wiley Ltd, G.P.O. Box 859, Brisbane,
Queensland 4001, Australia

John Wiley & Sons (Canada) Ltd, 22 Worcester Road,
Rexdale, Ontario M9W 1L1, Canada

John Wiley & Sons (SEA) Pte Ltd, 37 Jalan Pemimpin #05–04.
Block B, Union Industrial Building, Singapore 2057

British Library Cataloguing in Publication Data:
International review of studies on emotion.
  Vol I.
  1. Man. Emotions   EDITED BY: K.T. STRONGMAN (1991)
  152.4

  ISBN 0-471-92831-3

Typeset by Dobbie Typesetting Limited, Tavistock, Devon
Printed and bound by Courier International, Tiptree, Essex

Contents

List of Contributors

James R. Averill
University of Massachusetts, Amherst, USA

Ross W. Buck
University of Connecticut, Storrs, USA

Linda Camras
DePaul University, Chicago, USA

L. Clayton Culver
New School for Social Research, New York, USA

Phoebe C. Ellsworth
University of Michigan, Ann Arbor, USA

Nico H. Frijda
University of Amsterdam, Amsterdam, The Netherlands

Theodore D. Kemper
St John's University, New York, USA

Carroll Izard
University of Delaware, Newark, USA

Carol Z. Malatesta-Magai
Long Island University, New York, USA

Batja Mesquita
University of Amsterdam, Amsterdam, The Netherlands

Jaak Panksepp
Bowling Green University, Bowling Green, USA

James W. Pennebaker
Southern Methodist University, Dallas, USA

Robert Plutchik
Albert Einstein College, New York, USA

Robert J. Robinson
Stanford University, Stanford, USA

Stephanie A. Shields
University of California, Davis, USA

Joep Sonnemans
University of Amsterdam, Amsterdam, The Netherlands

Carol Thomas-Knowles
University of Massachusetts, Amherst, USA

Stephanie Van Goozen
University of Amsterdam, Amsterdam, The Netherlands

Preface

When approached by Michael Coombs of Wiley about the possibility of editing a regular series of volumes on emotion, I sprang at the opportunity. Two reasons drove my enthusiasm. First, and most important, occasions are all too rare when one is persuaded to do something one wishes to do anyway. It struck me as an honour to be asked, and simultaneously to be given a chance to make a further contribution to a field of endeavour to which I had long been committed. In spite of the tribulations of editorship, this view remains unchanged.

The second prompt to my enthusiasm came from what operant psychologists used to term a negative baseline; perhaps they still do. Over some years, I have become increasingly disaffected with the style of journal articles. With few exceptions, cautious journal editors and prissy reviewers, in a misplaced *folie à deux*, have been creating and helping in the evolution of a style of communication that, ironically, becomes ever less communicative. Academic psychology is becoming so precious and refined that it can be followed with interest by increasingly fewer of its collegial members. It is my suspicion that as the journals proliferate and more and more people contribute to them, so they are read by fewer and fewer people. Unless the ideas that an article happens to embrace are of particular significance, the tedious turgidity of the style which editors insist on usually makes it most unattractive. Here, then, was the opportunity to try to bring back a little freedom into style with a publication which, although not quite a journal, was at least tending in that direction.

It was decided that IRSE was to be a biannual publication, each volume to consist of 10–12 invited critical assays on emotion, mainly, but not entirely, from a psychological perspective. Each volume would also contain a contribution from an emotion scholar in a discipline related to psychology. And there would also be a section of shorter position pieces, intended to be both timely and provocative.

It was explained to the potential authors of the first volume that the primary emphasis of the series is theoretical, but the aim is also for the contributors to consider whatever is worthwhile in recent research, rather than to list exhaustively *all* that there is. The authors were encouraged to be relatively free in their writing style and to aim at being speculative and creative as well as precise and scholarly. The goal is to stimulate thought as well as providing something of an overview of recent developments. Above all, the contents of each volume should be interesting to read rather than resembling the shopping lists of references so often found in standard review articles. In short, wherever possible, they should be genuine essays.

To begin with, the aim of the series is to cover the main areas of emotion in which there have been recent developments. These would include, for example, cognition, biology and physiology, social psychology, particularly emphasizing the constructionist viewpoint, and the application of research in emotion to other fields, particularly those involving health and disorder but also perhaps reaching as far as the industrial/organizational world. Although the overall structure of each volume will remain similar, the precise content will vary considerably.

It was suggested to authors that they should aim their level of exposition somewhere between the *Psychological Review* and the *Annual Review of Psychology*, although the style should be less obscure and dense than is typically found in this type of journal. The readership is expected to consist largely of academic scholars, from postgraduate students on. However, the goal is to produce essays that can be read and enjoyed by advanced undergraduates and by academics in areas of psychology other than emotion.

The publishers made it plain that responsibility for the final form of each volume rests with the editor. So far, this responsibility has been taken seriously in order to produce as good a first volume in the series as possible. However, I have not attempted to exert an inhibitory influence on content or style as long as both are of merit. In a scholarly context I believe it is possible to define merit in many different ways and to produce writing of quality which is not necessarily to a narrow formula. In short, within reason, idiosyncracies have been and will be tolerated, not to say encouraged.

In these and other matters I have enjoyed the assistance of a small editorial board consisting of Carroll Izard, Carol Malatesta-Magai, Jaak Panksepp and Klaus Scherer. I thank them all, but particularly Carol Malatesta-Magai, for their invaluable help. They are partly responsible for the better aspects of what follows, but I reassure their friends and colleagues that the responsibility for what some people describe euphemistically as infelicities remains mine.

The order in which the contributions appear reflects little more than an idiosyncratic attempt to achieve an amalgam of fluency and categorization. The ice is broken with two very different views of infant emotion debated by Carol Malatesta-Magai and Carroll Izard on one side and Linda Camras on the other. Following this, the biological aspects of emotion are dealt with by Robert Plutchik in his most recent evolutionary account and then in the form of a tough-minded conceptual neurobiological model by Jaak Panksepp.

A link between the biological and the increasingly dominant cognitive approach is made by Ross Buck via his thoroughly researched consideration of motivation, emotion and cognition. From there, Phoebe Ellsworth takes us through some erudite and fascinating ideas she has been pursuing on cognitive appraisal, a topic often mentioned but rarely developed with this lucidity.

Two contributions are concerned with what might be termed the slower aspects of emotion; as it happens, they both have interesting methodological implications as well. Carol Malatesta-Magai and Clayton Culver consider the links between mood and personality and Nico Frijda and a series of co-workers grapple with the question of the general duration of emotion, partly in an attempt to reintroduce ideas of sentiments and passions into psychology. Stephanie Shields also makes trenchant and timely methodological points in a position piece on emotion and gender. After reading this, mention sex differences at your peril.

Finally, there are contributions in a more applied vein. Rob Robinson and Jamie Pennebaker provide a penetrating integration of emotion and health in a position piece. Assisted by Carol Thomas-Knowles, Jim Averill takes his usual enviably creative and learned social constructionist approach, but on this occasion to the beguiling topic of emotional creativity. Last, but certainly not least, Dave Kemper, a most welcome visitor from sociology, provides an elegantly written overview of the sociology of emotion sufficiently compelling to have a permanent effect on the way in which psychologists look at emotion.

KTS

1 Conceptualizing Early Infant Affect; Emotions as Fact, Fiction or Artifact?

CAROL Z. MALATESTA-MAGAI
Long Island University, 1 University Plaza, Brooklyn, NY 11201, USA

CARROLL IZARD
Department of Psychology, University of Delaware, Newark, DE 19711, USA

LINDA CAMRAS
Department of Psychology, DePaul University, 2323 North Seminary Avenue, Chicago IL 60614, USA

Among social or gregarious animals the ability to communicate is vital to survival, and it is no less the case among humans. However, with humans, the situation is somewhat more complicated. In these special forebrain-hypertrophied, symbol-manipulating animals, there are two systems of communication—the verbal and the non-verbal. Classically, philosophers and other critics of the human condition have tended to view the verbal system as the more important one since it is such a singular psychological phenomenon—and an existentially salient aspect of being human. Within psychology as well, especially developmental psychology, the verbal mode of communication has commanded the greater degree of attention and research.

However, in recent times, the rediscovery of the emotions has stimulated a resurgence of interest in non-verbal communication such as facial expressions and intonational patterns. Moreover, within the field of developmental psychology, emotional expressions are increasingly viewed as fundamental building blocks for the development and elaboration of human social relationships. Consequently, developmentalists have been drawn into the enterprise of charting the course of expressive development during the critical years of infancy and early childhood.

As one surveys the corpus of research literature, it is clear that much headway has been made in advancing the state of our knowledge about expressive development over the past two decades. Equally, it is clear that there are still a great number of unanswered questions, some of which have evolved in the course of coming to terms with earlier ones. The first volume of IRSE seems an opportune time to take stock of the state of the art. In this chapter devoted to developmental aspects of emotion, the editorial board has decided to invite

International Review of Studies on Emotion, Vol. 1. Edited by K. T. Strongman
©1991 John Wiley & Sons Ltd

authors whose research has centered on early development to comment on one of the most controversial of issues—the status of early infant affect. Carol Malatesta, Carroll Izard, and Linda Camras were invited to contemplate the following question: when in development can we legitimately begin to talk about human emotions?

Malatesta and Izard have chosen to examine this question from the perspective of differential emotions theory—a functionalist, developmental evolutionary view which maintains that there are a limited number of discrete emotional expressions, each of which is associated with distinctively different motivational goals and feeling states. The theory furthermore assumes that emotion expressions and their underlying feeling states are prewired, preadapted propensities, but that they operate flexibly in adaptation and development.

Camras, in contrast, presents a modified cognitive/constructivist view which incorporates elements of a dynamical systems framework. The cognitive/constructivist position, as represented by such authors as Alan Sroufe and Michael Lewis, tends to embrace a differentiation theory of emotion. In various versions of this theory, emotions begin as undifferentiated precursor states of distress or general negative affect and differentiate into specific emotions only gradually. Camras' analysis of the relevant literature is that various anomalies in early infant development sustain a differentiation view and she uses concepts from dynamical systems theory to examine and predict transition points.

The following presents the authors' views as well as their replies to one another.

VIEW I: THE PERSPECTIVE FROM DIFFERENTIAL EMOTIONS THEORY

Carol Malatesta-Magai and Carroll Izard

It is only within recent times that scientists and medical practitioners have conceded that it is possible that young babies may experience something like emotional states. The tendency to deny infant affect is nowhere more clearly instantiated than in the medical practice of foregoing anesthesia during surgery on young infants. Established medical canon has been that infants are too immature to experience pain and discomfort. That position has undergone reevaluation lately and corresponding changes in medical policy have resulted.

The denial of sentience in infants has a history reaching back into antiquity, as voiced variously by philosophers, physicians, and, most recently, by psychologists. Dietrich Tiedemann, a professor of Greek and philosophy at the University of Marburg, writing in 1787, cites the then prevalent view that the first quarter of the first year of life was an "age of stupor", though his own painstaking observational study of his infant son convinced him otherwise. In 1903, Sully, a psychologist, was to describe the young infant as "dim and mindless". Within contemporary psychology, the issue of early infant feeling or sentience is still a topic of considerable debate. In this article we take the opportunity to present the view of differential emotions theory (Izard, 1971, 1977; Izard & Malatesta, 1987; Malatesta & Wilson, 1988; Malatesta *et al.*, 1989).

The issue is complex: do infants have feelings? How do we know? Young infants display emotional expressions that show a remarkable resemblance to those of adults, but is there a correspondence between expressive behavior and feeling states during early infancy or is this only something that emerges over time? Are early expressive behaviors artifactual—ie random and meaningless?

Given the present technology and the non-verbal status of the infant, the question of whether or not there is a connection between infants' expressive displays and their feeling states would seem more epistemological that empirical. How can one know another's feeling state in the absence of verbal confirmation? Difficult as this may be to certify even in adults, as Kenny (1963) has illustrated, it is even more problematic in infants. The essential problem is that since feelings are internal states, and thus are unverifiable to another person who does not have access to the same inner world, they are unknowable, unsayable, things— *Undingen*, to use Wittgenstein's term. To be sure, we can never know for certain what another person is really feeling. However, humans are capable of introspecting and reporting their internal states. In the case of emotions, there is an additional source of information about feelings that is not generally available for other internal states—and that is expressive behavior. Although adults can certainly control facial display (and to a lesser extent other non-verbal channels) to mask real internal states, there is enough regular correspondence to make an orderly and reliable social life possible. Social interactants trust that the display behaviors of their social partners communicate their motivational states. One only has to imagine what social life would be like if the pathways between feelings and displays were to become temporarily crossed for certain individuals—disgust being displayed when a smile was expected—to realize how much one depends on the veridicality of display behavior in interpersonal interaction.

Infants present us with additional complications. Although they show expressive behavior, they are unable to report their experiences, and hence it would appear that we have no way of ascertaining what their experiences might be. There is also a fairly well-established bias against attributing human-like capabilities to infants—as though we still believed Haeckel's recapitulation doctrine and viewed infants as adult forms of lower-order animal ancestors. Although we no longer regard infancy as a period devoid of cognitive awareness, we have been less willing to relinquish the idea of infants as affectively vacant. How do we go about ascertaining what the inner motivational and feeling states of infants might be and verifying the connection between state and behavior?

Although classically it has been difficult to get non-verbal organisms to "report" their experiences, researchers have recently had success using a conditioning model with lower organisms. Lubinski and Thompson (1987) induced differential internal states in pigeons via pharmacological agents and trained them to communicate with one another through the exchange of discriminative stimuli. They showed that the performances subsequently generalized to untrained pharmacological agents. The authors suggest that the training procedure used in the study may model the way in which humans learn to report on private events. Although this kind of procedure has not yet been used with infants, it is conceivable that it might profitably be applied towards answering a number of "inner state" questions in the preverbal child.

In the meantime, we can pursue the issue further through the application of ethological approaches to the problem of motivation. Animals, like human infants, cannot speak, but ethologists use other behaviors to make inferences about motivational states. Typically, inferences about the meaning of a behavior are made on the basis of (a) its phylogenetic continuity with similar forms of behaviors in other species (the analogy or homology argument of Eibl-Eibesfeldt, 1979)); (b) its resemblance to other forms of behavior whose meaning is better understood; (c) its context (what precedes and follows it); and (d) in terms of multiple common forms of the behavior, its functional relationship to the ongoing social or physical environment.

There is now a fair degree of consensus that at least some human facial expressions are phylogenetically continuous with those of non-human primates, for example, the human smile is said to be homologous to the silent bared-teeth display of monkeys and apes, and human laughter is thought to be homologous to their relaxed open-mouth display (van Hooff, 1972). In addition, human infant expressions appear to be morphologically and functionally continuous with adult expressions (Izard & Malatesta, 1987; Malatesta et al., 1989).

The questions then become: do infant expressive behaviors occur in the same kinds of contexts as adult expressions (are they preceded (elicited) by the same kinds of events and followed by the same kinds of responses); and (2) are they functionally relevant as adaptations, or are they meaningless, random events? Traditionally, the answer to the first question has been negative and the answer to the second affirmative. The perception that infant expressions are random, unreliable, and unrelated to goals is created, in part, by an adult chauvinism that has clouded our ability to perceive continuities in structure, function and process. Granted, the continuities are sometimes hard to establish; in particular, difficulties abound in dealing with functional equivalence of behavior across developmental epochs—the reciprocal of the problem of task equivalence while assessing abilities across developmental periods. The perception of randomness with respect to facial activity is further reinforced when infants fail to meet certain established criteria—criteria which, as we will see, turn out to be more conservative than is warranted—namely, that categories of infant behavior always be preceded by the same precipitating events and that there be specificity of response to individual events.

Here we attempt to resolve these problems and demonstrate that infant expressive behavior is not random, chaotic, or discontinuous with later expressive behavior. We begin by discussing the concept of elicitors and then consider whether there is specificity of event–emotion linkages—ie whether infant expressions are reliably preceded by certain kinds of specific events, and whether there is selectivity in terms of what kinds of events precipitate what kinds of expressions.

EMOTION–EVENT RELATIONSHIPS: RANDOM OR ORGANIZED?

Virtually all theories of emotion assume that emotions are prompted, released, or triggered in some way, and that different emotions are prompted, released, or triggered by different kinds of circumstances. For example, Lewis and Michalson (1983) describe emotional elicitors as "situations or stimulus events that trigger an organism's emotional receptors" (p. 31). Roseman (1979) has proposed that different emotions are elicited by different "appraisals", or cognitive judgments; the kind of emotion elicited on any given occasion is said to be systematically related to the pattern of appraisals experienced. For example, anger is said to be provoked when there is a conjunction of appraisals about having and losing power, and about negative events. Sadness is provoked when there is a conjunction of appraisals about lack of power, and about negative events. Campos *et al.* (1983) assert that the primary emotions are "evoked in relationship to biological goals, although they eventually are evoked in relationship to socialized goals as well" (p. 820); each primary emotion is identified as having a different combination of goals and appreciations (which are appraisal-like perceptions).

In looking at the various models of emotion that have been proposed in recent times, one is struck by the fact that various systems seem to be specifying similar eliciting conditions for each of the specific emotions found in most basic-emotion lexicons. Fear is typically discussed as being connected with situations of danger, anger with frustrating events, and so on (though the definition of what constitutes a dangerous or frustrating circumstance can vary across cultures, as congruent with the fact of differential socialization practices (Scherer *et al.*, 1988). This degree of consensus is what one would expect in the case of a fairly reliable response system. It is now commonly accepted that the emotion system is part of a prewired evolutionary adaptation (Issacson, 1982; Panksepp, 1982; Eibl-Eibesfeldt, 1979), and orchestrated at the level of the nervous sytem. Cross-cultural research has indicated that certain emotion expressions are recognized and labelled in the same way (Ekman, Sorenson & Friesen, 1969; Izard, 1971), which would appear to support the argument that there is a basic set of "universal" human emotions. Ekman (1973) has cautioned that similarities across cultures could equally be explained by similar species-typical learning experiences; however, newly accumulated data on expression ontogeny now render this explanation untenable (Izard & Malatesta, 1987).

THE "PROBLEM" OF DEVELOPMENTAL DISCONTINUITY

It is only recently that the issue of developmental continuity with respect to elicitors has been addressed. The question is: are people responsive to the same kinds of elicitors in the same kind of way irrespective of developmental status? In the past, this was not much of an issue because emotions theorists tended not to have developmental backgrounds, and because infants were assumed to be devoid of affective capabilities in any case. During the 1970s, as developmental psychology began to grapple with issues of socioemotional development in earnest, researchers were confronted with certain anomalous findings—such as neonatal smiles observed during sleep (Emde, Gaensbauer & Harmon, 1976). In such cases, although the infant was demonstrably showing evidence of "emotional behavior", the behavior seemed unconnected to any appropriate eliciting event. Moreover, in awake infants, smiles could sometimes be elicited by non-social objects such as a bulls-eye design or other unusual visual stimuli. Because these smiles occurred under conditions other than those most adults view as probable and apt cause for smiling (social interaction, humorous interchange), there was a tendency to reject them as behaviors associated with real feeling states. These and other observed oddities in the circumstances that seemed to provoke infant affect not only reinforced the notion that such expressions in infants were developmentally discontinuous at some fundamental affective level with later emotional expressions, but probably also reinforced the bias of those who were inclined to view infants as stuporous, dim, mindless and chaotic.

Today there is still a strong inclination to disqualify infant emotion expressions as indexing true emotion states; this is partly due to the tendency to subordinate emotion to cognition. For example, "genuine" emotions are said not to occur before certain cognitive milestones have been achieved, such as reflective self-awareness (Kagan, 1984). A number of authors have also noted that the elicitors of early infant affective expressions are more likely to involve physical than psychological stimuli (Campos et al., 1983; Lewis & Michalson, 1983; Izard & Malatesta, 1987), which alone would seem to set them apart. In addition, others have pointed out that the band of elicitors for single categories of emotion seems to be broad and unfocused. For example, Camras (1988) kept a diary and film record of the emotional expressive development of her daughter, Justine, during the first year of life. She recorded instances of affective expressions as well as noting the circumstances surrounding the affective events. Camras found that anger expressions occurred under a variety of conditions— when a pacifier was removed, when Justine's bath was drained, at inoculation, during times of hunger, and in response to the cessation of the motion of a swing. Disgust expressions were seen to a wide band of stimuli as well, including head and limb restraint, aspiration of the nostrils, taking vitamins, being poked in the face, and so on. She also found that expressions of anger, sadness, and pain not only occurred in similar situational contexts, but that they also tended to "co-occur" during a single bout of crying. She regards these kind of data, as well as the findings of other studies that seem to show a lack of specificity between eliciting circumstances and emotional expressions, as weakening the argument that these infant facial displays are expressions of discrete emotions as opposed to more generalized negative affect states.

The apparent lack of specificity between elicitor events and emotion expression responses can leave the impression that infant behavior is random and unorganized. This would seem to challenge the differential emotions position that emotion expressions in early infancy index corresponding feeling states, as well as the supposition that there is a fundamental identity in feeling states that lies behind the similar expressive behaviors of adult and infant. Moreover, the observation that young infants tend to react to the physical rather than the psychological parameters of stimuli would seem to support the notion of discontinuity in development, which again would seem to challenge the differential emotions thesis. Nevertheless, a few writers have begun to search for the thread that might link early manifestations of affect with those seen later in development (eg Campos & Barrett, 1984), and indeed, when one applies a different kind of analysis—that derived from an evolutionary-developmental and functionalist perspective—one is led to a different conclusion, as we will show.

Malatesta and Wilson (1988) have proposed that a discrete emotions, functionalist analysis of emotions can illuminate certain developmental paradoxes as well as explain differential personality development. In their conceptualization, the emotion system is part of a behavioral system that has evolved to serve species survival. Emotions mediate crucial adaptive functions largely via a sophisticated signaling system that provides motivational information to the self and to others. While animal ethologists tend to emphasize the value of emotion signals to conspecifics, ie as expressive behaviors that reveal dispositional tendencies, more recent evolutionary-developmental treatments (Buck, 1984; Izard, 1977; Plutchik, 1980) place equal emphasis on the feedback component as a signal to the self and stress the role of emotional information in self-evaluation and self-regulation. Malatesta and Wilson (1988) have specified the self-related and other-related adaptive functions of the signals associated with each of the 10 primary emotions described by Izard (1977). For example, the experience of anger functions in the self system to motivate behavior designed to eliminate barriers; its function within the interpersonal system is to warn others of the possibility of impending attack. In the case of shame/shyness experiences/expressions, the emotion produces behavior (gaze avoidance, hiding, etc) that serves to protect the self against unwanted exposures; as a signal to others, it motivates compliance with the signaler's attempt to achieve privacy. Each emotion expression implies a specific, differentiated functional relationship with respect to self-regulation and with respect to social relationships. Moreover, since emotions evolved as adaptations to environmental incentives or threats and since they ordinarily function in everyday contexts to promote individual goals, elicitors and emotions should be related to one another in a complementary way. Anger is associated with the event of frustration, fear with threats to safety and security, and so on. It should be noted that elicitors are defined in such a way that they connote "families" of environmental events rather than single, specific events. Thus, there is not a one-to-one correspondence between a particular stimulus and a particular emotional response, nor should we expect there to be from a psychoevolutionary point of view. Emotions are complex behavioral patterns, not reflexes. According to MacLean (1973), social behaviors among mammals evolved along with the limbic (emotional) brain. In fact, the emotion system is deeply involved in establishing and maintaining social bonds and social order. As Hinde (1985) has noted, emotions are not isolated events; they are embedded in ongoing social relationships, and involve "negotiation" between interactants.

Izard & Malatesta (1987) have also emphasized the distinction between instinctual and reflexive behavior and note that emotions are more instinct-like than reflex-like in nature (Epstein, 1979). As such, human emotion expressions resemble the modal action patterns of the contemporary ethological literature (Gould, 1982)—that is, species-typical behavior that is coherent and patterned but flexible. Let us take an example of a fixed action pattern in birds. The Australian brush turkey (*Alectura lathami*)—a large bird that inhabits the mountains of the Great Dividing Range—builds a peculiar kind of nest in which it will incubate its eggs. The nest consists of a large, rounded mound of specialized organic material, which will, over time, decompose and in so doing generate heat that will incubate the eggs buried at the mound's center. The bird must adjust the nesting materials from time to time to keep the temperature at a constant 33 degrees. The bird's behavior is both reliable and variable.

It is variable in that the bird adjusts its behavior—adding or subtracting nest material—in response to fluctuations in the temperature of the materials covering the eggs. But the behavior is also reliable, in that the nest building and maintaining behavior is species-specific and is a predictable response following mating. The bird's behavior follows an instinctual program which is flexible within certain limits. But it is hardly reflexive behavior. Nor are the motor patterns associated with human emotion expressions.

If emotions were reflexes, we would be justified in expecting a one-to-one correspondence between a particular elicitor and a particular response. But once we abandon this conception, the lack of correspondence between a particular stimulus and a particular emotional response is no longer surprising nor is it problematic.

Let us return to the "anomalies" in infant affective behavior noted earlier. First, we address the challenge that infant expressive behavior is random and unorganized (ie several different types of stimuli elicit the same emotional expression, and the same stimulus elicits several different emotional expressions). Take the case of disgust. Camras' (1988) report discloses various instances in which the disgust facial display is found to occur under non-equivalent circumstances. For example, Justine is found to show one of the disgust variants under the following situations: being fed sour vitamins, having her face washed, having water poured over her body, having her head restrained, having her nostrils aspirated, having her body or face poked, and being pulled from a reclining position.

In surveying these various eliciting conditions, it becomes apparent that all involve the infant experiencing some kind of intrusive, noxious stimulation (Camras, 1988). As indicated in Malatesta and Wilson's (1988) functionalist analysis, disgust is elicited under conditions of the "perception of noxious substances/individuals". Theories dating back to Darwin (1872) note that the adaptive (functional) significance of the disgust expression is to remove the self from further contact with repellent stimuli. Closing the face, eyes and nostrils, retraction of the body and averting the head produce effects that accomplish this "goal" or adaptation. This kind of analysis seems to work for the other emotions as well. For example, recall that Camras found that her infant's anger expressions occurred in response to pacifier removal, the draining of her bath, inoculation procedures, hunger, and cessation of the motion of swing; all of these events could be collectively understood as engendering the blockage of goals and the creation of frustration—the incentive conditions for anger, as described in the functionalist analysis of Malatesta and Wilson (1988). And so on. Thus, that which at first appears to be a randomness and lack of specificity with respect to elicitors for a given emotion during the time of early infancy is revealed as having its own internal coherency.

What about the finding that common stimuli provoke variable emotional responses? For example, the Camras data indicated that the removal of a pacifier was associated with facial expressions of distress-pain, anger and sadness. The observation of "co-occurrence" leads Camras to entertain the possibility that the facial patterns described for distress-pain, anger and sadness may not be tied to discrete emotions during the first months of life. Instead she suggests that "these expression patterns may become associated with discrete emotions through a process of differentiation", although the process by which emotions become differentiated is not specified. In using the terms "co-occurrence" and "undifferentiated", Camras seems to be implying both that the expressive behaviors are unconnected with differentiated internal states and that the configurational aspects (morphology) of the expressions may be expressed in a less articulated form early on, or in a jumbled-up fashion. In reality, she is chiefly referring to the fact that facial expressions of emotion fluctuate rapidly during a distressful provocation, at least during early infancy (Camras, personal communication). However, since others have raised questions about morphology, and since the term "differentiation" can refer to morphological as well as psychological differentiation, we take up both issues.

Are emotion expressions connected to internal states? The observation that infant facial expressions fluctuate rapidly, even in the case of a "single" stimulus event, is sometimes regarded as evidence that infant expressions and states are not linked; the assumptions is that it is unlikely that infants can be having the kinds of rapid emotional oscillations implied by the facial changes. Interestingly, by requiring infants to feel/express only one emotion in response to an event, we are holding them to standards that we do not impose on adults. For example, it would not seem at all paradoxical for adults to experience, alternately, sadness, anger, and pain during an emotionally disturbing event. Why, then, not infants? The double standard appears attributable to fundamental assumptions about limitations on infant information-processing capabilities. If we assume that emotions are intrinsically related to appraisal processes—as we do in the case of the adult (Roseman, 1979)—the infant would appear to suffer by comparison. On the face of it, infants' cognitive immaturity would seem to exclude the possibility that they could shift rapidly from one emotional state to another. However, it is becoming apparent that the information-processing functions in question need not involve sophisticated cognitive processes. Emotion can be activated by precognitive evaluative processes mediated by subcortical structures (LeDoux, 1987). Furthermore, emerging data are beginning to indicate that infants are capable of fairly well-differentiated appraisals and that their emotional responses are appropriately matched to them. For example, Sullivan and Lewis (1989) have demonstrated that 4–6-month-old infants in a contingency learning task display different patterns of emotion expression at different points in the learning curve. Specifically, the infants showed an increase in their level of interest during the early stage of learning, a decrease in their expression of fear over the acquisition period (in contrast to a control group), an increase in surprise over time until the one minute prior to the peak level of responding, and the appearance of sadness after the acquisition phase. In addition, in learning paradigms that involve conditioning/extinction phases, young infants show an increase in anger expression during the extinction phase (DeCasper & Carstens,

1981). It is worth noting that the emotions of fear, sadness, and surprise have traditionally been viewed as either not in the infant repertoire before six months, or, if behaviorally in the repertoire, functionally irrelevant (eg Sroufe, 1979).

Facial expressions have also been found to relate meaningful to contingency learning in older infants, as in Sullivan and Lewis's (1988) study of one-year-olds, but the rate of change of facial expressions is not as rapid as that found in the younger infant. Similarly, Malatesta and Haviland (1982) found that the rate of infant facial expressions during mother–infant face-to-face play decreases from the third to the sixth month. Thus, emotion expression appears to become less labile over time, but this need not imply that the more rapidly changing expressions are unconnected to state, as we see from Sullivan and Lewis's work.

In summary, emotional expressions during learning and extinction training in both younger and older infants appear related to the infants' appreciation of the relation between their own behavior and other events; as the understanding changes as a function of location in the learning curve, there are corresponding changes in facial expressions. The expressive changes are exactly those one would predict if infants were experiencing their successes and failures in an emotionally differentiated, versus random, fashion. Similarly, it is possible that the fluctuations among various negative states in response to a "single" stimulus event (as in the case of anger, sadness, and pain expressions during a single bout of crying) represent something other than random noise. Once one accepts the possibility that the expressions and states are differentiated (though unstable), one can entertain the possibility that rapid fluctuations in facial expressions are meaningful, and that they can be understood from a developmental perspective. Rapidity of change in infant facial expressions and feeling states may well be linked to the rapidity with which neural activity builds up within the several neural command circuits associated with the primary emotions (Panksepp, 1982, 1986); electrical currents can spread rapidly within the immature nervous system. Tomkins (1962, 1963) has suggested that sadness can readily degrade into anger when the level of neural stimulation is prolonged or especially intense.

Infant emotion expression morphology: random and poorly articulated, or morphologically mature? Recent work from our own laboratories addresses the question of just how differentiated early infant affect expressions are in terms of configuration.

Izard, Haynes and Slomine (submitted) studied the ontogeny of emotion expressions of 2½–9-month-old infants in a variety of positive and negative mother–infant interactions, including play, mother enacting still face, simulated anger and sadness, and mother's contingent and non-contingent responding. The expressions were coded and frequencies of each type of emotion were calculated, summing across subjects and conditions. Four categories of expression—interest, joy, sadness, and anger—were observed with sufficient frequency and duration to be examined systematically. In each category there were four forms of expression: full face (same category signals in upper and lower face), partial (signal or a single emotion in one region of the face and no movement in the other), partly obscured (an emotion signal in one region, while the other region is obscured), and expression blends (simultaneous movement cues or signals for different emotions, usually in different regions of the face).

Results indicated that discrete emotion signals, both full-face and partial expressions for the four emotions, are present by two and a half months of age. More importantly for the issue of differentiation, the data indicated that the frequencies of discrete expressions far exceed the frequency of blends (which holds for all four emotions) and that there is morphological stability of emotion expression across subjects and situations. Thus, at least by as early as two and a half months, these emotion expressions are already morphologically mature; they do not enter the repertoire later in development as more morphologically coordinated or more fully articulated. This would appear to challenge the notion (cf Bridges, 1932) that postneonatal expressive behavior develops from global undifferentiated actions to differentiated, specific ones that eventually become hierarchically organized. This is not to say that there may not be changes in the *frequency* with which the different emotions may be expressed for specific events over different developmental epochs. For example, mother's anger expression or leavetaking would certainly be expected to change in significance for the infant between the ages of two and a half and nine months. Several lines of recent research bear this out (Izard, Haynes & Slomine, submitted; Malatesta *et al.*, 1989). We also point out that the Izard, Haynes and Slomine (submitted) study does not resolve the differentiation issue with respect to *very* early infant affect, since the youngest subjects in that study were already two and a half months old.

In passing, it is worth mentioning that the above study produced data that also have a bearing on the earlier question of the link between expressive behavior and internal state. First, discrete signals of sadness and anger were more frequent under the stress conditions (eg still face) and interest and joy were more frequent in the playful conditions. Secondly, emotion signals entered into blends in a non-random fashion and the patterning in these blends was explainable in terms of the valence of the emotions signaled and the innate and learned relations between them (Izard, 1972; Blumberg & Izard, 1986).

CONCLUDING REMARKS

The perspective that emotion expressions are well differentiated and most likely connected to internal states at an early age seems perfectly compatible with an evolutionary-developmental theoretical framework as well as with Carmichael's (1971) law of prenatal neurogenesis, which states that many physiological and behavioral systems are functionally mature before birth. In addition, we believe that it is more reasonable to assume that state/behavior linkages exist early on than to make this an accomplishment of the maturation of some as yet unspecified developmental process linked to advanced cognition and learning (Lewis & Michalson, 1983; Campos & Barrett, 1984). If we are correct, then the task of development becomes one of learning to control state fluctuations and modulate expressivity. Indeed, research on toddlers indicates that the developmental pattern is one of learning to disconnect state from behavior at the service of affect regulation and impression management (Malatesta *et al.*, 1989).

In summary, once we assume that emotions are instinct-like behaviors, satisfying the same ends as other organized patterns of behavior in lower organisms, it prompts a different level of analysis and sheds a new light on certain developmental anomalies. It is important to look at event–emotion sequences not as instances of stimulus–response reflex arcs, but as instances of functional adaptations to categories of goals. Moreover, goals will be related to categories of stimuli. As such, developmental coherences may be discovered if, despite differences in the physical parameters of stimuli, emotional responses to this collection of stimuli or events are seen as being at the service of a common functional goal.

REFERENCES

Blumberg, S. H. & Izard, C. E. (1986). Discriminating patterns of emotions in 10- and 11-year-old children's anxiety and depression. *Journal of Personality and Social Psychology*, **51**, 852–857.

Bridges, K. M. B. (1932). Emotional development in early infancy. *Child Development*, **3**, 324–341.

Buck, R. (1984). *The Communication of Emotion*. New York: Guilford Press.

Campos, J. J. & Barrett, K. C. (1984) Toward a new understanding of emotions and their development. In C. E. Izard, J. Kagan & R. B. Zajonc (Eds), *Emotions, Cognition, and Behavior*. New York: Cambridge University Press.

Campos, J. J., Barrett, K. C., Lamb, M. E., Goldsmith, H. H. & Stenberg, C. (1983). Socioemotional development. In M. M. Haith (Ed.), P. H. Mussen (Series Ed.), *Handbook of Child Psychology: Vol. 2. Infancy and Developmental Psychobiology*. New York: Wiley, pp. 783–916.

Camras, L. A. (1988). Darwin revisited: An infant's first emotional facial expressions. Paper presented at the International Conference on Infant Studies, Washington, DC.

Carmichael, L. (1971) The onset and early development of behavior. In P. H. Mussen (Ed.), *Carmichael's Manual of Child Psychology*. New York: Wiley.

Darwin, C. (1872/1965). *The Expression of Emotions in Man and Animals*. London: John Murray (Chicago: University of Chicago Press).

DeCasper, A. J. & Carstens, A. A. (1981). Contingencies of stimulation: Effects on learning and motivation. *Infant Behavior and Development*, **4**, 19–35.

Eibl-Eibesfeldt, I. (1979). Human ethology: Concepts and implications for the science of man. *Behavioral and Brain Sciences*, **2**, 1–57.

Ekman, P. (1973). Cross-cultural studies of facial expression. In P. Ekman (Ed.), *Darwin and Facial Expression*. New York: Academic Press, pp. 169–222.

Ekman, P., Sorenson, E. R. & Friesen, W. V. (1969). Pan-cultural elements in facial displays of emotion. *Science*, **164**, 86–88.

Emde, R. N., Gaensbauer, T. J. & Harmon, R. J. (1976). *Emotional Expression in Infancy*. New York: International Universities Press.

Epstein S. (1979). The stability of behavior: I. On predicting most of the people much of the time. *Journal of Personality and Social Psychology*, **37**, 1097–1126.

Gould, J. L. (1982). *Ethology*. New York: W. W. Norton.

Hinde, R. (1985). Expression and negotiation. In G. Zivin (Ed.), *The Development of Expressive Behavior*. New York: Academic Press, pp. 103–116.

Issacson, R. L. (1982). *The Limbic System*. New York: Plenum.

Izard, C. E. (1971). *The Face of Emotion*. New York: Appleton-Century-Crofts.

Izard, C. E. (1972). *Patterns of Emotion: A New Analysis of Anxiety and Depression*. New York: Academic Press.

Izard, C. E. (1977). *Human Emotion*. New York: Plenum.

Izard, C. E., Haynes, O. M. & Slomine, B. S. (submitted). Infants' full-face expressions, partial expressions, and expressive blends during playful and stressful interactions with their mothers.

Izard, C. E. & Malatesta, C. Z. (1987). Perspectives on emotional development: I. Differential emotions theory of early emotional development. In J. D. Osofsky (Ed.), *Handbook of Infant Development* (2nd edn). New York: Wiley, pp. 494–554.

Kagan, J. (1984) The idea of emotion in human development. In C. E. Izard, J. Kagan & R. B. Zajonc (Eds), *Emotions, Cognition, and Behavior*. New York: Cambridge University Press, pp. 38–72.

Kenny, A. (1963). *Action, Emotion and Will*. London: Routledge & Kegan Paul.

LeDoux, J. E. (1987). Emotion. In F. Plum (Ed.), *Handbook of Physiology: The Nervous System*. Washington, DC: American Physiological Society, pp. 419–459.

Lewis, M. & Michalson, L. (1983). *Children's Emotions and Moods: Developmental Theory and Measurement*. New York: Plenum.

Lubinski, D. & Thompson, T. (1987). An animal model of the interpersonal communication of interoceptive (private) states. *Journal of the Experimental Analysis of Behavior*, **48**, 1–15.

MacLean, P. D. (1973). *A Triune Concept of the Brain and Behaviour*. (T. J. Boag & D. Campbell Eds). Toronto: University of Toronto Press.

Malatesta, C. Z., Culver, C., Tesman, J. R. & Shepard, B. (1989). *The Development of Emotion Expression During the First Two Years of Life*. Monograph of the Society for Research in Child Development, No. 219, Vol. 54, Nos. 1–2, pp. 1–104. Chicago: University of Chicago Press.

Malatesta, C. Z. & Haviland, J. M. (1982). Learning display rules: The socialization of emotion expression in infancy. *Child Development*, **53**, 991–1003.

Malatesta, C. Z. & Wilson, A. (1988). Emotion/cognition interaction in personality development: A discrete emotions, functionalist analysis. *British Journal of Social Psychology*, **27**, 91–112.

Panksepp, J. (1982). Toward a general psychobiological theory of emotions. *Behavioral and Brain Sciences*, **5**, 407–468.

Panksepp, J. (1986). The anatomy of emotions. In R. Plutchik & H. Kellerman (Eds), *Emotion: Theory, Research, and Experience*, Vol. 3. New York: Academic Press, pp. 91–124.

Plutchik, R. (1980). *Emotion: A Psychoevolutionary Synthesis*. New York: Harper & Row.

Roseman, I. (1979). Cognitive aspects of emotion and emotional behavior. Paper presented at the meeting of the American Psychological Association, New York.

Scherer, K. R., Wallbott, H. G., Matsumoto, D. & Kudoh, T. (1988) Emotional experience in cultural context: A comparison between Europe, Japan, and the United States. In K. R. Scherer (Ed.), *Facets of Emotion: Recent Research*. Hillsdale, NJ: Erlbaum, pp. 5–30.

Sroufe, L. A. (1979). Socioemotional development. In J. D. Osofsky (Ed.), *Handbook of Infant Development*. New York: Wiley, pp. 462–516.

Sully, J. (1903). *Studies of Childhood*. New York: Appleton.

Sullivan, M. W. & Lewis, M. (1988). Facial expressions during learning in 1-year-old infants. *Infant Behavior and Development*, **11**, 369–374.

Sullivan, M. W. & Lewis, M. (1989). Emotion and cognition in infancy: Facial expressions during contingency learning. *International Journal of Behavioral Development*, **12**, 221–236.

Tiedemann, D. (1787). Die Beobachtungen ueber die Entwickelung der Seelenfaehigkeiten bei Kindern. Translation and commentary by Murchison, C. & Langer, S. (1929), Tiedemann's observations on the development of the mental faculties of children. *Pedigogical Seminary*, **34**, 205–230.

Tomkins, S. S. (1962). *Affect, Imagery, and Consciousness: Vol. 1. The Positive Affects*. New York: Springer.

Tomkins, S. S. (1963). *Affect, Imagery, and Consciousness: Vol. 2. The Negative Affects*. New York: Springer.

van Hooff, J. A. R. A. M. (1972). A comparative approach to the phylogeny of laughter and smiling. In R. A. Hinde (Ed.), *Non-verbal Communication*. Cambridge: Cambridge University Press, pp. 209–38.

VIEW II: A DYNAMICAL SYSTEMS PERSPECTIVE ON EXPRESSIVE DEVELOPMENT

Linda Camras

The position presented here is a modified constructivist view of expression and emotional development. In essence, I will argue that affect-related facial expressions are present in early infancy but during the course of development they are both modified and integrated into larger emotion systems such as we conceive of in adults. At some level, such a premise is shared by both viewpoints presented in this chapter. In fact, one might argue that a considerable proportion of the current controversies on emotion involve matters of emphasis rather than matters of substance. However, beyond this, I will offer some specific hypotheses regarding the affective underpinning of infant emotional expressions that differ from those currently held by many investigators. In addition, I will present a conceptual framework incorporating elements of the dynamical systems perspective in order to account for several phenomena that are currently neglected in developmental theories. At present, my proposals are largely speculative, based on a critical evaluation of the current literature and some provocative observations made during a participant–observer study of my daughter Justine's early expressive development. However, by presenting them, I will be able to highlight some phenomena that must be confronted in formulating a theory of expressive development as well as offer a conceptual perspective that may serve as the basis for future investigation and the development of a more fully articulated theory.

RECENT RESEARCH ON INFANT EMOTIONAL FACIAL EXPRESSIONS

An extensive critical review of recent research on infant emotional facial expressions can be found in Camras, Malatesta and Izard (in press). Here, I will focus on a number of "orphan phenomena" described in that review, ie phenomena whose implications have been largely overlooked in current theories of emotional development. Perhaps most striking is the observation that several emotional expression patterns described for infants (Izard, Dougherty & Hembree, 1983)—in particular, surprise and fear—have only rarely been observed in situations that we believe are eliciting the corresponding emotion. For example, Hiatt, Campos and Emde (1979) found that 10-month-old infants seldom displayed components of the surprise and fear expression patterns although these same infants produced non-facial responses indicating that they were indeed surprised and frightened by the experimental manipulations (eg vanishing toy, impossible toy switch, visual cliff, and stranger approach procedure). Similar fear and surprise eliciting procedures have been used by numerous investigators, yet none has successfully produced the predicted expression patterns with substantial frequency.

Of equal importance, some emotional expression patterns have been observed in a number of situations in which we would not expect the corresponding emotion to be produced. For example, neonates have been observed to smile during REM sleep and many investigators have been reluctant to attribute the emotion of enjoyment/joy to infants under such circumstances (Campos & Barrett, 1984; Emde & Harmon, 1972; Sroufe, 1984; Wolff, 1987). Distress-pain configurations have also been observed in circumstances under which the hypothesized associated affect would seem unlikely. For example, Matias, Cohn and Ross (1989) coded a considerable number of distress-pain expressions in three-month-old infants during face-to-face interactions with their mothers. Similarly, during her first nine weeks, my daughter Justine frequently produced the physical distress-pain pattern in situations that appeared distressing but did not involve physical discomfort or pain (eg pacifier removal). One interpretation of these observations is that the distress-pain pattern is an expression of general distress rather than a specific pain or physical discomfort response (see also Camras, 1988 and Camras, Malatesta & Izard, 1990, for further supporting data and discussion).

The surprise configuration has also been observed in situations during which surprise would seem unlikely. For example, starting at about nine weeks of age, whenever Justine's infant seat was placed on the kitchen table under the soft light of the ceiling lamp, she would wave her arms, make soft panting noises and show the surprise expression pattern. Overall, the observed pattern of contextual occurrence for the "surprise" configuration suggested that the expression reflects excited attention rather than surprise in early infancy. This interpretation is also consistent with proposals made by Peiper (1963), who described the expression as part of a spreading orientation reaction.

In contrast to the distress-pain and surprise pattern, anger configurations have *not* been recorded in clearly inappropriate circumstances in infants. However, a review of the literature (Camras, Malatesta & Izard, in press) shows that the anger pattern is the most common negative facial response produced in *all* studies involving *any* form of negative elicitor presented to infants over two months of age: eg DPT inoculation (Izard *et al.* 1983; Izard, Hembree & Huebner, 1987), arm restraint (Stenberg & Campos, 1988), cookie removal (Stenberg, Campos & Emde, 1983), separation from mother (Hyson & Izard, 1985; Shiller, Izard & Hembree, 1986), contingency interruption (Lewis, Alessandri & Sullivan, 1989), mother's facial and vocal expressions of sadness (Termine & Izard, 1988). Since anger is an emotion that we might expect to occur in a wide range of negative circumstances, possibly infants indeed experienced this discrete emotion in all of the studies examined in the review. However, an alternative possibility is that the anger pattern is actually a general expression of negative affect or distress during the first few months of life. As Hiatt, Campos and Emde (1979) indicated over a decade ago, to demonstrate the discrete emotion status of a facial configuration, one must demonstrate discrimination in its occurrence across situations producing the target emotion versus other emotions from which it is to be discriminated (eg anger vs sadness, or anger vs distress). Alternatively, one perhaps might show discrimination in emotion-related non-facial behaviors accompanying the expressions. For the anger expression pattern, such discriminations have not been demonstrated. Thus the general distress interpretation remains a viable and possibly more parsimonious hypothesis.

In contrast to the anger pattern, the sadness configuration has *never* been observed to be the predominant facial response in any laboratory study of infant facial expression. On the other hand, in small numbers, sadness expressions have been observed in *all* studies that have comprehensively coded infants' facial responses to negative eliciting circumstances (eg Fox & Davidson, 1987; Izard, Hembree & Huebner, 1987; Shiller, Izard & Hembree, 1986; Sullivan & Lewis, 1989; Lewis, Alessandri & Sullivan, 1989). Consistent with this, in my study of Justine, I observed sadness patterns to be shown in the same types of circumstances that elicited the distress-pain and/or anger patterns (eg limb restraint, bath, sour vitamin, pacifier removal). Furthermore, I often observed that Justine cycled among these three facial patterns during a single bout of crying. During these bouts, the patterns of distress-pain and anger versus sadness appeared to be differentially associated with opening versus closing the mouth, and thus the waxing and waning of the crying response. This suggests the hypothesis that the sadness pattern in young infants reflects a waning or relatively low level of distress, while the anger and distress-pain patterns are distress responses of increasing intensity. Further arguments supporting these hypotheses may be found in Camras, Malatesta and Izard (in press) and Oster, Hegley and Nagel (1988).

If the affective bases of some infant facial expressions differ from those proposed by differential emotions theory (Izard & Malatesta, 1987), how can we account for the eventual association of these expression patterns with the discrete emotion labels used by adults? Below I will suggest that a dynamical systems perspective can provide us with some principles that might be useful in our reformulation of developmental theories of emotional expression.

THE DYNAMICAL SYSTEMS PERSPECTIVE

Related to the recent development of chaos theory (Fisher, 1985; Kelso, 1981), the dynamical systems perspective encompasses a number of concepts and principles that may be useful in describing complex systems of various sorts. Developed primarily in the domain of motor behavior and movement science (Kugler, Kelso & Turvey, 1980, 1982), the dynamical systems perspective may be literally applicable in other domains and/or may serve as a useful metaphoric heuristic. This brief presentation cannot hope to serve as a comprehensive treatment of the dynamical approach to systems analysis. However, by way of introduction, I will describe some major principles characterizing this perspective and relate them to emotion.

Dynamical systems theory is an attempt to account for the organized coordination of complex systems involving a nearly infinite number of possible actions or states (Schoner & Kelso, 1988; Thelen, 1985b). For example, in humans, the numerous muscles of the body potentially could be contracted in a virtually limitless number of combinations. Yet body movement appears to involve a far from infinite number of coordinated patterns (Bernstein, 1967; Kelso & Scholz, 1986; Fogel & Thelen, 1987). Of equal importance, however, these coordinated patterns are enacted with an almost infinite number of minor variations in order to accommodate to or compensate for variations in the action context. For example, no two acts of reaching are identical even when one is reaching twice for the same object.

How can one account for the control of such a system? One possibility is to propose a central executive agent or "command program" for each basic pattern that controls the selection and temporal sequencing of the pattern components. However, within the area of movement science (Bernstein, 1967; Kugler, Kelso & Turvey, 1980; Fogel & Thelen, 1987), this solution has not been deemed completely satisfactory, in part because it burdens the controlling mechanism with the need to perform a monumental number of computations to adjust for all the major variations in task demand and action context (eg position of body when reaching is initiated; location and characteristics of reaching target).

Dynamical systems proponents argue that the burden on the executive system can be significantly reduced by assuming a set of lower-order coordinated structures involving synergistic relations among elements. Thus, if any feature of the action context affects one element, the actions of other elements may also be influenced or even determined through their synergistic relationship with the affected component. For example, walking across slightly uneven ground involves synergistic compensations among lower-order muscle groups rather than continuous monitoring and adjustments by a higher-level motor program. Thus, according to the dynamical systems view, behavioral output is as much the result of context and task demands as it is of a central controlling agent (Fogel & Thelen, 1987; Thelen, 1989). Indeed, in radical versions of dynamical systems theory, the central controlling agent may be completely eliminated. In this case, the limit in number of stable coordinated behavior patterns results from limitations in critical contextual parameters rather than limitations in the number of central programs. Thus, to use a favorite dynamical systems dictum: the task assembles the behavior.

With regard to emotion, all current theories recognize emotions to be complex systems involving numerous components that are selected and organized within an emotion "episode". However, the manner in which such selection and organization occur has not been carefully explicated. According to the dynamical systems perspective, emotions may be viewed as self-organizing systems involving elements that may be synergistically related and/or not completely orchestrated by some central program. Thus, within an emotion episode, the components may be assembled in a task-specific manner, with some being determined directly by the context or by other components rather than being mediated through a central emotion-specific "command system". This view emphasizes variation among emotion episodes and would predict that no components (including facial expression) should be recruited for an emotion episode unless they are specifically appropriate (ie adaptive) to the action context. Thus, the dynamical systems perspective would allow us to retain the notion of facial expression as emotion signal while also accommodating recent data suggesting that these expressions sometimes are produced more often in social as opposed to non-social emotion contexts (Fridlund, in press; Gilbert, Fridlund & Sabini, 1987; Kraut & Johnson, 1979; but see also Ekman, 1972; Ekman & Ancoli, 1980). In addition, it can account for recent intriguing findings regarding the recruitment of ANS responses by the voluntary production of emotional facial expressions (Ekman, Levenson & Friesen, 1983; Levenson, Ekman & Friesen, 1990). Within the dynamical systems perspective, this would be a considered an example of synergistic relations among non-central components of the emotion system.

The dynamical systems approach has another important feature that is potentially relevant to the conceptualization of emotion. According to this view, an organism may shift from one major coordination pattern to another because of change in a single critical component (termed the "control parameter"; Kelso & Scholz, 1986; Schoner & Kelso, 1988). For example, when a horse increases its speed of locomotion beyond a critical threshold, its gait shifts from a trot to a gallop. This change is thought to occur because of lower-level anatomical constraints on muscle interactions. Thus, the shift in coordination pattern (termed a "phase shift") results from the dynamic interactions among lower-order elements rather than a shift at higher levels from one central program to another.

With respect to emotion, the notion of a lower-order-component-generated phase shift may be useful in explaining interindividual differences and intraindividual changes in emotional response to similar eliciting situations. For example, when the social context of a transgression becomes public (ie when the control parameter reaches critical threshold), a shift in emotion from guilt to shame may occur. This shift may involve a change in the coping strategies mandated by the context (including intrapsychic strategies) rather than a shift from one primary emotion program to another. Again, the advantage of such a formulation is a reduction in the number of central programs that must be produced. While this limitation is also provided for in other theories (eg the emotion–cognition blends of differential emotions theory; Izard, 1977), the dynamical systems formulation has the additional advantage of potentially motivating a more systematic search for control parameters, ie critical factors determining the selection among alternative emotional responses to similar eliciting situations.

The principles of dynamical systems have been extended into the realm of development to generate a number of novel and interesting proposals about the nature of developmental change (Fogel, 1987; Fogel & Thelen, 1987; Thelen, 1989). Most important, proponents of a dynamical systems perspective have argued that developmental "structures" (eg motor abilities, cognitive abilities) may be viewed as organized coordination patterns that change over time as the values of critical components change. For example, Thelen (Thelen, 1985a; Thelen & Fisher, 1982) has argued persuasively that the onset of walking occurs when the fat:muscle ratio in the infant's legs reach a critical value rather than when a centralized "walking program" matures. Thus the development of new abilities need not imply the emergence or maturation of a new "executive command system" or central orchestrating program.

Of equal importance, the components of an organized coordination pattern or structure (eg leg muscle, fat deposits for walking) may develop independently from each other and at different rates, ie heterochronically (Fogel, 1985; Fogel & Thelen, 1987). Consistent with the findings of early ethological studies of development, dynamical systems theory thus asserts that some components may be present before they function as part of a coordinated system because other critical elements of the system have not yet emerged or have not yet reached the values necessary to catalyze the system's organization and functioning (see also Carmichael's (1970) "law of anticipatory function"). Thelen's work again provides a good example of this heterochronicity in development. In her research, Thelen (Thelen, 1985a; Fogel & Thelen, 1987) has found components of the walking system to be present in the supine kicking of young infants whose fat:muscle ratios have not achieved their critical values. When this "control parameter" reaches threshold, the walking system will be organized and will include the patterned leg alternations observed earlier in supine kicking.

With respect to emotional development, the dynamical systems perspective would argue against the *a priori* acceptance of any particular "innate tie" hypothesis. If heterochronic development occurs, the presence of one component of the emotion system in early infancy (eg facial expression) would not necessarily imply the functioning of the entire system or any of its other critical components (eg an emotion-invariant core of subjective experience). Especially at the earliest stages, empirical evidence is required in order to establish the relationships among components of an emotion system. On the other hand, given the potential for intercomponent recruitment, the dynamical systems perspective does allow for the possibility that such relationships do exist.

A last important feature of the dynamical systems view of development is the notion that control parameters for a system may change with age (Fogel & Thelen, 1987; Thelen, 1989). For example, within the domain of motor development, the fat:muscle ratio in the legs may serve as a control parameter for the onset of walking but may not play a similar role in the development of reaching or stair climbing. With regard to emotional development, this implies that a theory of emotional development should not be wedded to any one factor, be it cognitive development, expressive development or the development of instrumental action capabilities. Changes in any of these factors at different points in time might catalyze a developmental "phase shift", ie a basic restructuring in the organization of emotion responding.

Beyond this, the dynamical systems perspective with its emphasis on heterochronicity and varying control parameters suggests that emotional or expressive development may not be best conceptualized as a unified whole involving synchronous changes across all emotions. Instead, the developmental story may differ for different emotions depending upon their particular affective, cognitive and instrumental constituents.

PROPOSALS REGARDING EXPRESSIVE AND EMOTIONAL DEVELOPMENT

As indicated earlier, based on a critical review of the literature and a contextual analysis of my daughter Justine's expressive development during the first nine weeks, I hypothesized that several emotional expression patterns originate as expressions of states and conditions related to but not identical to discrete emotions described for adults (Camras, 1988; Camras, Malatesta & Izard, in press). Thus, the surprise pattern is proposed to reflect excited attention. The distress-pain, anger, and sadness patterns are variants of a general distress response, with the anger and distress-pain patterns reflecting high intensities of distress and the sadness configuration reflecting a waning or lower intensity of distress. While these emotional expression patterns are thus systematic and do not reflect completely undifferentiated affect in newborn and very young infants, the states with which they are associated do not seem to be accurately or best described using the adult discrete emotion labels.

When and how do these expression patterns become associated with adult emotions? Because an invariant association has often been assumed, relatively little research has been conducted that directly sheds light on this issue. Therefore, I will begin by presenting a set of informal observations of Justine's expressive development after nine weeks of age focusing again on relationships between facial pattern and other observable aspects of emotion such as eliciting context and non-facial/instrumental and vocal behaviors. Subsequently I will use these observations as the basis for proposing a modified conceptualization of expressive development. Importantly, within this conceptualization, different emotional expressions can be seen as taking different courses of development.

Regarding the distress-pain configuration, this expression was observed to decrease in frequency after nine weeks of age. At this time, the distress-pain pattern appeared to be replaced by the anger configuration, which differs from it morphologically only in that the eyes are open for anger and tightly closed for distress-pain. The replacement of the distress-pain by the anger configuration corresponding to a general increase in Justine's tendency to maintain a more alert, open-eyed state. As before (see Camras, Malatesta & Izard, in press), the two expression patterns were produced in similar circumstances and sometimes occurred sequentially as Justine opened and closed her eyes during a single bout of crying. Even at two years, when Justine appeared to be extremely distressed (in both pain and non-pain situations), she occasionally tightly closed her eyes and thus displayed the distress-pain pattern. However, by the end of the first year, this intense response was relatively unusual and the anger configuration was the pattern more typically observed. Thus, the subsequent discussion will focus on use of the anger pattern in comparison to the sadness configuration.

Given Justine's limited action capabilities at nine weeks, not surprisingly I could not observe associations between either the anger or sadness expression pattern and non-facial instrumental actions that might readily be interpreted as indices of specific discrete emotions (eg striking out for anger). As Justine grew older, however, differential patterns of association between facial expressions, non-facial behaviors and also situational appraisals did appear to develop. For example, by two years of age (and probably considerably before that), Justine had developed two separate patterns of response associated with the anger versus sadness facial patterns. The anger-related pattern involved use of the anger facial configuration accompanied by loud crying and often (though not always) intense physical activity that might consist of potentially instrumental actions (eg grabbing a desired object, hitting an agent of frustration) or less potentially effective behaviors (eg waving her arms but not actually striking at the frustrating agent). The sadness-related response pattern involved the sadness facial expression, more restrained sobbing, and an absence of body activity or even a dramatic collapse to the floor (the "swooning response"). These patterns were sometimes elicited by similar frustrating events (eg being forbidden access to an object or activity) and seemed to reflect differences in arousal or intensity of distress or a "decision" to take an active versus passive approach to dealing with the frustration. However, gradually, Justine developed a tendency to display the sadness pattern during circumstances in which she knew from experience that the situation would not be altered to her satisfaction (eg having to hold mother's hand when crossing the street). Similarly, within the same situational episode, Justine often switched from the anger to the sadness pattern after a prolonged but ineffectual display of anger. Thus, by two years, Justine appeared to develop somewhat cohesive patterns of situation appraisal, facial expression and body activity that differentiated anger from sadness and seemed compatible with our adult notions of the distinction between these two emotions.

Nevertheless, even at two years, Justine's use of the anger pattern often seemed more consistent with a general distress rather than an anger interpretation. For example, after accidentally bumping an object and hurting herself, Justine often cried and turned to her mother for comfort, displaying a distress-pain to anger pattern sequence similar to that described by Izard in his inoculation studies (Izard, Hembree & Huebner, 1987). Although Justine faced her mother while showing the anger configuration, it seemed unlikely that mother was viewed as the culpable agent. Furthermore, Justine displayed no anger-indicating non-facial behaviors, instead seeking to be picked up and held. Such observations suggest that even in late infancy the anger facial pattern is not confined to circumstances in which one would plausibly infer the presence of anger as a discrete emotion.

Regarding the surprise expression patterns, as earlier described, this configuration was associated with a distinct pattern of non-facial behavior from the time it was first observed (ie soft panting and limb waving suggesting arousal and excited attention at nine weeks of age). Subsequently, the non-facial accompaniments of the surprise configuration appeared to change in correspondence to developments in the realm of motor behavior. For example, as Justine developed the capacity for directed reaching during the first three months, the surprise pattern was often observed in the context of this activity. At about the fifth month, the surprise configuration became associated with the often performed sequence of reaching, grabbing and mouthing of an object. Thus, the non-facial accompaniments of the surprise pattern were observed to change but might all be reasonably interpreted as indicating a state of attentive orientation rather than surprise.

By the end of the first year, use of the surprise facial pattern while reaching, grabbing and mouthing had declined and during the second year was no longer regularly observed to accompany this sequence of behavior. This is particularly noteworthy because it indicates that the expression's earlier occurrence was not merely an epiphenomenal anticipation of mouthing. Instead, again consistent with the views of Peiper (1963), this decline suggests that the surprise configuration indeed originates as a part of a spreading orientation reaction and, like other spreading reactions, drops out or decreases during the course of neurological development.

Although no longer produced with substantial frequency, during the second year the surprise configuration was occasionally observed in contexts very different from those in which it was originally seen. In particular, Justine occasionally produced the expression in imitation of adult emblematic usage. As can be readily observed, American adults often use the surprise pattern when they are not genuinely surprised but are instead attempting to attract and/or direct the infant's attention or to indicate that some object or event is worthy of notice. Infrequently, Justine also used the expression in this way, for example during an affect-sharing sequence in which she pointed to an object while alternating glances between her mother and the object.

Since the surprise expression pattern has not been regularly observed in surprise situations, when it becomes associated with this emotion remains to be determined. However, the observations described here in conjunction with previous failures to observe this expression during "surprise" experimental procedures suggest some intriguing possibilities. For example, the surprise pattern may only occur in some subset of surprise situations involving a "control parameter" that is at yet undetermined. Possible candidates for this control parameter might be nominated based on observations of the non-surprise uses of this expression in early development. These might include sudden redirection of attention or even a particular (undetermined) form of social context.

While the developmental course of the surprise expression pattern thus remains to be explicated or even fully described, it clearly differs substantially from the developmental courses of the distress-pain, anger, and sadness patterns. Any general theory of emotional expression development must be able to account for these differences.

Regarding such a theoretical overview, the above observations are still open to several possible developmental interpretations. First, as would be maintained by differential emotion theorists (Izard & Malatesta, 1987), possibly the several facial configurations discussed above were associated with discrete emotion programs (including invariant subjective experiences) right from the beginning. However, the behavioral and contextual correlates of these discrete emotions changed with age until they corresponded more closely to adult expectations. One problem with this view, however, is that it is not data-driven with respect to what one can actually observe in infants. That is, it involves the adultomorphic extension of our beliefs about face–feeling relationships in adults down to infancy. With regard to observations made on infants' use (or non-use) of the distress-pain and surprise patterns in particular, this extension seems implausible.

An alternative view is suggested by a dynamical systems perspective. According to this view, during the course of development, these facial expression patterns (and their associated states of attention or distress) become available for recruitment by developing emotion systems corresponding to the commonly used adult labels. Such systems might be hierarchically organized (in part) under the control of CNS command programs. However, in each emotion "episode", particular components may or may not be produced depending on the action context.

This view differs from differential emotions theory in that it gives no priority to any particular observable element (ie facial expression). Thus, it involves a shift away from an automatic read-out model which asserts that emotion expressions will automatically be produced in emotion episodes unless they are inhibited or replaced in accordance with personal and/or cultural display rules. As indicated above, the read-out model is challenged for both infants and adults by data suggesting that facial expressions do not always occur in situations where we believe the emotion to be present but have no reason to believe that an inhibitory display rule is operating. The dynamical systems alternative accommodates this possibility by suggesting a model in which all responses are recruited in a task-specific manner, ie the task assembles the behaviors. This shift puts facial expression more on a par with other behaviors that may be recruited in the service of emotion but (in contrast to some other proposed alternatives, Fridlund, in press) does not invite us to relinquish the notion of facial expression as emotion signal.

A third more provocative alternative might also be proposed by the radical wing of dynamical systems proponents. This alternative involves relinquishing the notion of central emotion programs in its entirety. According to this view, an emotion "system" in actuality consists of an often co-occurring set of responses produced by frequently occurring task demands, contextual and organismic constraints and synergistic relations among components. That is, emotion-relevant responses are individually produced in response to particular aspects of the task context. Emotion episodes are structured and episodes of the same emotion (ie two different episodes of anger) are related. However, the structure comes from the environment and the similarities among emotion episodes come from the common occurrence of task requirements and contextual constraints. This radical alternative has appealed to those who wish to completely eradicate the homunculus they see as hovering in the brain under the guise of a "command program".

SUMMARY AND CONCLUSION

In summary, a critical review of the recent research has revealed several observations inconsistent with assumptions widely held (at least implicitly) by many investigators and with the current formulation of differential emotions theory. These include: (1) situations in which we believe an emotion is present yet the facial expression is not seen, and (2) situations in which an expression is observed but does not appear to be best described using the discrete emotion categories of differential emotion theory. In a number of cases, I have offered alternative proposals regarding the affective bases of these expressions in infants. In addition, I have suggested that a dynamical systems perspective might productively guide our efforts to account for both the development of emotional facial expressions and their situationally selective use by infants and older individuals.

Based on these proposals, two profitable (and related) lines of future investigation may be identified. First, further naturalistic studies are needed to produce a stronger empirical foundation for theorizing about expressive development. That is, in order to generate alternative proposals regarding the affective bases of infant facial expressions, we need comprehensive descriptions of their contextual occurrence including their accompanying non-facial emotion-relevant behaviors. Secondly, experimental studies are needed to identify "control parameters" for facial expression production by both infants and older individuals. Increased understanding of the conditions and variables influencing facial expression production would make an important contribution to our general understanding of the organization of emotion responding and expressive development.

REFERENCES

Bernstein, N. (1967). *Coordination and Regulation of Movement*. New York: Pergamon.
Campos, W. & Barrett, K. (1984). Toward a new understanding of emotions and their development. In C. E. Izard, J. Kagan & R. Zajonc (Eds), *Emotions, Cognition, and Behavior*. New York: Cambridge University Press, pp. 229–263.

Camras, L. A. (1988). Darwin revisited: An infant's first emotional facial expressions. Paper presented at the International Conference on Infant Studies, Washington, DC.

Camras, L. A., Malatesta, C. Z. & Izard, C. (in press). The development of facial expressions in infancy. In R. Feldman & B. Rime (Eds), *Fundamentals of Nonverbal Behavior*. Cambridge: Cambridge University Press.

Carmichael, L. (1970). The onset and early development of behavior. In P. Mussen (Ed.), *Carmichael's Manual of Child Psychology*, 3rd edn. New York: Wiley.

Ekman, P. (1972). Universals and cultural differences in facial expressions of emotion. In *Nebraska Symposium on Motivation 1971*, pp. 207–283.

Ekman, P. & Ancoli, S. (1980). Facial signs of emotional experience. *Journal of Personality and Social Psychology*, **39** (6), 1125–1134.

Ekman, P., Levenson, R. & Friesen, W. (1983). Autonomic nervous system activity distinguishes among emotion. *Science*, **221**, 1208–1210.

Emde, R. & Harmon, R. (1972). Endogenous and exogenous smiling systems in early infancy. *Journal of Child Psychiatry*, **11** (2), 177–200.

Fisher, A. (1985). Chaos: the ultimate asymmetry. *Mosaic*, Jan./Feb., 25–33.

Fogel, A. (1985). Coordinative structures in the development of expressive behavior in early infancy. In G. Zivin (Ed.), *The Development of Expressive Behavior*. New York: Academic Press, pp. 249–267.

Fogel, A. (1987) Dynamic systems in human development: The inhibition of attention to mother in early infancy. Paper presented at the Dynamic Patterns in Complex Systems Conference, Fort Lauderdale, Florida.

Fogel, A. & Thelen, E. (1987). The development of early expressive and communicative action. *Developmental Psychology*, **23**, 747–761.

Fox, N. and Davidson, R. (1987). Electrocephalogram assymetry in response to the approach of a stranger and maternal separation in 10-month-old infants. *Developmental Psychology*, **23**, 233–240.

Fridlund, A. (in press). Evolution and facial action in reflex, social motive and paralanguage. In P. Ackles, J. Jennings & M. Coles (Eds), *Advances in Psychophysiology*, Vol. 4. Greenwich, Conn.: JAI Press.

Gilbert, A., Fridlund, A. & Sabini, J. (1987). Hedonic and social determinants of facial displays to odors. *Chemical Senses*, **12**, 355–363.

Hiatt, S., Campos, J. & Emde, R. (1979). Facial patterning and infant emotional expression: Happiness, surprise, and fear. *Child Development*, **50**, 1020–1035.

Hyson, M. & Izard C. E. (1985). Continuities and changes in emotion expressions during brief separation at 13 and 18 months. *Developmental Psychology*, **21** (6), 1165–1170.

Izard, C. E., Dougherty, L. & Hembree, E. (1983). A System for Identifying Affect Expression by Holistic Judgments (AFFEX). Newark, Del.: Instructional Resources Center, University of Delaware, Newark, Delaware, 19711.

Izard, C. E., Hembree, E., Dougherty, L. & Spizzirri, C. (1983). Changes in 2- to 19-month-old infants' facial expression following acute pain. *Developmental Psychology*, **19** (3), 418–426.

Izard, C. E., Hembree, E. & Huebner, R. (1987). Infants' emotional expression to acute pain: Developmental changes and stability of individual difference. *Developmental Psychology*, **23**, 105–113.

Izard, C. E. & Malatesta, C. Z. (1987). Perspectives on emotional development I: Differential emotions theory of early emotional development. In J. D. Osofsky (Ed.), *Handbook of Infant Development*. New York: Wiley, pp. 494–554.

Kelso, J. (1981). Contrasting perspectives on order and regulation in movement. In J. Long & A. Braddeley (Eds), *Attention and Performance*, Vol. 9. Hillsdale, NJ: Earlbaum, pp. 437–457.

Kelso, J. A. S. & Scholz, J. (1986). Cooperative phenomenon in biological motion.

In H. Haken (Ed.), *Synergetics of Complex Systems in Physics, Chemistry, and Biology*. New York: Springer-Verlag.

Kraut, R., & Johnson, R. (1979). Social and emotional messages of smiling; An ethological approach. *Journal of Personality and Social Psychology*, **37** (9), 1539–1553.

Kugler, P., Kelso, J. & Turvey, M. (1980). On the concept of coordinative structures as dissipative structures: I. Theoretical line. In G. Stelmach & J. Requin (Eds), *Tutorials in Motor Behavior*. Amsterdam: North-Holland, pp. 3–48.

Kugler, P., Kelso, J. & Turvey, M. (1982). On the control and co-ordination of naturally developing systems. In J. Kelso & J. Clark (Eds), *The Development of Movement Control and Co-ordination*. New York: Wiley, pp. 5–78.

Levenson, R., Ekman, P. & Friesen, W. (1990). Voluntary facial action generates emotion-specific autonomic nervous system activity. *Psychophysiology*, **27**, 363–384.

Lewis, M., Alessandri, S. & Sullivan, M. (1989). Expectancy, loss of control and anger expression in young infants. Unpublished manuscript.

Matias, R., Cohn, J. & Ross, S. (1989). A comparison of two systems that code infant affective expression. *Developmental Psychology*, **25** (4), 483–489.

Oster, H., Hegley, D. & Nagel, L. (1988). The differentiation of negative affect expressions in infants. Paper presented at the International Conference on Infant Studies, Washington DC.

Peiper, A. (1963). *Cerebral Function in Infancy and Childhood*. New York: NY Consultant's Bureau. (Translated by B. Nagler and H. Nagler.)

Schoner, G. & Kelso, J. (1988). Dynamic pattern generation in behavioral and neural systems. *Science*, **239**, 1513–1520.

Schwartz, G., Izard, C. & Ansul, S. (1982). Heart rate and facial response to novelty in 7- and 13-month old infants. Paper presented at the International Conference on Infant Studies, Austin, Texas.

Shiller, V., Izard, C. E. & Hembree, E. (1986). Patterns of emotion expression during separation in the strange-situation. *Developmental Psychology*, **22** (3), 378–383.

Sroufe, L. A. (1984). The organization of emotional development. In K. Scherer & P. Ekman (Eds), *Approaches to Emotion*. Hillsdale, NJ: Erlbaum, pp. 109–128.

Stenberg, C. & Campos, J. (1988). The development of anger expression in infancy. Unpublished manuscript.

Stenberg, C., Campos, J. & Emde, R. (1983). The facial expression of anger in seven month old infants. *Child Development*, **54**, 178–184.

Sullivan, M. & Lewis, M. (1989). Emotion and cognition in infancy: Facial expression during contingency learning. *International Journal of Behavioral Development*, **12** (2), 221–237.

Termine, N. & Izard, C. (1988). Infants' responses to their mothers' expressions of joy and sadness. *Developmental Psychology*, **24** (2), 223–229.

Thelen, E. (1985a). Developmental origins of motor coordination: Leg movements in human infants. *Development Psychobiology*, **18** (1), 1–22.

Thelen, E. (1985b). Expression as action. In G. Zivin (Ed.), *The Development of Expressive Behavior*. New York: Academic Press, pp. 223–248.

Thelen, E. (1989). Conceptualizing development from a dynamical systems perspective. In B. Bertenthal, A. Fogel, L. Smith & E. Thelen (Chairs), Dynamical systems in development. Society for Research in Child Development Pre-Conference Workshop, Kansas City.

Thelen, E. & Fisher, D. (1982). Newborn stepping: An explanation for a "disappearing reflex". *Development Psychology*, **18**, 760–775.

Wolff, P. (1987). *The Development of Behavioral States and the Expression of Emotions in Early Infancy*. Chicago: University of Chicago Press.

REPLY BY CARROLL IZARD AND CAROL MALATESTA-MAGAI

Camras has presented an interesting alternative to the differential emotions theory view of emotional development. While we see promise in the perspective, there are a number of important points on which we disagree. We see dynamical systems theory as a useful theoretical framework but believe that its application to expressive behavior may be limited.

Fogel and Thelen (1987) were the first to propose a dynamical systems analysis of expressive development. They put forward some intriguing possibilities, though certain suggestions are clearly not in accordance with the available empirical data. For example, their discussion of the theory implies that the change from the zygomatic smile to the smile involving the zygomatic muscle and the orbicularis oculi muscle is some kind of developmental transition. We have examined hundreds of infants' smiles from ages two and a half to nine months and have found both types of smiles during this period and no evidence of a developmental trend in the morphology of the smile (Izard, Haynes & Slomine, 1989). Expressive movements do not show postnatal developmental changes in the way implied by dynamical systems theory.

We have similar problems with some of the theses suggested by Camras. She has proposed that sadness reflects the waning of the intensity of distress. If this were the case, why would we not always see sadness following an intense pain or anger expression? There are abundant data to show that this is clearly not the case (Izard, Hembree & Huebner, 1987). It happens on some occasions and not on others.

Camras also casts doubt on the specificity of the pain-distress expression because infants have been observed to emit pain-distress expressions during face-to-face interaction with their mothers—as evident in the work of Matias, Cohn & Ross (1989). We have observed these expressions on occasion during mother–infant interaction sessions as well (Malatesta & Haviland, 1982; Malatesta *et al.*, 1986), but do not find this surprising or anomalous. Laboratory face-to-face "play" sessions often engender discomfort for young infants due to conditions of filming—bright lights, being immobilized in ways that cause pain, and sometimes being unable to escape from well-meaning but overstimulating mothers. On the occasions where we observed infant pain-distress expressions, there were multiple indicators of discomfort, including facial and vocal expressions of discomfort and body movements obviously oriented towards reposturing the self. Moreover, these bursts of discomfort expression tended to occur towards the end of the session rather than the beginning, and during episodes where there were indicators of gastric pain.

EMOTION FEELINGS AND THE COGNITIVE REPRESENTATION OF FEELINGS

An essential point in understanding the differences between our differential emotions theory (DET) and Camras' view of dynamical systems theory is that the former clearly distinguishes among the neural, expressive, and experiential aspects of emotion and defines the latter in terms of feeling states. Although the neural component subserves both expression and feeling (and all other psychological phenomena), it can be recognized as a distinct mode or level for analysis and investigation. Clearly, expression and experience must be distinguished as functionally separable components, because it is possible to completely dissociate emotion feeling and observable expression.

The most important distinction, for present purposes, relates to the experiential component of emotion. DET defines the third component of emotion as a feeling state and proposes that feelings can exist in consciousness without being cognitively represented. Relevant to this point is the research of LeDoux (1987) showing that emotions can be activated in subcortical pathways that process information in rapid, automatic fashion unencumbered by the cognitive processes mediated by neocortex. Moreover, according to the latest neurophysiological data (LeDoux, 1990), the brain structure that appears to be the primary "computational" core for the registration and processing of emotional stimuli is the amygdala. This structure receives direct sensory input from the thalamus and thus does not require prior cognitive processing for affective "comprehension" by the individual. Importantly, both the thalamus and the amygdala tend to mature earlier than higher-order cortical areas. LeDoux suggests that the amygdala may well be functioning in the early days and weeks of life.

When we make and carefully maintain the distinction between feeling state and the cognitive meaning of that state, then it no longer seems incongruous that infants would show a sequence of discrete expressions (and corresponding feelings) to a particular stimulus, with some of the expressions (and corresponding feelings) appearing inappropriate to the adult's eye. It is through cognitive and motor development and the development of all the other systems of the individual that the cognitive meaning of discrete emotion states becomes finely tuned to the great variety of events in the social and physical environment. In this way emotion response systems come to function more and more "appropriately" in an endless variety of circumstances.

That an infant's emotion expression appears inappropriate to an adult does not mean that the corresponding feeling is not present. The feeling may be "inappropriate" as well. Why should all the infant's emotion–response systems be perfectly tuned to all stimulus events at birth? We do not expect this in any other response system. Arm flailing and leg kicking are inappropriate responses to frustration by adult standards.

When feelings obtain in consciousness without being cognitively represented, they are incompletely integrated with cognitive processes and movements. This may help account for the seeming "irrationality" of some infant emotion expressions (that seem inappropriate by adult standards), as well as some adult behavior.

INVARIANCE OF FEELINGS AND DEVELOPMENTAL CHANGES IN EMOTION–COGNITION–ACTION SEQUENCES

The distinction between emotion feeling state and the cognitive representation of that state is important in understanding the DET postulates of (a) the continuity of emotion feelings and (b) the development of diverse emotion–cognition–action sequences. Obviously, the cognitive meaning of a feeling changes with cognitive development. Joyful imagery becomes richer as memory functions mature and anticipation becomes possible. Sadness becomes more profound as the individual becomes more capable of comprehending the extent and consequences of the loss of a loved one. Similarly, the actions that are organized and motivated by joy or sadness change significantly with age. Yet, the core feeling states of joy and sadness remain invariant. It is this invariance in feeling/motivational state that guarantees the adaptiveness of the emotions. What changes with development is the network of cognitions and actions associated with these feelings.

In short, we see that achievement of appropriate emotion–cognition–action sequences to the more or less infinite variety of the world's events and situations as the key set of processes in human development. These developmental processes continue throughout life.

HIERARCHICAL–DYNAMICAL ORGANIZATION OF EMOTIONS

We have long maintained that emotions are hierarchically organized and dynamically related (Izard, 1977; Izard & Malatesta, 1987). These characteristics of the emotions system mean that a certain pattern or cluster of discrete fundamental emotions may operate as an apparently unitary dimension. The data for this come from the still growing body of dimensional studies of emotion. Watson and Clark (in press) have shown that at least for self-reported emotions one can demonstrate a very neat hierarchy, with the discrete fundamental emotions as the building blocks or primaries at the bottom of the pyramid, clusters like the hostility triad (anger, disgust, and contempt) in the middle and the global dimensions of negativity and positivity at the top. Discreteness can exist as points on a broader dimension. For example, the hostility triad, identified by different investigators (Izard, 1971; Watson and Clark, in press), is certainly something that emerges with development. We know that expressions of anger and disgust exist in early infancy, but no one would ever think of suggesting that the infant is capable of a hostility response that includes feelings of anger, disgust, and contempt.

The occurrence of multiple emotion expressions to the same stimulus (eg pain, separation) during early infancy may be explained in part by the instability of emotion responses that are not cognitively represented and in part by the fact that the discrete emotions are hierarchically organized and dynamically related. By a dynamic relation we mean that some sets of emotions are more likely to co-occur than other sets. That more than one emotion occurs in response to pain is no more of an argument against expression–feeling specificity than it is for the dynamic relations among emotions or the flexibility of the emotion–response systems.

REFERENCES

Fogel, A. & Thelen, F. (1987). Development of early expressive and communicative action: Reinterpreting the evidence from a dynamic systems perspective. *Developmental Psychology*, **23** (6), 747–761.

Izard, C. E. (1971). *The Face of Emotion*. New York: Plenum.

Izard, C. E. (1972). *Pattern of Emotions: A New Analysis of Anxiety and Depression*. New York: Academic Press.

Izard, C. E. (1977). *Human Emotions*. New York: Plenum.

Izard, C. E. and Malatesta, C. Z. (1987). Perspectives on emotional development: I. differential emotions theory of early emotional development. In J. D. Osofsky (Ed.), *Handbook of Infant Development*, 2nd edn. New York: Wiley, pp. 494–554.

Izard, C. E., Haynes, O. M. & Slomine, B. S. (1989). Infants' full-face expressions, partial expressions, and expressive blends during playful and stressful interactions with their mothers. Unpublished manuscript.

Izard, C. E., Hembree, E. A. & Huebner, R. R. (1987). Infants' emotion expressions to acute pain: Developmental change and stability of individual differences. *Developmental Psychology*, **23** (1), 105–113.

LeDoux, J. E. (1987). Emotion. In F. Plum (Ed.), *Handbook of Physiology—The Nervous System V*. Washington, DC: American Physiological Society, pp. 419–459.

LeDoux, J. E. (1990). Cognitive–emotional interactions in the brain. *Cognition and Emotion*, **3**, 267–290.

Malatesta, C. Z., Grigoryev, P., Lamb, C., Albin, M. & Culver, C. (1986). Emotion socialization and expressive development in preterm and full term infants. *Child Development*, **57**, 316–330.

Malatesta, C. Z. & Haviland, J. M. (1982). Learning display rules: The socialization of emotion expression in infancy. *Child Development*, **53**, 991–1003.

Matias, R., Cohn, J. and Ross, S. (1989). A comparison of the two systems that code infant affective expression. *Developmental Psychology*, **25** (4), 483–489.

Watson, D. & Clark, L. A. (in press). Affects separable and inseparable: A hierarchical model of emotional experience.

REPLY BY LINDA CAMRAS

It is heartening to be able to discern several critical areas of agreement in the two positions presented in this chapter. All authors agree that infant facial expressions can no longer be considered random or chaotic although we may differ in our analysis of their systematic basis. Furthermore, both positions recognize the important adaptive function of emotions and emotional facial expression. Lastly, all of us acknowledge the difficulty of resolving some of our critical points of disagreement since we are dealing with issues for which direct and incontrovertible evidence is difficult to obtain. Thus, confronted with a complex set of data on infant facial behavior, we propose somewhat different models to be evaluated and perhaps synthesized in the future.

To facilitate this process, I will here reiterate two differences that I see as the most central points of disagreement between the two positions. The first key difference involves the notion of facial expressions as direct read-outs of emotion in infants. This notion has enormous pragmatic significance in that if infant emotions were isomorphic with infant facial expressions, expression could be used as a free-standing index of emotion. Unfortunately, there are compelling reasons for rejecting this attractive and expedient supposition. For example, as described above, it has been long known that several laboratory situations we believe to elicit infant emotions do not elicit corresponding facial expressions as described by differential emotions theory. This orphan phenomenon has both methodological and theoretical implications. First, it implies that non-facial as well as facial indices of emotion should be used in infant studies. Secondly, it implies that we must reformulate our theories to account for the non-isomorphic relationship between facial and non-facial emotion behaviors in infants. An example of an effort made in this direction is the family relationship model presented by Barrett and Campos (1987). This model describes how phenotypically different emotion episodes may all be considered members of the same emotion family. The dynamical systems perspective can also accommodate disjunctions between facial expression and other aspects of emotion. Furthermore, it more explicitly motivates a search for synergistic relationships and contextual factors that determine whether or not an emotional expression will be produced in an emotion situation. Thus Izard and Malatesta are correct to point out that if sadness expressions reflect a low level or waning of the distress response (as I have tentatively proposed), we must still determine why they are not produced in all instances of distress reduction. Similarly, we must determine why fear and surprise expressions are not produced in all fear and surprise situations. When we have done so, we will have learned something important about emotion and emotional expression. Perhaps we will also have learned when we can legitimately use facial expression as our sole index of emotion.

The second key difference between differential emotions theory and the alternative position presented in this chapter involves the interpretation of several expressions that have been observed in infants. In particular, these are the expressions described by Affex for distress-pain, anger, and sadness and also the expression of surprise. Differential emotions theory proposes that the Affex-specified expressions reflect the same emotions (ie "invariant core of subjective experience") both in adults and young infants. In contrast, I have argued that the emotion status of these facial expressions may change during the course of development and have proposed some alternative interpretations of these expressions for infants.

What evidence can be adduced for each of these positions? As described above and in Camras, Malatesta and Izard (1990), the hypotheses I have proposed are based on both an analysis of data reported in previous studies and observations of naturally occurring expressive behavior in a wider range of circumstances than has been observed in laboratory studies. In the tradition of ethology, these hypotheses reflect an empirically driven effort to deduce common factors underlying the situations in which the expressions have been observed. Potentially these factors might differ for the Affex-described expressions of distress-pain, anger, and sadness, and furthermore their essential features might plausibly be linked to the discrete affects or emotions of distress-pain, anger, and sadness. However, because such differentiation has not been demonstrated, I have argued for a revised interpretation of the negative expressions at least during early infancy. This revised interpretation reflects the observation that all three expressions are associated with a wide range of negative elicitors, suggesting that they might better be described as expressions of non-specific distress at least during the first few months of life. Similarly, the range of circumstances in which the surprise expression has been observed suggests its reinterpretation as reflecting excited attention.

What evidence is adduced for the proposal that the Affex-described expressions represent the discrete negative emotions proposed by differential emotions theory? Two types of arguments have been presented in Izard and Malatesta's commentary. First, the authors have proposed that infant expressions may occur in seemingly inappropriate situations because they are produced via appraisal processes (such as those described by LeDoux, 1990) that do not involve the cognitive analysis of stimulus input that differentiates these emotions in adults. These non-cognitive appraisal processes also serve to explain the frequent occurrence of multiple expressive responses (and thus multiple emotions) to the same eliciting situation. Izard and Malatesta's proposal is certainly plausible. However, while such non-cognitive appraisals may indeed take place, their existence does not necessarily argue for invariance in the relationship between facial expression and emotion throughout the lifespan. That is, development might still bring changes in the emotions elicited by non-cognitive appraisal processes.

Secondly, Izard and Malatesta have argued that invariance in expression–feeling relationships guarantees adaptiveness, ie is adaptive presumably because it guarantees that the expressions will be appropriately interpreted by the infants' caretakers. However, arguments about evolutionary adaptiveness are notoriously ephemeral (Hailman, 1982; Kitcher, 1985). Why would it be particularly adaptive for infants to experience anger and sadness as discrete emotions during the first few months of life? One could easily argue that general distress would be a more adaptive response on the part of an infant too young to be differentially motivated by the discrete emotions of anger and sadness. Furthermore, adaptive communication between infants and adults might still take place even if the emotion status of these facial expressions was modified in the course of development. Within the field of ethology, it is well recognized that species with considerably less cognitive sophistication than humans are able to appropriately and differentially respond to signals whose meaning changes with development (eg begging postures in fledgling vs adult songbirds; Smith, 1977). In line with this, recent studies (Oster, Hegley & Nagel, 1990) suggest that adults may actually perceive infant negative expressions as less discrete than negative expressions in adults and may prefer to label Affex-specified negative expressions as ''distress'' when they are shown by young infants.

Beyond these arguments, a more central problem may be discerned regarding the role of phenomenological experience in emotion theory. Izard and Malatesta propose the existence of an invariant core of subject experience that provides continuity throughout development. However, subjective experience in infants cannot be measured and their hypothesis is thus unfalsifiable. Furthermore, even if this invariant core exists, Izard and Malatesta agree that it becomes incorporated into more advanced and sophisticated emotion structures that include richer and more profound subjective experience. Might it not make sense to define emotional development in terms of these larger structures—especially if this allows us to achieve greater consistency between our theoretical description and the observable correlates of emotional expression?

To conclude on a positive note, the alternative position I have presented in this chapter is not incompatible with many important tenets of differential emotions theory. Primarily, it represents an attempt to account for certain puzzling observations on infant expressive behavior and provide a more empirically driven account of infant emotional development. As Izard and Malatesta have indicated in their commentary, dynamic relations among emotions are not precluded by the assumptions of differential emotions theory. I would suggest that other aspects of the dynamical systems perspective as well as some modifications in expression interpretation might also be incorporated. Thus we may look forward to a synthesis of viewpoints as we acquire further empirical data on emotional behavior in infancy and beyond.

REFERENCES

Barrett, K. Campos, J. (1987). Perspectives on emotional development II: A functionalist approach to emotions. In J. Osofsky (Ed.), *Handbook of Infant Development*, 2nd edn. New York: Wiley, pp. 555–578.

Camras, L. A., Malatesta, C. & Izard, C. (1990). The development of facial expressions in infancy. In R. Feldman & B. Rime (Eds), *Fundamentals of Nonverbal Behavior*. Cambridge: Cambridge University Press.

Hailman, J. (1982). Evolution and behavior. In H. Plotkin (Ed.), *Learning, Development and Culture*. New York: Wiley, pp. 205–254.

Kitcher, P. (1985). *Vaulting Ambition*. Cambridge, Mass: MIT Press.

LeDoux, J. (1990). Cognitive–emotional interactions in the brain. *Cognition and Emotion*, **3**, 267–290.

Oster, H., Hegley, D. & Nagel, L. (1990). Adult judgements and fine-grained analysis of infant facial expressions. Unpublished manuscript.

Smith, W. J. (1977). *The Behavior of Communicating*. Cambridge, Mass: Harvard University Press.

2 Emotions and Evolution

ROBERT PLUTCHIK
Department of Psychiatry, Albert Einstein College of Medicine,
1300 Morris Park Avenue, Bronx, New York 10461, USA

By the year 1838, Darwin "was already inclined to believe in the principle of evolution, or of the derivation of species from other and lower forms" (Darwin, 1872/1965). He recognized that the process of evolution applied not only to anatomic structures but to an animal's "mind" and expressive behavior as well. He assumed that intelligence, reasoning ability, memory, and emotions all had an evolutionary history and that all could be identified at different phylogenetic levels. He further assumed that each emotional expression demanded a rational explanation. This belief led Darwin to collect information on the expressive behavior of humans and lower animals which led eventually to his book *The Expression of the Emotions in Man and Animals*, published in 1872. With regard to humans, he obtained information on expressive behavior in infants, in the mentally deranged, in the works of great masters of painting and sculpture, in various races of mankind, particularly those who had had little contact with Europeans, and in a man who permitted electrical stimulation of his facial muscles. He also studied expressions in the commoner animals.

In his effort to explain the various expressions observed in humans and lower animals Darwin suggested three hypotheses, or "principles". The first principle was that some expressions or actions are of value in gratifying desires and that these expressions may sometimes occur in situations where they have no use (eg cats trying to cover up excrement by pawing at a concrete pavement). The second principle (of antithesis) claimed that since certain states of mind lead to certain useful actions, then opposite states of mind lead to the performance of movements of a directly opposite nature (eg an animal's expressions preparatory to attack are often opposite to those shown in submission). The third principle (of direct action of the nervous system) stated that strong excitation of the nervous system affects various systems of the body (eg sweating, trembling of the muscles, color changes in the skin, voiding of the bladder, fainting, etc). Darwin used his various sources of information and these principles to try to account for the particular forms taken by expressions of pain, anxiety, grief, love, hatred, anger, contempt, disgust, guilt, pride, surprise, fear, shame, shyness, and other emotions. The evidence he presented was designed to illustrate the basic continuity of emotional expressions from lower animals to humans. He suggested that the baring of the fangs of the dog or wolf is related to the sneer of the human adult. He noted that flushing of the

International Review of Studies on Emotion, Vol. 1. Edited by K. T. Strongman
©1991 John Wiley & Sons Ltd

face in anger has been reported in widely diverse human races, as well as in certain species of monkeys. Defecation and urination in association with fear has been observed in rats, cats, dogs, monkeys, and humans.

Some of the flavor of Darwin's description is revealed through his discussion of one of the expressive signs of fear and anger, namely, apparent enlargement of body size. He wrote: "Hardly any expressive movement is so general as the involuntary erection of the hairs, feathers or other dermal appendages for it is common throughout three of the great vertebrate classes. These appendages are erected under the excitement of anger or terror; more especially when these emotions are combined, or quickly succeed each other. The action serves to make the animal appear larger and more frightful to its enemies or rivals, and is generally accompanied by various voluntary movements adapted for the same purpose, and by the utterance of savage sounds."

To support these generalizations, Darwin cited observations made of chimps, orangutans and gorillas in a zoo. He also pointed to the bristling of the mane in lions and the erection of hair at the time of fear or threat in hyenas, dogs, cats, horses, cattle, pigs, elk, goats, antelope, anteaters, rats, and bats.

This kind of adaptive behavior has been observed in many different species of animal. Birds ruffle their feathers when threatened by other animals, and Darwin cited similar observations made of chickens, roosters, swans, owls, hawks, parrots, finches, warblers, and quail. Some reptiles have been observed during courtship fights to expand their throat pouches or frills and erect their dorsal crests. Toads, frogs, and chameleons take in air and swell up in size; and it has been reported that when a frog is seized by a snake, the swelling of the body sometimes allows escape. In humans a somewhat parallel expansion of apparent body size occurs in anger as reflected by expansion of the chest, thrusting the head forward, standing more erect, and sometimes by erection of body hair.

On the basis of these kinds of examples it is evident that Darwin's view of expressive behavior is a functional one. Emotional expressions serve some functions in the lives of animals. They act as signals and as preparations for action. They communicate information from one animal to another about what is likely to happen and thereby affect the chances of survival.

What are some implications of Darwin's views? One implication of an evolutionary perspective is that many aspects of expressive (emotional) behavior are innate. This means that there are genetic programs that influence the form of emotional expression. It is important to emphasize that to say something is innate or genetically influenced is not the same as saying that its expression is invariant or unchangeable. Flying is innate in birds, but if a bird's wings are clipped it will not fly. Bird song is innate, yet some birds will sing in the pattern of another species if they are adopted early enough. In addition, the precise pattern or expression of emotions depends on the extent to which multiple emotions are simultaneously aroused. As has been shown in a number of instances, the simultaneous arousal of fear and anger produces different patterns of expressions than either anger or fear alone (Morris, 1954; Leyhausen, 1956; Lorenz, 1952).

Another result of Darwin's views on emotion is to direct research attention to the issues of how particular emotional expressions influence survival and exactly what they communicate. The recent literature on ethology is filled with studies on the survival implications of particular patterns of behavior as well as on the communication content of expressions. For example, the function of song in a Florida population of Scott's seaside sparrows was studied by temporarily muting male birds in the field. This procedure left the birds songless for about two weeks before recovery. During this time the songless birds did not acquire mates, or lost previously acquired mates. Their territories either shrank or were lost, although new territories were established after voice recovery. The muted birds also experienced more close-range aggressive behavior than controls (McDonald, 1989). It thus appears that bird song in this species influences both reproductive behavior and aggressive interactions. Similarly, studies of the ferret revealed that anal drags seemed to act as an olfactory signature providing an association between a resident and its defended territory. Ferrets who meet each other apparently identify a resident by matching the odor of the anal region with that of recently encountered scent marks. This process helps an intruder evaluate the degree of motivation of the resident to defend its territory and in turn helps to assess the relative outcome of a possible contest. A different behavior pattern called body rubbing occurred most frequently in the spring at breeding time, when males defend their territories most aggressively. It also occurs most in males and at the boundaries of the enclosures where most encounters take place. This pattern was interpreted as a threat signal that functions to intimidate opponents (Clapperton, 1989).

Another implication of the Darwinian evolutionary perspective on emotions is that all emotional expressions can be considered in terms of at least five fundamental questions. These are: (1) What is the precise nature of the expression being observed? (2) What are the developmental origins of this behavior? (3) What are the phylogenetic origins of this behavior? (4) What are the specific stimuli and internal states that interact to bring about this behavior (proximate causation)? (5) What are the ultimate survival implications of this behavior (ultimate causation)? The disciplines that attempt to answer these questions represent the heritage of Darwin's theory of evolution. The following sections will briefly illustrate how research has attempted to deal with each of the questions.

DESCRIBING EMOTIONAL EXPRESSIONS

Birds exhibit an extensive diversity of sound productions. Some species develop only a single song, while others may sing thousands. In some species mates sing in duet, but in most species the females do not sing. Birds of some species may learn new songs throughout life, while in most species song learning terminates after a few months.

Many studies have been carried out to determine the exact nature of the songs exhibited by birds at different ages and the nature of the conditions under which songs are sung. It has been discovered, for example, that almost all birds have a sensitive period during which they learn their songs. This period typically varies from two or three weeks after birth to about seven to 10 weeks (Kroodsma, 1978). Sonograms have been made of bird songs showing the fine structure of the frequency and intensity patterns for different types of songs.

Many birds develop song dialects, that is, songs that vary somewhat from the ones learned from the male parent. These dialects generally develop after the bird disperses to a new environment and the dialect represents a match to the song of conspecific adult males in adjacent territories. The precise nature of the dialect is largely dependent on how many different song patterns are in the repertoire of the individual; dialect changes are more likely when only one song is present in a repertoire than when many are. Other studies have demonstrated that songs are involved in mate attraction and territory defense (Wilson, 1975).

Another illustration of an attempt to define the precise nature of emotional interactions may be seen in the work of Scaife (1976a,b). He was interested in the stimulus value of eyes in causing avoidance responses in birds. This problem was studied by exposing young chickens to a predator (a stuffed hawk) and to a strange bird (a stuffed kiwi) both bearing the same glass eyes. They were also separately tested with round or square-shaped "eyes" that looked at or looked away from the chick. It was found that the chicks avoided the hawk but approached the kiwi. Obscuring the hawk's eyes decreased avoidance of the hawk. Accentuating the kiwi's eyes increased avoidance. The chicks also avoided the two tracking eyelike shapes the most. These results suggest that birds, or at least chickens, are strongly avoidant of staring eyelike shapes, particularly when associated with following movements.

A final example of the importance of precise description of emotional (as well as other) behaviors may be seen in the work of Jane Goodall (Lawick-Goodall, 1973). In 1960, she began a longitudinal study of free-living chimpanzees in the Gombe National Park in Tanzania, East Africa. She and her associates observed a population of about 100 chimpanzees living in several smaller communities and she described their social and emotional interactions in great detail. She noticed, for example, that there is a well-defined hierarchy dominated by males. The animals are promiscuous in that a female, during her periods of oestrus, may be mated by many males and no stable pair bonds are formed.

Among the many interesting observations are the following. Young chimpanzees are not weaned from their mothers until five or six years of age. Quite often a young chimpanzee will go through a period of apparent depression at the time of weaning. This is indicated by a reversion to earlier forms of infantile behavior such as clinging to the mother, decreased play behavior, and listless and apathetic behavior.

Although no permanent pair bonds develop between male and female, there appear to be strong affectionate bonds between mothers and their offspring, and between siblings. It is also of interest that there have been no observations of a sexually mature male attempting to mate with his mother.

Sexual advances by males often consist of gestures that also occur in aggressive contexts; some females become fearful initially and may try to escape when a male approaches for copulation. Male chimpanzees often hunt in groups and show behavior that can clearly be labeled as cooperative. When prey is killed many chimpanzees gather round the hunters and beg for a share of the food. "When begging, a chimpanzee may hold his hand to the mouth of an eating individual in the hope that he will be given the remains of a mouthful, or he may hold out his hand toward the other, palm up, in the typical begging gesture of man" (Lawick-Goodall, 1973, p. 9).

It is in considering non-verbal communication that the most extensive similarities to human behavior are found. Chimpanzees hold hands, touch and pat each other, embrace, kiss, bite, punch, kick, scratch and pull each other's hair in contexts that are similar to those seen when humans demonstrate the same behavior. Greeting patterns are similar, as are aggressive behaviors. The chimpanzee also has a wide range of vocalizations, and each appears to be related to a specific emotion; screams are associated with fear, barks with aggression, etc. In more recent years evidence has been found of cannibalism as well as the killing of members of one group of chimpanzees by another (Goodall, 1986). These various detailed observations show many behavioral similarities between chimpanzees and human beings and are consistent with their similarities in chromosomes, blood proteins, immune responses and DNA.

DEVELOPMENTAL ORIGINS OF EMOTIONS

Examples from fish and reptiles will be given of studies of the development of emotional interactions. In salmon there are major differences in behavior before and after the time of emergence of embryos from their gravel beds. Prior to emergence, embryos are capable of a number of sensory and motor reactions. They tend to avoid the light, and stay close to the ground.

These characteristics help to avoid predators. After emergence from the gravel there is an abrupt change in pattern with an onset of eating and agonistic behavior. The agonistic behavior following emergence consists of attacks, chases, and/or bites and it has been suggested that agonistic patterns develop from ingestive patterns. As time goes on, the social encounters become more complex, with threat postures (head down and dorsal fin up) replacing overt attack. Similarly, with experience, feeding responses become narrowly directed towards certain food objects, a pattern that is relatively unaffected by food deprivation (Noakes, 1978).

Studies of development in reptiles demonstrate that many reptiles shortly after birth engage in such defensive behaviors as flight, or, when seized, biting, tail lashing, defecation and writhing. Young crocodiles, when threatened, will often vocalize a destructive call that appears to attract nearby adults. In baby iguanas, flight reactions to danger have been identified in the form of climbing up and jumping from trees, swimming, diving, cryptic color changes, tonic immobility and tail loss when grabbed. As reptiles become adult their weight is often hundreds of times greater than that of newborns (eg crocodiles) and they live in quite different environments. Their relationship to predators changes and so do the forms of defense. Expressive signals are much more used in agonistic encounters between adults than between newborns (Burghardt, 1978).

PHYLOGENETIC ORIGINS OF BEHAVIOR

Darwin paid particular attention to this point in his book. In discussing the emission of sounds, he pointed out that vocalizations are a means of communication in lower animals as well as in humans. Certain distinct sounds appear to be associated with pain, fear, anger, courtship and sex. For example, observation of cebus monkeys indicated that they expressed anger by repeating the sound *hu hu* in a deep grunting voice, and fright or pain by shrill screams. In addition, as fear tends to cause the muscles of the body to tremble, the sounds connected with fear tend to be tremulous. Pigs grunt when satisfied and scream shrilly when distressed. Such screams are considered by Darwin to be calls for assistance and their intense, high-pitched quality tends to make them heard over long distance. Darwin believed that similar patterns of focal expression of emotions can be heard in humans as well. Recent research has largely confirmed this.

As a result of spectographic analysis of animal calls, Tembrock (1975) has concluded that there are connections between certain social states and vocalizations. When an animal appears relaxed or is playing, sounds tend to be repeated low-frequency sounds. Prolonged low-frequency sounds are associated with threat calls. Defense calls tend to be short, and loud with a broad frequency range. Submission sounds tend to be described as repeated high-frequency tones that are prolonged. In this study and others like it, the emotional state of the animal is generally inferred on the basis of the stimuli that produce the behavior, the consequences of the animal's actions, and the behavior of other animals to the sounds.

The consistency of these patterns of sounds with human vocalizations has been demonstrated by Scherer (1989), who notes that animal sounds are most like the non-linguistic interjections (cries, moans, screams, shouts) of humans. Ordinary speech is a complex mixture of symbolic and affective elements.

One additional example may be given. Darwin reports on several observations of the snarl in dogs. He describes the action as one that uncovers a canine tooth along with a characteristic furrowing of the cheek and wrinkling under one eye. This pattern generally occurs at times of threat and involves showing this facial pattern to the antagonist. The snarl pattern is sometimes seen in humans, in which case it is referred to as a sneer. Darwin also suggests that a trace of the same expression is evident in a derisive or sardonic smile.

These examples, and the ones given earlier concerning body size, are illustrations of the fact that many emotional expressions have an evolutionary history.

THE CONCEPT OF PROXIMATE CAUSATION

If we accept an evolutionary framework for looking at human behavior, we recognize that most transactions with the environment (both human and non-human) are in the service of survival. There are, however, two senses in which the term survival is used. In the more familiar sense, the term refers to survival of the individual as a total organism over a length of time that is characteristic of the species (one's lifespan). In the biological sense, survival means genetic representation in succeeding generations, what the sociobiologists call inclusive fitness. The two are clearly not the same. Some individuals will give up their lives to save that of their offspring.

These two types of survival create different problems for the individual, and the differences are reflected by some of the different concerns of ethologists and sociobiologists. Ethologists have tended to focus their attention on variables that influence important interpersonal behaviors such as displacements, intention movements, rituals, appeasement gestures, fragmentations, and displays. All of these patterns influence the probability of individual survival. In contrast, sociobiologists have been largely concerned with concepts that are related to gene distributions in different populations, concepts such as reciprocal altruism, parental investment, courtship strategies, evolutionarily stable strategies, and inclusive fitness. Although the two sets of concepts are interrelated, there are some differences that deal with the issue of proximate versus ultimate causation.

Two examples of studies concerned with proximate causation will be given. One deals with the appearance of display behaviors in a group of Japanese macaques living in a seminatural setting. In this study, four types of displays were observed and the conditions under which they appeared recorded. These displays were: shaking an object, leaping up and down in the air, tossing one's head back and forth, and swinging on a branch. In addition to these displays, the frequency of adult aggressive interactions was noted as well as mounts, play, courtship behavior, and ejaculations (Modahl & Eaton, 1977).

The data revealed that males tended to show these displays more frequently than did females and this was particularly true during the mating season. In addition, individual males who displayed most frequently during the mating season also ejaculated most frequently. Social dominance levels and mating success (frequency of ejaculation) was found not to be related to plasma levels of testosterone. Castration and androgen replacement failed to alter genital display behavior in dominant squirrel monkeys and it is probably unlikely to be relevant in this case. The patterns of display behaviors described here apparently function to attract females for courtship and mating although few of the contributing internal variables have yet been identified.

A second illustration of a concern with proximate causation is one that deals with the appearance of a particular behavior that can be observed in most ungulates (horses, cows, goats, buffalo, deer, etc). This pattern is called "flehman" and consists of the animal standing open-mouthed, with head extended and elevated while the upper lip is retracted, wrinkling the nose and baring the gum. The question at issue was: what is the meaning of this facial expression often seen in horses? In an effort to answer this, Crowell-Davis and Houpt (1985) recorded all incidents of flehman in a group of mares, fillies, and colts. Temporally related behaviors including urination, defecation and sniffing were also recorded.

Results demonstrated that flehman incidents occurred significantly more often in colts than in either fillies or mares. On the average, flehman occurred about once per four hours in colts, once per nine hours in fillies, and once per 50 hours in mares. The rate of showing flehman expressions decreased linearly in colts during their first 20 weeks of life, while it remained relatively unchanged and at a low rate in fillies.

Evaluation of the records of events immediately preceding, during and after each flehman incident revealed that most responses were to the urine of another horse or to one's own urine. In many cases, the flehman expression was followed by urination by the pony that had performed the flehman. The conclusion reached by these researchers was that flehman is primarily oriented to sampling the urinary pheromones of females. A further speculation is that detection of pheromones by the vomeronasal organ is important for sexual maturation and growth.

THE CONCEPT OF ULTIMATE CAUSATION

There are several ways one might explain the phenomenon of changes in apparent size that many animals show when dealing with an aggressive encounter. Numerous animals exhibit threat postures that involve standing erect (as, for example, in canines and rodents) and raising the neck hairs. The manes of lions erect, fish expand their fins, birds extend their wings and fluff their feathers, while lizards and some frogs have inflatable pouches.

One level of explanation for such behavior attempts to trace the stimulus conditions that precipitate the increase in apparent size and to identify the hormonal and neurophysiological changes that are associated with it. Another level of explanation uses sociobiologic concepts such as "resource holding power". Since size is a cue used by an animal to assess the ability of another animal to successfully defend a territory, the selection of mechanisms that increase apparent size has occurred during the course of evolution in widely dispersed species. The capacity to use size cues to defend resources is thus related to inclusive fitness (Parker, 1974).

The two concepts cited here, "resource holding power" and "inclusive fitness", are sociobiological ones that are concerned with the mechanisms underlying survival of one's genetic endowment in the long run. Sociobiological concepts are thus concerned primarily with population characteristics. Two studies of dominance behavior will illustrate this point.

In one study (Samuels, Silk & Rodman, 1984) 76 bonnet macaques were systematically observed in a large enclosure. Observations of aggressive and submissive behavior directed by one animal towards another were used to determine dominance ranks. In any given year, the dominance ranks tended to be relatively stable. Observations were also made of the extent to which each animal entered into a consort relationship, that is, a prolonged and continuous association between a male and a receptive female.

The results showed that only high-ranking males became the primary companions of conceiving females. The three highest-ranking males were responsible for nearly three-quarters of all copulations with conceiving females, and the high-ranking males copulated primarily with high-ranking females. Males who rose in rank spent increasing amounts of time with conceiving high-ranking females. The relationships described tend to increase the inclusive fitness of high-ranking males because the offspring of high-ranking females are more likely to survive.

Dominance relationships are found not only in lower animals but in humans as well. Because of its widespread occurrence, dominance is considered to be a phylogenetically conservative trait (Wilson, 1975). In lower primates most evidence reveals that high-ranking males have the most access to high-ranking females and that survival of their offspring is relatively high. Thus dominance increases inclusive fitness. A corollary of this observation is that dominant males are more likely to be relatively more attractive to females. This hypothesis provided the basis for a study of college students who were asked to rate the sexual attractiveness of opposite-sex models who engaged in either dominant or non-dominant behaviors (Sadalla, Kenrick & Vershura, 1987).

In this study subjects watched a silent one-minute videotape of actors, two men or two women, who engaged in either high or low dominant behavior in a simulated professor–student interaction. Subjects then rated each stimulus person on several bipolar scales including "physically attractive–physically unattractive" and "desirable as a date–undesirable as a date". Results of this study indicated that dominance behavior increased the sexual attractiveness of the males. The same findings were obtained in a further study using a method that presented verbal descriptions of dominant or non-dominant people. In both studies high-dominant females were not judged as more attractive than low-dominant females.

The authors conclude that "male dominance is an attribute whose genetic mechanism spread because it conferred a reproductive advantage to its carriers. . . (It appears that) dominance hierarchies are universal in human societies; dominance appears to be an attribute of the male role in all human cultures; male sex hormones are associated with an increased masculinization of anatomical and behavioral traits, including an increase in dominance behaviors; display of rank, skill and achievement by men are commonly part of the human courtship ritual; and females appear to be attracted to dominant males in the majority of primate species" (p. 737).

The various examples that have been cited illustrate how ethologists and sociobiologists consider concepts related to emotions (eg dominance and sexuality). The following section will briefly discuss some attempts by evolutionary biologists to relate other biological concepts to emotions.

EMOTIONS IN THE CONTEXT OF EVOLUTIONARY BIOLOGY

Trivers (1971) has described the emotional implications of reciprocal altruism, that is, cooperation between unrelated members of the same or different species. He points out that altruistic behavior is understandable in an evolutionary context. If one risks one's life for a close relative, any offspring left by the relative will contain some of one's own genes. However, altruistic behavior directed towards unrelated individuals is more difficult to understand. To account for such behavior, Trivers (1971) assumes that altruistic behavior towards others makes sense only if they are willing to show altruistic behavior in return. Such mutual concern is highly adaptive and is likely to increase the inclusive fitness of both parties. The major problem that occurs in this context is that some people are "cheaters" and will accept altruistic behavior but not express it. The existence of cheaters in turn leads to an increased ability to assess or evaluate others as a counterstrategy. In addition, the emotions of "moralistic anger", "gratitude", "sympathy", "guilt", "trust", and "suspicion" are assumed by Trivers to have evolved, in part, as a result of natural selection for reciprocal altruism.

To explicate these ideas, Trivers (1971) suggests, for example, that "moralistic anger" evolved as a way to avoid victimization and to increase the chances that one's own altruism would be reciprocated. The emotion of "gratitude" is assumed to be a motivator to reciprocate acts of altruism from others. "Guilt" is interpreted as an unpleasant emotion that tends to discourage the individual from exploiting others.

Trivers (1972) has also suggested that "coyness" is a characteristic feminine trait because of the relative difference in parental investment in offspring. Because the female incurs a larger parental investment once she gets pregnant, she tries to gain assurance before mating that the male will assist her in raising her young. The courtship ritual involves the presentation of mixed signals ("teasing") until an assessment has been made about the likely degree of commitment of the male. In contrast, for a male to commit himself to the long process of child rearing, his interest is to make sure that he does not raise another male's offspring. To guard against such a threat to his inclusive fitness, the male tends to be aggressive towards rivals. This is the probable basis for the fact that jealousy is the most frequent cause of murder within a group in most cultures of the world (Freedman, 1974).

Evolutionary biologists have also made some comments on several other emotions. Almost all animals have inhibitions about killing members of their own species. These inhibitions are expressed in the form of rituals, for example appeasement rituals, greeting rituals, combat rituals, and defeat rituals. Such rituals are found in humans as well as in lower animals. Eibl-Eibesfeldt (1975) assumes that the subjective emotion of "pity" is a correlate of some of these rituals, just as "fear" is a correlate of others. He also suggests that gregarious mammals become apathetic when they are kept alone; they suffer from "loneliness". Most important of all is the fact that animals exhibit different and often opposing emotions. The same individuals that are capable of sociability, altruism, and love are also capable of jealousy, hatred, and aggression. None of these relations are more (or less) "natural" than the others, but all reflect aspects of the human ethogram.

In one of the few sociobiological papers dealing primarily with the subject of emotion, Weinrich (1980) points out that (1) every emotion must have an evolutionary history; and (2) as evolutionary adaptations based on natural selection, emotions are all fundamentally "positive" in that they are ways that help individuals increase their reproductive success.

COGNITIONS IN THE CONTEXT OF EVOLUTION

The existence of emotion implies evaluation (Lazarus, Kanner & Folkman, 1980). However, evaluations are not always conscious or reportable. They are more like "cognitive maps" or "hypotheses" whose existence can only be inferred from various kinds of evidence. Such inferred evaluations may be quite primitive, as Zajonc (1980) suggests, or complex and based on extensive experience. They may sometimes be in error, but on the average, most evaluations must be reasonably accurate if an individual is to survive.

Cognitive capacities in lower animals and in humans have evolved with the evolution of the brain. The main function of a large brain and a highly developed cognitive system is to ensure survival. Survival is ensured by increasing the ability of the organism to predict the future. Cognition provides a model of the environment and codes information in a neural code. The predictions that are made are clearly in the service of biological needs such as hunger, sex, and nurturance.

Most organisms come into the world genetically equipped with a cognitive system that is precoded for response to certain events (Breland & Breland, 1966).

For most organisms there are special stimuli in their environment that tend to release characteristic species-typical responses. Such releasing stimuli function to promote group cohesion, initiate courtship behavior, initiate greeting or submissive behavior, warn conspecifics, or serve as threat signals. Many young animals are protected from aggression by adults because of their infantile appearance (Eibl-Eibesfeldt, 1975). For a given type of environment many organisms (such as insects and most birds) "know," without the need for a learning period, which events are dangerous or safe, what signals indicate a mate or a non-mate, and what foods are edible. In higher organisms (mammals and primates) there are fewer innate responses to particular stimuli. Instead, there is a genetically based "curiosity" that impels the animal to explore its environment and gradually to develop an internal "map" of it. The successful exploration of a large home range requires the ability to remember features of the terrain, food areas, prey, and predators. Cognitive abilities thus contribute directly to inclusive fitness. What is available is a cognitive system—sensory mechanisms, memory stores, coordinating circuits, and so on—whose parameters have to be established by learning experiences of various kinds. In exactly the same way, the capacity for speech and conceptual thought is innate; only the symbols themselves must be learned.

G. A. Parker (1974) has pointed out that fighting behavior functions to assess the relative resource-holding power of the combatants. This means that cognitive capacities must be sufficiently developed to be able to identify displays, threats, and attacks and to judge comparative fighting ability. In species where strong dominance–submission hierarchies exist, there is considerable value for future reproductive success in being able to recognize one's relative position in the hierarchy, and in being able to choose the best time for challenging and overthrowing an ageing dominant animal. This requires the cognitive capacity to assess the existing strengths and weaknesses of all parties to the conflict, and the ability to predict the outcome of a fight with some degree of accuracy.

Similarly, the fact that reciprocal altruism gives cheaters a possible advantage suggests that there must be strong selective pressures for the cognitive capacity to identify cheaters and to recognize trustworthiness in others. The appropriateness of an emotional response can determine whether the individual lives or dies. The whole cognitive process evolved over millions of years in order to make the evaluation of stimulus events more correct and the predictions more precise so that the emotional behavior that finally resulted would be adaptively related to the stimulus events. *Emotional behavior, therefore, is the proximate basis for the ultimate outcome of increased inclusive fitness.* This same idea has been expressed by Barash (1982). He points out that "the major biological function of male–female pair-bonding is the production of successful offspring. Love, companionship and sexual satisfaction are proximate means for achieving this ultimate end" (p. 295). Similarly, Alexander (1987) suggests that happiness is "a proximate mechanism that leads us to perform and repeat acts that in the environments of history, at least would have led to greater reproductive success

. . . Humans should always experience pleasure when they gain in status or increase their control of resources . . . and they should experience some converse feeling when they lose status or resource control" (p. 26).

These various points of view suggest that emotions are evolutionary adaptations, and, as such, are fundamentally "positive" in the sense that they all tend to contribute to survival by increasing the chances of reproductive success.

Another important idea, consistent with biologic thinking, is that emotions can be grouped into a few basic patterns (types) that can be identified at almost all phylogenetic levels and in almost all species. This notion of types, or what I prefer to call "emotion prototypes", reflects the idea that the environments of all organisms have much in common and thus create similar functional needs in different individuals. All organisms need to take in energy supplies from the environment and to deal with issues of reproduction, predation, and elimination of wastes or unpalatable objects. Emotions are adaptive mechanisms that help carry out these tasks successfully.

In order for these various functions to be performed successfully, the organism must be able to make reasonably correct discriminations and evaluations of its social and physical environment. It needs to be able to make predictions about weather, food, the environment, and the relative resource holding power of other individuals. It needs to be able to distinguish cheaters from trustworthy individuals, estimate relative social rank of other members of its group, and distinguish between those who belong to the group and those who do not. The ability to interpret the motives of others is also an important skill for social organisms. These various discriminations and evaluations represent the cognitive functions needed for survival.

Another important idea about emotions that relates to evolution is the view that emotions are forms of behavioral homeostasis. In other words, emotions are activated in an individual when issues of survival are raised in fact or by implication (eg threats, attacks, poisons, or potential mates). The effect of the emotional state is to create an interaction between the individual and the event (or stimulus) that precipitated the emotion in the first place. This interaction is usually an attempt to reduce the disequilibrium and to reestablish a state of comparative rest.

Another important emotion idea that biologists should find congenial is the concept that an emotion should not be defined solely as a subjective feeling state. Such a narrow definition is one factor that makes it difficult for biologists to use the concept of emotion in their work with animals. However, if one recognizes that an emotion is a complex chain of loosely connected events that begins with a stimulus and includes feelings, physiological changes, impulses to action, and specific goal-directed behavior, one can see the application of these ideas to all species.

FOUR BILLION YEARS OF EVOLUTION

If one considers the patterns of changes that have occurred over four billion years of evolution, it may be easier to accept the idea of emotions as adaptive patterns of reaction to significant stimuli in the life of organisms. However life started, self-replication of living cells required four processes: some form of utilization of energy from sunlight, accurate replication of genetic information, accurate translation of genetic information into proteins, and metabolism (Loomis, 1988). This occurred first in small bacteria (prokaryotes). A bacterial cell with 2000 genes could carry out a large number of metabolic activities and could replicate and divide accurately. It could also flourish in diverse environments.

One of the major reasons life was confined to the seas for the first three billion years of this planet is that cells can escape the lethal effects of ultraviolet radiation by staying under water. Only very gradually did oxygen develop in the atmosphere, permitting the gradual development of an ozone layer. Protection against lethal radiation came about in a variety of ways, for example by encasing the embryo in a shell, or by internal development of embryos, or by plants sending their germinative roots underground. In addition to local or periodic changes in environmental conditions, the major environmental event was the gradual change on the earth from an atmosphere without oxygen to one with it. This led to a large increase in the size of cells (eukaryotes) and to a change in their system of metabolism. "As oxidative metabolism came on line, there was sufficient chemical energy available for bacteria to explore the possibilities of directed cell movement. A set of genes evolved to generate flagella and twirl them such that they moved the whole cell toward attractive compounds and away from repellants. In this way metabolism became coupled to adaptive behavior" (Loomis, 1988, p. 136).

Because no environment is optimum for growth indefinitely, there is a strong selective advantage to moving around. The large eukaryotes became predators that engulfed the smaller bacteria. They evolved nuclei, internal membranes to encase their chromosomes, and special intracellular proteins, all adaptations which are found in many current living cells. In fact, "all eukaryotic organisms, from algae to trees to elephants, appear to have descended from a single protoeukaryotic cell" (Loomis, 1988, p. 161). Evidence for this comes from work in molecular biology. A related idea is that various systems developed millions of years ago that worked so well they have never been improved upon. For example, mammalian sperm now use the same flagellum for locomotion that evolved 600 million years ago to keep algae cells near the surface of water. Similarly, the amino acid sequences for both X and B tubulin (the bases of the microtubules that form flagellae) are more than 70% similar in yeast, algae, sea urchins, chickens, rats, pigs, and humans.

Another illustration of the same point is that a small, acidic protein called calmodulin that binds free calcium has an amino acid structure that is almost identical from the amoebae to humans. The same basic histone proteins and nucleosome structure is found in the chromosomes of all eukaryotic cells throughout the plant and animal kingdoms. The gene order on the sex chromosome of mice (the X chromosome) is almost identical with that on the human X chromosome. The development of sexual dimorphism (specialization of males for sperm production and females for egg production) is also extremely widespread. The advantage of this system is that the variability of genetic potentials increases the chances of the individual successfully dealing with changing or catastrophic environments.

Similarities in evolutionary patterns are also found through studies of development. For example, the similarity of developmental patterns in limb bones is evidence that amphibians, reptiles, and mammals all evolved from a common stock of lobe-fin fish. More than 100 years ago it had been noted that there are remarkable similarities in the structures that appeared in the early stages of embryogenesis in mammals, amphibians, birds, reptiles, and fish. A small number of developmental genes can radically alter the behavior of cells and change an amoeba into a multicelled organism. Loomis (1988) estimates that fewer than 1400 developmental genes may have been sufficient for the evolution of simple cells into fish, and fewer than 2500 developmental genes may be sufficient for the embryogenesis of humans. "The important evolutionary differences between a guppy and a primate probably lie in only a few hundred genes" (Loomis, 1988, p. 216).

These various observations, from evolutionary and molecular biology, are presented to emphasize the points that Darwin first made: namely, that evolutionary continuities of structure, function and development imply continuities of behavioral adaptations and mental life.

A PSYCHOEVOLUTIONARY THEORY OF EMOTION

During the past three decades I have been developing a theory of emotion which I refer to as a psychoevolutionary theory. It is based on the Darwinian assumption that emotions are modes of adaptation to significant events in an organism's environment, and that they are complex processes having functional value both for purposes of communication and to increase an individual's chances of survival. Emotions represent proximate methods to achieve ultimate goals of inclusive fitness (Plutchik, 1962, 1980, 1989). The general theory includes three subsidiary models: a structural model, a sequential model, and a derivatives model.

The structural model

This aspect of the theory assumes that emotions may be conceptualized in a fashion analogous to colors and that the relations among emotions can be represented by a three-dimensional model shaped like a cone. The vertical dimension represents the intensity of emotions, the circle defines degree of similarity of emotions, and polarity is represented by the opposite emotions on the circle. This postulate also includes the idea that some emotions are primary and others are derivatives or blends in the sense that some colors are primary and others are mixed. A number of studies have been published showing that the language of emotions can be represented by means of a circle or circumplex (Fisher *et al.*, 1985; Conte & Plutchik, 1981; Plutchik, 1980; Russell, 1989; Wiggins & Broughton, 1985).

The structural model also assumes that emotions are hypothetical constructs or inferences based on various classes of evidence. The kinds of evidence we use to infer the existence of emotions include (1) knowledge of stimulus conditions, (2) knowledge of an organism's behavior in a variety of settings, (3) knowledge of what species-typical behavior is, (4) knowledge of how an organism's peers react to it, and (5) knowledge of the effect of an individual's behavior on others (Plutchik, 1980a). One of the more important reasons that emotional states are difficult to define unequivocally is that more than one emotion can occur at the same time. Any given overt display of emotions can reflect such complex states as approach and avoidance, attack and flight, sex and aggression, or fear and pleasure.

This model also implies that emotions, like colors, have a genetic basis. Darwin (1872/1965) first suggested at least four types of evidence one can use for establishing a genetic basis for emotions. First, he noted that some emotional expressions appear in similar form in many lower animals (for example the apparent increase in body size during rage or agonistic interactions due to erection of body hair or feathers, changes in postures, or expansion of air pouches). Secondly, some emotional expressions appear in infants in the same form as in adults (smiling and frowning, for example). Thirdly, some emotional expressions are shown by those born blind in identical ways to those who are normally sighted (pouting and laughter, for example). And fourthly, some emotional expressions appear in similar form in widely separated races and groups of humans (Eibl-Eibesfeldt, 1975; Ekman & Friesen, 1971).

Recent genetic studies comparing monozygotic and dizygotic twins, cross-adoption studies, and other methods have revealed hereditary contributions to such temperamental (emotional) qualities as aggressiveness (Fuller, 1986; Wimer & Wimer, 1985), timidity or fearfulness (Goddard & Beilharz, 1985), assertiveness (Loehlin, Horn & Williams, 1981), and shyness (Stevenson-Hinde & Simpson, 1982), as well as many others.

Genetic theory indicates that individuals do not inherit behavior *per se* but only the structural and physiological mechanisms that mediate behavior. Genes influence threshholds of sensitivity, perceptual inclinations, cellular structures, and biochemical events. They determine epigenetic rules that act as filters limiting the kind of information allowed into the system and how that information is to be processed. For example, most animals appear to have auditory detectors "tuned" to signals that are of special significance for their survival (Lumsden & Wilson, 1981). Most, but not all, emotional expressions are based on genetic templates or schemata that determine the generality of emotional development and reactions to probable events in the environment (Plutchik, 1983).

The sequential model

This model assumes that emotions are complex chains of events with stabilizing feedback loops that tend to produce some kind of behavioral homeostasis. Figure 2.1 illustrates this idea. Emotions are triggered by various events. These events must be cognitively evaluated as being of significance to the well-being or integrity of the individual. If such a determination is made, various feelings as well as a pattern of physiological changes will result. These physiological changes have the character of anticipatory reactions associated with various types of exertions or impulses, such as the urge to explore, to attack, to retreat, or to mate. Depending on the relative strengths of these various impulses, a final vectorial resultant will occur in the form of overt action that is designed to have an effect on the stimulus that triggered this chain of events in the first place. For example, distress signals by a puppy or the crying of an infant will increase the probability that the mother or a mother substitute will arrive on the scene. The overall effect of this complex feedback system is to reduce the threat or to change the emergency situation in such a way as to achieve a temporary behavioral homeostatic balance.

The derivatives model

The concept of primary and derived emotions implies that emotions are related to a number of derivative conceptual domains. This idea has been explored in a number of different ways. For example, it has been shown that the language of mixed emotions is identical to the language of personality traits. Hostility has been judged to be composed of anger and disgust, sociability is a blend of joy and acceptance, and guilt is a combination of pleasure plus fear. Emotional components have been identified for hundreds of personality traits. In addition, there is now clear-cut evidence that personality traits also exhibit a circumplex structure just as emotions do (Conte & Plutchik, 1981; Russell, 1989; Wiggins & Broughton, 1985).

The idea of derivatives can be extended further. Diagnostic terms such as "depressed", "manic", and "paranoid" can be conceived as extreme expressions of such basic emotions as sadness, joy, and disgust. Several studies have also revealed that the language of diagnosis shares a circumplex structure

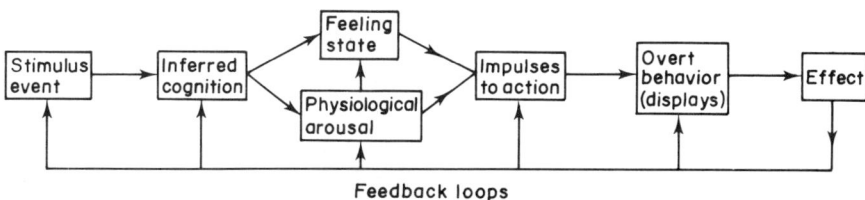

Figure 2.1. The complex chain of events defining an emotion

Table 2.1. Emotions and their derivatives

Subjective language	Behavioral language	Functional language	Trait language	Diagnostic language	Ego defense language	Coping style language
Fear	Escape	Protection	Timid	Passive	Repression	Suppression
Anger	Attack	Destruction	Quarrelsome	Antisocial	Displacement	Substitution
Joy	Mate	Reproduction	Sociable	Manic	Reaction formation	Reversal
Sadness	Cry	Reintegration	Gloomy	Depressed	Compensation	Replacement
Acceptance	Groom	Incorporation	Trusting	Histrionic	Denial	Minimization
Disgust	Vomit	Rejection	Hostile	Paranoid	Projection	Fault-finding
Expectation	Map	Exploration	Demanding	Obsessive–compulsive	Intellectualization	Mapping
Surprise	Stop	Orientation	Indecisive	Borderline	Regression	Help-seeking

with emotions (Plutchik & Platman, 1977; Schaefer & Plutchik, 1966; Plutchik & Conte, 1985).

Carrying the notion of derivatives still further, our research has shown that the language of ego defense can also be conceptualized as being related to emotions. For example, displacement can be conceptualized as an unconscious way to deal with anger that cannot be directly expressed without punishment. Similarly, projection can be conceptualized as an unconscious way to deal with a feeling of disgust for (or rejection of) oneself by attributing this feeling to outsiders. Parallels of this sort have been drawn for each of the primary emotions and are described in detail in Kellerman (1979) and Plutchik, Kellerman and Conte (1979). The concept of derivatives is illustrated more fully in Table 2.1, where the conceptual links between affects, behavior, functions, personality traits, diagnoses, and ego defenses are shown. Also added is the domain of coping styles, which can be hypothesized as the conscious derivatives of the unconscious ego defenses. Thus, fault-finding corresponds to projection, reversal to reaction formation, and mapping to intellectualization. Other derivative domains have also been proposed (Plutchik, 1984b, 1989).

IMPLICATIONS OF THE PSYCHOEVOLUTIONARY THEORY

The theory states that emotions represent fundamental adaptive mechanisms related to interorganismic communication and personal as well as genetic survival. Emotions have a genetic substitute, and can be identified in functional terms at all phylogenetic levels. This theory is parsimonious in that the same set of assumptions has relevance and explanatory value for a number of conceptual domains (affects, personality, defenses, diagnoses, coping styles). It has predicted some new observations that have been empirically confirmed (the circumplex structure of affects, personality traits, diagnoses, and defenses). It has also provided some new insights into specific issues such as the relations between emotions and motivations (Plutchik, 1980), emotions and cognitions (Plutchik, 1977), emotions and imagery (Plutchik, 1984a), emotions and temperament (Plutchik, 1971, 1985), emotions and empathy (Plutchik, 1987), emotions and nightmares (Kellerman, 1987), emotions and primary processes (Kellerman, 1990), and emotions and projective tests (Kellerman, 1989). Also of great importance, it has provided a theoretical rationale for the construction of a number of new test instruments designed to measure affects (Plutchik, 1966, 1971, 1989), personality (Plutchik & Kellerman, 1974), ego defenses (Plutchik, Kellerman & Conte, 1979), and coping styles (Buckley *et al.*, 1984; Wilder & Plutchik, 1982). The theory thus provides a guide for research, shows connectedness between diverse domains, and predicts some relationships that have been empirically confirmed.

REFERENCES

Alexander, R. D. (1987). *The Biology of Moral Systems*. New York: Aldine de Gruyter.
Barash, D. P. (1982). *Sociobiology and Behavior*. New York: Elsevier.

Breland, K. & Breland, M. (1966). *Animal Behavior*. New York: MacMillan.

Buckley, P., Conte, H. R., Plutchik, R., Wild, K. V. & Karasu, T. B. (1984). Psychodynamic variables as predictors of psychotherapy outcome. *American Journal of Psychiatry*, **141**, 742–748.

Buirski, P., Plutchik, R. & Kellerman, H. (1978). Sex differences, dominance, and personality in the chimpanzee. *Animal Behavior*, **26**, 123–129.

Burghardt, G. M. (1978). Behavioral ontogeny of reptiles: whence, whither, and why? In G. M. Burghardt & M. Bekoff (Eds), *The Development of Behavior: Comparative and Evolutionary Aspects*. New York: Garland STPM Press.

Clapperton, B. K. (1989). Scent-marking behavior of the ferret, *Mustela furo L. Animal Behavior*, **38**: 436–446.

Conte, H. R. & Plutchik, R. (1981). A circumplex model for interpersonal traits. *Journal of Personality and Social Psychology*, **2**, 823–830.

Crowell-Davis, S. & Houpt, K. A. (1985). The ontogeny of flehman in horses. *Animal Behavior*, **33**, 739–745.

Darwin, C. (1965). *The Expression of the Emotions in Man and Animals*. Chicago, Ill. University of Chicago Press. (Original work published 1872)

Eibl-Eibesfeldt, I. (1975). *Ethology: The Biology of Behavior*, 2nd edn. New York: Holt.

Ekman, P. & Friesen, W. V. (1971). Constants across cultures in the face and emotions. *Journal of Personality and Social Psychology*, **17**, 124–129.

Fisher, G. A., Heise, D. R., Bohrnstedt, G. W. & Lucke, J. Z. (1985). Evidence for extending the circumplex model of personality trait language to self-reported moods. *Journal of Personality and Social Psychology*, **49**: 233–242.

Freedman, D. G. (1974). *Human Infancy: An Ethological Perspective*. Hillsdale, NJ: Erlbaum.

Fuller, J. L. (1986). Genetics and emotions. In R. Plutchik & H. Kellerman (Eds), *Emotion: Theory, Research, and Experience*: *Vol. 3. Biological Foundation of Emotion*. Orlando, Fl.: Academic Press.

Goddard, M. E. & Beilharz, R. G. (1985). A multivariate analysis of the genetics of fearfulness in potential guide dogs. *Behavior Genetics*, **15**, 69–89.

Goodall, J. (1986). *The Chimpanzees of Gombe: Patterns of Behavior*. Cambridge, Mass: Belknap.

Kellerman, H. (1979). *Group Therapy and Personality. Intersecting Structures*. New York: Grune & Stratton.

Kellerman, H. (1987). Nightmares and the structure of personality. In H. Kellerman (Ed.), *The Nightmare: Psychological and Biological Formulations*. New York: Columbia University Press.

Kellerman, H. (1989). Projective measures of emotion. In R. Plutchik & H. Kellerman (Eds), *Emotion: Theory, Research, and Experience*: *Vol. 4. The Measurement of Emotions*. San Diego, Ca: Academic Press.

Kellerman, H. (1990). Emotion and the organization of primary process. In R. Plutchik and H. Kellerman (Eds), *Emotion Psychopathology and Psychotherapy, Vol. 5*. San Diego, Ca: Academic Press.

Kroodsma, D. E. (1978). Aspects of learning in the ontogeny of bird song: Where, from whom, when, how many, and how accurately? In G. M. Burghardt & M. Bekoff (Eds), *The Development of Behavior: Comparative and Evolutionary Aspects*. New York: Garland STPM Press.

Lawick-Goodall, J. van (1973). The behavior of chimpanzees in their natural habitat. *American Journal of Psychiatry*, **130**, 1–12.

Lazarus, R. S., Kanner, A. D. & Folkman, S. (1980). Emotions: A cognitive-phenomenological analysis. In R. Plutchik & H. Kellerman (Eds), *Emotion: Theory, Research, and Experience*: *Vol. 1. Theories of Emotion*. New York: Academic Press.

Leyhausen, P. (1956). Verhaltens—studien bei katzen. *Zeitschischrift fur Tierpyschologie*, **2**. Cited in Hinde, R. A., *Animal Behavior*, 1966.

Loehlin, J. C., Horn, J. M. & Williams, L. (1981). Personality resemblance in adoptive families. *Behavior Genetics*, **11**, 309–320.

Loomis, W. F. (1988). *Four Billion Years*. Sunderland, Mass: Sinauer Associates.

Lorenz, K. (1952). Cited in Eibl-Eibesfeldt, I. *Love and Hate*, 1971, Holt, Rinehart & Winston.

Lumsden, C. J. & Wilson, E. O. (1981). *Genes, Mind and Culture: The Coevolutionary Process*. Cambridge, Mass: Harvard University Press.

McDonald, M. V. (1989). Function of song in Scott's seaside sparrow, *Ammodramus maritimus peninsulae*. *Animal Behavior*, **38**, 468–485.

Modahl, K. B. & Eaton, G. G. (1977). Display behavior in a confined troop of Japanese macques (Macaca fuscata). *Animal Behavior*, **25**, 525–535.

Morris, D. J. (1954). The reproductive behavior of the zebra finch (Peophila guttata) with special reference to pseudofemale behavior and displacement activities. *Behaviour*, **6**, 271–322.

Noakes, D. L. G. (1978). Ontogeny of behavior in fishes: A survey and suggestions. In G. M. Burghardt & M. Bekoff (Eds), *The Development of Behavior: Comparative and Evolutionary Aspects*. New York: Garland STPM Press.

Parker, G. A. (1974). Assessment strategy and the evolution of fighting behavior. *Journal of Theoretical Biology*, **47**, 223–243.

Plutchik, R. (1962). *The Emotions: Facts, Theories and a New Model*. New York: Random House.

Plutchik, R. (1966). Multiple rating scales for the measurement of affective states. *Journal of Clinical Psychology*, **22**, 423–425.

Plutchik, R. (1971). Individual and breed differences in approach and withdrawal in dogs. *Behavior*, **40**, 302–311.

Plutchik, R. (1977). Cognitions in the service of emotion. In D. R. Candland, J. P. Fell, E. Kean, A. I. Leshner, R. Plutchik & R. M. Tharpy (Eds), *Emotion*. Monterey, Ca: Brooks/Cole.

Plutchik, R. (1980). *Emotions: A Psychoevolutionary Synthesis*. New York: Harper & Row.

Plutchik, R. (1983). Emotions in early development: A psychoevolutionary approach. In R. Plutchik & H. Kellerman (Eds), *Emotion: Theory, Research, and Experience: Vol. 2, Emotions in Early Development*. New York: Academic Press.

Plutchik, R. (1984a). Emotions and imagery. *Journal of Mental Imagery*, **8**, 105–112.

Plutchik, R. (1984b). Emotions: A general psychoevolutionary theory. In K. R. Scherer & P. Ekman (Eds), *Approaches to Emotion*. Hillsdale, NJ: Erlbaum.

Plutchik, R. (1985). Emotion and temperament. Paper presented at the symposium on "Biology and temperament" at the meeting of the American Psychological Association, Los Angeles, California.

Plutchik, R. (1987). Evolutionary bases of empathy. In N. Eisenberg and J. Strayer (Eds) *Empathy and Its Development*. New York: Cambridge University Press.

Plutchik, R. (1989). Measuring emotions and their derivatives. In R. Plutchik & H. Kellerman (Eds), *Emotion: Theory, Research, and Experience*: Vol. 4, *The Measurement of Emotions*. San Diego, Ca: Academic Press.

Plutchik, R. & Conte, H. R. (1985). Quantitative assessment of personality disorders. In R. Michels, J. O. Cavenar, Jr, H. K. H. Brodie *et al.* (Eds), *Psychiatry* (Vol. 1). Philadelphia, Pa: Lippincott.

Plutchik, R. & Kellerman, H. (1974). *Manual of the Emotions Profile Index*. Los Angeles, Ca: Western Psychological Services.

Plutchik, R., Kellerman H. & Conte, H. R. (1979). A structural theory of ego defenses. In C. E. Izard (Ed.), *Emotions, Personality and Psychopathology*. New York: Plenum.

Plutchik, R. & Platman, S. R. (1977). Personality connotations of psychiatric diagnoses, *Journal of Nervous and Mental Disease*, **165**, 418–422.

Russell, J. A. (1989). Verbal measures of emotion. In R. Plutchik & H. Kellerman (Eds), *Emotion: Theory, Research and Experience: Vol. 4. The Measurement of Emotions*. San Diego, Ca: Academic Press.

Sadalla, E. K., Kenrick, D. T. & Vershura. B. (1987). Dominance and heterosexual attraction. *Journal of Personality and Social Psychology*, **52**, 730–738.

Samuels, A., Silk, J. B. & Rodman, P. S. (1984). Changes in the dominance rank and reproductive behavior of male bonnet macques (Macaca radiata). *Animal Behavior*, **32**, 994–1003.

Scaife, M. (1976a). The response to eye-like shapes by birds I. The effect of context: A predator and a strange bird. *Animal Behavior*, **24**, 195–199.

Scaife, M. (1976b). The response to eye-like shapes by birds II. The importance of staring, pairedness, and shape. *Animal Behavior*, **24**, 200–206.

Schaefer, E. S., and Plutchik, R. (1966). Interrelationships of emotions, traits, and diagnostic constructs. *Psychological Reports*, **18**, 399–410.

Scherer, K. R. (1989). Vocal measurement of emotion. In R. Plutchik & H. Kellerman (Eds), *Emotion: Theory, Research and Experience: Vol. 4. The Measurement of Emotions*. San Diego, Ca: Academic Press.

Stevenson-Hinde, J. & Simpson, A. E. (1982). Temperament and relationships. In R. Porter & G. M. Collins (Eds), *Temperamental Differences in Infants and Young Children*. London: Pitman.

Tembrock, G. (1975). Die Erforschung des tierlichen Stimmausdrucks (Bioakustik). In F. Trojan (Ed.), *Biophonetick*. Mannheim: Bibliographisches Institut.

Trivers, R. L. (1971). The evolution of reciprocal altruism. *Quarterly Review of Biology*, **46**, 35–57.

Trivers, R. L. (1972). Parental investment and sexual selection. In B. Campbell (Ed.), *Sexual Selection and the Descent of Man*. Chicago, Ill.: Aldine.

Weinrich, J. D. (1980). Toward a sociobiological theory of the emotions. In R. Plutchik & H. Kellerman (Eds), *Emotions: Theory, Research, and Experience. Vol. 1. Theories of Emotion*. New York: Academic Press.

Wiggins, J. S. & Broughton, R. (1985). The interpersonal circle: A structural model for the integration of personality research. *Perspectives in Personality*, **1**, 1–47.

Wilder, J. F. & Plutchik, R. (1982). Preparing the professional. Building prevention into training. In W. S. Paine (Ed.), *Job Stress and Burnout*. Beverly Hills, Ca: Sage.

Wilson, E. O. (1975). *Sociobiology: The New Synthesis*. Cambridge, Mass: Harvard University Press.

Wimer, R. E. & Wimer, C. C. (1985). Animal behavior genetics: A search for the biological foundations of behavior. *Annual Review of Psychology*, **36**, 171–218.

Zajonc, R. B. (1980). Feeling and thinking: Preferences need no inferences. *American Psychologist*, **35**, 151–175.

3 Affective Neuroscience: A Conceptual Framework for the Neurobiological Study of Emotions

JAAK PANKSEPP

Department of Psychology, Bowling Green State University, Bowling Green, Ohio 43403, USA

That the experience-hypothesis, as ordinarily understood, is inadequate to account for emotional phenomena, will be sufficiently manifest. If possible, it is even more at fault in respect to the emotions than in respect to the cognitions. The doctrine maintained by some philosophers, that all the desires, all the sentiments, are generated by the experiences of the individual, is so glaringly at variance with hosts of facts, that I cannot but wonder how any one should ever have entertained it.

Herbert Spencer (1855) *Principles of Psychology*, p. 606

The study of emotions is one of the most important and one of the most neglected areas of behavioral neuroscience. The failure of brain research to deal effectively with emotions is highlighted each year by the schedule of events of the Annual Meeting of the Society for Neuroscience in the States. Since the inaugural meeting of that society (in October of 1971), there has yet to be a session devoted exclusively to emotions (not to mention any specific emotion such as "fear", "rage", "separation distress/grief", "anticipatory eagerness", "joy/play", "sexual lust", or "maternal nurturance/acceptance"), although there are routinely multiple sessions on more limited topics. This reflects the microanalytical bias of the times—the current emphasis on discovering more and more about less and less at the expense of dealing with systemic issues of brain organization. The neglect of emotionality also results from its subjective neurodynamic nature—which is presently impossible to measure directly in animals or humans. Since it is much easier to study neurobehavioral specifics than the intrinsic organizational principles which control behavioral states, many important aspects of brain function continue to be neglected by neuroscientists.

Our understanding of both brain and behavior continues to be impoverished by this neglect. Since the 1990s have been designated the "Decade of the brain" by congressional resolution in the United States, it seems timely once more to promote a vigorous empirical confrontation with this most important neglected area of brain research—the psychoneurological nature of emotionality. To achieve this, we need to fully acknowledge that psychology is not simply

International Review of Studies on Emotion, Vol. 1. Edited by K. T. Strongman
© 1991 John Wiley & Sons Ltd

"the study of behavior" as the glib pedagogic assertion used to go, but rather "the study of all psychobehavioral brain functions—many of which can only be indirectly observed through the study of behavior". This is an essential assumption for progress to be made in understanding the various endogenous central state control mechanisms of the brain. Although this battle has been won in cognitive psychology, it has not in other areas of experimental psychology, especially among those of us who focus our empirical analysis on animal behavior. One can envision such a reorientation leading to a new hybrid discipline of "affective neuroscience", which could be as potent a force in understanding the basis of psychological and behavioral processes as its prospering sister discipline of cognitive neuroscience. Unlike cognitive neuroscience, however, most of the work in the area of affective neuroscience will, by necessity, have to be pursued in carefully selected animal models. A general overview of where such a discipline would fit into the broad arena of the behavioral/brain sciences is presented in Figure 3.1. To achieve such a hybrid science we must acknowledge that other mammals probably also have internal emotional states and experiences which reflect the operation of a shared neurodynamic (ie psychological) heritage and be willing to study them in earnest. In this scheme, anthropomorphism may be a beneficial guide to empirical inquiries as opposed to the mentalistic sin it has always been deemed to be.

It is understandable why the development of a substantive affective neuroscience has been long delayed. The concept of emotion is notoriously hard to define in scientifically useful ways, and it is difficult to extract empirically useful and conceptually consistent guidelines from the vast array of existing perspectives (see Kleinginna & Kleinginna, 1981; Plutchik, 1980; Strongman, 1987). For such reasons, the "behaviorism" of the first two-thirds of this century discarded all mentalistic and innate concepts (including emotions and instincts) which had previously been used in circular ways to explain complex behaviors via unobservable internal causes. However, the behaviorist tradition failed to offer an alternative way to study and understand the nature of central state processes. It merely pretended such concepts were irrelevant for a clear-headed understanding of behavior and did away with them by fiat. This pretty much remains the *modus operandi* of modern behavioral neuroscience. Although it is certain that emotional concepts (as semantic entities) cannot serve as *scientific* explanations of either human or animal behavior, such processes (at a neural level) may instigate and orchestrate many of the spontaneous as well as learned behavioral sequences animals exhibit. Sensitive observers down through the ages have agreed that primal emotive tendencies are the deep neuropsychic triggers which instigate and channel much of human thought and action. Although cognitions and emotions are intimately interrelated at various locations within the nervous system, emotions may well be more influential than cognitions in guiding choices among courses of action which confront organisms during their lifespans in the real world.

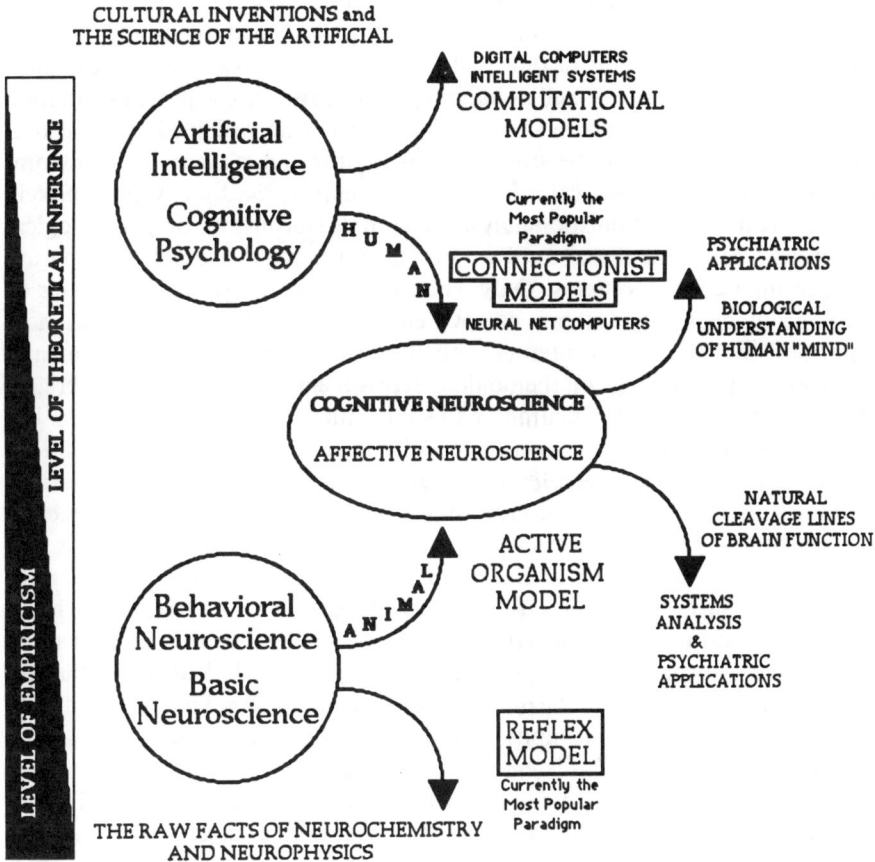

CULTURAL INVENTIONS and
THE SCIENCE OF THE ARTIFICIAL

DIGITAL COMPUTERS
INTELLIGENT SYSTEMS
COMPUTATIONAL
MODELS

LEVEL OF THEORETICAL INFERENCE

LEVEL OF EMPIRICISM

Artificial
Intelligence

Cognitive
Psychology

H U M A N

Currently the
Most Popular
Paradigm

CONNECTIONIST
MODELS

NEURAL NET COMPUTERS

PSYCHIATRIC
APPLICATIONS

BIOLOGICAL
UNDERSTANDING
OF HUMAN "MIND"

COGNITIVE NEUROSCIENCE

AFFECTIVE NEUROSCIENCE

NATURAL
CLEAVAGE LINES
OF BRAIN FUNCTION

ACTIVE
ORGANISM
MODEL

Behavioral
Neuroscience

Basic
Neuroscience

A N I M A L

SYSTEMS
ANALYSIS
&
PSYCHIATRIC
APPLICATIONS

REFLEX
MODEL

Currently the
Most Popular
Paradigm

THE RAW FACTS OF NEUROCHEMISTRY
AND NEUROPHYSICS

Figure 3.1. A conceptual model of relations between the major cognitive and neuroscience approaches to understanding central nervous system processes. As one ascends from basic neuroscience to higher cognitive approaches, the level of the theoretical inference must increase by necessity and hence the level of raw empiricism diminishes. While artificial intelligence and basic neuroscience tend to yield facts which do not readily fit into what we can actually know about the overall *functional* organization of the brain at the present time, cognitive neuroscience and affective neuroscience attempt to deal with intermediate levels of evidence which can relate more directly to such global issues of brain organization. While cognitive neuroscience aspires to understand human mental functions which are difficult to probe in animal models, affective neuroscience can aspire to understand the basic ancient operating systems the animals and humans share in "hard-wired" neural circuitry. Affective neuroscience assumes an "active organism" approach, namely, that inherited central state processes rather than reflexes are the major source of behavioral coherence that animals normally exhibit

It is certain that within the evolutionary layers of brain function there reside many central state regulators which resemble the "hidden units" of neural net computers, which are undoubtedly hard to conceptualize objectively. Such mechanisms, which may represent genetically ordained read-only-memory (ROM) operating systems in the brain, cannot be addressed empirically until we (animal behaviorists as well as human psychologists) are willing, as a unified discipline, to accept the existence of intrinsic, genetically ordained psychoneural processes which can only be studied indirectly through a rigorous behavioral analysis guided by theoretical inference (Panksepp, 1989a,b). It seems unlikely that a credible reductionistic analysis of complex behaviors or psychological "energies" can be achieved until we first decipher the neurobiological nature of such innate brain systems. Only when we fathom the neural substrates of these brain operating systems can we endeavor to credibly determine how emotions help organisms interact with the infinite variety of environmental complexities that impinge on the random-access-memory analogs of their brains. Without the intervening neural analysis of the ROMs that evolution has constructed into neural tissue, we are left with little else than surface descriptions of the relationships between semantic, behavioral and autonomic regularities and the subjectively emotional responses which are triggered by environmental occurrences. Although there is a vast area of descriptive research such as that which remains to be done at the periphery, especially when combined with sensitive measures of human self-disclosure, the peripheral and subjective levels of analysis must remain perpetually "superficial", at least from a hard scientific perspective. A penetrating analysis requires that we try to link affective changes in some credible manner to the underlying neural dynamics. That is a hard task. Some dualists say it is an impossible one. But they are wrong.

Behaviorism, by actively disregarding the workings of the brain (of the "black box" as it was so euphemistically called), could stand firm in its denial of the scientific utility of central state concepts (for critique see Bunge, 1990; Panksepp, 1988, 1989a,b, 1990a). Without a neurological analysis, emotional and other "mental" concepts can all too readily be deemed to be scientifically insubstantial, especially as far as animal psychology is concerned. Although modern cognitive approaches have accepted the reality of hidden psychological processes which direct behavior, without the assistance of a neural analysis cognitive approaches cannot deal effectively with the nature of the basic emotions. Indeed, until recently, cognitive psychology largely ignored emotional issues because it had no substantive way to deal with brain processes that could not be reduced to environmental-informational events or simpler verbal/mental concepts. However, it is perplexing that modern functional neuroscience has "chosen" to follow the lead of behaviorism in disregarding emotional issues. Only from a superficial methodological perspective is the neglect understandable. The tenets of a visually based radical positivism are easier to agree upon than the vagaries of theoretical inference. However, by ignoring such key psychoneural issues, modern neuroscience has helped sustain a form of neodualism (ie that certain dynamic brain functions are not capable of being scientifically understood) as did behaviorism before it. The realization that there is no credible alternative to a neurotheoretical approach to understanding the emotional organization of the brain has yet to become common currency. The option has been to ignore or abandon the field, and behavioral neuroscience presently still proceeds on that course.

Hence, our mechanistic understanding of emotionality remains primitive, and there is not even a provisionally accepted consensus of taxonomies and subtypes of emotional systems of the brain which reflect the natural fracture lines of brain organization, but at least two data-based neurotaxonomies have been proposed (Henry, 1986; Panksepp, 1982). If predictable relations do in fact exist between certain traditional emotional concepts and the activities of distinct neural systems of the brain, then neurobiological work on the mechanisms of emotion could succeed quite rapidly. On the other hand, if emotions are simply social constructions reflecting the higher brain's interpretation and verbal labelings of various forms of bodily turmoil (ie variants of the James–Lange theory), as many cognitively oriented investigators are prone to believe, then the prospect of a coherent neurobiological analysis of emotion is remote. Indeed, if the social constructivist view is correct, animal research would have little role in elucidating the nature of human emotions. However, I would suggest that that view, at least as far as the basic emotions are concerned, is quite simply wrong (as the early associationist Herbert Spencer acknowledged forcefully over a century ago, see above). I am tempted to add, at risk of causing offense, that the social constructivist view is a uniquely human, self-centered, and an anti-evolutionary perspective. The weight of existing evidence suggests that all mammals share essentially identical primary process emotional circuits, subcortically situated.

Thus, the present perspective rests on the empirically based premise that primal emotions do have coherent neural underpinnings in the mammalian brain (LeDoux, 1987; MacLean, 1990; Panksepp, 1981a, 1982, 1986a, 1988, 1989a,b). However, it is probably fair to say that the majority of behaviorally oriented investigators of the brain have not yet accepted such a view—indeed, it is not uncommon for such a view to be disparaged (eg Vanderwolf et al., 1988). Such criticisms, I believe, reflect the residual influence of an outmoded James–Langian conception of emotionality, where emotion was deemed to be a monolithic entity akin to arousal, with only the dimensions of intensity and positive and negative affect giving it further resolution. In fact, the brain appears to contain a number of functionally and anatomically distinct emotional circuits. Still, regardless of one's theoretical position, it is undeniable that emotions cannot be measured directly as empirical dependent variables in either animal or human research. To proceed empirically, one must assume that emotional functions of the brain can be indexed reasonably accurately via a careful analysis of behavior in conjunction with related autonomic changes.

The perspective advocated in this chapter is that primary emotive processes can be studied effectively in common laboratory animals through the analysis of brain mechanisms which control certain simple *unconditional* behaviors which most humans spontaneously recognize as reflective of internal emotional content (ie we seem to have feature detectors for such behaviors because in addition to organizing behavioral coping strategies, some emotions also have important interanimal signaling functions). From this perspective, a somatic analysis may be more important for understanding the nature of emotions than a visceral analysis. Visceral changes instigated by emotional circuits are better conceptualized as support systems which facilitate the behavioral ends of emotive circuits (Mancia & Zanchetti, 1981). For instance, in order for anger to be an effective energizer of behavior, there must be an accompanying increase in heart rate. Although visceral changes may well feed back onto the nervous system and give color and added "energy" to emotions, there is presently no cogent reason to believe such visceral inputs constitute the essence of emotions as social constructivist theories have posited. Rather, emotionality is instigated directly by arousal of executive circuits of the brain which were designed through evolutionary selection to induce rapid bodily, behavioral and psychological coherence when organisms are confronted by various threatening, thwarting and instigating circumstances. This is a straightforward approach, but for the preceding historical reasons it remains to be widely deployed in neuroscience research. Hence, the token chapter on emotions in most psychobiological texts remains meagre indeed.

THE NATURE OF EMOTIONS AND EMOTIONAL SYSTEMS

A full understanding of basic emotional processes will require the emergence of a fruitful empirical and conceptual interchange between those who study the subjective neurocognitive dynamics of human emotions and fantasies, and behavioral neuroscientists who analyze brain mechanisms which govern the spontaneous action tendencies of animals. We need a language that all interested parties can understand and are willing to use. Effective interchange and fruitful hybridization between the relevant scientific cultures—the psychological, behavioral and neurological—has long been stifled by vastly different languages and conceptions of what is "proper science". While most psychological research proceeds at a molar conceptual and descriptive level of analysis, most behaviorists and neuroscientists aspire toward a molecular causal analysis of simple units of behavior. An intermediate system's approach, using a common language of basic emotions (probably a natural language that already exists in folk psychology), is needed to bring the two sides together.

Obviously, emotionality is a multilevel process in the brain, and substantive progress cannot be made on all fronts. Emotionality encompasses many fuzzy concepts such as moods, feelings, affective states and sentiments that can only be arbitrarily/creatively defined at the present time but which surely are closely linked to the neural processes which subserve emotions and motivations. Although there is a common tendency to believe that emotions are felt subjectively by the higher reaches of the brain, that is an assumption based on practically no evidence. Indeed, it is almost impossible to evoke emotional feelings by electrically stimulating the human neocortex. I think it is more reasonable to suppose that the basic neural schema for affective self-awareness is an ancient neural faculty (which allowed organisms to compete for resources more effectively), and that emotional systems exert most of their hedonic effects at quite primitive levels of brain organization. Indeed, it is clear from repeated experiments during this century that decorticate animals express and appear to experience emotions more intensely than those having intact brains. Apparently, the neocortex achieves its higher functions at least partially by inhibiting more primitive affective tendencies. In any event, the basic emotional systems appear to be ancient subcortical action instigating and coordinating systems. These executive systems probably inherently promote a certain degree of behavioral flexibility which can be molded by reinforcement mechanisms which themselves may be closely linked, perhaps even isomorphic with, fluctuations in the neural activities of the emotional systems. For instance, one possibility, akin to the discarded "drive-reduction theory of reinforcement", is that the rapid decline in activity of an emotional system can strengthen ("reinforce") immediately preceding behaviors and cognitions (Panksepp, 1986a).

Until demonstrated otherwise, it is most reasonable to assume that the executive emotive circuits, or closely related systems, directly instigate internal feeling states because they were designed to impose values and priorities on events and courses of action. For effective arousal of coordinated action, a variety of bodily and cognitive changes have to be simultaneously recruited. From such a vantage, both the autonomic and cognitive consequences of emotional arousal may be largely the products rather than the causes of activity in emotive circuits. This is not to suggest that during ontogeny cognitions do not develop access routes to emotional circuits (perhaps via the aforementioned "reinforcement" processes), but that that type of control is a secondary development (one that may require the prior epigenetic development of cognitive structures under the permissive guidance of emotive circuits). In other words, some evolutionarily "prepared" sensations and perceptions have strong access routes to emotional circuits. Most exteroceptive stimuli are neutral (ie have only weak interactions with emotive circuits) and they can come to elicit emotions only as a function of the neural mysteries that yield classical conditioning. Indeed, recent work with sound-cued fear conditioning indicates that such conditional access routes can be totally subcortical (LeDoux, Sakaguchi & Reis, 1984). Whether these sensory access routes should be considered cognitive or not (eg see the Lazarus, 1984 vs Zajonc, 1984 debate) is a moot point. When conceptualized in this way (as fundamental, unconditional ROM circuits of the brain), emotional systems become readily amenable to a reductionistic analysis. If primal emotions are defined with respect to provisional neural circuit characteristics—for instance as executive command systems for the activation and synchronization of psychobehavioral classes—we can emerge from the conceptual morass of disparate and often undefinable affective terms and begin to work, in earnest, on the common brain mechanisms which underlie emotionality in all mammals. If one accepts this view, the search to understand the fundamental nature of emotionality becomes largely a neurobehavioral question that can be most effectively studied in carefully selected animal models.

One additional problem in studying emotionality is that in the higher reaches of the human brain, emotional systems appear to help create many subtleties of subjective experience which help guide behavioral choices. At present, that level of analysis remains quite unworkable in animal brain research. We will never know, with any certainty, what types of subjective emotional feelings other animals have, nor whether they can prioritize their actions indirectly on the basis of such internal states. For present purposes, however, it is not necessary to be able to measure the subjective dynamics of other animals. It is a sufficiently pressing task simply to determine which brain circuits generate the various classes of unconditional emotive behaviors which seem to represent the direct operation of emotional processes in the brain and to determine whether the activities of these circuits have affective consequences for animals (as can be measured in various ways, especially via the study of conditioned preferences and aversions). Once we have sufficient clarity at that level, we can then potentially inquire whether emotional feelings in humans emanate from homologous circuits, and if they do (as presently seems likely—see, Panksepp, 1985), then we may be in a position to develop more direct ways to index the putative feeling states of other animals via objective behavioral, neurophysiological and neurochemical measures.

In short, emotions can only be used as scientific explanations for animal behavior when we have some substantial neurobiological understanding of emotional circuits. Since that level of knowledge remains to be achieved, animal behaviorists rightfully avoid emotional concepts (for without the neurological knowledge, emotional explanations must remain perpetually circular). Unfortunately, animal behaviorists also tend to avoid the neurobiological study of emotional concepts, and all too often discourage and disparage the study of such concepts since they cannot be adequately defined or validated. Of course, it is absurd to request definitions for primary brain processes at the outset of research—the proper definition of a central state can only emerge from the cogent study of the underlying neural mechanisms. It is the end-point rather than the beginning of a research program. To proceed empirically, all we need are well-operationalized measures which can be provisionally used to index the arrays of emotional states that animals seem to possess. Their validity can only be judged by the coherence of the results produced and ultimately, if one is willing to accept the probability of homologies, by the relationship of the results to human subjective and clinical experiences. Until such knowledge is achieved, animal behaviorists might simply encourage more neurobiological research in the area and advisedly entertain the use of an "as if" semantic strategy to discuss the role of emotions in the control of animal behavior (for further discussion of this option, see the penultimate section of this chapter).

SOME RECURRENT PROBLEMS WITH THE USE OF EMOTIONAL EXPLANATIONS FOR BEHAVIOR

Besides problems which arise from definitions and the subjective nature of emotional experiences, behaviorally oriented investigators also typically do not like emotional explanations for animal actions because they often seem excessively complex and unparsimonious. Every time someone suggests a specific emotional explanation for a learned behavioral change, skilled thinkers in the field can suggest equally simple logical alternatives. To take one example. The possible explanations of how anxiolytic drugs such as benzodiazepines reduce conditioned emotional responses (CERs) are many. In addition to anxiety-fear reduction, perhaps the minor tranquilizers produce (i) analgesia, (ii) amnesia, (iii) general disinhibition of behavior, (iv) enhanced appetite for the positive reward that is sustaining baseline operant behavior, or even (v) perceptual derangements such as impaired discrimination of temporal relationships between conditional and unconditional stimuli. No study in the vast CER/punishment/psychopharmacology literature, to my knowledge, has tried to address all such control issues in a single project.

Obviously, the utility of an emotional analysis of animal actions depends ultimately on the nature of the underlying neural systems which control behaviour. I would argue that by entertaining the existence of emotional realities in the animal brain, we can vastly change, in potentially productive directions, the way behavioral phenomena are conceptualized. Consider the case of stress-induced analgesia, a seemingly cruel area of research that has grown enormously during the past two decades (see Kelly, 1986 and Rodgers & Randall, 1988 for overviews). The phenomenon itself is quite straightforward—animals exhibit an apparent elevation of pain sensitivity following imposition of a variety of stressors—but the meaning of the response change is not. Because animal behaviorists have been loathe to entertain the existence of neuropsychic responses, they have come to accept the behavioral end-point of a change in pain responsivity as an adequate reflection of a change in pain sensitivity (ie "analgesia" as operationally defined), even though some of the pertinent experiments are methodologically silly. For instance, cold-water swimming is used as a stressor and then pain sensitivity is measured by applying radiant heat to the resulting cold tail, with no straightforward "cold-tail control" groups being run (ie only the tail of an animal which has been immersed). Also, no one has yet entertained the simple possibility that stressors change blood flow to the tail and hence change the local neural dynamics in the tail. The so-called "analgesia" could simply be a biophysical response of the tail. In any event, because of the behaviorist tradition, there is practically no discussion in the literature of such alternative psychobiological explanations. "Stress-induced analgesia" is accepted as an important phenomenon at a simple-minded operational level.

Despite the penetrance of signal-detection theory throughout psychology, little attention is paid to the fact that attentional changes and other response bias changes may also explain the apparent pain sensitivity changes. Even less consideration is devoted to the possibility that the neuropsychic changes associated with the offset of the stressor (ie relief) are critical for the "analgesic" phenomena—even though in practically all published experiments of this genera, changes in pain "sensitivity" are measured following the offset rather than during the imposition of the stressor. In such circumstances, both stress onset and offset-related processes should obviously be deemed as equally logical alternatives for explaining changes in pain responsivity. Thus, so-called "stress-induced analgesia" may in fact turn out to be relief-induced analgesia. In this context, it is especially noteworthy that brain opioid release (ie a component of some forms of "stress-induced analgesia") appears to be more closely linked to the offset than to the actual imposition of the stressor (Seeger *et al.*, 1984). Indeed, recent evidence indicates that bodily (spinal) analgesia following stress, as commonly measured by tail-flicks to radiant heat, is not accompanied by a central (supraspinal) analgesia. Squealing to electric tail-shock is actually facilitated by the same stressors which increase tail-flick latencies (Kiyatkin, 1989). By accepting the potential existence of a seemingly self-evident neuroemotional reality in the brain (ie relief), a novel conception of a well-established behavioral phenomenon becomes apparent and diverse new experiments suggest themselves. Which conception is correct needs to be resolved by theoretically guided work. Avoidance of emotional concepts in animal behavior research has simply discouraged adequate consideration of such alternative views.

Of course, emotional interpretations of behavioral change can often be incorrect. For instance, a prominent past mistake is the suggestion that anxiety in the brain is mediated by brain serotonin release simply on the basis of the fact that disinhibition of punished behaviors could be induced by agents which reduce serotonergic activity (for a summary of that theory see Soubrie, 1986 and discussants). In fact, reduction of serotonergic activity disinhibits practically all behaviors, including those learned behaviors which have been inhibited by anxiety. Indeed, it is the premise of this chapter that relatively complex learned behaviors are especially susceptible to faulty interpretation with regard to emotional factors. Because of past problems and mistakes, it would seem that the most effective deployment of emotional concepts would be in the analysis of simple unconditional behavioral tendencies, where alternative explanations can be evaluated most readily. Complex learned behaviors (the traditional fare of behaviorists) are best avoided in basic emotion research for some time to come. In other words, the neurological organization of specific emotions will be best served via the study of unconditional behavioral indicator variables as well as by the analysis of simple, spontaneously learned ("autoshaped") behaviors which are not intentionally reinforced by the investigator (such as freezing and potentiated startle for fear and anticipatory eagerness for predictable appetitive rewards). When we understand such spontaneous emotive processes at the neuronal level, we may eventually be able to utilize that knowledge rigorously to determine how the underlying emotional systems control learned behaviors in more complex situations.

But, of course, the analysis of unconditional behavioral indicators of emotional change will be confronted by interpretive difficulties. Take the seemingly straightforward case of isolation-induced crying as a measure of the intensity of separation distress. It is clear that this measure of protest is reduced by social comfort, but it can also be reduced by other comforting stimuli such as warmth and food. But even more troublesome is the fact that it can be reduced by negative stimuli such as those which produce fear, as well as negative psychological states such as malaise and depression. Although a surface behaviorist analysis may choose to disregard such interpretive issues, any central state analysis must attempt to grapple with the psychoneural meaning of any documented response change. This can only be accomplished through the concurrent use of a variety of analyses which attempt to converge upon coherent explanatory principles.

UNCONDITIONAL BEHAVIORS AS INDICATORS OF THE UNCONDITIONAL EMOTIONAL PROCESSES OF THE BRAIN

As already mentioned, emotions are here viewed as certain types of synchronizing/coordinating processes of the brain which trigger coherent action tendencies in the nervous system which have sensory, perceptual and conscious attributes (for a further discussion of pertinent issues as well as a preliminary neuroscience-type definition of emotions, see Panksepp, 1982, 1986a). Which behaviors, then, shall we justifiably use as indicator variables for emotive states? No foolproof dicta can be prescribed, but to the present writer it seems that several sources of knowledge must be used concurrently: (i) in line with Darwin's original approach as summarized in *The Expression of Emotions in Man and Animals*, our initial emotive taxonomies have to be based on "self-evident" resemblances between universal human experiences and expressions of emotions and the natural (ie unconditional) categories of animal behavior; (ii) thus, the selected behavioral indicator variables for individual emotions should be ones which most intelligent observers of animal behavior in different cultures readily agree as having face validity; and (iii) we should formally seek to demonstrate that the selected emotive categories and behavioral indicators are congruent with formal ethological analyses of spontaneous classes of behaviors across diverse mammalian species. In short, we can assume that certain unconditional emotive behaviors are "evolutionarily derived operants" reflecting various central state controls which are prepared to guide additional learning. Once there is some agreement as to what types of behaviors can be considered to be the most promising indicator variables, they can be used to pursue systematic research programs into primary-process emotive mechanisms of the brain. Of course, this has all of the problems of traditional theoretical approaches to understanding nature whereby we have to deploy the logical fallacy of affirming consequents (Figure 3.2). We can only hope that the weight of evidence will prevail and that

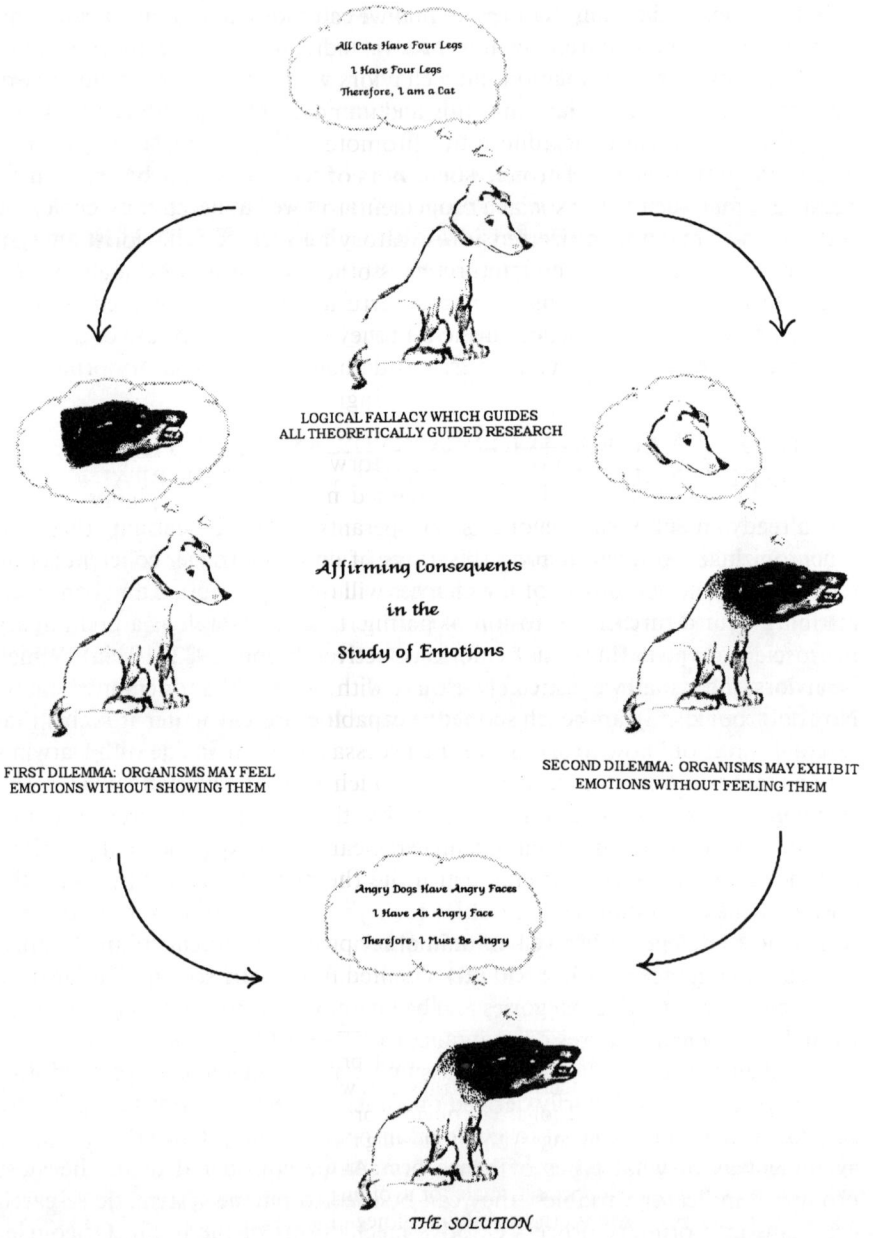

All Cats Have Four Legs
I Have Four Legs
Therefore, I am a Cat

LOGICAL FALLACY WHICH GUIDES
ALL THEORETICALLY GUIDED RESEARCH

Affirming Consequents

in the

Study of Emotions

FIRST DILEMMA: ORGANISMS MAY FEEL
EMOTIONS WITHOUT SHOWING THEM

SECOND DILEMMA: ORGANISMS MAY EXHIBIT
EMOTIONS WITHOUT FEELING THEM

Angry Dogs Have Angry Faces
I Have An Angry Face
Therefore, I Must Be Angry

THE SOLUTION

the inevitable mistakes will be adequately corrected by subsequent experiments designed to disconfirm or negate our provisional theoretical conceptions.

In sum, the argument of this chapter that we can effectively monitor emotional processes in the brain by using such behavioral indices—the harsh insistent hitting and biting behaviors of anger (ie the behaviors which occur in fits of temper); the running away, trembling, squealing and immobility of fear (ie the behaviors which limit behavioral flexibility and promote escape when an organism is threatened); the crying and dejected behaviors of the panic–sadness continuum; various forms of intense social engagement for joy play; the characteristic energization of forward-directed investigatory activity and jumpiness during states of anticipation–craving; and perhaps others such as sexual prowling for male lust circuits and maternal care for nurturance/acceptance circuits. Such behaviors can be well operationalized, and they have considerable face validity and cross-species generality. It is assumed that these behaviors are ancient "evolutionary operants" which have been ingrained within neural genetically ordained neural circuits via the "reinforcement" processes of evolutionary selection. Although this approach is straightforward, the investment of research in developing such approaches has remained modest. In this chapter, I will summarize the use of such "evolutionary operants" (ie unconditional behaviors) as index variables for evaluating the status of certain basic emotive processes in the brain. The remainder of the chapter will discuss specific aspects of such a theory-guided approach to investigating the neurobiological nature of emotional processes. If the basic human affective tendencies do emerge, in fact, from the primitive emotive circuits we share with other mammals in homologous fashion, this strategic approach should be capable of revealing the primal nature of human emotional systems. Since the necessary brain research is essentially impossible in humans, there should be a much greater devotion to the study of animal models of human emotionality than presently exists. But the perspective that such approaches can shed clear light on the biological nature of human emotionality has yet to permeate the scientific *zeitgeist* of current psychology and neuroscience.

Although the brain may well contain other primal emotional systems, there is presently adequate evidence for only a limited few. Although I have addressed

---

Figure 3.2 (opposite) Theoretical research must proceed by effective deployment of "affirming consequents" concerning central states which can only indirectly be indexed by spontaneous animal expressions. The obvious problem with such an approach is that organisms may experience feelings without showing them and that organisms may express emotive states without actually experiencing them. Although these dilemmas must always be kept in mind, they are a poor rationale for avoiding theoretically guided research into animal emotions. Presumably, the possibility of negating theoretical propositions as well as the possible accumulation of convergent evidence can salvage the approach from the inevitable mistakes that will be made. The angry canine face was adapted from Darwin's *The Expression of Emotion in Man and Animals*, and the body of the dog as well as the humorous affirmation of the consequent was adapted from a cartoon by S. Harris

them several times before (Panksepp, 1981a,b, 1982, 1986a,b 1988, 1989a,b, 1990a,b), I will provide here a brief status report of each.

THE SEPARATION DISTRESS, PANIC SYSTEM

All young mammals and avian species that have been studied exhibit distinct calls when they are forcibly or accidentally separated from their homes and social environments (Newman, 1988). It is also part of human nature to be emotionally dependent on home cues and social support networks, and to protest vigorously if separated from such sources of comfort (Lester & Boukydis, 1985). If such support is not available, we ultimately feel loneliness, sorrow, grief, despair and eventually have a greater susceptibility to depression. Like animals, we humans have a much greater tendency to panic and cry following enforced social separation (all the more so if we are young and helpless). These emotions and behavioral responses are not learned but appear to emerge from the ingrained structures of mammalian and avian brain organization (although the responses may also become learned operants to manipulate one's social environment). According to the research paradigm advocated here, it is assumed that the executive structure of the emotive system which governs separation-induced crying patterns is the primal source of emotions which emerge from social separation, and hence the study of the underlying neural systems is assumed to be the key to understanding the neural infrastructure of emotions such as loneliness, sorrow, grief and isolation-induced panic. Although it may well be the case that the affect emerges from more distant circuitries that interact with the crying circuits, it is presently more parsimonious to assume that the neural force for each emotional feeling emerges rather directly from the neurochemical tides of the primitive circuits which orchestrate and coordinate the emotive response pattern. Our past empirical work on the crying system has been summarized elsewhere (Panksepp et al., 1980; Panksepp, 1981a,b; Panksepp, Siviy & Normansell, 1985; Panksepp, 1986b; Panksepp et al., 1988), and only selected issues will be touched upon here.

The isolation call is a relatively stereotyped response whose frequency, intensity and duration (both as a singular unit of behavior as well as a protracted behavioral response) can be readily measured. It can be simply induced by briefly separating young animals from their social environments. The brain circuitry underlying the response can be estimated by localized electrical stimulation of the brain (ESB) in both awake and anesthetized animals (although it is noteworthy that above the mesencephalon the DVs are usually emitted at ESB offset). Unlike most other basic emotions, positive electrode sites are more heavily represented in dorsomedial thalamic zones than in hypothalamic areas (Herman & Panksepp, 1981; Panksepp et al., 1988). This somatic localization of separation distress circuitry is reasonable, for the function of this emotion is to sustain contact with exteroceptive stimuli which indicate social presence. The spectral characteristics of the ESB-induced vocalizations are usually identical to those emitted naturally (Figure 3.3). Our impression, at present, is that there is relatively little important information concerning the executive operation of the emotive system in analyzing the fine-grained spectral properties of the vocalization itself (which probably reflect characteristics of the final motor pattern generator as well as the peripheral vocal apparatus, as opposed to the executive emotive influences which govern the activity of this response system). Although the duration of natural DVs does tend to get longer as guinea-pigs approach puberty, and sometime the ascending frequency rise becomes more shallow (Figure 3.3), the vocalizations do remain relatively stereotyped and stable throughout early life. Hence, we believe the major dependent measures of the executive operation of the emotive brain system would consist of the measurement of the momentary incidence frequency (number of DVs per unit of time), the sound amplitudes, the bursting patterns, and their overall persistence across prolonged periods of isolation. Although our own work has been restricted to measurement of the incidence frequency of DVs during set periods of isolation (largely because of the limited resources presently available for such work), we certainly advocate a comprehensive analysis of all parameters. The number of questions to be asked about this dependent measure remains vast.

A key neuroscience task at present is the determination of the precise neural pathways and neurochemistries which govern this response. Extensive neuropharmacological data have now been collected for several distant species. Most of our own data (for overview, see Table 3.1) have been obtained from the young domestic chick (which is an excellent model, especially for central neuropeptide work since intraventricular injections can be done rapidly using free-hand procedures). It may presently seem doubtful that this work will generalize to mammalian species since recent research with young rat pups is not affirming all of the patterns that have been observed in young chicks. For instance, clonidine powerfully reduces DVs in chicks (Rossi, Sahley & Panksepp, 1983) and monkeys (Kalin & Shelton, 1990), with evident sedation, but increases DVs in rat pups (Kehoe, 1988). However, it is noteworthy that primates respond more like chicks than rats. In quite a similar way, benzodiazepines have a weak inhibitory effect in chicks (Panksepp, Meeker & Bean, 1980) dogs (Scott, 1974) and monkeys (Kalin, Shelton & Barksdale, 1987) but a powerful effect in rat pups (Insel, Hill & Mayor, 1986). Of course, the difference may be "trivial", simply reflecting that certain circuits or types of receptors (eg autoreceptors on norepinepherine cell bodies) have not matured in the brains of altricial rats. In this context, it is also worth noting that altricial rodents show a very short period of time during early life when they exhibit a clear separation response, and their unusual pharmacological responsivity may be due to the immaturity of their nervous systems during that time. In studying infant dogs (during the first three weeks of life), we have observed very dramatic changes in drug effects on stress-induced vocalizations which are emitted during separation (strong reductions following amphetamine and dramatic agitation and crying with methysergide) but similar pharmacological effects are not present at older ages

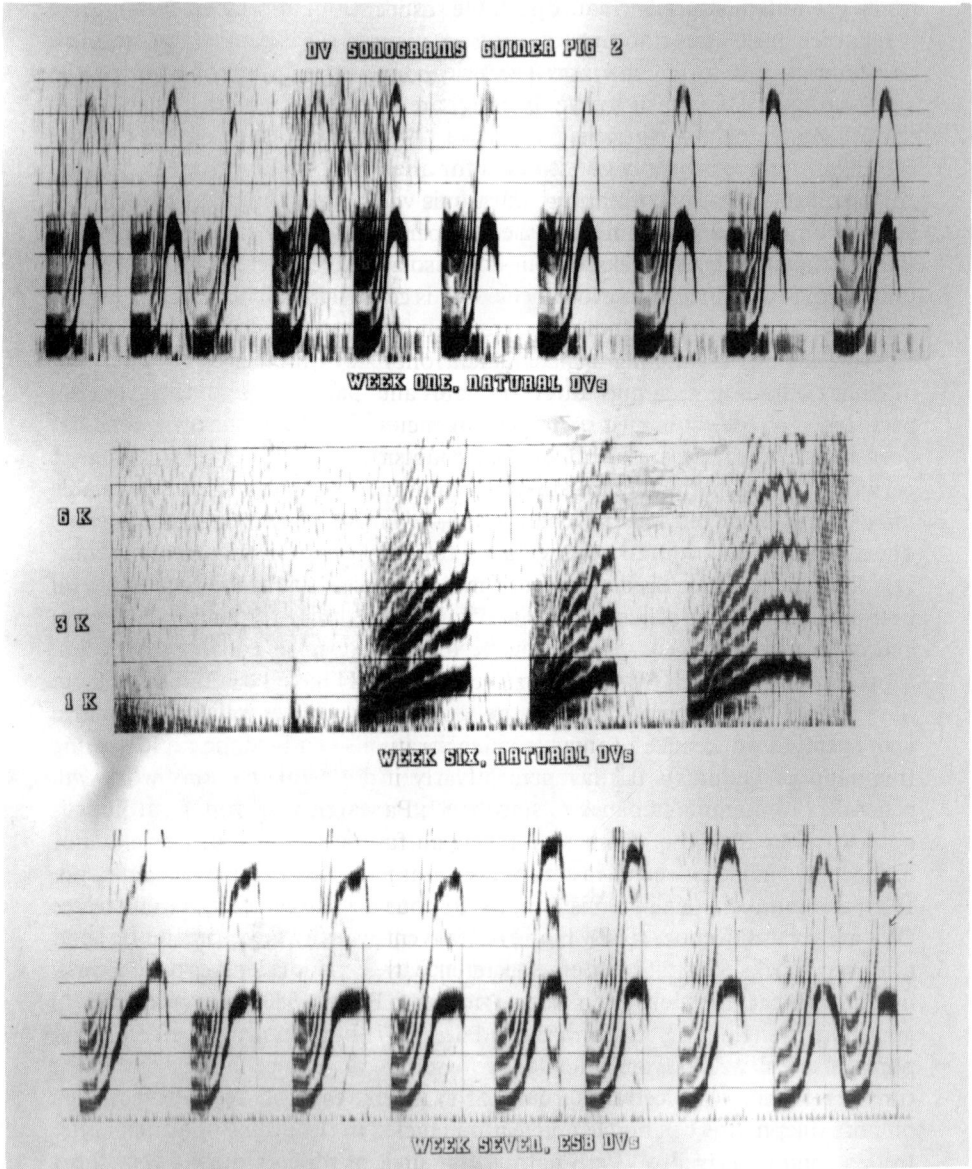

Figure 3.3. Sonographic analysis of natural guinea-pig DVs evoked by social separation at one week of age (top tracing) and six weeks of age (middle tracing). The vocalization pattern exhibited age-dependent changes in spectral characteristics, but ESB of the bed nucleus of the stria terminalis at seven weeks of age (bottom tracing) reevoked the infantile pattern of DVs. This same infantile pattern could be activated at all ages as a poststimulation phenomenon. Tracings according to Sahley and Panksepp (unpublished data, 1981)

when the animal's eyes and ears open. We suspect that the vocalizations during these early ages are not true separation responses, but rather discomfort responses engendered by thermoregulatory and other stresses. In our experience, if young puppies (ie prior to eye opening) are kept warm on a cuddly blanket, social isolation is not sufficient to evoke DVs. Thus, we do not believe the altricial rat is an especially good model for analyzing social separation distress mechanisms. Indeed, it is clear that ultrasonic vocalizations are emitted by infant rats for other reasons than prior social experience (Hofer *et al.*, 1989). Also, we know that in young chicks kept in social isolation separation from their home environment is sufficient to evoke DVs, so it is certainly not just a social isolation response but one that can indicate separation from existing circumstances (with the social dimension being a most salient one).

Unlike chicks, guinea-pigs, dogs, primates and humans, the juvenile rat does not appear to exhibit robust social dependencies during juvenile development. Also, since infant rat social-bonding mechanisms seem to be largely based on olfactory information, perhaps they are a poor model for other mammals which use visual, auditory, and somatosensory information to sustain social dependencies. Accordingly, we presently believe that the DV data from young rats may highlight the operation of immature stress mechanisms of the infant brain more than the neurodynamics of a fully developed separation distress system, which is better studied in species which are truly socially dependent for a prolonged period of juvenile life.

At present, we hypothesize that corticotrophin release factor (CRF) circuits may serve a key executive function in elaborating separation distress, because this peptide, administered intraventricularly in chicks, can turn on the DV response (Panksepp, Crepau & Clynes, 1987; Panksepp *et al.*, 1988). However, more recent work with infant rats has again failed to confirm that finding—indeed, CRF reduced the ultrasonic calls of rat pups (Insel & Harbaugh, 1989). In chicks the CRF was administered to the fourth ventricle region while in the rat it was placed more rostrally in the lateral ventricles; hence it remains possible that rather than being a true species difference, the rostral injections were simply not optimally placed. There is abundant DV circuitry adjacent to the fourth ventricle (in the intercollicular area and central gray) but next to none around the lateral ventricles to our knowledge. Another inconsistency is the ability of choleocystokinin to reduce DVs in infant rats (Weller & Blass, 1988), even though in our experience it has no clear effect on chick DVs when administered either peripherally or centrally (Panksepp, 1984, unpublished data).

Although there appear to be an ever increasing number of discrepancies among species at the present time (with the rat pup typically the odd one out), I suspect that many of the inconsistencies will turn out to be minor variations on a common theme once more data become available. We are not yet ready to concede that the neurochemical control for separation distress has exhibited as much divergent evolution as the infant rat data presently suggest. At the same time, it should be noted that the most powerful inhibitory modulators of the

Table 3.1. Neurochemical effects on separation calls

Psychopharmaceuticals	Neuropeptides
Large reductions in DVs (all peptides have to be given intraventricularly)	
All opiates (which stimulate mu receptors)	D-Ala^{2}Met-enkephalin
Morphine & oxymorphine	All endorphins
Alpha-2-norepinephrine agonists	Casomorphins & DAGO
Clonidine	
Glutamate receptor antagonists	Somatostatin
APV & DGG	Oxytocin & vasotocin
Large increases in DVs (all agents only work when given directly into ventricular system)	
Kainic acid and NMDA (N-methyl-D-aspartate)	**CRF (corticotrophin releasing factor)**
Curare	
Modest reliable reductions in DVs	
Quipazine	D-Ala^2-Leu-enkephalin
Yohimbine	D-Pen^2, L-Pen^5-enkephalin
Phenelzine	DSLET and DPDPE
Apomorphine	Vasoactive intestinal peptide
Carbachol	Human pancreatic protein
Imipramine	Thyrotrophin release hormone
(species variation)	
Modest reliable increases in DVs	
Naltrexone	alpha-MSH (biphasic effect)
Naloxone	ACTH (1–24) (biphasic effect)
Chlornaltrexamine	ICI-149129

(Cont'd)

Table 3.1. (*Cont'd*)

	Arginine-vasopressin
MR-2266	
Fenfluramine (decreases (as well as increases)	Neurotensin and substance P
Scopolamine	Choleocystokinin and bombesin
Atropine	LH-RH, DSIP and FMRF amide
Methysergide	Dynorphin (1–13) and (1–8)
d- and l-amphetamine	MIF-1 and Tyr-PRO-LEU-GLY
	Growth hormone RH fragment (1–29)

Little specific effect on DVs

Propranolol
Sotalol
GABA
Glutamate
Pyridoxine
Nimodipine
Pilocarpine
Procaine
Bicuculline
Glycine
Ascorbate
Buspirone
Haloperidol
Sodium pentobarbital
Hexamethonium
Strychnine
Quisqualic acid
Diphenylhydantoin

separation response are still brain opioids (mu receptor ligands) and that effect has been consistent in the young of all species that have been tested. The opioid results have precipitated an opioid-excess theory of early childhood autism (Gillberg, 1988; Panksepp, 1979; Panksepp & Sahley, 1987), which is yielding positive therapeutic results in preliminary tests with naltrexone (Campbell *et al.*, 1988; Herman *et al.*, 1987; Leboyer, Bouvard & Dugas, 1988; Lensing *et al.*, 1989). Although there are bound to be many species specifics to be documented, at present there is relatively little reason to believe that the lessons learned about the executive circuits of one species which exhibits strong and clear separation responses will not translate effectively to other species which protest vigorously following enforced social isolation (with no other stressors being present in the situation).

Of course, as more work is conducted, there are bound to be many disagreements which will need to be addressed. Controversy is an essential ingredient of theoretically guided research. For example, another useful measure of the separation response is plasma cortisol secretion (Coe *et al.*, 1985), and recently Levine and colleagues have confirmed our finding that opiates greatly reduce separation DVs, but they also found that opiates do not reduce separation-induced cortisol secretion in rhesus monkeys (Wiener, Coe & Levine, 1988). Hence, they suggested that cortisol secretion may be a better indicator of separation distress than DVs. Although there are presently not enough data to adjudicate on the matter, we believe the reverse—that the behavioral rather than hormonal measure is a better indicator of the emotional response. For instance, it is possible that social isolation concurrently evokes several distinct emotions—perhaps both separation distress and fear, as well as a generalized stress response—and the pituitary adrenal axis may be activated non-specifically by all these stressors. If facilitation of brain opioid activity specifically attenuates separation distress without a full attenuation of the concurrent fear, then the above data may merely affirm the long-standing belief that pituitary–adrenal arousal is a general index of emotional stress rather than of any specific emotional response.

At present, DV circuitry remains the premier example of the type of emotional brain system which is very capable of being analyzed with the modern tools of neuroscience (see Newman, 1988). Why this system has not received the attention it deserves in biological psychiatry is, I suspect, the result of the anti-instinct bias of the era of behaviorism (which is all the more paradoxical since the DV is such an objective behavioral response). Although our preliminary theoretical assumption is that this circuit is the ultimate neural substrate for the primary-process feelings of grief and sorrow in humans, we will, of course, not know to what extent that is true until appropriate empirical data can be collected from humans. In any event, there are many reasons to believe that the trepidation which emerges from social isolation is distinct from the fear which arises from more direct threats to survival. Typically, fear stimuli tend to reduce the frequency of separation calls (Davis, Gurski & Scott, 1976), and it is now well appreciated that pharmacological treatments which reduce anticipatory anxiety are not especially effective in reducing panic attacks, and *vice versa* (Klein, 1981). Fear and separation distress/panic appear to arise from distinct brain mechanisms.

ANALYSIS OF FEAR IN THE BRAIN

Considering the importance of fear in understanding psychiatric disorders, it is remarkable how little work, at a basic neuroethological level, has been done on fear systems of the brain. Although there is a great deal of information about how various neurobiological manipulations affect learned avoidance behaviors as well as how minor tranquilizers of the benzodiazepine class affect brain activity, there is only modest work on how unconditional behaviors indicative of fear are organized in the brain (for recent summaries of available work see Gray, 1987 and Panksepp, 1990a,b).

Much of the recent behavioral research on "fear" has been done under the rubric of the "defense motivation system" (Adams, 1979; Bolles & Fanselow, 1980; Masterson & Crawford, 1982), which semantically recognizes that fear processes were designed by evolution to provide one type of defensive maneuver against impending threats to bodily integrity. There are a number of innate "evolutionary operants" which appear unconditionally to index the activity of fear circuitry. An especially simple behavioral reflex which can be used to index fear is "potentiated" startle. Many animals exhibit this behavior as the initial component of their flight response, and cues which predict danger lead to a clear potentiation of acoustically elicited startle (Davis, 1986). The flight behavior that is set in motion can take many forms, including vigorous running away from threatening objects and circumstances (flight), with strong hind leg thrusting which leads to the characteristic jumping and flailing when an animal is caught by a predator. It is noteworthy that several somatic reflections of the flight process (hyperpnea and hind leg thrusting) can be observed during electrical stimulation of hypothalamic and mesencephalic "fear" circuits of the fully anesthetized animal (rats and guinea pigs: Panksepp, Sacks & Crepeau, 1987, unpublished observations). Also, threatened animals exhibit several types of rapid fear conditioning which can be easily measured, including potentiated startle (Davis, 1986; Leaton & Borszcz, 1985), defensive burying (Pinel & Treit, 1979), defensive attack (Blanchard *et al.*, 1980) and freezing (Blanchard, Fukunaga & Blanchard, 1976; Fanselow, 1984). We have recently summarized that research (Panksepp *et al.*, 1990; Panksepp, 1990b), so I will only focus on the measure of terror-stricken immobility here.

Freezing may be especially useful as a generalized measure of conditioned fear since it does not require interaction with objects in the world, and could be easily quantified using automated procedures (via sensitive activity platforms which can detect minimal body movements). Cues which have been associated with stimuli (such as electric shock) which provoke unconditional flight appear spontaneously to generate the opponent process of flight on future occasions, namely the curtailment of all external activity—a sustained and tense bodily immobility. Only sporadically has freezing been used as a measure of fear in psychobiological research (see Blanchard & Blanchard, 1969; Bolles & Collier, 1976; Fanselow & Lester, 1988), and it deserves greater attention than it has yet received. For instance, by the use of this measure one can ask whether hypothalamic ESB which evokes vigorous flight has experiential attributes of fear. This is a key issue because past work suggests that animals will not readily avoid such ESB, raising the possibility that the stimulation has merely evoked an emotive response pattern with no accompanying affect. Accordingly, we have determined whether conditional freezing will be exhibited in the presence of the contextual cues in which flight-producing ESB had been applied. Such conditional freezing to hypothalamic stimulation did indeed develop rapidly (Figure 3.4), suggesting that rats do experience a true affective state during such ESB (Sacks & Panksepp, 1987). Also, we have found that ESB which evokes flight at high intensities can unconditionally potentiate freezing at much lower, subflight, intensities (Sacks & Panksepp, 1988, unpublished data), suggesting that freezing and flight may represent differential arousal of a unitary fear system of the brain. Modest activation leads to tense immobility, and stronger stimulation to an increasing arousal which culminates in flight (Panksepp et al., 1990).

All of the unconditional indices of fear mentioned above deserve more experimental attention than they have yet received. Because of the large number of useful measures presently available, it should be possible to evaluate empirically whether there is a generalized system for fear in the brain. One candidate for such a system is the septohippocampal behavioral inhibition system (Gray, 1987); another is ascending NE circuitry (Redmond, 1979); and another is the circuitry where flight is evoked by localized ESB (Panksepp, 1982, 1990b). During the 1970s and early 1980s there was relatively little work on this fear–flight system (for summaries see Panksepp et al., 1990), but recently work on the functions of such circuits has increased (eg Cazala & Schmitt, 1987; Di Scala et al., 1987; Iwata, Chida & LeDoux, 1987; Roberts & Cox, 1987; Sacks & Panksepp, 1987; Sandner, Schmitt & Karli, 1985). Continuance of such work should allow us to understand the unconditional brain mechanisms which elaborate fear, and should allow us to begin probing how such systems interact with more recently evolved systems of the brain to yield the vast complexity of trepidation observed in the real world interactions.

THE RAGE SYSTEM OF THE BRAIN

Because of the spectacular intensity of the rage response in many species, this emotional system has received more attention from neuroscientists than the others (for recent reviews see Bandler, 1988; Siegel & Pott, 1988). Affective attack elicited by brain stimulation and various related behavioral indices of

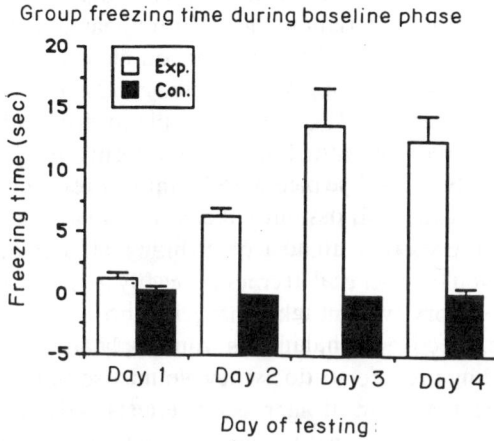

Group freezing time during baseline phase

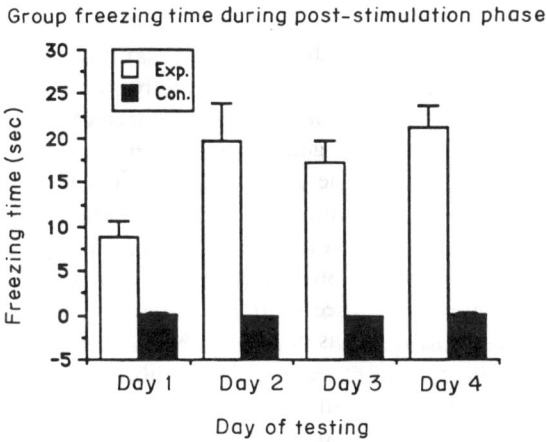

Group freezing time during post-stimulation phase

Figure 3.4. On four successive days, 12 rats with chronically implanted electrodes into flight zones of the anterior hypothalamus (AH) were administered "fear"-provoking ESB systematically on four successive days. On each test day, there was an initial five-minute "baseline" observation phase (top graph), which was followed by a stimulation phase consisting of five successive 10-sec periods AH stimulation (18--30 uA sine wave), each separated by 1 min. This was followed by another five-minute post-stimulation phase (bottom graph) when no more ESB was applied. Freezing was measured by duration of inhibition of all motor movement (ie sustained crouching) with rapid diaphragmatic respiration). Clearly, freezing was increased immediately by the stimulation (day 1) and sustained for all days of testing, while prestimulation conditional freezing developed more slowly (data from Sacks & Panksepp, 1987)

threat such as hissing in cats have been the main reflections of activity in this system, and it is possible to discriminate rage-like aggression from other forms of aggression by various criteria. On the basis of apparent behavioral differences, Flynn (1967) initially divided feline aggression elicited by ESB into affective and quiet-biting attack categories. When these aggression systems in the rat brain were mapped (Panksepp, 1971), it was possible to distinguish affective attack from quiet-biting predatory attack not only in terms of the apparent outward behavior patterns but also by differential stimulus responsivities: (1) animals would uniformly escape ESB that provoked affective attack but would typically self-stimulate for ESB that evoked quiet-biting attack; (2) during affective attack, animals would target conspecifics as readily as prey animals such as mice, while during predatory-type attack conspecifics were left in peace; (3) during ESB evoking the affective form, animals would only attack live animals whereas during ESB yielding predatory attack they would also bite dead prey. It seemed that only the affective form of aggression reflects activity of a "rage/anger" emotional system in the brain. It remains quite possible that quiet-biting (ie predatory) attack may reflect the species-typical operation of the appetitive/investigatory (self-stimulation) emotive system of the feline brain. Available evidence suggests the homologous circuits mediate vigorous self-stimulation behavior in rats. The outward behavioral differences between the two species may be explained by the fact that rats forage for their food while cats hunt for theirs. These surface differences may have led to two distinct areas of research which may need to be conceptually joined.

Problems which can arise from allowing surface characteristics as opposed to deeper functional issues to guide our thinking are also highlighted by the common label of "defense motivation system" which is used to describe the affective rage that can be evoked by ESB. My reading of the evidence is that affective rage and fear–flight systems are highly overlapping in the brain (since they normally must work in close conjunction with each other), and that the ESB-induced "defensive" attack reflects an epiphenomenon of concurrent activation of these distinct nearby systems by the artificial maneuver of ESB. I believe the continuance of Cannon's old combinatorial "fight/flight" system, as if it were a single entity, continues to muddy thinking in the area. Instead, there appear to be two nearby, highly interacting systems (fear and rage) which can be jointly aroused to get defense but which are distinct and capable of being empirically dissected.

At present, the use of freely behaving protagonists does not seem to be an optimal way to systematically study the activity of these circuits, for both ethical and practical reasons. A more systematic procedure might be to study various energized somatic activities ("fits of temper") which might be especially indicative of activity in the system. Although angry animals exhibit vigorous pouncing types of behavior which resemble energized staccato movements similar to humans "pounding the table", it is not presently clear whether the trajectories and force of angry movements can be sufficiently differentiated from other types of energized somatic movements. Perhaps the most easily measured response associated with anger is emotional biting (ie vigorous jaw clenching). Such a response could be objectively studied in a restrained, artificially irritated animal which is permitted to bite down on objects which contain pressure transducers to monitor the vigor of the response (as done by Hutchinson & Renfrew, 1978). Also, research has affirmed that hypothalamic stimulation which provokes attack sensitizes perioral trigger zones for orientation and biting reflex (Flynn, 1967), and it has been shown that the biting reflex is modulated by hypothalamic aggression circuitry (Landgren & Olsson, 1980). These observations raise the possibility that activity of the system could be analyzed in mildly anesthetized animals. For instance, one could artificially elicit the Masseter reflex by electrically stimulating the motor nucleus of the trigeminal, and determine how higher emotive circuits modulate this reflex (also see Chase & Morales, 1990). Also, ESB which precipitates affective attack in awake rats commonly evokes teeth-chattering when stimulation is applied during light anesthesia (Panksepp, 1971). In sum, the routine use of simplified model systems could greatly enhance our ability to dissect the nature of the underlying systems. Although a great deal is already known about the brain organization of rage, and the executive circuits have been probed with the new generation of neuroanatomical tools (eg see Bandler, 1988; Fuchs, Edinger & Siegel, 1985; Fuchs & Siegel, 1984), the command neurochemistries remain to be identified. Work along these lines is the most promising way to understand the psychologically irreducible but neurobiologically complex nature of anger.

THE "CURIOSITY/FORAGING/ANTICIPATION/ CRAVING/EXPECTANCY" SYSTEM OF THE BRAIN

An evident class of behaviors that most animals exhibit is exploratory searching (foraging) when they are under the sway of homeostatic imbalances and bouncy energization (anticipatory eagerness) when they are expecting desired positive incentives. These behaviors reflect the shared emotive components of all appetitive behaviors, but such response patterns have rarely been studied systematically. The behaviors are apparently designed to seek and anticipate forthcoming events so that the animal can optimize its opportunities to interact with desired objects (ie objects that can sustain homeostatic balances, ranging from food to sex). In their extreme form, such behaviors have a persistent, addictive, craving character to them, as if the animals are being driven by irresistible internal urges (perhaps obsessive–compulsive behaviors reflect thwarting of such "energies"). For some time I have argued that this primal emotive system has long been studied under the guise of brain reward/reinforcement systems via the epiphenomenon of intracranial self-stimulation along the trajectory of the medial forebrain bundle (Panksepp, 1981a, 1982, 1986a). It has been called the "reinforcement" and the "pleasure" system, but the underlying circuit function appears to be the instigation of exploratory–investigatory–appetitive behavior. Gray (1987) has called this the behavioral activation system, and more recently clinical psychologists have started to conceptualize this circuitry as the behavioral facilitation system (see Depue & Iacono, 1989). Behaviorists are more prone to view this as a primary reward or incentive motivation system (Wise & Rompre, 1989), a concept that goes back to the analysis of self-stimulation by Olds (1955), Trowill, Panksepp and Gandelman (1969) and Crow (1972). Perhaps the simplest view is that this system mediates investigatory/exploratory activity which in its conditional form is anticipatory eagerness (Panksepp, 1981a). The outward behavior of rats clearly bears this out.

When we simply observe rats forcibly administered this kind of ESB, several clear behaviors emerge most of which remain to be formally analyzed: (1) the animals exhibit persistent forward locomotion; (2) they investigate prominent protuberances, objects and recesses of their environment; and (3) they exhibit persistent sniffing. Although all of these behaviors need to be studied more systematically, sniffing may be an especially direct indicator variable for the status of the system. Sniffing can be evoked by lateral hypothalamic stimulation even in the totally anesthetized rat, and can thus be used as an indicator that an electrode site will yield self-stimulation (in practice, when one is lowering an electrode through the lateral hypothalamic area one first passes through a zone where stimulation produces a tonic forward sweep of the vibrissae, the actual sniffing zone, which is best gauged by the rhythmic movement of the nostrils just below this area). The current levels for self-stimulation and sniffing are highly correlated suggesting they reflect the same underlying process, but the thresholds are always lower for sniffing, suggesting that it is a more primal reflection of activity in the system (Rossi & Panksepp, 1983). The sniffing measure can be easily objectified and automated (Clarke, Panksepp & Trowill, 1970) and yields a measure of spontaneous appetitive conditioning processes of the brain (Clarke, 1971; Clarke & Trowill, 1971). The technique needs to be more extensively deployed in studies of this basic "search system" of the brain. Although ascending mesolimbic dopamine circuitry seems to be at the heart of this system, descending pathways are also critical in its overall organization (Wise & Rompre, 1989). In preliminary work we have made unilateral brainstem cuts several millimeters in front of or behind electrodes which activate sniffing, but only the caudal cuts eliminate the response (Panksepp, 1987, unpublished observations). The sniffing system appears to be descending and not to require dopamine release. At present, our best guess is that it is glutaminergic.

Of course, thanks to the willingness of animals to vigorously turn on such brain stimulation, perhaps partly because they place themselves into a foraging–curiosity "do-loop", we presently know a great deal about the underlying organization of this putative foraging/expectancy circuitry (Liebman & Cooper, 1989). However, considering that this system is a fundamental substrate for the energization of all positively motivated seeking and goal-directed behaviors, it is remarkable how little work has been done on basic measures of "anticipatory eagerness". When an animal is expecting positive rewards, it often literally bounds around with excitement, which appears to be a highly energized form of investigatory curiosity. This bouncy behavior is sufficiently distinct to be objectively measured, and it may tell us much about the fundamental nature of brain dopamine systems as well as the addictive urges which emerge from this system (Wise & Rompre, 1989). Recently, Phillips, Blaha & Fibiger (1989) have demonstrated that dopamine release from this system is very vigorous when male rats are enticed with receptive female rats (ie during the appetitive phase of behavior), but comparatively low during the ensuing sexual activity. The subtlety of behavioral research on this system would be enriched if we were to conceptualize the underlying substrate in an emotive rather than a reward/reinforcement way. Indeed, the mechanisms of reinforcement may be more closely linked to offset rather than onset of activity in the system. Many years ago Grastyan *et al.* (1968) demonstrated that cats would seek out objects in the environment where such stimulation ceased as opposed to objects near which the ESB was initiated! Also, once we understand the emotive functions which emerge from this circuitry, we may be in a better position to conceptualize psychiatric disorders, such as certain forms of schizophrenia and mania, which emerge from the deranged dynamics of this and related brain systems (Schultz & Tamminga, 1989).

THE STUDY OF LUDIC (PLAYFUL) PROCESSES OF THE BRAIN

Play circuitry is a fundamental heritage of the mammalian brain (MacLean, 1985). All young mammals spontaneously exhibit carefree social interactions which most people promptly recognize as play, and despite the misgivings of behaviorism about such concepts, it turns out that social play is remarkably easy to operationalize and measure in animals. Perhaps certain affective brain states which are typically labelled "joy" and "fun" emerge from the activities of such circuits. Although it is important to consider that positive subjective feelings may be linked to the activity of play circuits, it is scientifically more pertinent to emphasize that play circuitry can be as systematically studied as any other neurobehavioral process that animals exhibit. It seems unlikely that a coherent understanding of the sources of social, emotional and various behavioral skills can be gained without an understanding of the neural pathways for play. Ludic processes have received very little attention by modern neuroscience, and this is especially surprising since rodent play is so easy to study systematically (Panksepp, Siviy & Normansell, 1984).

When one puts several young rats together who have not been given an opportunity to play for several hours (by either individual housing or housing with a non-playful adult) they promptly begin to exhibit vigorous chasing, pouncing, and wrestling with frequent and rapid shifts in positions and "roles".

A remarkable amount of behavioral activity is exhibited during these play bouts, and a fine-grained analysis of the motor movements would be a Herculean task. Still, if one assumes that the behaviors emerge from a coherently operating brain system, one may be able to index the amount, intensity and duration of play by utilization of various easily quantified indicator variables. After years of observation, we have settled on the following: (1) the counting of the frequency and duration of pinning behavior where one animal ends up on its back (with at least three feet off the ground) with the other animal on top; we assume this measure to reflect the consummatory aspects of play; (2) the counting of the frequency of times that one animal touches the other animal on the dorsal surface with its two paws. We assume this measure reflects play solicitation and hence the appetitive phase of play; (3) we measure the total amount of activity that is generated on a stabilimeter movement platform upon which the play chamber is situated. This measure yields an overall estimate of the amount of rough-and-tumble activity. In addition, there are many forms of chasing and specific forms of sparring that occur during play. They could be quantified, but only with great difficulty if scoring is attempted on-line. Hence, we have decided to forgo the evaluation of those measures.

Although the "playful" activity is assertive (and some have even suggested it is aggressive), we know from learning tests that both animals of a play pair find the activity to be a positive experience, as indicated by their willingness to work for opportunities to engage in it (Normansell & Panksepp, 1990). Also, in our experience, specific anti-aggressive drugs such as fluprazine do not reduce play fighting. In addition, if true aggression were involved in this assertive behavior, we would expect that the "losers" would tend to avoid locations in which they had been "trounced". They do not. Also, a recent formal analysis of the behavior sequences seen during aggression and play indicates that they are quite distinct (Pellis & Pellis, 1987). This does not mean that play cannot escalate into serious fighting, but whenever such rare events transpire, playful interactions promptly cease (Panksepp, 1986b). In sum, rough-and-tumble play seems to be elaborated by a coherent system of the brain that probably has widespread ramifications for promoting the ultimate adult competence of an organism (enhancing various types of learning abilities and the ability of an animal to fit emotionally into its social environment). No function of play has yet been conclusively demonstrated, but we suspect that it may have direct effects on aspects of brain growth, especially of emotional systems (Panksepp, 1986a).

The identification and study of play circuits poses a special challenge for neuroscience. It is hard to imagine that recording of electrical activity of the brain can be conducted accurately when animals are exhibiting such flurries of wild activity. We have tried radioactive 2-DG studies, but nothing obvious has emerged, perhaps because so much of brain activity is recruited in the midst of play. Subtractive autoradiography studies suggest brain opioid activity is enhanced throughout the brain, with perhaps some greater activity in preoptic areas which are known to participate in sexual and other social behaviors

(Panksepp & Bishop, 1981; Panksepp, 1981b). Pharmacological and brain injection approaches could be employed, as they have been quite extensively (see Panksepp *et al.*, 1987 for review), but it is hard to imagine that they could be used to localize the circuits. Perhaps new approaches such as the identification of brain circuits which begin to express oncogenes like *c-fos* during neuronal firing (Sagar, Sharp & Curran, 1988; Sudol, 1988) can help identify the neuronal fields that are highly aroused during play. The brain lesion approach, problematic as it is for unambiguous interpretations, is still one of the most robust that can be taken to the issues of play circuit localization (eg Siviy & Panksepp, 1985, 1987a).

Indeed, we have pursued the lesion approach for some time, in conjunction with an analysis of the sensory systems which control play. Past work has indicated that rats play essentially normally even though they cannot see or smell. Although hearing may have some modest effect, our analysis suggests that somatosensory senses are most important for the normal elaboration of play (Siviy & Panksepp, 1987b). Sensations from the anterior dorsal surface of the animal appear to be especially important, which has led us to believe that mammals may have specific play–skin trigger zones on their bodies (which, by reasoning from potential homologies, may explain why human children laugh and become especially playful when their ribs are tickled). In any event, we have systematically lesioned various areas of the somatosensory system and the data suggest that the non-specific somatosensory projection areas of the posterior thalamus and parafascicular may be important for receiving such playful messages (Siviy & Panksepp, 1985, 1987a). Various control studies suggest the observed play deficits are behaviorally specific. Having identified one area of the brain which contains specific play circuitry makes the further analysis of the system slightly easier. The anterograde and retrograde connectivities of the parafascicular should yield a set of candidates for other major components of play circuitry, which could then be evaluated by direct manipulation of the candidate systems. Once the broad outlines of play circuitry have been identified, we may be in a much better position to try to implement more molecular tools. Unlike the other emotive systems discussed above, we have yet to find a procedure to index the activity of this system in the anesthetized animal. The psychiatric implications of understanding this system remain ambiguous, but the nature of hyperkinesis, autism, Tourette's and mania may be clarified by such knowledge.

OTHER EMOTIONS

I would by no means wish to intimate that the emotive processes I have discussed are the only ones that exist in the brain. Although initially it would seem wise to focus research on fairly straightforward, self-evident emotive processes, other intervening brain processes surely exist (both emotive and cognitive) which cannot be as easily studied because obvious unconditional behavioral measures are not yet available to index their operation. How many other basic emotive systems there are and how they will be studied will constitute an intriguing future chapter of functional brain research. However, it is only worth speculating on these matters when clear ways can be suggested to study them.

There are several systems which are almost ready to be conceptualized. For instance, a prominent class of animal behaviors is competition for resources. Are there hard-wired emotive pathways for monopolizing resources, or are all competitive behaviors learned? Take "greed" as an example. Many species clearly exhibit specific behavioral tendencies when they seek to keep certain resources for themselves, for instance hoarding behavior. Likewise, when two cohabiting rats are given a single desirable object, the animal that possesses the object tries to keep it from the other animal by a stereotyped series of bodily actions. It pivots away each time the other animal approaches the desirable object that is being held, and the behavior stops as soon as the object of desire has been consumed. This is an exquisitely concrete behavior that deserves closer empirical scrutiny (we are developing frequency of "possessive pivoting" as a dependent measure and a much more elegant but time-consuming quantitative approach has been pursued by Whishaw & Tomie, 1988). Under appropriate circumstances, one can elicit this type of pivoting by simply approaching a target animal with an anesthetized rat held in one's hand, whereas a comparable inanimate object is not effective (Panksepp, unpublished data, 1985). Young chickens exhibit a similar behavior. If one throws a worm-like object into a flock, one animal picks it up and others immediately begin to chase the owner. After a few moments, the cage resembles a soccer field, with chicks chasing each other and the "object of desire" being repeatedly exchanged on the field of competition (Panksepp, unpublished data, 1984). The behavior almost seems playful, and perhaps we will be able to evaluate whether it is homologous to mammalian play once we learn enough about the underlying brain circuitries of both behaviors.

Also, there are reasons to suspect that the brain contains basic emotive systems for sexual appetitive and reproductive behaviors. For instance, the male-typical tendency to prowl in search of a mate may be distinct from brain systems which generate other types of foraging. It is surprising that with the vast amount of work that has been done on the consummatory phase of sexual behavior, so little has been carried out on the appetitive phase (which may be mediated by distinct emotive circuits). Brain vasopressin circuits have characteristics which would commend them as potential executive systems for male lust (De Vries *et al.*, 1985).

There are surely brain circuits which mediate maternal intent, and help organize the many diverse nurturant behaviors that animals exhibit quite spontaneously near the onset of parturition. Indeed, the oxytocin circuitry of the brain is a promising candidate for executive circuitry of maternal acceptance (Jirikowski *et al.*, 1989; Pedersen *et al.*, 1985). The ability of oxytocin to dramatically reduce separation distress is congruent with such a function

(Panksepp, 1989c). Further, the possibility that much of female sexuality emerges from such nurturance circuits requires attention, and from that perspective, the ability of medial hypothalamic oxytocinergic systems to mediate female receptivity is intriguing indeed (Caldwell, Prange & Pedersen, 1986). These fascinating emotive behaviors surely emerge from coherently operating brain systems which have powerful affective consequences for the animal, and there is presently every reason to suspect that the ultimate sources of human passions reside within this neural infrastructure for emotive behaviors in animals. Parenthetically, it should again be noted that this perspective puts emotional behavior at the forefront of any analysis of animal emotions, leaving autonomic effects as secondary issues. The primary function of emotional systems is to generate coherent behavioral tendencies, and the autonomic changes may be subservient to the behavioral ends that are built into the emotional circuitries. Only when we have a basic understanding of such ROM functions of the brain will we be ready to analyze mechanistically the emotional underpinnings of more complex behaviors.

THOUGHTS ON AN "AS IF" SCIENCE OF EMOTIONS

Considering the fact that humans can communicate directly (albeit poorly) about their subjective emotional states, and considering the abundant evidence that these feelings emerge from subcortical circuits which we share with other animals (Panksepp, 1985), it is probably scientifically wise (as an initial simplifying maneuver) to assume monistically that both feeling states and spontaneous, unconditional emotional behaviors emerge, at least initially during early development, from the same primal executive substrates of the brain. If correct, such an assumption could eventually provide a useful two-way avenue of anthropomorphic–neuroscientific discourse between general human experiences of emotions and animal brain research—an approach which I would call "comparative psychoneurophenomenology". If the assumption is incorrect, then I suspect the objective data which such a liberalized approach to understanding animal behavior would generate will have been well worth the effort.

It will be some time before we have a definitive foundation concerning the precise nature of emotional circuits in the brain, and investigators may wish to use emotive terms before adequate knowledge of the underlying circuits is available. For a long time the use of affective terminology has been discouraged in scientific writing about animal behavior, largely because such semantics implied a level of understanding we really do not have (and some skeptics claimed "could never have", since animal "emotions" were a figment of the human imagination). Emotional explanations were also typically circular. Indeed, it is still sadly common at neuroscience meetings for investigators who study various animal models of fear to apologize for using words such as "anxiogenic" and "anxiolytic"' which suggest that animals experience anxiety. My recommendation is that we liberalize strictures against such terminology by developing a habit of speaking which implicitly recognizes how we utilize emotive words. They need not be used foolishly as a final explanation of behavior, but rather as shorthand ways of saying that an investigator assumes that underlying emotive systems were critically engaged in mediating the behavior.

It should not be detrimental to the rigor, richness, or subtlety of behavioral research if we consider using an "as if" approach to discussing how emotions may participate in the elaboration of the complex behaviors which are objectively quantified. Indeed, such usages could promote certain lines of empirical inquiry which would be hard to initiate otherwise. Our failure to use emotional words can be a straightjacket which prevents creative research. Thus, as a first approximation, I would suggest that investigators should feel free to describe behavior by statements such as "so-and-so behaved '*as if*' motivated by a such-and-such an emotion". We should accept emotional terminology as long as the behavioral data on which such statements are based are clear and unambiguous, and as long as there are data available to support the existence of "such-and-such" an emotive system in the brain. In the absence of comprehensive knowledge of how such an emotional system operates, it should still be permissible to discuss the observed behaviors theoretically in terms of the operation of the putative underlying circuitries. Although this would not constitute an explanation of the behavior any more than describing external events which precipitate certain behaviors, it could be a shorthand way of describing the theoretical perspective that one is taking with respect to the type of neural mechanism which may be contributing to the behavior.

WHEN IS AN EMOTION NOT AN EMOTION?

As mentioned before, the most persistent logical argument against the use of emotional concepts is that we can never have direct knowledge about the subjective experiences of other creatures (Figure 3.2). This is a poor reason for ignoring phenomena for which there are abundant surface manifestations for an important hidden structure. For instance, because of the nature of their subject matter, subatomic physicists accept that they must be satisfied, perhaps forever, with probing the organization of matter indirectly. Indeed, just at the time when Watsonian behaviorism was encouraging psychology to model itself after classical physics, modern physics was abandoning the surface level of analysis and starting to probe the hidden structure of matter using highly theoretical approaches. But psychology failed to emulate the approaches of the new physics. The present perspective is an advocacy of such an approach. In our search for the hidden structure of psychobehavioral realities, we, as the physicists before us, will be beguiled and deluded by attractive concepts of little substance. Such errors are bound to occur. However, we should no longer evade the issues but proceed in the only way possible—via theoretical inference. The overall research strategy I have advocated is that central feeling states and externally manifested emotive behaviors ultimately arise from the same executive structures of the brain. Although this approach has chosen to ignore many important issues concerning emotions, this has been done purposefully. I do not think it is worth spending much semantic effort on issues that cannot be empirically adjudicated. Obviously, our objective measurements of behavior may, at times, not accurately reflect the operation of the central affective dynamics they were designed to measure (Figure 3.2). As most of us know from personal experience, external indices of emotion can be dissociated from the subjective substrates. This is probably more of a problem in human than in animal research. We humans can all too readily put on faces which do not reflect our true feelings. Nature has also provided poignant dissociations between emotional feelings and emotional expressions which emerge during certain forms of neural dissolution. For instance, individuals with brainstem demyelination, such as in amyelotrophic lateral sclerosis, exhibit the laughter of apparent joy and the tears of apparent sorrow with no corresponding subjective feelings (Poeck, 1969).

Dissociations between emotional expressions and central emotive states can surely also occur in some animal studies. For instance, ESB-induced threat behaviors do not always reflect a willingness to attack on the part of the stimulated animal. Indeed, it has frequently been claimed that such animals are not experiencing true affect, but rather that only their motor pattern generators for emotive behavior have been activated (Delgado, 1969; Masserman, 1941). Such dissociations between affect and behavior are bound to occur, especially at levels of the neuroaxis where the motor pattern generators are situated. Thus it will always be essential to try to evaluate directly whether animals are truly experiencing affective states following specific brain manipulations. The only known way to do this is via "secondary reinforcement" learning paradigms that evaluate the willingness of animals to approach and avoid neutral cues which have been paired with the supposed emotive states. Such avoidance and place preference studies (Carr, Fibiger & Phillips, 1989) can provide strong evidence concerning the affective meaning of a situation for the animal, and should be done routinely to evaluate the internal affective valence induced by the circumstances in which emotive behaviors are observed. These studies have indicated that stimulation of the foraging/expectancy circuits has true affective content for the animal (Trowill & Hynek, 1970), and recent studies analyzing the "fear" system have also supported the existence of a felt (ie conditionable) trepidation during such forms of ESB (DiScala et al., 1987; Roberts & Cox, 1987; Sacks & Panksepp, 1987). Also, the human data quite consistently support the conclusion that activation of these systems instigates affective experiences which are indistinguishable from the "real thing", and when such systems are damaged it is difficult for humans to experience certain emotional states (for review, see Panksepp, 1985).

A SYNOPSIS OF THE PRESENT RATIONALE

Neuroanatomy tells us in no uncertain terms that a variety of coherent influences—some learned, some instinctual—converge on final motor pathways.

Functional brain science has no alternative but to accept the inherent theoretical uncertainties posed by such intrinsic intervening brain functions, and to proceed with the postulation of coherent hypothetical constructs and testable neurotheoretical models. Basic emotions seem to be theoretically useful constructs, handed down in human languages as important entities (some of which probably reflect coherent brain circuits) which should be scientifically probed rather than ignored. I would again emphasize: although emotional constructs cannot be used as coherent non-circular explanations for most behaviors at the present time, they can help identify the types of questions that must be asked about the brain, and they can help us identify certain types of functional systems in the brain and guide us in their empirical analysis. We can use emotional concepts rigorously, but only if we define each emotion operationally with respect to quantifiable behaviors, and conceptually, at least in part, by concrete neurological end-points—whether brain areas, neurochemical systems, or specific circuits. Without abundant possibilities for neural and neurochemical anchor points, such as those provided by the last few decades of basic neuroscience (see Panksepp, 1986b), the utilization of emotive concepts in rigorous behavioral research could only have been a sterile exercise in pseudoscience. No substantive level of causal analysis could have been achieved without such basic information, and it will be wise to keep our emotional analyses minimalist in case the project be dissipated by verbal excesses that have all too easily been generated on behalf of emotional theory in the past. However, we now have a vast storehouse of knowledge concerning the neural and chemical organization of that "great intermediate net" (to use Nauta's (Nauta & Feirtag, 1979) cautious terminology) which lies between sensory and motor systems of the brain. This "great intermediate net" is ripe for theoretically guided investigations of neuroemotional processes which can be only indirectly observed with objective behavioral, neurophysiological and neurochemical tools.

Although there are bound to be many controversies and mistakes in this field, the general approach that needs to be implemented seems clear. It is unabashedly theoretical, unabashedly neurobiological and unabashedly behavioral. But behavior must be used as an index variable to guide a deeper search into the biopsychological nature of the mind/brain. It is similar to the path which particle physics has had to follow since the dawn of the nuclear era. Through such theoretically guided research, the emotive processes of the mammalian brain can finally be brought under the viewing-glass of reductionistic neuroscience methodologies. We are finally in a position to begin conceptualizing how psychological complexity emerges from the "simplicity" of brain processes that the reinforcement history of evolutionary change has bestowed within our "mammalian brain". The assumption of the present approach is that the executive core structures for the primary emotions were an early evolutionary solution to life-challenging circumstances that have been conserved in all mammalian species, and that it is primarily the emotional expressions that have undergone great diversification because of the variety of ecological niches that different species have been forced to confront. Once we understand the nature of these core systems in other animals, we will probably have an essential understanding of them in humans. That type of knowledge, once firmly established, could serve as a solid foundation pillar for modern psychology and psychiatry.

REFERENCES

Adams, D. B. (1979). Brain mechanisms for offense, defense and submission. *Behavioral and Brain Sciences*, **2**, 201–242.

Bandler, R. (1988). Brain mechanisms of aggression as revealed by electrical and chemical stimulation: Suggestion of a central role for the midbrain periaqueductal grey region. In A. N. Epstein & A. R. Morrison (Eds), *Progress in Psychobiology and Physiological Psychology*, Vol. 13. New York: Academic Press, pp. 67–154.

Blanchard, R. J. & Blanchard, D. C. (1969). Passive and active reactions to fear-eliciting stimuli. *Journal of Comparative and Physiological Psychology*, **68**, 129–135.

Blanchard, R. J., Fukunaga, K. K. & Blanchard, D. C. (1976). Environmental control of defensive reactions to a cat. *Bulletin of the Psychonom. Society*, **8L**, 179–181.

Blanchard, R. J., Klienschmidt, C. F., Fukunaga-Atinson, C. & Blanchard, C. (1980). Defensive attack behavior in male and female rats. *Animal Learning and Behavior*, **8**, 177–183.

Bolles, R. C. & Collier, A. C. (1976). The effect of predictive cues on freezing in rats. *Animal Learning and Behavior*, **4**, 6–8.

Bolles, R. C. & Fanselow, M. S. (1980). A perceptual–defense–recuperative model of fear and pain. *Behavioral and Brain Sciences*, **3**, 290–323.

Bunge, M. (1990). What kind of discipline is psychology: Autonomous or dependent, humanistic or scientific, biological or sociological? *New Ideas in Psychology*, **8**, 121–137.

Caldwell, J. D., Prange, A. J., Jr & Pedersen, C. A. (1986). Oxytocin facilitates the sexual receptivity of estrogen-treated female rats. *Neuropeptides*, **7**, 175–189.

Campbell, M., Perry, R., Small, A., McVeigh Tesch, L. & Curren, E. (1988). Naltexone in infantile autism. *Psychopharmacology Bulletin*, **24**, 135–139.

Carr, G. D., Fibiger, H. C. & Phillips, A. G. (1989). Conditioned place preference as a measure of drug reward. In J. M. Liebman & S. J. Cooper (Eds), *The Neuropharmacological Basis of Reward*. Oxford: Clarendon Press, pp. 264–319.

Cazala, P. & Schmitt, P. (1987). Dorso-ventral variation in the attenuating effects of lateral hypothalamic stimulation on the switch-off response elicited from the mesecephalic gray area. *Physiology & Behavior*, **40**, 625–629.

Chase, M. H. & Morales, F. R. (1990). The atonia and myoclonia of active (REM) sleep. *Annual Review of Psychology*, **42**, 557–558.

Clarke, S. (1971). Sniffing and fixed-ratio behavior in sucrose and brain stimulation reward in the rat. *Physiology & Behavior* **7**, 695–699.

Clarke, S., Panksepp, J. & Trowill, J. A. (1970). A method of recording sniffing in the free-moving rat. *Physiology and Behavior*, **5**, 125–126.

Clarke, S. & Trowill, J. A. (1971). Sniffing and motivated behavior in the rat. *Physiology & Behavior*, **6**, 49–52.

Coe, C. L., Wiener, S. G., Rosenberg, L. T. & Levine, S. (1985). Endocrine and immune responses to separation and maternal loss in nonhuman primates. In M. Reite & T. Fields (Eds), *The Psychobiology of Attachment and Separation*. New York: Academic Press, pp. 163–200.

Crow, T. J. (1972). A map of the rat mesencephalon for electrical self-stimulation. *Brain Research*, **36**, 265–273.

Davis, M. (1986). Pharmacological and anatomical analyses of fear conditioning using the fear-potentiated startle pardigm. *Behavioral Neuroscience*, **100**, 814–824.

Davis, K. L., Gurski, J. C. & Scott, J. P. (1976). Interaction of separation distress with fear in infant dogs. *Developmental Psychobiology*, **10**, 203–212.

Delgado, J. M. R. (1969). *Physical Control of the Mind: Toward a Psychocivilized Society*. New York: Harper & Row.

Depue, R. A. & Iacono, W. G. (1989). Neurobehavioral aspects of affective disorders. *Annual Review of Psychology*, **40**, 457–492.

De Vries, C. J., Buijs, R. M., Van Leeuwen, F. W., Caffe, A. R. & Swaab, D. F. (1985). The vasopressinergic innervation of the brain in normal and castrated rats. *The Journal of Comparative Neurology*, **233**, 236–254.

Di Scala, G., Mana, M. J., Jacobs, W. J. & Phillips, A. G. (1987). Evidence of Pavlovian conditioned fear following electrical stimulation of the periaqueductal grey in the rat. *Physiology & Behavior*, **40**, 55–63.

Fanselow, M. S. (1984). What is conditioned fear. *Trends in Neuroscience*, **7**, 460–462.

Fanselow, M. S. & Helstetter, F. J. (1988). Conditional analgesia, defensive freezing, and benzodiazepines. *Behavioral Neuroscience*, **102**, 233–243.

Fanselow, M. S. & Lester, L. S. (1988). A functional behavioristic approach to aversively motivated behavior: Predatory imminence as a determinant of the topography of defensive behavior. In R. C. Bolles & M. D. Beecher (Eds), *Evolution and Learning*. Hillsdale, NJ: Lawrence Erlbaum, pp. 185–212.

Flynn, J. P. (1967). The neural basis of aggression in cats. In D. C. Glass (Ed.), *Neurophysiology and Emotion*. New York: Rockefeller University Press.

Fuchs, S. A. G., Edinger, H. M. & Siegel, A. (1985). The organization of the hypothalamic pathway mediating affective defense behavior in the cat. *Brain Research*, **330**, 77–92.

Fuchs, S. A. G. & Siegel, A. (1984). Neural pathways mediating hypothalamically elicited flight behavior in the cat. *Brain Research*, **306**, 263–281.

Gillberg, C. (1988). The role of the endogenous opioids in autism and possible relationships to clinical features. In L. Wing (Ed.), *Aspects of Autism: Biological Research*. Oxford: Alden Press, pp. 31–37.

Grastyan, E., Szabo, I., Molnar, P. & Kolta, P. (1968). Rebound, reinforcement, and self-stimulation. *Communications in Behavioral Biology*, **2**, 235–266.

Gray, J. A. (1987). *The Psychology of Fear and Stress*. Cambridge: Cambridge University Press.

Henry, J. P. (1986). Neuroendocrine patterns of emotional response. In R. Plutchik & H. Kellerman (Eds), *Emotion: Theory, Research, and Experience, Vol. 3, Biological Foundations of Emotions*. New York: Academic Press, pp. 37–60.

Herman, B., Hammock, K., Arthur-Smith, A., Egan, J., Chatoor, I., Werner, A. & Zelnick, N. (1987). Naltrexone decreases self-injurious behavior. *Annals of Neurology*, **22**, 550–552.

Herman, B. H. & Panksepp, J. (1981). Ascending endorphin inhibition of distress vocalization. *Science*, **211**, 1060–1062.

Hofer, M. A., Shair, H. N. & Murowchick, E. (1989). Isolation distress and maternal comfort responses of two-week-old rat pups reared in social isolation. *Developmental Psychobiology*, **11**, 553–566.

Hutchinson, R. R. & Renfrew, J. W. (1978). Functional parallels between the neural and environmental antecedents of aggression. *Neuroscience & Biobehavioral Reviews*, **2**, 33–58.

Insel, T. R. & Harbaugh, C. R. (1989). Central administration of corticotropin releasing factor alters rat pup isolation calls. Pharmacology Biochemistry & Behavior, **32**, 197–201.

Insel, T. R., Hill, J. & Mayor, R. B. (1986). Rat pup ultrasonic isolation calls: Possible mediation by the benzodiazepine receptor complex. *Pharmacology Biochemistry and Behavior*, **24**, 1263–1267.

Iwata, J., Chida, K. & LeDoux, J. E. (1987). Cardiovascular responses elicited by stimulation of neurons in the central amygdaloid nucleus in awake but not anesthetized rats resemble conditioned emotional responses. *Brain Research*, **418**, 183–188.

Jirikowski, G. F., Caldwell, J. D., Pilgrim, C., Stumpf, W. E. & Pedersen, C. A. (1989). Changes in immunostaining for oxytocin in the forebrain of the female rat during late pregnancy, parturition and early lactation, *Cell and Tissue Research*, **256**, 411–417.

Kalin, N. H. & Shelton, S. E. (1990). Effects of clonidine and propranolol on separation-induced distress in infant rhesus monkeys. *Brain Research*, in press.

Kalin, N. H., Shelton, S. E. & Barksdale, C. M. (1987). Separation distress in infant rhesus monkeys: Effects of diazepam and Ro 15-1788. *Brain Research*, **408**, 192–198.

Kehoe, P. (1988). Ontogeny of adrenergic and opioid effects on separation vocalizations in rats. In J. D. Newman (Ed.), *The Physiological Control of Mammalian Vocalization*. New York: Plenum Press, pp. 301–320.

Kelly, D. D. (1986). Stress-induced analgesia. *Annals of the New York Academy of Sciences*, **467**, 1–449.

Kiyatkin, E. A. (1989). Nociceptive sensitivity/behavioral reactivity regulation in rats during aversive states of different nature: Its mediation by opioid peptides. *International Journal of Neuroscience*, **44**, 91–110.

Klein, D. F. (1981). Anxiety reconceptualized. In D. F. Klein & J. Rabkin (Eds), *Anxiety: New Research and Changing Concepts*. New York: Raven Press, pp. 235–264.

Kleinginna, P. R. & Kleinginna, A. M. (1981). A categorized list of emotion definitions, with suggestions for a consensual definition. *Motivation & Emotions*, **5**, 345–379.

Landgren, S. & Olsson, K. A. (1980). The effect of electrical stimulation in the hypothalamus on the monosynaptic jaw closing and the disynaptic jaw opening reflexes in the cat. *Experimental Brain Research*, **39**, 389–400.

Lazarus, R. S. (1984). On the primacy of cognition. *American Psychologist*, **39**, 124–129.

Leaton, R. N. & Borszcz, G. S. (1985). Potentiated startle: Its relation to freezing and shock intensity in rats. *Journal of Experimental Psychology: Animal Behavior Processes*, **11**, 421–428.

Leboyer, M., Bouvard, M. & Dugas, M. (1988). Effects of naltrexone on infantile autism. *The Lancet*, **26**, 715.

LeDoux, J. E. (1987). Emotion. In V. Mountcastle, F. Plum & S. R. Geiger (Eds), *Handbook of Physiology, Section 1: The Nervous System, Vol. V. Higher Functions of the Brain, Part 1*. Bethesda, Maryland: American Physiological Society, pp. 419–459.

LeDoux, J. E., Sakaguchi, A. & Reis, D. J. (1984). Subcortical efferent projections of the medial geniculate nucleus mediate emotional responses conditioned to acoustic stimuli. *Journal of Neuroscience*, **4**, 683–698.

Lensing, P., Klinger, D., Gerstl, W. & Panksepp, J. (1989). Clinical notes on naltrexone therapy for five autistic children: Provisional guidelines for future research. Collected Papers of the Autism Research Unit Meeting on the "Experimental Biology of the Autistic Syndromes", Sunderland Polytechnic, England.

Lester, B. M. & Boukydis, C. F. Z. (Eds) (1985). *Infant Crying: Theoretical and Research Perspectives*. New York: Plenum Press.

Liebman, J. M. & Cooper, S. J. (Eds) (1989). *The Neuropharmacological Basis of Reward*. Oxford: Clarendon Press.

MacLean, P. D. (1985). Brain evolution relating to family, play and the separation call. *Archives of General Psychiatry*, **42**, 405–417.

MacLean, P. D. (1990). *The Triune Brain in Evolution*. New York: Plenum Press.

Mancia, G. & Zanchetti, A. (1981). Hypothalamic control of autonomic functions. In P. J. Morgane & J. Panksepp (Eds), *Handbook of the Hypothalamus, Vol. 3B, Behavioral Studies of the Hypothalamus*. New York: Marcel Dekker, pp. 147–202.

Masserman, J. H. (1941). Is the hypothalamus a center of emotion? *Psychosomatic Medicine*, **3**, 3–25.

Masterson, F. A. & Crawford, M. (1982). The defense motivation system: A theory of avoidance behavior. *Behavioral and Brain Sciences*, **5**, 661–696.

Nauta, W. J. H. & Feirtag, M. (1979). The organization of the brain. *Scientific American*, **241**, 88–111.

Newman, J. D. (Ed.) (1988). *The Physiological Control of Mammalian Vocalizations*. New York: Plenum Press

Normansell, L. & Panksepp, J. (1990). Effects of morphine and naloxone on play-rewarded spatial discrimination in juvenile rats. *Developmental Psychobiology*, **23**, 75–83.

Olds, J. (1955). Physiological mechanisms of reward. In M. R. Jones (Ed.), *Nebraska Symposium on Motivation*. Lincoln: University of Nebraska Press, pp. 73–138.

Panksepp, J. (1971). Aggression elicited by electrical stimulation of the hypothalamus in albino rats. *Physiology and Behavior*, **6**, 311–316.

Panksepp, J. (1979). A neurochemical theory of autism. *Trends in Neuroscience*, **2**, 174–177.

Panksepp, J. (1981a). Hypothalamic integration of behavior: Rewards, punishments, and related psychobiological process. In P. J. Morgane & J. Panksepp (Eds), *Handbook of the Hypothalamus, Vol. 3, Part A. Behavioral Studies of the Hypothalamus*. New York: Marcel Dekker, pp. 289–487.

Panksepp, J. (1981b). Brain opioids: A neurochemical substrate for narcotic and social dependence. In S. Cooper (Ed.), *Progress in Theory in Psychopharmacology*. London: Academic Press, 149–175.

Panksepp, J. (1982). Toward a general psychobiological theory of emotions. *The Behavioral and Brain Sciences*, **5**, 407–467.

Panksepp, J. (1985). Mood changes. In *Handbook of Clinical Neurology. Vol. 1. (45): Clinical Neuropsychology*. Amsterdam: Elsevier Science Publishers, pp. 271–285.

Panksepp, J. (1986a). The anatomy of emotions. In R. Plutchik (Ed.), *Emotion: Theory, Research and Experience. Vol. III. Biological Foundations of Emotions*. New York: Academic Press, pp. 91–124.

Panksepp, J. (1986b). The psychobiology of prosocial behaviors: Separation distress, play, and altruism. In C. Zahn-Waxler, E. M. Cummings & R. Iannotti (Eds), *Altruism and Aggression, Biological and Social Origins*. Cambridge: Cambridge University Press, pp. 19–57.

Panksepp, J. (1986c). The neurochemistry of behavior. *Annual Review of Psychology*, **37**, 77–107.

Panksepp, J. (1988). Brain emotional circuits and psychopathologies, In M. Clynes & J. Panksepp (Eds), *Emotions and Psychopathology*. New York: Plenum Press, pp. 37–76.

Panksepp, J. (1989a). The neurobiology of emotions: Of animal brains and human feelings. In H. Wagner & T. Manstead (Eds), *Handbook of Social Psychophysiology*. Chichester: Wiley, pp. 5–26.

Panksepp, J. (1989b). The psychobiology of emotions: The animal side of human feelings. In G. Gaionotti & C. Caltagirone (Eds), *Experimental Brain Research, Series 18, Emotions and the Dual Brain*. Heidelberg: Springer-Verlag, pp. 31–55.

Panksepp, J. (1989c). Les circuits des emotions. *Science & Vie*, No. 168, Sept., 58–67.

Panksepp, J. (1990a). Psychology's search of identity: Can "mind" and behavior be understood without understanding the brain? *New Ideas in Psychology*, **8**, 139–149.

Panksepp, J. (1990b). The psychoneurology of fear: Evolutionary perspectives and the role of animal models in understanding human anxiety. In R. Burrows (Ed.), *Handbook of Anxiety*, Vol. 3, Amsterdam: Elsevier, pp. 3–58.

Panksepp, J. & Bishop, P. (1981). An autoradiographic map of the (^{3}H) diprenorphine binding in rat brain: Effects of social interaction. *Brain Research Bulletin*, **7**, 405–410.

Panksepp, J., Crepeau, L. & Clynes, M. (1987). Effects of CRF on separation distress and juvenile play. *Neuroscience Abstracts*, **13**, 1320.

Panksepp, J., Herman, B. H., Villberg, T., Bishop, P. & DeEskinazi, F. G. (1980). Endogenous opioids and social behavior. *Neuroscience & Biobehavioral Reviews*, **4**, 473–487.

Panksepp, J., Meeker, R. & Bean, N. J. (1980). The neurochemical control of crying. *Pharmacology, Biochemistry and Behavior*, **12**, 437–443.

Panksepp, J., Normansell, L., Cox, J. F., Crepeau, L. J. & Sacks, D. S. (1987). Psychopharmacology of social play. In J. Mos (Ed.), *Ethnopharmacology of Social Behavior*. Duphar: Holland, pp. 132–144.

Panksepp, J., Normansell, L., Herman, B., Bishop, P. & Crepeau, L. (1988). Neural and neurochemical control of the separation distress call. In J. D. Newman (Ed.), *The Physiological Control of Mammalian Vocalizations*. New York: Plenum Press, pp. 263–299.

Panksepp, J., Sacks, D. S., Crepeau, L. J. & Abbott, B. B. (1991). The psycho- and neuro-biology of fear systems in the brain. In M. R. Denny (Ed.), *Aversive Events and Behavior*. Hillsdale, NJ: Erlbaum, pp. 7–54.

Panksepp, J. & Sahley, T. (1987). Possible brain opioid involvement in disrupted social intent and language development of autism. In E. Schopler & G. Mesibov (Eds), *Neurobiological Issues in Autism*. New York: Plenum Press, pp. 357–373.

Panksepp, J., Siviy, S. & Normansell, L. (1984). The psychobiology of play: Theoretical and methodological perspectives. *Neuroscience & Biobehavioral Reviews*, **8**, 465–492.

Panksepp, J., Siviy, S. M. & Normansell, L. A. (1985). Brain opioids and social emotions. In M. Reite & T. Fields (Eds), *The Psychobiology of Attachment and Separation*. New York: Academic Press, pp. 3–49.

Pedersen, C. A., Asher, J. A., Monroe, Y. L. & Prange, A. J. Jr (1985). Oxytocin induces maternal behavior in virgin female rats. *Science*, **216**, 648–649.

Pellis, S. M. & Pellis, V. C. (1987). Play-fighting differs from serious fighting in both target of attack and tactics of fighting in the laboratory rat *Rattus norvegicus*. *Aggressive Behavior*, **13**, 227–242.

Phillips, A. G., Blaha, C. D. & Fibiger, H. C. (1989). Neurochemical correlates of brain-stimulation reward measured by *ex vivo* and *in vivo* analyses. *Neuroscience & Biobehavioral Reviews*, **13**, 99–104.

Pinel, J. P. J. & Treit, D. (1978). Burying as a defensive response in rats. *Journal of Comparative and Physiological Psychology*, **92**, 708–712.

Plutchik, R. (1980). *Emotion: A Psychoevolutionary Synthesis*. New York: Harper & Row.

Poeck, K. (1969). Pathophysiology of emotional disorders associated with brain damage. In P. J. Vinken & G. W. Bruyn (Eds), *Handbook of Clinical Neurology, Vol. 3, Disorders of Higher Nervous Activity*, Amsterdam: North-Holland, pp. 343–367.

Redmond, D. E., Jr (1979). New and old evidence for the involvement of a brain norepinephrine system in anxiety. In W. G. Fann *et al.* (Eds), *Phenomenology and Treatment of Anxiety*. New York: Spectrum, pp. 153–203.

Roberts, V. J. & Cox, V. C. (1987). Active avoidance conditioning with dorsal central gray stimulation in a place preference paradigm. *Psychobiology*, **15**, 167–170.

Rodgers, R. J. & Randall, J. I. (1988). Environmentally induced analgesia: Situational factors, mechanisms and significance. In R. J. Rodgers & S. J. Cooper (Eds), *Endorphins, Opiates and Behavioural Processes*. Chichester: Wiley, pp. 107–142.

Rossi, J. III & Panksepp, J. (1983). The relationship between electrically elicited sniffing and self-stimulation in the rat. *Neuroscience Abstracts*, **9**, 564.

Rossi, J. III, Sahley, T. L. & Panksepp, J. (1983). The role of brain norepinephrine in clonidine suppression of isolation-induced distress in the domestic chick. *Psychopharmacology*, **79**, 338–342.

Sacks, D. S. & Panksepp, J. (1987). Electrical stimulation of the lateral hypothalamic fear/flight sites in rats produces conditional freezing. *Neuroscience Abstracts*, **13**, 452.

Sagar, S. M., Sharp, F. R. & Curran, T. (1988). Expression of *c-fos* protein in brain: Metabolic mapping at the cellular level. *Science*, **240**, 1328–1331.

Sandner, G., Schmitt, P. & Karli, P. (1985). Effects of hypothalamic lesions on central gray stimulation induced escape behavior and on withdrawal reactions in the rat. *Physiology & Behavior*, **34**, 291–297.

Schultz, S. C. & Tamminga, C. A. (Eds) (1989). *Schizophrenia: Scientific Progress*. New York: Oxford University Press.

Scott, J. P. (1974). Effects of psychotropic drugs on separation distress in dogs. *Proceedings of IX Congress of the Collegium International Neuropsychpharmacologicum*, Exerpta Medica International Congress Series No. 359, pp. 735–745.

Seeger, T. F., Sforzo, G. A., Pert, C. B. & Pert, A. (1984). *In vivo* autoradiography: Visualization of stress-induced changes in opiate receptor occupancy in the rat brain. *Brain Research*, **305**, 303–311.

Siegel, A. & Pott, C. B. (1988). Neural substrates of aggression and flight in the cat. *Progress in Neurobiology*, **32**, 261–283.

Siviy, S. & Panksepp, J. (1985). Dorsomedial diencephalic involvement in the juvenile play of rats. *Behavioral Neuroscience*, **99**, 1103–1113.

Siviy, S. M. & Panksepp, J. (1987a). Juvenile play in the rat: Thalamic and brain stem involvement. *Physiology & Behavior*, **41**, 103–114.

Siviy S. & Panksepp, J. (1987b). Sensory modulation of juvenile play in rats. *Developmental Psychobiology*, **20**, 39–55.

Soubrie, P. (1986). Reconciling the role of central serotonin neurons in human and animal behavior. *Behavioral and Brain Sciences*, **9**, 319–364.

Strongman, K. T. (1987). *The Psychology of Emotion*. Chichester: Wiley.

Sudol, M. (1988). Expression of proto-oncogenes in neural tissues. *Brain Research Reviews*, **13**, 391–403.

Thor, D. H. & Holloway, W. R. Jr (1984). Social play in juvenile rats: A decade of methodological and experimental research. *Neuroscience & Biobehavioral Reviews*, **8**, 455–464.

Trowill, J. & Hynek, K. (1970). Secondary reinforcement based on primary brain stimulation reward. *Psychological Reports*, **27**, 715–718.

Trowill, J. A., Panksepp, J. & Gandelman, R. (1969). An incentive model of rewarding brain stimulation. *Psychological Review*, **76**, 264–281.

Vanderwolf, C. H., Kelly, M. E., Kraemer, P. & Streather, A. (1988). Are emotion and motivation localized in the limbic system and nucleus accumbens? *Behavioral Brain Research*, **27**, 45–55.

Weller, A. & Blass, E. M. (1988). Behavioral evidence for cholecystokinin-opiate interactions in neonatal rats. *American Journal of Physiology*, **255**, R901–R907.

Wishaw, I. Q. & Tomie, J.-A. (1988). Food wresting and dodging: Strategies used by rats (*Rattus norvegicus*) for obtaining and protecting food from conspecifics. *Journal of Comparative Psychology*, **101**, 202–209.

White, N. M. & Franklin, K. B. J. (1989). The Neural Basis of Reward and Reinforcement: A Conference in Honour of Peter M. Milner. *Neuroscience & Biobehavioral Reviews* (Special Issue, Volume 13).

Wiener, S. G., Coe, C. L., & Levine, S. (1988). Endocrine and neurochemical sequelae of primate vocalizations. In J. D. Newman (Ed.), *The Physiological Control of Mammalian Vocalization*. New York: Plenum Press, pp. 367–394.

Wise, R. A. & Rompre, P.-P. (1989). Brain dopamine and reward. *Annual Review of Psychology*, **40**, 191–225.

Zajonc, R. B. (1984). On the primacy of affect. *American Psychologist*, **39**, 117–123.

4 Motivation, Emotion and Cognition: A Developmental–Interactionist View

ROSS BUCK
Department of Communication Science, University of Connecticut, Storrs, Connecticut 06268, USA

This chapter will first present briefly some of the central concepts of a developmental–interactionist theory of motivation, emotion, and cognition which is based upon the notion of an interaction of special-purpose, general-purpose, and linguistic systems of behavior control operating in a developmental context. It will then present a view of the attribution/appraisal process, which contrasts with many "cognitive" approaches which view emotion as an outcome of appraisal. In contrast, developmental–interactionist theory views emotion as contributing structured input into the attribution/appraisal process, so that emotion is really a type of knowledge: a type of "cognition". Following this, the chapter will describe a research program investigating the spontaneous communication of motivation and emotion and discuss how spontaneous emotional communication fosters emotional education and emotional competence. Finally, it will review briefly the implications of this point of view for understanding (a) the emotional bases of personal relationships; (b) psychosocial aspects of coping with disease; and (c) the role of media in providing the emotional basis for a "global village".

THE DEVELOPMENTAL–INTERACTIONIST VIEW

Historical antecedents

The interactionist view presented here has its roots in the Schachter & Singer (1962) self-attribution theory of emotion as an interaction between "cognitive" and "physiological" systems. This basic interactionist notion was put forward in the 1920s by Gustave Maranon and Bertrand Russell (see Russell, 1961). My version of the theory differs from the earlier versions in several ways. First, the "physiological factors" in previous theories tended to emphasize peripheral autonomic/endocrine responding that contributes relatively diffuse and unstructured information to the cognitive system, which then supposedly sorts it all out according to external cues. In my view, the body actually provides well-differentiated structured information to the organism via the activation of innate knowledge systems (LeDoux, 1986). This knowledge comes from

International Review of Studies on Emotion, Vol. 1. Edited by K. T. Strongman
©1991 John Wiley & Sons Ltd

special-purpose processing systems that have been structured over the course of evolution: ie structured by *phylogeny*. A second difference is that, in place of the "cognitive factors" in previous theories (in which "cognition" was not well defined), I put general-purpose processing systems of associative and instrumental learning which evolved to be sensitive to the experience of the individual organism with external (and internal) reality. These systems are therefore structured by experience over the course of individual development: ie structured by *ontogeny*. Thirdly, in contrast to previous theories, my view emphasizes the process of individual development in determining the nature of the interaction between special-purpose and general-purpose processing systems. Fourthly, my view emphasizes the special importance of *linguistic competence* as constituting a third system of behavior control: a formal means of information processing that is perhaps unique to human beings. The three systems of behavior control and their characteristics are summarized in Figure 4.1.

The primes

The biologically based special-purpose processing systems exist in a hierarchy of primary motivational/emotional systems, or primes. These interact increasingly with general-purpose processing systems as one goes up the hierarchy. The hierarchy of primes is illustrated in Figure 4.2.

Reflexes, instincts, drives, primary affects, and effectance motivation are all seen to be primes at different hierarchical levels in the nervous system. Reflexes (and also what have been termed taxes, tropisms, and endogenous automatic movements) are unconditioned actions that are released by specific external or internal stimuli and perform highly specific, albeit vital, functions (see Buck, 1985; Cofer & Appley, 1964). They exist outside the central nervous system and in the spinal cord: examples include the knee-jerk response initiated by the neurologist's tap on the knee and the activation of melanin within skin cells by solar radiation that produces suntanning. Instincts (or fixed action patterns) are innate tendencies to perform specific actions and action sequences which may culminate in an orderly but stereotyped series of behaviors which are characteristic of a given species. They are activated by specific releasers. Instincts

Biological	Learned	Linguistic
Special-purpose control systems structured by evolution (Phylogeny)	General-purpose control systems structured by individual experience (Ontogeny)	Formal ways of categorizing and organizing information about the internal and external environment
Reflexes, instincts, drives, affects, effectance motivation	Conditioning, instrumental learning, cognition	Language, mathematics, logic

Figure 4.1. Systems of behavior control. Reproduced by permission from Buck (1988a)

Linguistically based motives and emotions

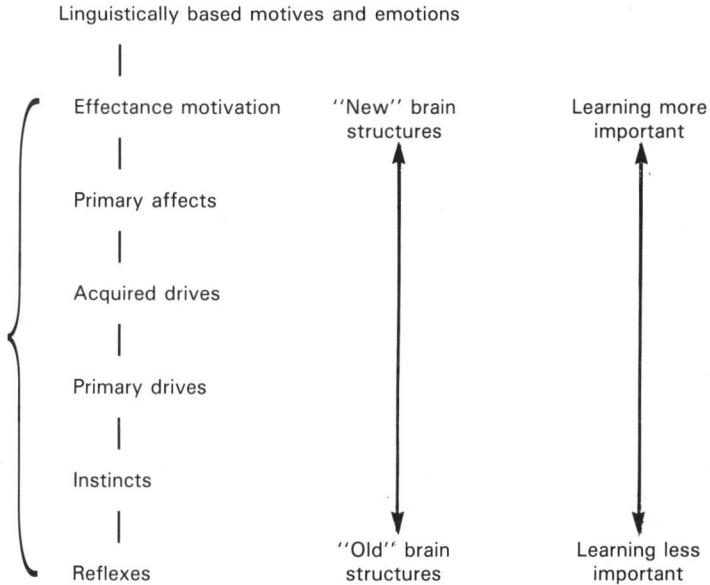

Figure 4.2. Hierarchy of motivational–emotional systems. Reproduced by permission from Buck (1988a)

can often be localized in the brainstem, and examples include the migratory behaviors of fish and birds and imprinting.

Primary drives are associated with natural tissue needs, such as the needs for air, water, food, sex, sleep, temperature regulation, and pain avoidance. They tend to be activated by stimuli relevant to these needs, but unlike instincts they are activated only when the need is present and they do not result in a stereotyped behavior sequence. Instead, they energize behavior, causing the organism to search the environment for stimuli that satisfy the need. This satisfaction (drive reduction) serves to reinforce the successful responses and thereby encourages the learning of a variable behavior sequence leading to a relatively fixed goal. In the case of acquired or secondary drives, the organism also learns the reinforcement value of initially neutral stimuli that are associated with drive reduction, so that such stimuli become incentives. In the brain, drives are particularly associated with neurochemical systems in the hypothalamus which interact with peripheral (autonomic, endocrine, etc) systems.

Primary affects are the systems most commonly associated with "emotion", and include at least happiness, sadness, fear, anger, surprise, and disgust (Ekman & Friesen, 1975; Tomkins, 1962, 1963). The capacity to experience and express the affects is innate and unlearned, but the circumstances under which they are experienced, and the ways in which they are expressed, are learned. The affects are not associated with such specific behavior sequences or goals as are instincts and drives: instead they activate general response tendencies *vis-à-vis* the environment. In the brain they are particularly associated with limbic system structures.

Effectance motivation involves an intrinsic need for an effective interaction with the environment (White, 1959). It is associated with curiosity, which motivates the exploratory behaviors by which new information is assimilated and accommodated by the organism. Effectance motivation is activated by stimuli termed "aliments" that are partially but not completely assimilated (Piaget, 1971). In the brain, effectance motivation is perhaps most associated with neocortical systems.

The primes are structured by evolution: ie by natural selection, or phylogeny. They are phylogenetic adaptations in that they have evolved because they have helped organisms to survive in their characteristic environmental niche.

The general nature of the relationship between special-purpose processing systems and general-purpose processing systems is suggested in Figure 4.3. The primes are special-purpose processing systems that interact increasingly with general-purpose processing systems involving conditioning and learning as one goes up the hierarchy. Reflexes are relatively fixed and immutable. Instincts, drives, and affects are increasingly open to influence by learning; effectance motivation is the motivational force behind the functioning of general-purpose systems.

Defining motivation, emotion, and cognition

In the view of developmental–interactionist theory, all of the primes—even the simplest—have motivational, emotional, and cognitive aspects. For example, suntanning occurs when skin-darkening melanin is released in skin cells under the influence of ultraviolet light. The ultraviolet light is the challenging stimulus that provokes the cognitive aspect: it is an event which provides information

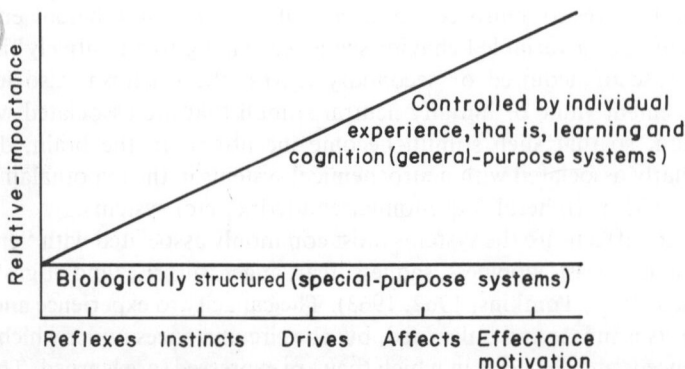

Figure 4.3. Relative importance of biological factors versus learning and cognition in the control of behavior based on the primes. Reproduced by permission from Buck (1988a)

to which the body responds with a kind of innate knowledge. In other words, a primary motivational/emotional system has evolved with the motivational potential to respond to this information with an emotional "readout" which in this case consists of the release of the melanin. The notion of suntanning as an emotion may well be received with some skepticism (although colleagues from California have told me that it makes sense) but it illustrates the notion basic to developmental–interactionist theory that motivation, emotion, and cognition are different aspects of the functioning of the primes. One cannot be defined or meaningfully conceptualized in isolation from the others. They are three sides, so to speak, of the same coin.

Motivation

Motivation is defined generally as the potential for behavior that is built into a system of behavior control. Biological motivation is the potential for behavior built into the biologically structured primes (see Buck, 1985).

Emotion

Emotion is defined generally as the readout of motivational potential when activated by a challenging stimulus. Biological emotion is defined as the readout of information from primes to systems involving adaptation homeostasis (emotion I), social expression (emotion II), and subjective experience (emotion III; see Buck, 1985).

The relationship of motivation and emotion

This view of motivation and emotion is consistent with the common Latin root of both words: the verb *movere*, to move. Motivation is viewed as the potential to movement, broadly conceived, while emotion is the expression, or readout, of that potential in actual "movement".

The relationship between motivational potential and emotional readout is analogous to the relationship between energy and matter: the potential is not seen, only the manifestation of that potential when activated by a proper stimulus. Potential energy (as in a weight raised to a height) is not seen, rather its manifestation in force, heat, light, etc, when activated. In the same way, motivation is not seen, but rather its manifestation in emotion.

The readout process

The three general ways in which motivational potential is manifested are illustrated in Figure 4.4. The activation of each prime should produce some adaptive bodily emotion I response which should, in principle, be measurable. Expressive emotion II responses should ·be present only when the prime in

Readout source	Readout process	Readout target	Readout function
Motivation Potential for behavior inherent in neurochemical structures (primes)	Emotion Realization of motivational potential when activated by challenging stimuli	III. Syncretic cognition II. Expressive behavior I. Autonomic/endocrine/ immune system response	Subjective experience / Self-regulation Spontaneous communication / Social coordination Adaptation/ homeostasis

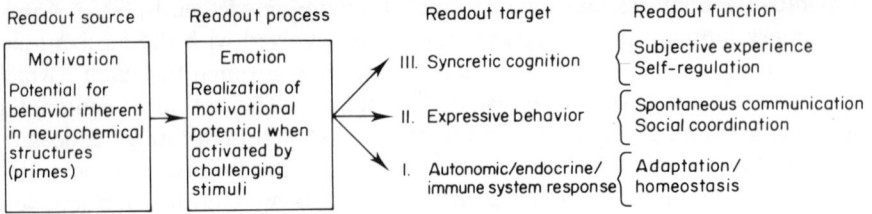

Figure 4.4. The readout process: sources, targets, and functions served. Reproduced by permission from Buck (1988a)

question has significance for social organization. Subjective emotion III responses are present only when internal feedback about the state of the prime is important for self-regulation. Many drives (hunger, thirst) are accessible to subjective experience (emotion III readout) but are not associated with specific emotion II displays. The classic primary affects of Tomkins (1962, 1963) and Ekman and Friesen (1975) have all three sorts of readout.

The primes' readout interacts with general-purpose processing systems of conditioning and learning which are structured by the organism's experience. The special-purpose primes are seen to be distinct systems which interact with general-purpose processing systems: the two sorts of system are *not* usefully considered to be two ends of the same continuum. Rather, the nature of the relationship between the primes and general-purpose processing systems is as indicated in Figure 4.3. As it suggests, special-purpose processing systems always exert some influence over responding, while the influence of general-purpose systems may be entirely absent or relatively more important. The ordinate of Figure 4.3 can be considered to be a continuum. It might be the primes (going from reflexes on the left to effectance motivation on the right). Alternatively, one could regard it as a continuum of communication situations, ranging from unbridled passion on the left to a preponderance of carefully reasoned argument on the right. One could also regard it as a developmental continuum, with the newborn infant on the left and the mature adult on the right. Or, it could be a phylogenetic scale with relatively simple organisms—ants, termites, even algae and single-celled creatures—on the left and humans on the right. In general, this continuum can be viewed as reflecting an increasing relative contribution of complex neurochemical activity—and in vertebrates cortical activity—as opposed to the activity of simpler neurochemical systems in the determination of behavior.

An example

An example of the three readouts of emotion is shown in Figure 4.5. Imagine that a young child (C) is frustrated while building blocks, screams and throws a block at an adult (A). Developmental–interactionist theory argues that this behavior is accompanied by subjective experience, or emotion III. This is presumably associated with neurochemical activity in the general region of the amygdalae. Independent of subjective experience, in a system constructed by different selection pressures over the course of evolution, is the emotion II display: the scream, the vigor of the throw, and probably the characteristic facial expression of anger. Thirdly, there is a tendency for a pattern of peripheral physiological responding—the fight-or-flight response—that serves basic adaptive/homeostatic functions (emotion I). We shall return to this interaction of A and C later in the chapter.

Cognition

The notion of subjective experience is controversial, and it is important here to define carefully what one means by "experience". This is relevant in turn to the definition of cognition. In developmental–interactionist theory cognition is defined broadly as knowledge, and in this sense subjective emotional

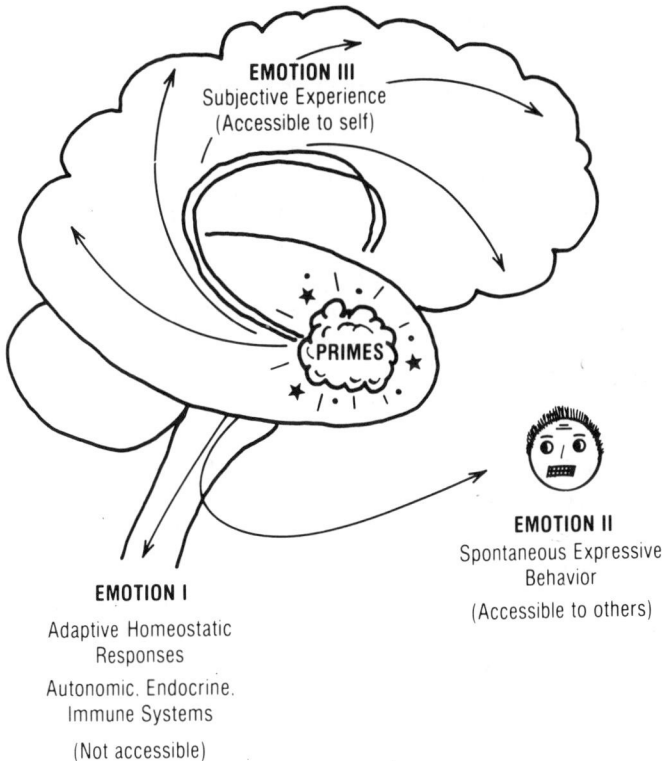

EMOTION III
Subjective Experience
(Accessible to self)

PRIMES

EMOTION II
Spontaneous Expressive
Behavior
(Accessible to others)

EMOTION I
Adaptive Homeostatic
Responses
Autonomic. Endocrine.
Immune Systems
(Not accessible)

Figure 4.5. Accessibility of the three readouts of the primes

experience constitutes a kind of cognition. However, some define cognition quite differently, insisting that cognition must constitute not only knowledge, but knowledge *about* something.

These two views of cognition have roots in epistemelogical theory that go back at least to St Augustine. Thus, William James, Bertrand Russell, and many others have distinguished between knowledge-by-acquaintance and knowledge-by-description. Knowledge-by-acquaintance is direct sensory awareness, the "presentational immediacy of experience" that is completely self-evident (Russell, 1912, p. 73), while knowledge-by-description is knowledge about such sense data. James defined knowledge-by-acquaintance as follows: "I know the color blue when I see it, and the flavor of a pear when I taste it . . . but *about* the inner nature of these facts or what makes them what they are I can say nothing at all. I cannot impart acquaintance with them to any one who has not made it himself . . . At most, I can say to my friends, 'Go to certain places and act in certain ways, and these objects will probably come'. All the elementary natures of the world . . . must either not be known at all, or known in this dumb way of acquaintance without *knowing about*" (p. 221, italics in the original).

Knowledge-by-description in contrast involves knowledge *about* sense data, and this varies in quality with *how much* we "know about" the phenomenon in question. "In general, the less we analyze a thing . . . the less we know about it and the more our familiarity of it is of the acquaintance-type" (p. 221). James relates his distinction to the grammatical sentence: "Its 'subject' stands for an object of acquaintance which, by the addition of the predicate, is to get something known about it" (p. 222). He adds, "The minimum of grammatical subject, of objective presence, of reality known about, the mere beginning of knowledge, must be named by the word that says the least. Such a word is the interjection, as *lo*! *there*! *ecco*! *voila*! or the article or demonstrative pronoun introducing the sentence, as *the*, *it*, *that*" (p. 222).

Knowledge-by-description can be very simple, as in Pavlovian conditioning. For example, the marine snail *Hermissenda crassicornis* naturally responds to rotation (which mimics ocean turbulence) by flexing its foot so as to anchor itself. If rotation is paired with a light, the snail learns to flex its foot to the light (Alkon, 1988, 1989). In effect, the snail has learned something *about* the light: that is associated with rotation. Alkon (1988, 1989) has described a detailed model of how the memory of such an association is stored by changes in nerve cell membranes which may selectively alter synaptic branching.

Another distinction between knowledge-by-acquaintance and knowledge-by-description is that knowledge-by-acquaintance may be particularly associated with the holistic and synthetic kind of cognitive processing that Tucker (1981) labeled "syncretic", while knowledge-by-description is associated with "analytic" sequential linear cognitive processing. These kinds of cognitive processing are in turn respectively associated with the right and left hemispheres (see Buck, 1984, 1988a).

The primacy of emotion vs cognition

One of the most important areas of controversy in contemporary theories of emotion is the question of whether cognition is a necessary part of emotion, and if so whether emotion or cognition is primary in the response of the organism to the environment. On one side are those who argue that the organism cannot respond emotionally to an event unless it can first appraise the significance of that event—you must in effect know what the event is before you can like it, or fear it, or ignore it. On the other side are those who argue that the initial emotional response of the organism can be in effect "automatic", not requiring cognitive knowledge of the event.

Richard Lazarus (1984) defines appraisal as an evaluation by the individual of the harmful or beneficial significance of some event. He regards this as central to emotion: "cognitive activity is a necessary precondition of emotion because to experience an emotion, people must comprehend . . . that their well-being is implicated in a transaction, for better or worse" (p. 124). This need not, however, be a conscious, rational sort of cognition. Lazarus states that appraisal can involve a conscious, rational, symbolic process but that it can also be a "primitive evaluative perception" (1984, p. 124) that is "global or spherical" (1982, p. 1020). Lazarus appears to be making a distinction here between two different sorts of cognition, but this is not explicitly acknowledged.

Studies by Robert Zajonc and his colleagues suggested that an individual could respond preferentially to stimuli before knowing what they were (Kunst-Wilson & Zajonc, 1980; Wilson, 1979; Zajonc, 1980, 1984). On this and other evidence, Zajonc argued that affect occurs prior to, and independently of, cognition. This argument drew strong criticism from Lazarus (1982, 1984).

Examination of the arguments used by Zajonc and Lazarus reveals that their disagreement rests upon what each considers to be "cognition". Lazarus (1984) acknowledged that the comprehension that one's well-being is at stake may take the form of a "primitive evaluative perception" (p. 124), but Zajonc (1984) replied that cognition must require some sort of transformation of sensory input: some kind of "mental work". Zajonc stated: "Lazarus has broadened the definition of cognitive appraisal to include even the most primitive forms of sensory excitation" (p. 117). Thus, Zajonc and Lazarus agree that *some* form of sensory information is necessary for emotion, but disagree about what would constitute "cognition". Specifically, Lazarus defines cognition in terms of knowledge-by-acquaintance and Zajonc in terms of knowledge-by-description, and the controversy between them can be resolved by this distinction (Buck, 1988a).

Thus, developmental–interactionist theory suggests that knowledge-by-acquaintance is itself an affective process, and that it precedes, and determines the nature of, knowledge-by-description. This analysis is consistent with James' position, for he notes that "through feelings we become acquainted with things, but only by our thoughts do we know about them. Feelings are the germ and starting point for cognition, thoughts the developed tree" (James, 1890, p. 222).

At some point, knowledge-by-acquaintance must be transformed into knowledge-by-description. Raw sensory and emotional information must become transformed into knowledge *about* this information. Developmental–interactionist theory suggests that it is this process that can most usefully be termed "appraisal".

Appraisal

Only a fraction of the vast number of events available to the brain is ever attended to. How does the brain know how to process a given event without knowing what that event is? And if the brain knows that an event should be processed, has it not already been processed? This implies an impossible infinite regress of processing mechanisms. In response to this riddle, the perception theorist J. J. Gibson argued that such a regress is avoided only if one assumes that the organism is not active in the initial pickup of events. The registration of events must be *direct* and unmediated (see Alley, 1988; Gibson, 1966, 1979).

The filter

In Gibson's theory, organisms become increasingly efficient at noticing potential uses of objects (affordances) through an education of attention (Goldfield, 1983), and they thereby come to attend to some events in the environment and to ignore others. This determines the impact of a particular event for a particular individual. Terms like "evaluation" or "appraisal" are often applied to this process, but such terms have information-processing connotations. Both terms imply the process of finding the value or "praiseworthiness" of an event, suggesting the operation of instrumental learning and memory in the service of comprehending the implications of an event for one's well-being. Because of these connotations, developmental–interactionist theory suggests that the term "filter" is more appropriate in describing the earliest—subcortical and paleocortical—phases in the pickup of events (Buck, 1986, 1988a).

A specific example of such a filter is provided by the tiny muscles behind the eardrum that contract involuntarily when a person is exposed to a loud noise (Borg & Counter, 1989). These function to dampen the sound vibrations that are transmitted to the cochlea, thereby preventing sensory overload and injury, among other things. Borg and Counter (1989) describe the pathways in the lower brainstem that are responsible for this. There is clearly no time for the organism to comprehend that its well-being is implicated when a sudden loud noise occurs. The event presents a general challenge that has been dealt with by a phylogenetic adaptation: in this case an elegant and sensitive reflex.

Like reflexes, instincts, drives, and affects have evolved as phylogenetic adaptations, at progressively higher levels in the nervous system (Buck, 1985). They too are activated directly by appropriate events, and it is they that arguably direct the pickup of "raw" knowledge-by-acquaintance. For example, there is evidence that sensory stimuli are processed at the cortex only if they are accompanied by non-specific influences from the reticular formation. We are not aware of the feel of comfortable shoes because even though sensory information about the feel of those shoes is available to the brain, it is usually ignored. The reticular formation does not *know* what the feel of comfortable shoes is like any more than the middle-ear reflex "knows" what loud noise is. Rather, in both cases basic decision rules are used. With the reticular formation, the rule is that of habituation. If the stimulation is weak or repetitive, it is filtered out and thereby ignored.

Emotional filters

Basic decision rules also attach emotional significance to events. Some events acquired importance during evolution: for example releasers in the process of ritualization (Eibl-Eibesfeldt, 1970). Other events acquire importance during individual development, ie a stimulus that evokes a conditioned emotional response. The result is what Ohman (1986) has described as a "preattentive stimulus analysis" (p. 123) involving a "fast, involuntary, holistic, and automatic analysis of an emotionally relevant stimulus" (p. 138).

The process of emotional filtering may be based upon sensory input to subcortical and palaeocortical structures that is more direct and therefore faster than input to the classical sensory areas in the neocortex. LeDoux (1986) has noted that projections direct from the retina to the hypothalamus—predicted by Papez (1937)—have been identified (Pickard & Silverman, 1981), as have projections from sensory regions of the thalamus to the hypothalamus and amygdalae (see LeDoux, Sakaguchi & Reis, 1984). The amygdalae appear to be particularly important in this regard. LeDoux (1986) states that the amygdalae receive sensory input from the thalamus and also from the neocortex, but that the thalamic pathway is several synapses shorter. The early input reaching the amygdalae may "prime the area to receive the better analyzed neocortical inputs, providing a crude picture of what is to come, narrowing the affective possibilities, and perhaps even organizing possible and actual responses" (LeDoux, 1986, pp. 345–346). In an elegant series of studies, LeDoux (1986) has tracked the neural pathways by which a conditioned emotional response (CER) involving autonomic (blood pressure) and behavioral (freeze) responses is evoked by an auditory stimulus. He demonstrated that fibers containing the excitatory amino acid glutimate go directly from the classic auditory tract in the medial geniculate bodies to synapse in the lateral amygdalae and on to the central amygdalae, from where they affect blood pressure (via the lateral hypothalamus) and behavior (via the midbrain central gray).

If the system is disrupted, as in bilateral amygdalectomy, the sensory/perceptual qualities of stimuli are divorced from their emotional qualities: "Objects are still perceived and emotional reactions are still expressed, but these functions are no longer coupled in the brain" (LeDoux, 1986, p. 341). The result is the Kluver–Bucy syndrome, where an amygdalectomized monkey might mouth feces, a burning match, or a usually feared snake.

Taken together, the reticular formation, hypothalamus, amygdalae, and other limbic system mechanisms constitute a filter that determines the impact of a particular event for a particular individual. The result is knowledge-by-acquaintance: the individual attends to the event and experiences an immediate awareness of it. Thus, basic motivational/emotional systems direct the initial stages of knowledge (Buck, 1986, p. 363). However, although we know directly the event, we as yet know nothing *about* it, for the event is not yet known by description.

Agnosia

Knowing an event directly yet knowing nothing about it seems impossible, but it is a relatively common occurrence in cases of brain damage: it is known as agnosia. Agnosias are disorders of recognition that are not due to sensory dysfunction or unfamiliarity. The normal perceptual process is somehow "stripped of meaning" (Bauer, 1984, p. 457). In effect, knowledge-by-description is disrupted, while knowledge-by-acquaintance is apparently unaffected. For example, prosopagnosia involves the inability to recognize and discriminate faces. Prosopagnosic patients know that a face is a face, can name it as such, and can name the parts of the face and point to them. Yet they cannot recognize the familiar faces of loved ones and/or famous persons (Etkoff, 1984).

There is evidence that familiar faces may be discriminated on an "unconscious" level in prosopagnosic patients. Bauer (1984) and Tranel and Damasio (1985) showed prosopagnosic patients pictures of family members and famous persons. The patients could not recognize any of the pictures, but did show electrodermal responses when the correct names were presented, suggesting that the faces were "recognized" at some level.

A model of agnosia

Damasio, Damasio and Van Hoesen (1982) suggest that the common factor in prosopagnosia is an inability to recognize a particular stimulus with which the patient has a history of contact: "recognition of the generic class to which the stimulus belongs presents no difficulty, but recognition of an individual member of that class, whose identity had previously been learned, is impaired" (p. 337). Furthermore, they suggest that the primary defect in agnosia is a failure of the stimulus to evoke the previously acquired information regarding that *particular* stimulus. Elementary perception is intact, and the patient has a store of memories that can be evoked, but that stimulus can no longer evoke those memories.

The Damasio, Damasio and Van Hoesen (1982) model suggests that conscious face recognition involves four steps: (a) perception; (b) the arousal by the perceptual event of a "template" based on past visual experience with that face;

(c) the activation of multimodal memories associated with the face; and (d) a conscious "readout", including feelings of familiarity and an ability to recall the memories. Tranel and Damasio (1985) suggest that in prosopagnosia the template is intact but prevented from activating memory stores—there is "a complete or partial blocking of the activation that normally would be triggered by template matching" (p. 1454)—but that the template matching can in itself trigger autonomic responding resulting in evidence of unconscious discrimination.

A model of appraisal

I suggest that the shift in processing at the different steps of the Damasio, Damasio and Van Hoesen (1982) model represents a basic change in the way that the facial stimulus is "known". Specifically, it represents a shift from knowledge-by-acquaintance to knowledge-by-description.

The Damasio *et al.* model can be combined with the evidence for a subcortical–paleocortical filter to arrive at a general model of appraisal (Buck, 1988a, 1989). This model is presented in Figure 4.6. Sensory systems project into the reticular formation, which functions to arouse the cortex to strong and/or unusual events. Sensory pathways also project directly to the hypothalamus. They also synapse in the thalamus, and from there project into the amygdalae and other limbic system structures. These respond to conditioned or innate emotional qualities in the event (LeDoux, 1986). This input into subcortical/paleocortical systems may correspond to the initial steps of the Damasio *et al.* model, perception and template matching, and it may in itself trigger the autonomic responses that are intact in agnosia.

The sensory pathways also proceed via the thalamus to the primary sensory areas of the cortex, where together with input from the subcortical/paleocortical systems they result in knowledge-by-acquaintance of the event. This normally leads to the arousal of the appropriate templates which activate multimodal memories *about* the event. The conscious readout of this memory activation, with feelings of familiarity and ability to give appropriate responses (ie verbal accounts), constitutes knowledge-by-description of the event. This corresponds to the subsequent steps in the Damasio *et al.* model: the activation of memory and feelings of familiarity that are disrupted in agnosia.

In summary, I am suggesting that subcortical/paleocortical systems function as filters to guide the initial pickup of events and so determine the input to the appraisal process, which in turn is the integration of the filtered event combining the knowledge-by-acquaintance of the event with motivational/emotional responses and memories associated with the event into the knowledge-by-description of the event. This process can be interfered with in several ways, resulting in disconnection syndromes where sensory pathways are intact but the ability to respond appropriately to sensory stimulation is disrupted. The cutting of the reticular formation from the rest of the brain, or *cerveau isole* (A), results in coma; bilateral amygdalectomy (B) results in the Kluver–Bucy syndrome, certain kinds of cortical damage (C) result in agnosia.

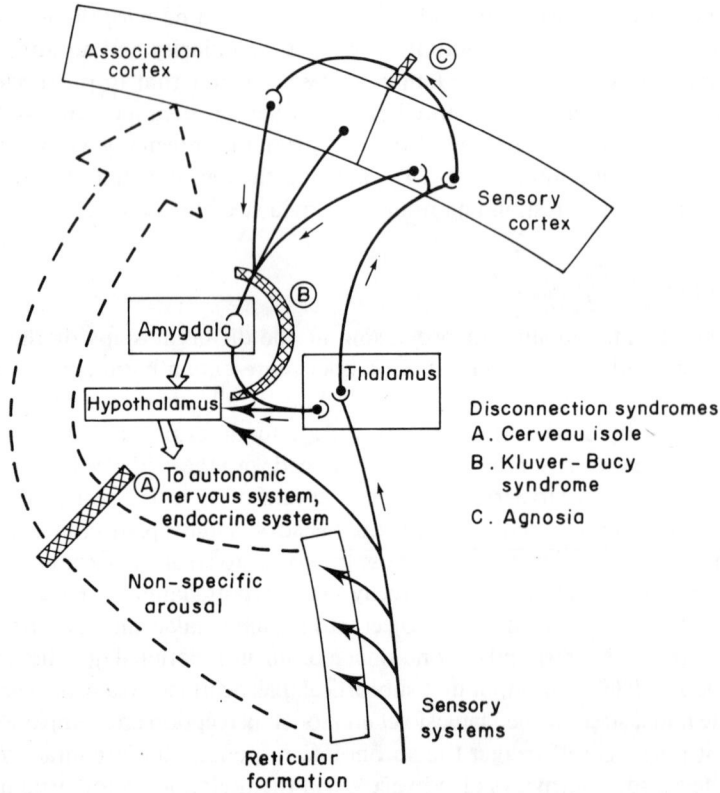

Figure 4.6. A model of appraisal. Disconnection syndromes affect different aspects of the appraisal process. Cerveau isole (A) separates the reticular formation from the rest of the brain, resulting in coma. Bilateral amygdalectomy (B) results in the Kluver–Bucy syndrome, which is an "emotional agnosia". The separation of neocortical sensory areas with their relevant association areas results (C) in modality-specific agnosias. Reproduced by permission from Buck (1988a)

Appraisal and subjective experience

The analysis of knowledge in developmental–interactionist theory has been greatly influenced by Gibson's ecological theory of perception. This emphasizes how perceptual systems have evolved to be sensitive to, or to "pick up", very particular aspects of the environment: those "affordances" that are critical for survival. The environment includes many "events", or physical changes, only a few of which have come to constitute "information". Information consists quite literally of events that inform: that are picked up directly via perceptual systems.

The Gibsonians argue that the perceptual process "is not one of *construction* but of *extraction* of structured information that is present in the light, in the air, on the skin, in short, in the world'' (E. J. Gibson. Quoted by Gibbs, 1985, p. 114). The result is an ecological theory of perception that emphasizes the constraints introduced by the terrestrial environment which have determined the evolutionary pressures which shaped the human perceptual system. This approach tends to emphasize what the head is inside of, rather than what goes on inside the head (Mark, Shaw & Pittenger, 1988, p. 16). But then, what the head is inside of has after all created what goes on inside the head.

The head is in the external environment, and the Gibsonians tend to emphasize the perception of the properties of the external environment in their studies. However, the head is also in the body. I argue that perceptual systems have evolved to pick up certain important events in the internal bodily environment, and that these constitute information: the raw material for subjective feelings and desires. This includes the experience of pain and temperature; drives of hunger, thirst, and sexual arousal; and primary affects such as happiness, sadness, fear, anger, surprise, and disgust (Buck, 1988a, 1989). Such subjective experience is always with us. We can recognize it easily: a perpetually updated progress report informing us constantly about the state of the body. However, like the appearance of the color blue or the taste of a pear, one's personal knowledge-by-acquaintance of these states resists description.

We have seen that events in the external environment may be ''filtered out'' if they are weak, repetitive, or do not otherwise meet criteria for attention built into the organism by phylogeny, conditioning, or the education of attention. In the same way, events in the internal environment are often filtered, as when experiences of motivational/emotional states are ignored in favor of ongoing tasks. We can call forth our subjective experience of these states just as we can call forth our subjective experience of the feel of comfortable shoes. Typically, these experiences are at weak levels, or one would notice them. These levels rise when attention is activated by appropriate external events (appetizing food, potential sexual partners) and the experience of relevant motivational/emotional states then commands attention and is consciously noticed. Some suggest that motivational/emotional states *occur* only when they are consciously noticed, but such approaches analyze motivational/emotional states at their extremes. Developmental–interactionist theory emphasizes that the prime states are *always* functioning, albeit usually at weak levels. The same subcortical and palaeo-cortical systems involved in filtering external events are presumably involved in filtering information about internal motivational/emotional states.

Some doubt the reality of subjective experience. Ludwig Wittgenstein, for example, writes: ''There is a kind of general disease of thinking which always looks for (and finds) what would be called a mental state from which all our acts spring'' (1965, p. 143). Wittgenstein considers the ''feeling of familiarity'' in some detail in *The Brown Book*, and concludes that ''. . . after abstracting all those experiences that we might call the experiences of expressing the feeling'', nothing remains (p. 184). He goes on, ''I am inclined to suggest to you to put the expression of our experience in place of the experience'' (p. 184). However, it seems clear that the loss in prosopagnosia cannot be attributed to a loss in expression. Instead, it is a loss of a direct readout of biologically structured information associated with recognition and memory activation which we have come to call a "feeling of familiarity". It is not necessary to call this a "mental state": it does seem to be related on the one hand to events in the brain which, in principle, are specifiable and on the other to reports of subjective experience.

Emotional education

I have argued that the basic "raw" experience of feelings and desires is known by acquaintance. The brain "knows" how to experience directly such states just as it knows how to experience directly the color blue or the taste of a pear. However, this experience itself can become an object of knowledge-by-description: the responder may learn much *about* feelings and desires which may (or may not) be useful and adaptive. The child must learn to deal with this structured information, internal to the body, just as the child must learn to deal with information in the external environment. This is the process of emotional education in which the child comes to first attend to some events in the internal environment and ignore others (the education of attention), to second understand these events poorly or well, and to third respond appropriately or inappropriately to them, resulting in a certain level of emotional competence.

The process by which this occurs is analogous to the process of perceptual learning in Gibson's theory, with one major difference. In normal perceptual learning the object of perception is accessible to both the child and the socialization agent. However, as B. F. Skinner (1953) discussed in his analysis of private events, the state of the primes as subjective experience is directly accessible to the child but not the socialization agent. The socialization agent has access instead to the child's expressive behavior associated with the primes. That brings us to the empirical part of this chapter, which emphasizes emotional communication.

THE COMMUNICATION OF AFFECT PARADIGM

Miller's studies

The study of the communication process requires particular techniques that are sensitive to its essentially dyadic nature. The unit of analysis in psychology tends to be the individual, and the unit in sociology tends to be the group. Both of these are unitary concepts. In contrast, the unit of analysis in communication is inherently dyadic, in that one must have both a sender and a receiver for communication to occur. This requires a dyadic assessment situation including a sender, receiver, and message. One way to do this is through experimental tasks whose solution requires accurate communication. An example is the cooperative conditioning task developed by Robert E. Miller and his colleagues to measure the communication of affect in rhesus monkeys.

Initial experiments

The cooperative conditioning procedure evolved from studies demonstrating interanimal conditioning: that rhesus monkeys can be conditioned to respond to affective states in other monkeys, apparently because of expressive cues involving at least facial expression and posture (Miller, Murphy & Mirsky, 1959; Murphy, Miller & Mirsky, 1955). To study this phenomenon more directly, Miller, Banks and Ogawa (1962) developed a procedure in which two animals were taught to press a bar within six seconds of the presentation of a light in order to avoid an electric shock. The animals were then paired so that one, the "sender", could see the light but not press the bar, while the other, "receiver", could press the bar but not see the light. The receiver could, however, see the sender's response: in the 1962 study the animals were in the same room, later the sender was presented to the receiver via closed-circuit television (Miller, Banks & Ogawa, 1963) or film (Miller, 1967).

Results indicated that when the light came on, the sender made characteristic facial expressions and postural adjustments that signaled the receiver to press the bar, thus avoiding the shock for both animals. Moreover, the monkeys performed in the paired tests virtually as well as they did individually, and successful communication was apparent from the first paired sessions. Miller, Banks & Ogawa (1962) stated: ". . . through nonverbal communication of affect an efficient mutual avoidance was performed. It was concluded that this paradigm is an exceptionally efficient and sensitive method for investigations of nonverbal communication" (p. 348).

Subsequent experiments

Subsequent studies demonstrated cooperative reward conditioning, using food rewards (Miller, Banks & Kuwahara, 1966). Also, it was found that monkeys from Harlow's laboratory who had been reared in isolation from other monkeys for the first year of life could neither send nor receive in the cooperative conditioning situation even though they were able to solve the initial avoidance task (Miller, Caul & Mirsky, 1967). This was interpreted as consistent with Mason's (1961) hypothesis that the social deficits observed in adulthood, in rhesus monkeys deprived of social contact in infancy, are due to their lack of opportunity to acquire important communication skills.

Other studies investigated the effects of psychoactive drugs upon sending and receiving tendencies. One of the motivating factors behind drug use might be the effect of the drug upon communication, and therefore social behavior: shy persons may use certain drugs to increase expressiveness and lower social inhibitions, while socially overstimulated persons may use other drugs to "cut themselves off" from social stimuli. Miller and his colleagues found that the stimulant amphetamine did indeed improve communication in the cooperative conditioning situation, the tranquilizer chlorapromazine markedly reduced both sending and receiving accuracy, and a hallucinogen (phencyclidine hydrochloride or Sernyl) did not markedly alter communication accuracy (Miller, Levine & Mirsky, 1973). Also, Miller and Deets (1974) found that THC (the active ingredient in marijuana) decreases sending accuracy but increases the ability to receive from other monkeys. These effects were apparent despite the fact that the dosage of drugs was low and did not greatly affect motoric abilities.

Studies with humans

Miller's studies with monkeys were followed by analogous studies of communication of affect in humans. The emotional stimuli used with the monkeys— food reward and electric shock—did not seem appropriate for use with humans. After considerable searching, we hit upon a reliable and flexible way to present emotional stimuli to humans: via emotionally loaded color slides.

Studies with adults

The first studies were conducted with college-age subjects recruited through advertisements and paid for participation. The subject was seated in a dental chair, which effectively served to restrict movement, and heart rate and skin conductance electrodes were attached. The subject was told that the purpose of the experiment was to relate physiological responses to the verbal report of subjective emotional experience as one viewed a series of emotionally loaded color slides. The slides would be presented on a back-lit screen (which allowed the use of normal room illumination), and the subjects were asked to silently view the slide until cued by a light and at that point to speak into a microphone and describe the "subjective experience that the slide evoked". When the light and slide were extinguished, the subject was asked to rate his or her emotional experience along two scales—one ranging from strong to weak and the other from pleasant to unpleasant—by saying the appropriate number into the microphone. Then the subject was left alone and the experiment run from the adjoining room.

Five kinds of slides were presented: sexual slides showed nude or seminude males and females together; scenic slides showed pleasant landscapes; pleasant people slides showed happy-looking persons; unpleasant slides showed severe burns and facial injuries; and unusual slides showed strange photographic effects (double exposures, time exposures).

Unknown to the subject, a television camera was concealed behind the back-lighted screen and was focused on the subject's upper torso and face. The camera was turned on two seconds before the slide was presented and televised the subject's initial reaction to the slide, his or her continuing responses for 10 seconds while the slide remained on (slide period), and the subject's response while discussing his/her emotional experience (talk period). After the light and slide were turned off, the camera was turned off as well.

In the initial studies, before videotaping was available, a "receiver" subject sat in another room with a television monitor. He or she viewed the subject's reaction (without audio) and attempted to guess what type of slide was shown (sexual, scenic, pleasant people, unpleasant, or unusual). The receivers also rated how certain they were of the choice, and how strong or weak, and pleasant or unpleasant, the subject's emotional response was to each slide. This produced two sorts of communication accuracy scores: the per cent of slides correctly categorized (per cent correct measure) and the correlation between the receiver's and the sender's ratings of strength and pleasantness over the 25 slides (strength and pleasantness measures, respectively).

Results indicated that, for the per cent correct and pleasantness measures, communication accuracy was statistically significant at beyond the 0.001 level, although the average communication scores were well below 100%. This moderate overall level of communication masked very large individual differences in expressiveness, or sending accuracy: some persons were very accurate senders while others were virtually at chance levels. These differences in samples of western adults were related to sex: females were significantly better senders on both the per cent correct measure (females = 35%; males = 28%; chance = 20%) and the pleasantness measure (females' $r = 0.42$; males' $r = 0.25$; combined data from Buck et al., 1972; Buck, Miller & Caul, 1974). The strength measure showed significant overall communication only for female senders ($r = 0.22$) and it was dropped from most subsequent studies.

Unexpectedly, the pleasantness measure of sending accuracy was negatively related (between subjects) to physiological responding: to the change in the number of skin conductance responses from before to after the slide was presented (combined $r = -0.50$), and to the accelerative heart rate response from before the slide was presented to the talk period (combined $r = -0.35$). This finding was consistent with the results of Lanzetta and Kleck (1970), who were independently working with the Miller procedure, and with other findings on the (negative) relationship of overt and electrodermal responding (see Buck, 1979, 1984; Manstead, 1990). The latter includes the data on externalizing vs internalizing modes of response to emotion found by Jones (1935) in his work on the Berkeley Growth Study. It should perhaps be stressed that this negative relationship appears only in between-subjects analyses. Within subjects, relationships between expressiveness and physiological responses were positive ($r = 0.15$), as one would expect if some slides were generally more emotionally arousing than others (see Buck, 1979, 1980).

It should also be stressed that it was the change in the number of SC responses, not the size (in micromhos) of those responses, that was negatively related to expressiveness. It is noteworthy that SC deflections are regarded as indicants of central inhibitory processes (Fowles, 1980), so that the result suggests that a central inhibitory tendency may produce both lessened spontaneous expressiveness and a greater number of skin conductance deflections. This is consistent with Gray's (1982) theorizing on the bases of extraversion–introversion, with Kagan's work on temperament in young children (Kagan *et al.*, 1984), with animal research on the septal syndrome (Gorenstein & Newman, 1980), and with a mass of other information relating systems of behavioral inhibition and excitation with personality and temperament (see Buck, 1979, 1984).

Studies with preschool children

To investigate further the sex difference in expressiveness and the relationship between expressiveness and SC responding, a study with preschool children was planned (Buck, 1975). This used new categories of slides: sexual slides were of course omitted, and less upsetting unpleasant slides (showing a grotesque clown, a crying woman, etc) were substituted for the originals. The most useful sort of slide category for the children turned out to be a "familiar people" category: pictures of the children themselves and their friends and teachers at the preschool. This was a very effective emotional stimulus, but unlike most effective emotional stimuli it was strongly positive, and in fact the existence of these slides generally made the experience of being in the experiment a pleasant one for subjects and experimenters alike.

To gain evidence of external validity for the sending accuracy measure, the Affect Expression Rating Scale (AERS) was constructed from previous studies which distinguished the characteristics of high and low electrodermal reactors (Block, 1957; Jones, 1960). This 37-item scale was given to the teachers in the preschool, three of whom rated all of the children in the experiment based on their behavior in the preschool.

The child was brought to the experiment by his or her mother, who was escorted to an observation room while the child was asked about game preferences by an experimenter (who was acquainted with the child from the preschool). The child was visible on a television set in the observation room; the picture was zoomed back compared with the view of the adults because the children tended to squirm in their seats. A second experimenter explained the situation to the mother, showed her examples of the slides the child would see, and gave her rating forms on which to rate the type of slide viewed by the child and the pleasantness/unpleasantness of the child's response.

The experimenter with the child was trained to allow the child to express him/herself naturally. She sat next to the child facing the back-lighted screen, and when a slide came on she looked at it for five seconds without comment and then (if the child had remained silent) said "Who's that?" or "What's that?" as appropriate while continuing to look at the slide. If the child spoke the experimenter answered in a natural way but continued to look at the slide. After 15–20 seconds the slide and videotape recorder were turned off, so that the image of the child disappeared from the mother's screen and she made her ratings. At this point, the experimenter turned to show the child a series of faces that went from "very happy" to "very unhappy" and asked the child to point to the face that matched how the slide made him/her feel. It might be noted that

[handwritten margin note: children can make emotional discriminations of their own feelings]

a recent study has shown that children successfully discriminate between pictures of "best friends" and "least preferred friends" both in their expressive behavior and in ratings of emotional response (Goldman, 1989).

The videotapes of the children's expressions were later shown to groups of undergraduates, who made ratings similar to those made by the mother. Results indicated that, as in the study with adults, significant communication occurred with very large individual differences in expressiveness. However, there was no evidence of a large sex difference in sending accuracy, although undergraduates were somewhat more accurate with girls than boys on the categorization measure. Most significantly, sending accuracy was related to teachers' ratings on the AERS: expressive children were rated to be active and sociable, but also aggressive, bossy, and impulsive; inexpressive children were rated as shy and emotionally inhibited, but also cooperative and controlled.

A subsequent replication (Buck, 1977) showed that the per cent correct measure of sending accuracy was negatively related to the change in SC deflections ($r = -0.42$, $p < 0.06$), and that teachers' ratings of expressiveness were positively related with the per cent correct measure and negatively related with the change in SC deflections. A factor analysis of the AERS scale revealed three factors: these were named (I) expressive vs inhibited (extraverted and sociable vs quiet, reserved, emotionally inhibited); (II) antagonistic vs cooperative (often shows aggression, often hard to get along with vs good-natured, cooperative); and (III) independent vs dependent (is independent of adults vs is unusually dependent, seeks reassurance). Interestingly, an "externalizing" pattern of high sending accuracy and low SC responding was associated in boys with high ratings on the expressiveness dimension, while the same pattern in girls was associated with high ratings on the antagonism dimension (see Buck, 1977).

Also interestingly, the combined data from the studies with children revealed a significant negative relationship between expressiveness and age for boys ($r = -0.52$, $p < 0.005$) but not girls ($r = 0.01$, NS), suggesting that between the ages of four and six boys were learning to inhibit and mask their spontaneous expression of emotion. A more recent study, however, has not replicated the negative relationship of expressiveness and age with boys, finding instead a positive relationship with both boys and girls (Goldman, 1989). Also, Goldman (1989) found evidence of greater expressiveness among boys than girls in her study. Clearly, the study of sex differences in spontaneous expressiveness in young children requires further investigation.

Non-verbal receiving ability and the CARAT test

The search for a useful measure of interpersonal sensitivity or "empathy" has eluded psychology since the 1920s, but it appeared possible to a number of investigators that measures of non-verbal receiving ability, using the new technology of videotape, might provide such a measure (see Buck, 1982; Ekman

& Friesen, 1974; Rosenthal *et al.*, 1975). The same data that yield measures of sending accuracy when averaged across receivers yield measures of receiving ability when averaged across senders. The measures of sending accuracy taken in the initial slide-viewing studies showed considerable evidence of construct validity: they were significantly related in meaningful ways with autonomic responding, personality measures, teachers' ratings, etc. The same, however, was not true of measures of receiving ability: they did not relate strongly with other measures.

To assess receiving ability more carefully, a standard test was constructed using 600 sequences of spontaneous facial/gestural expressions as potential "items" and subjecting them to item analyses. First, 120 items were selected and divided into two 60-item forms which were rated by large groups of subjects. This initial collection had an estimated coefficient alpha of 0.57. Items which correlated best with the total scores were then combined into another 60-item form and shown to additional large groups. From this, a 32-item final form was constructed which included two males and two females viewing each of four kinds of emotionally loaded slides. Theoretically, this process of item analysis should result in an increase in coefficient alpha, but in this case the alpha of the final instrument was 0.56 (Buck, 1976).

One of the perks involved in constructing a test is to invent an acronym, and in this case the instrument was called the Communication of Affect Receiving Ability Test, or CARAT. It was administered as follows. Standard instructions were videotaped at the beginning which told the subject to guess the kind of slide being viewed by the sender on each trial and showed examples of the slides. There was some initial evidence for construct validity: business and fine arts majors scored higher than science majors for example (Buck, 1976). However, when CARAT was given with other tests of non-verbal receiving ability, such as the Rosenthal *et al.* (1975) Profile of Nonverbal Sensitivity (PONS), the sizes of the resulting intercorrelations were disappointing. This was mirrored in the low intercorrelations between other measures of receiving ability as well (Buck, 1982).

The accumulated evidence—the lack of construct validity, the failure to increase coefficient alpha, the low intercorrelations between tests designed to measure the same thing—suggested that there may be a problem with the basic conceptualization of non-verbal receiving ability assumed by CARAT and similar instruments. Specifically, it may be that in presenting the videotaped expressions of strangers in a non-interactive setting, and specifically instructing subjects to attend to those expressions, CARAT may be missing the most important features of true receiving ability, or "empathy". It may be that empathy must be measured interactively, instead, in settings where there is a choice of what to attend to, and perhaps in the context of a specific personal relationship rather than with a stranger (see Buck, 1982, 1984).

Communication within specific relationships

Later studies using the slide-viewing procedure in fact investigated the "specific sensitivity" of speech clinicians to the expressions of their own school-age clients versus clients of other clinicians (Buck & Lerman, 1979) and communication patterns within intimate (dating and married) dyads (Sabatelli, Buck & Dreyer, 1982, 1983). The latter studies suggested that very specific aspects of the patterns of communication in dyads were related to dyad satisfaction. For example, Sabatelli, Buck & Dreyer (1982) defined general sending accuracy as the ability of married couples to send to strangers; general receiving ability as the ability of couples to decode strangers (presented via the CARAT); specific receiving ability as the ability of couples to decode the spouse; and unique communication accuracy as the difference between the sending accuracy of a person to the spouse versus to strangers. Results indicated that overall communication scores were not related to measures of marital satisfaction. However, husbands were happier if their wives were generally expressive (ie high in general sending accuracy), and an internal analysis suggested that the wife's ability to decode the husband on trials where strangers could not was related to both the wife's and the husband's marital satisfaction.

The Sabatelli, Buck & Dreyer (1982) analysis was intriguing but cumbersome, depending upon complex analytic procedures. A more direct and elegant solution to the problem of breaking down specific aspects of the spontaneous communication process came in the form of Kenny's Social Relations Model (SRM: Kenny & LaVoie, 1984), which breaks the communication of A to B into the sending accuracy of A, the receiving ability of B, the specific or unique communication of A to B, and error. The SRM requires an approximation of a round robin design, and fortunately the Sabatelli, Buck & Dreyer (1982) study fits this requirement. It was therefore possible to reanalyze the data and show that the wife's general sending accuracy was indeed correlated with husband satisfaction. Also, the wife's specific ability to decode the husband was indeed related to satisfaction for the wife, but interestingly for the husband the SRM analysis found that this effect was restricted to the sexual slides. That is, the wife's specific ability to decode the husband on sexual slides was related to husband satisfaction (Sabatelli, Buck & Kenny, 1986).

The SRM produced a number of other interesting results, one of the most striking being that sending accuracy contributed more variance to the total communication score than did receiving ability. This is consistent with the general difficulty in finding consistent individual differences in non-verbal receiving ability noted above (Buck, 1982, 1984). The same pattern of strong sender and weak receiver effects has been replicated in a study of emotional expression in subjects from Taiwan and the People's Republic of China (PRC). Interestingly, the expected pattern of more accurate communication within cultural groups than between groups was not found. In fact, the best overall receivers turned out to be American students. Also interesting was the fact that the finding of greater expressiveness in females than males that is typical for western samples did not occur with the Chinese; in fact, there was a non-significant tendency for males to be more expressive than females. Also, the subjects from the PRC were significantly less expressive than persons from Taiwan (Buck et al., 1989).

The SRM results indicated that, although communication was not more accurate within than between cultures, there was evidence that communication was more consistent within cultures. That is, sender effects and relationship effects were higher when communication occurred within Taiwanese groups, or the PRC groups, than they were in cross-nationality pairings. This suggested that communication within groups is more structured by shared expectations, or decoding rules, and that these rules are applied more consistently if the other is of the same nationality than if cross-nationality pairings are involved. Interestingly, sender effects and relationships effects *vis à vis* the Taiwanese senders were also high with American receivers, suggesting greater consistency as well as greater accuracy (Buck *et al.*, 1989).

The segmentation technique

The SRM is proving useful in studying emotional communication patterns within the context of particular relationships. Another technique useful for analyzing data from the slide-viewing paradigm is the segmentation technique, in which subjects are asked to press a button when, in their opinion, "something meaningful" occurs. The resulting data are able to show "high-information points" in the stream of expression where observers agree that something meaningful has happened (Buck *et al.*, 1980; Buck, Baron & Barrette, 1982; Newtson, 1976). Information on whether a given receiver "hit" or "missed" such a high-information point allows for a new kind of "accuracy-in-process" approach to the study of non-verbal receiving ability, and information on what was happening in the sender's behavior at those points allows an efficient approach to studying the nature of the behaviors underlying spontaneous communication (Buck, 1984).

Studies with brain-damaged patients

The segmentation and SRM techniques provide ways of analyzing the stream of expression, and relating expressive communication to such important phenomena as the relationship between sender and receiver (Buck, 1984). However, the most important single study using the slide-viewing technique was undoubtedly that by Buck and Duffy (1980) on brain-damaged patients, for it was this study that clarified the nature of spontaneous communication and its differences from symbolic communication.

The Buck and Duffy (1980) study had its origin in the efforts of Robert Duffy and his colleagues to develop "non-verbal" techniques for the remediation of the communication deficits, or aphasias, brought about by damage in adulthood to the left cerebral hemisphere (Duffy, Duffy & Alderdice, 1977; Duffy, Duffy & Pearson, 1975). Duffy and his colleagues developed a program of remediation based upon pantomime, and developed instruments to measure the progress of aphasic patients in this program. These were the Pantomime Recognition

Test (PRT), in which the patient was taught to point to a picture that corresponded to a pantomimic action on the part of the experimenter (ie pretending to drink), and the Pantomime Expression Test (PET), in which the patient was shown a picture (ie of a drinking glass) and taught to pantomime its use. Unfortunately, the program was not very successful clinically, as it was found that the patients who could pantomime generally had residual verbal functioning as well, as measured by the standard Porch Index of Communicative Ability (PICA) (Porch, 1967).

It is apparent that the sort of "non-verbal communication" assessed by the PET and PRT is different from the sort measured by the slide-viewing technique, and in fact the difference seems to parallel a distinction long made in the aphasia literature between "propositionizing", or using words for the deliberate encoding of a message, and "emotional utterance", which is the use of words (such as expletives) for the expression of a presently existing emotional state. It is a common observation that emotional utterance may be relatively intact in aphasic patients while propositional speech shows severe deficits. Critchley (1975) suggested that an analogous distinction can be made for non-verbal behavior, with facial and bodily expression of a present emotional state similar to emotional utterance while intentionally posed expressions or pantomimes are similar to propositionizing.

The slide-viewing technique, by manipulating the present emotional state of the viewer, seems to be an excellent way to measure the non-verbal equivalent of emotional utterance. Indeed, Buck and Duffy (1980) found that left-hemisphere-damaged aphasic patients retained a level of expressiveness in the slide-viewing situation that was comparable to that of non-brain-damaged control patients, while right-hemisphere-damaged patients (who can use propositional speech) showed a relatively low level of expressiveness. The expressiveness of the right-hemisphere-damaged patients, in fact, did not differ significantly from the level of expressiveness found in patients with Parkinson's disease, a disorder which has long been associated clinically with a lack of facial and body expressiveness. The general pattern of results across the slide categories suggested that non-verbal "emotional utterance" is associated with right hemisphere activity, and that the left hemisphere is involved both in non-verbal "propositionizing" and in the control of the emotional expression via display rules (Buck & Duffy, 1980).

It seems clear from the results of this study, as well as other research, that the deficits associated with left hemisphere damage are not restricted to verbal behaviors. Duffy and Liles (1979) have suggested that left hemisphere damage is associated with a general inability to express symbols in any modality that is consistent with Finklnberg's (1870) characterization of aphasia as "asymbolia". Others suggest that left hemisphere damage does not represent a general communication deficit *per se*, but rather results in apraxia: an inability to perform *any* voluntary movement (Goodglass & Kaplan, 1963; Kimura, 1979).

Regardless of the outcome of this debate, the results of the Buck and Duffy (1980) study motivated the search for the distinguishing characteristics of non-verbal behavior as propositionizing versus as emotional utterance, and this led to the formal distinction in developmental–interactionist theory between symbolic and spontaneous communication (Buck, 1984, 1988b).

Spontaneous communication

The definition of "communication" in developmental–interactionist theory follows that of Wilson (1975): it occurs whenever the behavior of one organism influences the behavior of another. A's behavior X1 is defined as communicative if "the conditional probability that act X2 will be performed by individual B given that A performed X1 is not equal to the probability that B will perform X2 in the absence of X1" (Wilson, 1975, p. 194). This definition of communication can be applied to any species.

Spontaneous communication is defined as having the following qualities:

1. Spontaneous communication is based upon biologically structured sending and receiving mechanisms. According to Darwin's (1872) analysis, emotional expression evolved to foster social coordination necessary for survival (ie courting behaviors, warnings, threat and submission behaviors, etc). There is plentiful evidence that expressive displays with important social functions are innately organized in many species (see Buck & Ginsburg, 1990; Ginsburg, 1974). In addition, communication demands a receiver as well as a sender: displays are useless unless receiving tendencies exist which are sensitive to those displays and which alter behavior tendencies accordingly. In the terms of Gibsonian theory, emotional displays are social affordances. They have evolved hand-in-hand with the behavior tendencies of the receiver so that the nature of the display specifies the receiver's reaction in important ways.

    In other words, the basic function of spontaneous communication is social coordination, and it evolves because the transmission of certain kinds of motivational–emotional information is adaptive to a given species. For example, the social organization of an ant colony is based upon a system of chemical communication in which the sender produces pheromones which determine rather precisely the receiver's behavior.

2. The elements of spontaneous communication are signs, which are externally accessible aspects of the referent. Dark clouds are a sign of rain because the darkness of the clouds is an externally accessible aspect of their moisture content. Just so, the pheromones released by the ant, or the human, are externally accessible aspects of certain important motivational–emotional states.

3. Spontaneous communication is in no way intentional, although it can be suppressed or inhibited intentionally.

4. The content of spontaneous communication is non-propositional, since it cannot be false. Propositions must be capable of being subjected to logical

Characteristics	Spontaneous communication	Symbolic communication
Basis of signal system	Biologically shared	Learned, socially shared
Intentionality	Spontaneous conversation between limbic systems	Voluntary at some level
Elements	Signs: externally accessible aspect of referent	Symbols: arbitrary relationship with referent
Content	Non-propositional. Motivational/ emotional states	Propositions: expressions capable of logical analysis (test of truth/falsity)

Figure 4.7. Summary of the characteristics of spontaneous and symbolic communication

analysis, for example tests for truth or falsity. Since spontaneous communication is composed of signs, if the sign is present the referent by definition must be present. The content of spontaneous communication instead involves motivational–emotional states. The characteristics of spontaneous and symbolic communication are summarized in Figure 4.7.

Spontaneous communication evolves because the transmission of certain kinds of motivational–emotional information is adaptive to a given species. The social organization of an ant colony is based upon a system of chemical communication in which the sender produces pheromones which determine precisely the receiver's behavior. Mechanisms of spontaneous communication are necessary for any species which reproduces sexually (Buck, 1989). For example, sexual pheromones are released by algae to regulate activity in one another's sexual cells, resulting in the mix of male and female chromosomes (Maier & Muller, 1986). All of the elements of a basic communication system (Shannon & Weaver, 1949) are present in the behavior of these primordial organisms.

Spontaneous communication is always by definition direct and veridical, but emotional communication is not always spontaneous, for in both sender and receiver the biologically structured "special-purpose processing systems" interact with general-purpose systems structured by conditioning and learning. The latter process results in the construction of rules which regulate the emotional communication process. These include both display rules, which regulate the sender's display, and decoding rules, which regulate the receiver's patterns of attention to the sender's display. These impose the features of symbolic communication upon the emotional communication process (Buck, 1984, 1988a).

Symbolic communication

In contrast to spontaneous communication, symbolic communication is defined as being (1) learned and culturally patterned; (2) based upon symbols which have an arbitrary relationship with their referent; (3) at some level intentional;

and (4) composed of propositions (Buck, 1984). Spontaneous communication constitutes a conversation between limbic systems, a conversation between brainstems, etc, which is carried on simultaneously with the symbolic stream of communication. In effect, communication proceeds in two simultaneously occurring and interactive "streams": one biologically structured and non-voluntary, and the other intentional and structured by learning and experience.

The relationship of spontaneous and symbolic communication

Spontaneous and symbolic communication are not at different ends of a continuum but rather are related, as are other sorts of special-purpose versus general-purpose processing systems as depicted in Figure 4.3. As the figure indicates, it is possible to have spontaneous communication without symbolic communication, as in algae or an ant or termite colony. It is not, however, possible to have symbolic communication without spontaneous communication. Symbolic communication may dominate spontaneous communication, as in a dry but well-reasoned lecture, but there is always an element of spontaneous communication present mediated by the nuances of gesture, posture, facial expression, and tone of voice.

To recapitulate, spontaneous communication is based upon biologically structured special-purpose processing systems which interact with general-purpose processing systems structured by conditioning and learning. Symbolic communication, in contrast, is based upon these general-purpose processing systems. Spontaneous communication systems interact with symbolic communication systems, and any particular communication event involves an interaction of spontaneous communication and symbolic communication. This is true of both human communication and the communication of other animals. In humans, symbolic communication is given an additional level of complexity by linguistic competence.

"Non-verbal" communication

The distinction between spontaneous and symbolic communication is more fundamental and less confusing than the distinction between "verbal" and "non-verbal" communication because, as we have seen, communication can be either spontaneous "emotional utterance" or symbolic "propositionizing". Symbolic non-verbal communication includes culturally learned gestures which accompany language, including emblems, illustrators, and regulators (Ekman & Friesen, 1969a) as well as sign language and pantomime. We have seen that symbolic communication in humans, verbal or non-verbal, is associated with left hemisphere processing in most persons, while spontaneous communication is associated with right hemisphere processing (Buck & Duffy, 1980).

EMOTIONAL EDUCATION

The notion that there are two simultaneous streams of communication has important implications when we consider the relationship between special-purpose processing systems and general-purpose and linguistic processing systems. Spontaneous communication is based upon special-purpose systems: it has evolved to transmit specific sorts of messages that have been phylogenetically important. Like other special-purpose systems, however, there is an interaction between these "innate" systems and general-purpose systems of learning and, in humans, language. In the case of motivation and emotion, things become interesting because, as we have seen, the different aspects of the prime readouts are differentially accessible to the responder and the socialization agent: subjective experience (emotion III) is accessible only to the responder, spontaneous expressive behaviors (emotion II) are more accessible to the socialization agent, and homeostatic responses (emotion I) are normally not very accessible to anyone.

In other words, the bodily events that provide structured information about the primes to the responder in the form of subjectively experienced feelings and desires (hunger, sexual desire, anger) are unlike external events (like the color red) that are accessible to all and therefore relatively easily labeled and understood. But the child must learn about these internal events: first to simply attend to them and realize they are there; secondly to come to terms with them, accept them, label them, and understand what they are; and thirdly to know what should be done with them. As noted above, this is the emotion education process, which will lead to a greater or lesser degree of emotional competence. We are now ready to examine the role of spontaneous communication in this process.

Social biofeedback

If the foregoing analysis is correct, it follows that during interaction the other must function in ways analogous to a biofeedback device. If expressive behavior is more accessible to others than it is to the expresser, one of the means by which an individual comes to understand his or her feelings and desires, and to control his or her expressive displays, is by interpersonal feedback: by the response to those displays on the part of others.

Ekman and Friesen (1969b) discussed the process by which the individual learns to control expressive displays, suggesting that channels to which others respond quickly and reliably (such as, in our culture, facial expressions) become controlled by display rules, while expressive behaviors that are ignored by others (such as many body movements) are less controlled and may thus "leak" the individual's true feelings. This is equivalent to the Gibsonian process of the education of attention, where an individual's attention is drawn to those aspects of his or her own display that are responded to by others. A potentially less

In conclusion learning process

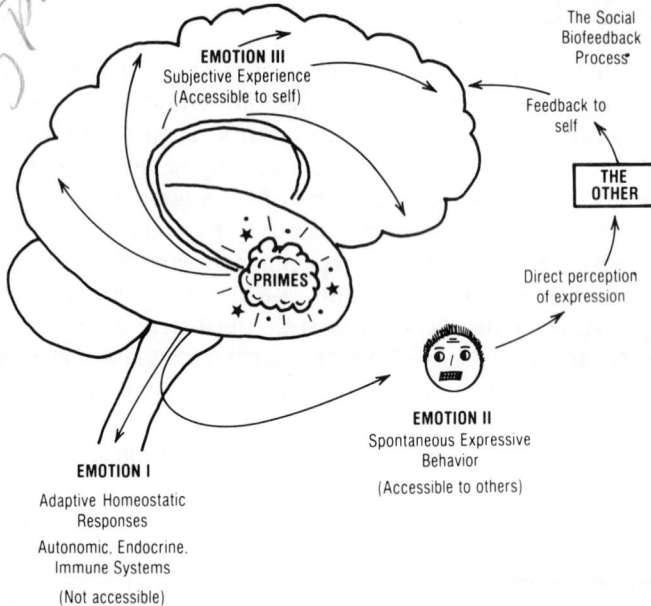

Figure 4.8. Emotional education: accessibility and the social biofeedback process

accessible response is rendered more accessible by feedback provided by other's behavior. This interpersonal feedback is analogous to the feedback provided by a biofeedback device, where a relatively inaccessible physiological response is rendered more accessible because of its association with the feedback signal (see Figure 4.8).

Developmental–interactionist theory makes two additions to the Ekman and Friesen (1969b) formulation: first, that the interpersonal feedback process involves spontaneous communication as defined above, and secondly, that one's attention to, understanding of, and ability to deal with one's subjective feelings and desires are also affected. Interpersonal feedback must have important implications for how one labels and interprets one's own feelings and desires: the emotion III readout from the prime states.

Let us go back to the example of the child (C) in Figure 4.5, who is frustrated while building blocks, screams, and throws a block at an adult (A). The subjectively experienced anger (emotion III), which is presumably associated in complex ways with neurochemical activity in the region of the amygdalae, is accessible only to C. The particular vocal quality of the scream, and the associated facial and bodily displays, are, however, more accessible to A via spontaneous communication, and the stage is set for A to respond both spontaneously and symbolically.

In general, the expressiveness and the attention patterns of the individuals involved determine the efficiency of social biofeedback. The ability of A to respond to C's feelings appropriately is first determined by the clarity of C's spontaneous expressions and the degree of A's attention to those expressions. If C is expressive and A is attentive, A will come to know C's emotional state directly via spontaneous communication. A may then express his or her reactions to C's display in a variety of ways. A may spontaneously express feelings about C's display. If A is expressive and C is attentive, C will come to know A's affective response to C's display via spontaneous communication.

In this example, A may respond to C's angry expression and behavior by saying: "You're angry. People sometimes get frustrated and angry, but you shouldn't throw things. Why don't you do something else for a while?" This response would give C a wealth of information about his or her subjective experience, its label, that it is OK to experience sometimes, and what one might do about it. Alternatively, A might say, "Don't be like that. It's naughty", or "You're a bad girl!", or simply smack C, and C would receive other sorts of lessons in emotional labeling and interpersonal relations. As in other kinds of education, emotional education may provide C with the wrong labels, or no labels at all, for certain experiences.

The net result of such experience is that the individual comes to respond more or less effectively in social contexts, being able to control his or her displays more or less appropriately. This occurs in animals as well as humans (see Harlow & Mears, 1983). In humans, an additional level of complexity is added by linguistic competence. Humans use their verbal and logical abilities in the exploration of the external physical environment, a process that is long acknowledged and much studied (eg Piaget, 1971). At the same time, humans must make connections between verbal labels and reasoning and the internal environment of their own bodies—the subjectively experienced world of feelings and desires.

Emotional competence

Competence in general is the ability to deal effectively with events (White, 1959). Social competence is the ability to deal effectively with other persons; emotional competence is the ability to deal with the internal environment of one's feelings and desires. Generally, social and emotional competence are mutually supportive: accurate emotional communication would tend to foster the ability to deal both with other persons and with one's own feelings and desires (Buck, 1991).

Both social and emotional competence are to some degree specific to a given personal or social relationship (Buck, 1989a; Hofer, 1984). One learns specific lessons about how to interact with the other as a relationship becomes more personal, and this applies as well to how to express and deal with one's feelings and desires *vis à vis* the other. The resulting relationship-specific emotional education process becomes useless when the relationship is lost, and some of the emotional turmoil associated with experiences like bereavement may be due to the resulting loss of emotional self-regulation (Hofer, 1984). On the other hand, the well-established and significant protective effects of social support on resistance to stress and illness may be related to the surfeit of emotional competence engendered by such support (Buck, 1988a).

As when the social environment changes, the emotional education process is challenged when the body changes. A dramatic example occurs at puberty, when in the words of one educator "kids get mugged by their hormones". Another example occurs with illness, particularly serious and chronic illness such as cancer (Reardon & Buck, 1989). There also are suggestions that the emotional education process breaks down in cases of psychopathology. Interestingly, there are indications that schizophrenics may be so sensitive to the emotional displays of others that they withdraw from communication as a defensive, self-protective device (Krause et al., 1989). Also, it is possible that emotional competence may be sacrificed in the service of social competence, and when a person learns to inhibit and suppress the expression of natural frustration and anger. An example is the "pathological niceness" of the type C behavior pattern linked in some studies with cancer (see Buck, 1988a).

Coping

Developmental–interactionist theory defines coping as reasoning about emotion: it is emotional reeducation made necessary by changes in the bodily or social–physical environments (Buck, 1988a; Reardon & Buck, 1989). Such changes affect social and/or emotional competence, and coping is seen as an attempt to restore such competence. More specifically, the theory recognizes three sources of "rules" in engendering social and emotional competence: the body, the self, and the external environment (ie the physical and social environments). These rules are established naturally during emotional education in a process analogous to the Piagetian assimilation, accommodation, and equilibration (Piaget, 1971). These rules among other things tell the person what to do with his or her feelings and desires, where, and with whom.

Partly through these rules the person develops a linguistically structured "self-image" in his or her specific bodily, social, and physical–environmental context. The rules adopted tend to be socially appropriate, consistent with the self-image, and effective in meeting personal goals (Reardon, 1981). Changes that alter the mix of information that supports these rules—changes in the body due to puberty or disease, or changes in the social environment due to leaving home, marriage, divorce, or bereavement—lead to challenges to the established rules, lessened social and/or emotional competence, and a pressure for emotional reeducation or coping.

Defining success or failure of a given "coping style" in this context is somewhat problematic, for success or failure is measured by different criteria depending upon whether one is looking at the social environment, the self, or the body. A coping style that is successful from the point of view of the self and the social environment, for example, may be disastrous to the body. On the other hand, part of the success of a coping style in protecting the body may be that whatever its nature it is acceptable from the point of view of the self or the social environment (see Reardon & Buck, 1989).

Social models and emotional education

The example of the emotional education process at puberty is interesting in that the feelings and desire awakened at that time prominently involve sexual and aggressive urges that are difficult to express in interpersonal settings, particularly to such "official" socialization agents as parents and teachers. Thus, the social biofeedback process is not so available for learning about such feelings. It may be that this explains in part the increased interest of young people in social models in media—literature, television, drama, popular music—and particularly in emotionally arousing media. Such models give among other things instruction in emotional experience and expression, and may thus constitute Piagetian "aliments" for emotional education (Buck, 1988a, 1989a).

This may also explain the curious human tendency to choose to experience really negative emotion, as when people (particularly young people) pay good money to be saddened (by "tear-jerkers"), frightened (by horror movies), and even disgusted (by "gross-out" exploitation films). Indeed, the quality of the experience seems generally defined by just how sad, frightened, or disgusted one is made. I think that this phenomenon is problematic for many "cognitive" theories of emotion that seem to imply that people should avoid such experiences. From the point of view of developmental–interactionist theory, such experiences are seen as aliments for emotional education, and it makes sense that they seem particularly attractive around puberty and adolescence (Buck, 1987, 1988a, 1989a).

Knowledge and communication

Above we considered knowledge of the external environment and of subjective experience. There remains the consideration of knowledge of "other minds". William James noted that "our senses only give us acquaintance with facts of the body, and of the mental states of other persons we have only conceptual knowledge" (1890, pp. 222–223). This is the basis of the other minds problem, which suggests that there is something puzzling about knowing another person's "inner meanings" when one has access only to the behaviors and physical states of the other (eg Austin, 1959).

Being biologically structured in both its sending and receiving aspects, spontaneous communication is direct. It requires no process of intention on the part of the sender or inference on the part of the receiver. It is a way in which the receiver has direct access to the motivational–emotional state of the sender. It thus answers the other minds problem. We know certain inner meanings—certain motivational/emotional states—in others because others are constructed to send information directly about these states and we are constructed to receive that information directly and to know its meaning directly. This knowledge is based upon eons of phylogenetic adaptation and is conferred on us through inheritance. Our knowledge-by-acquaintance of the motivational/emotional states of others via spontaneous communication is just as direct and biologically based as our knowledge-by-acquaintance of the feel of our shoe. In a very real sense, the individuals involved in spontaneous communication constitute a biological unit (Buck & Ginsburg, 1990).

Again Wittgenstein might argue with this position. At the end of *The Brown Book* he states that "when we communicate a feeling to someone, something which we can never know happens at the other end. All that we can receive from him is an expression" (1965, p. 185). But developmental–interactionist theory argues that an expression is all we need to know what has happened on the other end. To know about what has happened on the other end we need in addition emotional education.

We tend to think of direct contact with other minds as an advanced mental capacity: mental telepathy and the like. However, spontaneous communication is not advanced but ancient, indeed primordial. It can be seen in monkeys, rabbits, snails, ants, even algae. Yet spontaneous communication links humans directly to one another, and thereby hangs a tale.

Spontaneous communication, media, and the global village

Direct communication via media

Direct communication via media seems to be a contradiction in terms, but there is in fact evidence that spontaneous communication occurs via mass communication media and that this influence can be direct and unconscious. For example, a number of studies have used facial EMG to record minute tendencies to smile and frown that are not visible on the face or consciously noticed by the responder. This facial EMG technique was used to record the reactions of viewers to the videotaped smiles and frowns of Ronald Reagan and Walter Mondale during the 1986 presidential election debates (McHugo *et al.*, 1985). It was found that Reagan, known as a charismatic "great communicator", elicited tendencies towards similar facial behavior in viewers: when Reagan smiled the viewer tended to smile, when he frowned the viewer tended to frown. Mondale's expressions did not have this effect, and it was unrelated to the consciously expressed political preferences of the viewers. Apparently Reagan's expressions had a direct emotional impact on the viewer, even via videotape (McHugo *et al.*, 1985).

The implications of this from the point of view of developmental–interactionist theory are enormous (Buck, 1988b,c). First, there is evidence that spontaneous communication is sufficient to activate altruistic emotion: that the observation of the distress or joy of another is in itself sufficient to activate motives to minimize that distress or maximize that joy (Batson, 1983, 1990; Batson & Oleson, 1990; Hoffmann, 1977, 1981, 1986). Secondly, it seems clear that it is the emotional qualities of media that are particularly prized: it is the photograph, soap opera, situation comedy, or motion picture that most effectively arouses emotion that receives recognition, awards, and popular response. Also, the "charismatic" politician is the one who most effectively uses available media to arouse emotion. In the radio era of the 1930s and 1940s the politicians with ringing, resonant voices (Churchill, Roosevelt, Hitler) had the edge. This changes with the advent of television, and that change was perhaps heralded by the Kennedy–Nixon debates in the 1960 presidential election campaign: those who heard the debates over radio thought Nixon had won, those who saw them on television gave Kennedy the win. Today, the successful television style—sometimes called "sizzle"—is highly prized (albeit rarely found) among politicians. Arguably, spontaneous emotional expressiveness is at the heart of this style.

The global village

The growth of instant worldwide electronic communication has created what Marshall McLuhan (1964) termed a global village. McLuhan's ideas drew much attention during the 1960s, and in many respects they have become part of the conventional wisdom of our culture. When televised images of famine in Ethiopia galvanize an outpouring of support, or when popular revolution in China is mirrored by similar movements in Eastern Europe, it is common for commentators to point to the importance of media in creating a global village in which everyone is "involved" with everyone else. However, describing these events does not explain them, and McLuhan's own explanation, in terms of changes in perceptual habits, is not very convincing (Buck, 1988c).

The growth of the global village is, however, explainable if spontaneous communication occurs via media and activates altruistic motivation. The new visual, immediate electronic media afford spontaneous communication at an unprecedented level, arguably resulting in the emotional basis for a fundamentally new, global, social organization (Buck, 1988c).

The end of history

Francis Fukuyama (1989a, 1990) has created an intellectual uproar over his contention that history, in the Marxist–Hegelian sense has ended. By the end of history Fukuyama means the history of ideology, or of "thought about first principles governing political and social organization" (1989b, p. c1). It implies "not the end of worldly events, but the end of the evolution of human thought about such first principles" (p. c1). The end of history was first proclaimed at the beginning of the nineteenth century by Hegel, who saw it in the liberal and democratic revolutions instituted by the American and French revolutions.

The young Karl Marx reacted strongly against Hegel's position, feeling that "the manifest injustices of the society of his time belied Hegel's confident assertion that 'everything that is real is rational'" (Fukuyama, 1989b, p. c2). Marx spent his career trying to show that Hegel was wrong, that the end of history had not in fact already arrived. Fukuyama feels the experiment and resulting failure of communism to be a 150-year detour, that Hegel was in fact correct that liberal democracy is driven by the ultimate principles of political and social justice, and that history in this sense has in fact ended.

From the point of view of developmental–interactionist theory, it may be suggested that the global spontaneous communication engendered by electronic media has created the possibility of global altruistic motivation and consequently the emotional basis for a new global social organization: a global village. As far as the end of history is concerned, Hegel may be correct in his assessment that liberal democracy is driven by the ultimate principles in political and social justice, but these principles are based not upon reason but upon emotion. They are the principles of the morality of cooperation that Piaget (1948) found were arrived at in the games of children as they played with peers, the cornerstone of which is the golden rule that one should treat others as one would wish to be treated. More speculatively, they are the rules learned by social animals like canids (wolves, dogs) and non-human primates (rhesus monkeys, baboons, chimpanzees) in the course of early social experience (particularly play with peers). This biologically based and yet learned morality of cooperation is arguably based upon innate altruistic motives that are naturally evoked in the course of spontaneous emotional communication. Electronic media have perhaps transferred the morality of cooperation from the games of children (and other young animals) to the global arena.

Thus, Hegel was perhaps wrong after all in his conclusion that "everything that is real is rational". Everything that is real is emotional; the rational is our subsequent linguistically structured elaboration of that reality.

REFERENCES

Alkon, D. L. (1988). *Memory Traces in the Brain*. New York: Cambridge University Press.

Alkon, D. L. (1989). Memory storage and neural systems. *Scientific American*, **261**, 42–51.

Alkon, D. L. & Rasmussen, H. (1988). A spatial temporal model of cell activation. *Science*, **239** (4843), 998–1005.

Alley, T. R. (Ed.) (1988) *Social and Applied Aspects of Perceiving Faces*. Hillsdale, NJ: Erlbaum.

Austin, J. L. (1959). Other minds. In A. G. N. Flew (Ed.), *Logic and Language*. Oxford: Basil Blackwell.

Batson, C. D. (1983). Sociobiology and the role of religion in promoting prosocial behavior: An alternative view. *Journal of Personality and Social Psychology*, **45**, 1380–1385.

Batson, C. D. (1990). How social an animal? The human capacity for caring. *American Psychologist*, **45**, 336–346.

Batson, C. D. & Oleson, K. C. (1990). Current status of the empathy–altruism hypothesis. In M. S. Clark (Ed.), *Altruism and Prosocial Behavior. Review of Personality and Social Psychology.* Vol. 11. Newbury Park, Cal.: Sage.

Bauer, R. M. (1984). Autonomic recognition of names and faces in prosopagnosia: A neuropsychological application of the guilty knowledge test. *Neuropsychologia*, **22**, 456–469.

Block, J. A. (1957). A study of affective responsiveness in a lie detection situation. *Journal of Abnormal Psychology*, **55**, 11–15.

Borg, E. & Counter, S. A. (1989). The middle-ear muscles. *Scientific American*, **261**, 74–81.

Buck, R. (1975). Nonverbal communication of affect in children. *Journal of Personality and Social Psychology*, **31**, 644–653.

Buck, R. (1976). *Human Motivation and Emotion.* New York: Wiley.

Buck, R. (1977). Nonverbal communication accuracy in preschool children: Relationships with personality and skin conductance. *Journal of Personality and Social Psychology*, **33**, 225–236.

Buck, R. (1979). Individual differences in nonverbal sending accuracy and electrodermal responding: The externalizing–internalizing dimension. In R. Rosenthal (Ed.), *Skill in Nonverbal Communication: Individual Differences.* Cambridge, Mass: Oelgeschlager, Gunn and Hain.

Buck, R. (1980). Nonverbal behavior and the theory of emotion: The facial feedback hypothesis. *Journal of Personality and Social Psychology*, **38**, 811–824.

Buck, R. (1981). Sex differences in psychophysiological responding and subjective experience: A comment. *Psychophysiology*, **18**, 349–350.

Buck, R. (1982). Spontaneous and symbolic nonverbal behavior and the ontogeny of communication. In R. S. Feldman (Ed.), *The Development of Nonverbal Behavior in Children.* New York: Springer-Verlag.

Buck, R. (1983a). Emotional development and emotional education. In R. Plutchick & H. Kellerman (Eds), *Emotions in Early Development.* New York: Academic Press.

Buck, R. (1983b). Recent approaches to the study of nonverbal receiving ability. In J. Weimann & R. Harrison (Eds), *Nonverbal Communication: The Social Interaction Sphere.* New York: Sage.

Buck, R. (1984). *The Communication of Emotion.* New York: Guilford Press.

Buck, R. (1985). Prime theory: An integrated view of motivation and emotion. *Psychological Review*, **92**, 389–413.

Buck, R. (1986). The psychology of emotion. In J. LeDoux & W. F. Hirst (Eds), *Mind and Brain: Dialogues Between Cognitive Psychology and Neuroscience.* New York: Cambridge University Press.

Buck, R. (1987). Emotion and MTV: The emotional appeal of music videos. Unpublished paper, University of Connecticut, Storrs.

Buck, R. (1988a). *Human Motivation and Emotion*, 2nd edn. New York: Wiley.

Buck, R. (1988b). The perception of facial expression: Individual regulation and social coordination. In T. R. Alley & L. S. Mark (Eds), *Social and Applied Aspects of Perceiving Faces.* Hillsdale, NJ: Erlbaum.

Buck, R. (1988c). Emotional education and mass media: A new view of the global village. In R. Hawkins, J. Weimann & S. Pingree (Eds), *Advancing Communication Science: Merging Mass and Interpersonal Processes.* Vol. 16, Sage Annual Reviews of Communication Research. Beverly Hills, Ca: Sage.

Buck, R. (1989a). Emotional communication in personal relationships: A developmental-interactionist view. In C. D. Hendrick (Ed.), *Close Relationships. Review of Personality and Social Psychology*, Vol. 10. Newbury Park, Ca: Sage.

Buck, R. (1989b). Subjective, expressive, and peripheral bodily components of emotion. In H. L. Wagner & A. S. R. Manstead (Eds), *Handbook of Psychophysiology: Emotion and Social Behavior.* Chichester: Wiley, pp. 199–121.

Buck, R. (1991). Temperament, social skills, and the communication of emotion: A developmental–interactionist perspective. In D. Gilbert & J. J. Conley (Eds), *Personality, Social Skills, and Psychopathology: An Individual Differences Approach.* New York: Plenum.

Buck, R., Baron, R. & Barrette, D. (1982). The temporal organization of spontaneous emotional expression: A segmentation analysis. *Journal of Personality and Social Psychology*, **42**, 506–517.

Buck, R., Baron, R., Goodman, N. & Shapiro, N. (1980). The unitization of spontaneous nonverbal behavior in the study of emotion communication. *Journal of Personality and Social Psychology*, **39**, 522–529.

Buck, R. & Duffy, R. (1980). Nonverbal communication of affect in brain-damaged patients. *Cortex*, **16**, 351–362.

Buck, R. & Ginsburg, B. (1990). Emotional communication and altruism: The communicative gene hypothesis. In M. Clark, (Ed.), *Altruism. Review of Personality and Social Psychology*, Vol. 11. Newbury Park, Ca: Sage.

Buck, R. & Lerman, J. (1979). General vs. specific nonverbal sensitivity and clinical training. *Human Communication*, Summer, 267–274.

Buck, R. W., Miller, R. E. & Caul, W. F. (1974). Sex, personality and physiological variables in the communication of emotion via facial expression. *Journal of Personality and Social Psychology*, **30**, 587–596.

Buck, R., Savin, V. J., Miller, R. E. & Caul, W. F. (1972). Nonverbal communication of affect in humans. *Journal of Personality and Social Psychology*, **23**, 362–371.

Buck, R., Teng, W., Petersen, L., & Kenny, D. A. (1989). Spontaneous emotional communication in Chinese and Taiwanese students. Paper presented at the meeting of the International Communication Association, San Francisco, Ca, May 25–29.

Cofer, C. N. & Appley, M. H. (1964). *Motivation: Theory and Research*. New York: Wiley.

Critchley, M. (1975). *Silent Language*. London: Butterworths.

Damasio, A. R., Damasio, H., & Van Hoesen, G. W. (1982). Prosopagnosia: Anatomic basis and behavioral mechanisms. *Neurology*, **32**, 331–341.

Darwin, C. (1872). *Expression of the Emotions in Man and Animals*. New York: Philosophical Library Edition, published 1955.

Duffy, R. J., Duffy, J. R. & Alderdice, M. (1977). Limb apraxia and gestural impairment in aphasia. Paper presented at the Convention of the American Speech and Hearing Association, Chicago, 1977.

Duffy, R. J., Duffy, J. R. & Pearson, K. (1975). Pantomime recognition in aphasics. *Journal of Speech and Hearing Research*, **18**, 115–132.

Duffy, R. J. & Liles, B. Z. (1979). A translation of Finklnberg's (1870) lecture on aphasia as "asymbolia" with commentary. *Journal of Speech and Hearing Disorders*, **44**, 156–168.

Eibl-Eibesfeldt, I. (1970). *Ethology: The Biology of Behavior*, 2nd edn. New York: Holt, Rinehart and Winston.

Ekman, P. & Friesen, W. V. (1969a). The repertoire of nonverbal behavior: Categories, origins, usage and coding. *Semiotica*, **1**, 49–98.

Ekman, P. & Friesen, W. V. (1969b). Nonverbal leakage and clues to deception. *Psychiatry*, **32**, 88–105.

Ekman, P., & Friesen, W. V. (1974). Nonverbal behavior and psychopathology. In R. J. Friedman & H. M. Katz (Eds). *The Psychology of Depression: Contemporary Theory and Research*. New York: Wiley.

Ekman, P. & Friesen, W. V. (1975). *Unmasking the Face*. Englewood Cliffs, NJ: Prentice-Hall.

Etkoff, N. L. (1984). Selective attention to facial identity and facial emotion. *Neuropsychologia*, **22**, 281–295.

Fowles, D. C. (1980). The three arousal model: Implications of Gray's two-factor learning theory for heart rate, electrodermal activity, and psychotherapy. *Psychophysiology*, **17**, 87–104.

Fukuyama, F. (1989a). The end of history. *The National Interest*. Summer issue, **16**, 3–18.

Fukuyama, F. (1989b). Beyond the end of history. *The Hartford Courant: Commentary*. Sunday, December 17, pp. C1–C4.

Fukuyama, F. (1990). Are we at the end of history? *Fortune*, **121** (January 15), 75–78.

Gibbs, J. C. (1985). The problem of knowledge, still: A review of Liben's *Piaget and the Foundations of Knowledge*. *Merrill-Palmer Quarterly*, **31**, 11–15.

Gibson, J. J. (1966). *The Senses Considered as Perceptual Systems*. Boston: Houghton-Mifflin.

Gibson, J. J. (1979). *An Ecological Approach to Visual Perception*. Boston: Houghton-Mifflin.

Ginsburg, B. E. (1974). Nonverbal communication: The effect of affect on individual and group behavior. In P. Pliner, L. Krames & T. Alloway (Eds), *Nonverbal Communication of Aggression*. New York & London: Plenum, pp. 161–173.

Goldfield, E. (1983). The ecological approach to perceiving as a foundation for understanding the development of knowing in infancy. *Developmental Review*, **3**, 371–404.

Goldman, C. (1989). The relationship of inhibited and expressive emotional behavior to sending accuracy and peer relationships in kindergarten children. Unpublished MA thesis, University of Connecticut.

Goodglass, H. & Kaplan, E. (1963). Disturbance of gesture and pantomime in aphasia. *Brain*, **86**, 703–720.

Gorenstein, E. E. & Newman, J. P. (1980). Disinhibitory psychopathology: A new perspective and a model for research. *Psychological Review*, **87**, 301–315.

Gray, J. A. (1982). Precis of *The Neuropsychology of Anxiety. With Commentaries*. *The Behavioral and Brain Sciences*, **5**, 469–534.

Harlow, H. F. & Mears, C. E. (1983). Emotional sequences and consequences. In R. Plutchik & H. Kellerman (Eds), *Emotion: Theory, Research and Experience: Vol. 2. Emotions in Early Development*. New York: Academic Press.

Hofer, M. A. (1984). Relationships as regulators: A psychobiologic perspective on bereavement. *Psychosomatic Medicine*, **46**, 183–198.

Hoffman, M. L. (1977). Empathy: Its development and prosocial implications. In C. B. Keasey (Ed.), *Nebraska Symposium on Motivation*, Vol. 25. Lincoln: University of Nebraska Press.

Hoffman, M. L. (1981). Is altruism part of human nature? *Journal of Personality and Social Psychology*, **40**, 121–137.

Hoffman, M. L. (1986). Affect, cognition, and motivation. In R. M. Sorrentino & E. T. Higgins (Eds), *Handbook of Motivation and Cognition: Foundations of Social Behavior*. New York: Guilford Press, pp. 245–275.

James, W. (1890). *The Principles of Psychology*, Vol. 1. New York: Henry Holt.

Jones, H. E. (1935). The galvanic skin response as related to overt emotional expression. *American Journal of Psychology*, **47**, 241–251.

Jones, H. E. (1960). The longitudinal method in the study of personality. In I. Iscoe & H. W. Stevenson (Eds), *Personality Development in Children*. Chicago: University of Chicago Press.

Kagan, J., Reznick, J. S., Clarke, C., Snidman, N. & Garcia-Coll, C. (1984). Behavioral inhibition to the unfamiliar. *Child Development*, **55**, 2212–2225.

Kenny, D. H. & LaVoie, L. (1984). The social relations model. In L. Berkowitz (Ed.), *Advances in Experimental Social Psychology*. New York: Academic Press, pp. 141–182.

Kimura, D. (1979). Neuromotor mechanisms in the evolution of human communication. In H. D. Steklis & M. J. Raleigh (Eds), *Neurobiology of Social Communication in Primates*. New York: Academic Press, pp. 197–219.

Krause, R., Steimer, E., Sanger-Alt, C., & Wagner, G. (1989). Facial expression of schizophrenic patients and their interaction partners. *Psychiatry*, **52**, 1–12.

Kunst-Wilson, W. R. & Zajonc, R. B. (1980). Affective discrimination of stimuli that cannot be recognized. *Science*, **207**, 557–558.

Lanzetta, J. T. & Kleck, R. E. (1970). Encoding and decoding of nonverbal affect in humans. *Journal of Personality and Social Psychology*, **16**, 12–19.

Lazarus, R. S. (1982). Thoughts on the relations between emotion and cognition. *American Psychologist*, **37**, 1019–1024.

Lazarus, R. S. (1984). On the primacy of cognition. *American Psychologist*, **39**, 124–129.

LeDoux, J. (1986). A neurobiological view of the psychology of emotion. In J. LeDoux & W. Hirst (Eds), *Mind and Brain: Dialogues Between Cognitive Psychology and Neuroscience*. New York: Cambridge University Press.

LeDoux, J., Sakaguchi, A. & Reis, D. J. (1984). Subcortical afferent projections of the medulla geniculate nucleus mediate emotional responses conditioned to acoustic stimuli. *Journal of Neuroscience*, **4**, 683–698.

Maier, I. & Muller, D. G. (1986). Sexual phenomones in algae. *Biological Bulletin*, **170**, 145–176.

Manstead, A. S. R. (1990). Expressiveness as an individual difference. In R. S. Feldman & B. Rime (Eds), *Fundamentals of Nonverbal Behavior*. New York: Cambridge University Press.

Maranon, G. (1924). Contribution à l'étude de l'action emotive de l'adrenaline. *Revue Française d'endocrinologie*, **2**, 301–325.

Mark, L. S., Shaw, R. E. & Pittenger, J. B. (1988). Natural constraints, scales of analysis, and information for the perception of growing faces. In T. R. Alley (Ed.), *Social and Applied Aspects of Perceiving Faces*. Hillsdale, NJ: Erlbaum, pp. 11–50.

Mason, W. A. (1961). The effects of social restriction of the behavior of rhesus monkeys: III. Tests of gregariousness. *Journal of Comparative and Physiological Psychology*, **54**, 287–290.

McHugo, G. J., Lanzetta, J. T., Sullivan, D. G., Masters, R. D. & Englis, B. G. (1985). Emotional reactions to a political leader's expressive displays. *Journal of Personality and Social Psychology*, **49**, 1513–1529.

McLuhan, M. (1964). *Understanding Media: The Extensions of Man*. New York: McGraw-Hill.

Miller, R. E. (1967). Experimental approaches to the physiological and behavioral concomitants of affective communication in rhesus monkeys. In S. A. Altmann (Ed.), *Social Communication Among Primates*. Chicago: University of Chicago Press, pp. 125–134.

Miller, R. E. (1973). Social and pharmacological influences on nonverbal communication in monkeys and man. Paper presented to the Symposium on Communication and Affect, University of Toronto.

Miller, R. E., Banks, J. & Kuwahara, H. (1966). The communication of affects in monkeys: Cooperative reward conditioning. *Journal of Genetic Psychology*, **108**, 121–134.

Miller, R. E., Banks, J. & Ogawa, N. (1962). Communication of affect in "cooperative conditioning" of rhesus monkeys. *Journal of Abnormal and Social Psychology*, **64**, 343–348.

Miller, R. E., Banks, J. & Ogawa, N. (1963). Role of facial expression in "cooperative-avoidance conditioning" in monkeys. *Journal of Abnormal and Social Psychology*, **67**, 24–30.

Miller, R. E., Caul, W. F. & Mirsky, I. A. (1967). Communication of affects between feral and socially isolated monkeys. *Journal of Personality and Social Psychology*, **7**, 231–239.

Miller, R. E. & Deets, A. C. (1974). Delta-9-THC and nonverbal communication in monkeys. Unpublished paper, University of Pittsburgh Medical School.

Miller, R. E., Levine, J. M. & Mirsky, I. A. (1973). Effects of psychoactive drugs on nonverbal communication and group social behavior of monkeys. *Journal of Personality and Social Psychology*, **28**, 396–405.

Miller, R. E., Murphy, J. V. & Mirsky, I. A. (1959). Nonverbal communication of affect. *Journal of Clinical Psychology*, **15**, 155–158.

Murphy, J. V., Miller, R. E. & Mirsky, I. A. (1955). Interanimal conditioning in the monkey. *Journal of Comparative and Physiological Psychology*, **48**, 211–214.

Newtson, D. (1976). Foundations of attribution. The perception of ongoing behavior. In J. H. Harvey, W. J. Ickes & R. F. Kidd (Eds), *New Directions in Attribution Research*, Vol. 1. New York: Wiley.

Ohman, A. (1986). Presidential address, 1985; Face the beast and fear the face: Animal and social fears as prototypes for evolutionary analyses of emotion. *Psychophysiology*, **23**, 123–142.

Papez, J. W. (1937). A proposed mechanism of emotion. *Archives of Neurology and Psychiatry*, **35**, 725–43.

Piaget, J. (1948). *The moral judgment of the child*. Glencoe, Illinois: Free Press, (First published 1932).

Piaget, J. (1971). Piaget's theory. In P. Mussen (Ed.), *Handbook of Child Development*, Vol. 1. New York: Wiley.

Pickard, G. E. & Silverman, A. J. (1981). Direct retinal projections to the hypothalamus, piriform cortex, and accessory optic nuclei in the golden hamster as demonstrated by a sensitive anterograde horseradish peroxidase technique. *Journal of Comparative Neurology*, **196**, 155–172.

Porch, B. (1967). *Porch Index of Communicative Ability*, Consulting Psychologists Press, Palo Alto.

Reardon, K. K. (1981). *Persuasion: Theory and Context*. Beverly Hills, Ca: Sage.

Reardon, K. & Buck, R. (1989). Emotion, reason, and communication in coping with cancer. *Health Communication*, **1**, 41–54.

Rosenthal, R., Hall, J. A., DiMatteo, M. R., Rogers, P. L. & Archer, D. (1979). *Sensitivity to Nonverbal Communication: The PONS Test*. Baltimore: Johns Hopkins University.

Russell, B. (1912). *Problems of Philosophy*. New York: Simon and Schuster.

Russell, B. (1961). *An Outline of Philosophy*. Cleveland: World.

Sabatelli, R., Buck, R. & Dreyer, A. (1982). Nonverbal communication accuracy in married couples: Relationships with marital complaints. *Journal of Personality and Social Psychology*, **43**, 1088–1097.

Sabatelli, R., Buck, R. & Dreyer, A. (1983). Locus of control, interpersonal trust, and nonverbal communication accuracy. *Journal of Personality and Social Psychology*, **44**, 399–409.

Sabatelli, R., Buck, R. & Kenny, D. (1986). Nonverbal communication in married couples: A social relations analysis. *Journal of Personality*, **54** (3), 513–527.

Sabatelli, R., Dreyer, A. & Buck, R. (1979). Cognitive style and nonverbal sending accuracy. *Perceptual and Motor Skills*, **49**, 203–212.

Schachter, S. & Singer, J. (1962). Cognitive, social and physiological determinants of emotional state. *Psychological Review*, **69**, 379–399.

Shannon, C. E., & Weaver, W. (1949). *The Mathematical Theory of Communication*. Urbana: University of Illinois Press.

Skinner, B. F. (1953). *Science and Human Behavior*. New York, Macmillan.

Tomkins, S. (1962). *Affect, Imagery, and Consciousness: The Positive Affects*. New York: Springer.

Tomkins, S. (1963). *Affect, Imagery, and Consciousness: The Negative Affects*. New York: Springer.

Tranel, D. & Damasio, A. R. (1985). Knowledge without awareness: An autonomic index of facial recognition by prosopagnosics. *Science*, **228**, 1453–54.

Tucker, D. M. (1981). Lateral brain function, emotion, and conceptualization. *Psychological Bulletin*, **89**, 19–46.

White, R. W. (1959). Motivation reconsidered: The concept of competence. *Psychological Review*, **66**, 297–333.

Wilson, E. O. (1975). *Sociobiology: The New Synthesis*. Cambridge, Mass: Belknap.

Wilson, W. R. (1979). Feeling more than we can know: Exposure effects without learning. *Journal of Personality and Social Psychology*, **37**, 811–821.

Wittgenstein, L. (1965). *The Blue and the Brown Books*. New York: Philosophical Library Edition.

Zajonc, R. B. (1980). Feeling and thinking: Preferences need no inferences. *American Psychologist*, **35**, 151–175.

Zajonc, R. B. (1984). On the primacy of affect. *American Psychologist*, **39**, 117–123.

5 Some Implications of Cognitive Appraisal Theories of Emotion

PHOEBE C. ELLSWORTH

*Research Center for Group Dynamics, Institute for Social Research,
University of Michigan, Ann Arbor, MI 48106, USA*

The opposition of cognition and emotion in psychological theory has, I believe, been one of those "killer dichotomies" (Berthoff, 1990) like nature and nurture, or language and thought, that has advanced many a scientific career while muddling science itself. The idea that reason and passion are alternative ways of responding to events is an ancient and persistent one, often accompanied by the companion ideas that reason is the more highly evolved, the more mature, the more masculine, the more civilized, the superior alternative. Human emotion resides somewhere *beneath* human cognition, somewhere under the frontal lobes, where it is stimulated by the body, the autonomic nervous system, and the primal hormonal soup, but *not* by the heavenly cerebral hemispheres, whose only relation to the emotions is that of gentlemanly victim attacked by the riffraff, struggling to quell the rebellion. I have exaggerated this idea but not invented it. Like all such dicho-tomies it makes us attend to the rather barren question "whether", in this case whether cognition influences emotion, whether cognition is necessary for emotion, or whether cognition is antithetical to emotion, and not to the more interesting question "how". For the time being, I am taking the perspective that the relation between cognition and emotion is mutual, dialectical, and marvellous.

Stated in the abstract, this statement seems commonsensical. It is implied in the theories of famous peripheralists (eg William James 1890/1950; Tomkins, 1962, 1963) and in those of our grandmothers ("Look on the bright side, dear"). Stated in the abstract, it did not lead to much. Although cognition was implicit in the theory of William James, who referred to emotion-arousing perceptions like "being insulted by a rival" and "reading a letter announcing the death of a loved one", which clearly involve fairly complex cognitive processing, for the next three-quarters of a century the cognitive aspects of emotion were rarely singled out for theoretical attention. Cognitive components were *assumed*, of course, by most researchers who relied on their commonsense and intuition to create situations that they thought would make their subjects feel specific emotions—Landis (1924) had his bucket of frogs, Ax (1953) his exploding polygraph—but they received little theoretical attention. Finding a situation that would make subjects feel fearful or angry or happy was an *ad hoc* methodological issue, not a theoretical issue leading to any sort of general principles.

International Review of Studies on Emotion, Vol. 1. Edited by K. T. Strongman
©1991 John Wiley & Sons Ltd

In 1962, Schachter and Singer made explicit the idea that cognition was an essential component of emotion, and so helped bring the notion of a cognitive component into current prominence. Their theory, however, while generating an enormous amount of research and theory in a variety of areas (placebo effects, pain tolerance, and self-attribution more generally), did not significantly advance the study of emotion, except by stimulating those who profoundly disagreed with it. My own debut in the field of emotion (Ekman, Friesen & Ellsworth, 1972) was in part a reaction against Schachter and Singer's claim that the role of cognition was to provide emotional color to preexisting undifferentiated physiological arousal.

Although Schachter and Singer revitalized the idea that in order to understand the person's emotion it was necessary to understand the person's cognitive interpretation of the situation, they had little to say about the kinds of cognition that were important in differentiating among the emotions. Methodologically, like their predecessors, they relied on the face validity of *ad hoc* situational manipulations, while conceptually they referred generally to social comparison theory (Festinger, 1954), without specifying exactly how it applied to the domain of emotion.

In the early 1980s a number of researchers, working independently, began to develop models designed to go beyond the general statement that cognition is an important component of emotion, models that would specify the *kinds* of cognitive interpretations that lead to different emotions. The basic premise is that emotions result from the way people interpret or appraise their environment. Different patterns of appraisals result in different emotions. The reason sorrow is different from anger is that people who are sad see their situation (and themselves in relation to that situation) differently from people who are angry.

The term "appraisal", I believe, was first used in this context by Magda Arnold (1945, 1960), who argued that as organisms move through their physical or mental environments they are ceaselessly engaged in evaluating the significance of environmental changes for their own well-being. These appraisals result in Action Tendencies, which are felt as emotions. Although this general perspective started no immediate movement in the field, it was kept alive by Richard Lazarus (eg Lazarus, 1968). For Lazarus, the subjective experience of emotion includes the appraisal, the associated physiological feedback, and the motivation to relevant action. Unlike Arnold, Lazarus reasoned that since human beings have the capacity for immense variability in their appraisals of situations, human emotions should also be immensely various; the idea that the world of emotions is made up of a few large distinct categories (such as joy, sorrow, and fear) is misleading (Lazarus, Kanner & Folkman, 1980; see also Frijda, 1986, chapter 4).

Over the past decade, interest in this general perspective has spread widely, and there are now more than half a dozen appraisal models of emotion bearing a close family resemblence to each other (for example Frijda, 1986; Roseman, 1984; Scherer, 1984; Wiener, 1985). Each of these models differs in some ways from all the others, but there is also considerable overlap. There is general agreement that the emotions, including the "basic" emotions identified by categorical theorists, can be broken down into smaller components, and that many of these components correspond to cognitive appraisals (Ortony & Turner, 1990). The purpose of this chapter is to discuss some implications of this general point of view for a few issues that have been of perennial concern to students of emotion, and to suggest a few new hypotheses generated by an appraisal point of view. That is, rather than nitpicking about the relative virtues and vices of the varous members of this family of models, I want to talk about what the family as a whole has to offer. (I hasten to add that I have no idea whether the authors of the other models would agree with the ideas presented here.)

THE SMITH AND ELLSWORTH MODEL

In our first study (Smith & Ellsworth, 1985), Smith and I proposed eight dimensions of appraisal that differentiate emotional experience: attention, pleasantness, certainty, perceived obstacle, anticipated effort, responsibility, control and legitimacy. We asked people to remember and try to reexperience a specific situation in which they had experienced each of 15 different emotions, to describe the situation, and to rate their perceptions of the situation on scales designed to tap the eight appraisal dimensions. We found six orthogonal dimensions that reliably differentiated among the emotions. Four of these corresponded to our proposed appraisals of attention, pleasantness, certainty, and anticipated effort. The other two were combinations of our proposed responsibility and control dimensions. The first, human agency, reflected the perception that the event was caused by oneself (at one pole of the dimension) or by some other person (at the opposite pole). The second, situational control, reflected the perception that the event was caused by a human being (*any* human being or beings, oneself or someone else) or by impersonal circumstances beyond human control.

Thus for example, although fear, anger, and sadness were all unpleasant, fear was associated with moderately high anticipated effort and very high uncertainty; anger was associated with moderately high effort and certainty, and with a very strong perception that some other human being was responsible for the adversity; and sadness was associated with lower attention, lower perceived effort, and a very strong perception that the adversity was brought about by circumstances beyond anyone's control. Thirteen of the 15 emotions we studied were characterized by a unique constellation of appraisals (shame and guilt did not differ, nor did anger and contempt). Thus we have gone beyond previous work on dimensions of emotion, which has been dominated by studies of differences along simple pleasantness and activation dimensions, and have put some specific content into the cognitions associated with various emotions.

Whether these are the "right" dimensions or the only dimensions of appraisal is an open question, but it is not a question to be addressed in this chapter. I would be astonished if any one of the appraisal researchers had managed to get the details right in less than a decade of work, but I do not think the details should be our only concern. Leaving aside the particulars of the various appraisal theories, I want to examine the implications and the heuristic value of the general perspective.

BASIC EMOTIONS, UNIVERSAL EMOTIONS

Theories of emotion can be categorized in terms of the number of emotions they postulate: two, a few, quite a few, or an infinite number. Two-emotion theories are valence theories: the organism feels good and approaches, or feels bad and withdraws (Young, 1943; Zajonc, 1980). By adding an intensity or activation dimension, orthogonal to the valence dimension, many theorists have expanded the basic positive–negative dichotomy into a two-dimensional space into which many, possibly an infinite number of emotions can be fitted (Woodworth & Schlosberg, 1954; Russell, 1980). These models have been criticized on several grounds. In particular, the major negative emotions common to almost all categorical theories of emotion—grief, fear, and anger—are all intense, unpleasant states, and thus fall very close to each other in the two-dimensional space. Phenomenologically, something important seems to be missing from a scheme that characterizes fear as a more activated version of grief, or grief as a more unpleasant version of anger (Frijda, 1986, chapter 4).

Those who posit a few emotions (Tomkins, 1962, 1963; Ekman, 1984; Izard, 1977, among others) reject the notion that differences in activation and valence, or even differences along three dimensions (Wundt, 1907; Schlosberg, 1954; Osgood, 1966), can adequately capture the fundamental qualitative differences in the subjective experience of various emotions. Instead, they postulate a small number of innate, categorically distinct, hardwired neural programs corresponding to certain "basic" emotions: fear, sorrow, happiness and anger are included on the lists of almost all these categorical theorists; after that the lists diverge. Each of the basic emotions has distinct neurophysiological, expressive, and subjective characteristics.

There are two major problems that proponents of this categorical view-point have to face: the problem of subjective emotional experiences that do not fit into any of the basic categories (eg pride, frustration, jealousy, pity) and the problem of transitions between emotions. One common way of dealing with the first problem is simply to deny that these other affective states are emotions (Ekman, 1984). This tactic raises the awkward question, "What are they then, and what is their relationship to the states we have decided to define as true emotions?" Another common way of dealing with the first problem is to speak rather metaphorically of "blends". Thus, for example, Plutchik (1984) considers remorse to be a blend of the basic emotions of disgust and sadness, love to be a blend of joy and acceptance. While various versions of the blend idea may be more or less satisfactory on a metaphorical level, they all beg the question of what is actually happening. Are both neural programs firing simultaneously at partial strength? A similar problem arises with transitions between emotions, particularly gradual transitions. Consider the common transition from distress to anger. You come home late through the freezing rain and discover that you are locked out—the house key is not in its usual hiding-place. As you rack your brains about what to do and where the key might be and slowly come to the realization that your husband must have used it without remembering to put it back where it belongs, your initial distress changes to anger. Does the distress program switch off and the anger program on? Or does the distress program slowly wane while the anger program slowly waxes? In either case, why do these changes occur?

According to an appraisal point of view, a new appraisal has been added—you realize that *someone else* is responsible for your misery, and the emotion changes correspondingly from distress to anger. A dimensional, appraisal point of view is compatible with an infinite number of emotional states (Lazarus, Kanner & Folkman, 1980; Mandler, 1975). As a person's appraisal of the situation changes, so will his or her emotion, gradually or suddenly depending on the speed of the appraisal change.

One hypothesis raised by this point of view is that transitions between some emotions should be easier (more likely, faster) than transitions between other emotions, depending on the number of appraisals they have in common. In our theory, hope and fear are both characterized by high levels of uncertainty, high attention, and the perception of an obstacle, differing only on the dimension of pleasantness; therefore the transition from hope to fear should be an especially easy one. Someone waiting for news that may or may not be good provides a classic example of the vacillation between hope and fear as attention is focused first on the possible success, then on the possible failure. Fear and sadness are further apart in dimensional space (at least in our model), hope and sadness further still. Transitions between these states should be correspondingly more difficult.

A primary argument in favor of a limited number of primary emotions, raised by Darwin in 1872 and revived a hundred years later by Tomkins (1962), Izard (1971), and Ekman, (1972, 1984), is that there are distinctive, culturally universal facial expressions corresponding to some emotions but not others. These emotions, then, must be innate and somehow more basic than the others.

Cognitive appraisal theories propose that emotions are the resultants of a set of appraisals; what we feel is some sort of combination of appraisals. What does this suggest about emotional facial expressions? It suggests the hypothesis that the so-called basic facial expressions may also be composed of more primitive, but still meaningful elements—elements corresponding to the appraisals of pleasantness, certainty, and so on (Ortony & Turner, 1990). An examination of the proto-typical examples of the facial expressions corresponding to the basic emotions proposed by Tomkins (1962, 1963), Izard (1977), and Ekman and Friesan (1975) reveals that the expressions of different emotions have elements in common. The eyebrows and lids are raised in both fear and surprise, the brows are drawn together in both anger and disgust. Also, just as the same elements may appear in different emotions, so the "same" emotion may be expressed with somewhat different combinations of elements. Although all the published prototypical expressions of sadness are recognizably sad and the expressions of anger recognizably angry, they are not identical. Anger, for example, may be expressed with an open mouth that bares the teeth or with tightly compressed lips.

An appraisal point of view implies that angry faces resemble each other because the experience of anger is the product of a particular set of appraisals and it is these appraisals that are reflected on the face. Typically the angry person perceives an obstacle—this perception of an obstacle may be reflected in a frown. A frown will *also* occur, however, when people who are not angry perceive an obstacle—people who are fearful, for example, or simply puzzled. Likewise we may hypothesize that an angry person who is exercising a high level of control will have compressed lips, but an angry person who is less in control will have an open mouth.

In our initial research (Smith & Ellsworth, 1985), each time we asked our subjects to remember a particular emotion we also asked them to show us the corresponding facial expression. We found that a number of specific facial movements were significantly correlated with specific situational appraisals. While these results were encouraging, they were by no means conclusive. The expressions were posed, and the data were correlational.

In a follow-up study, Smith (1989) tested the hypothesis that the appraisal of *an obstacle* results in a frown—the eyebrows drawn together through the action of the corrugator muscle. Previous research and theory had generally designated the frown as a sign of negative affect; if, however, it also reflects the perception of an obstacle, it should show up in certain positive states as well, such as interest or challenge. Smith used a directed imagery task in which subjects were asked to imagine themselves in various pleasant situations. The appraisals of perceived obstacle and agency (self or other) were systematically varied across the situations. Challenging a friend to a race was an example of a high obstacle situation; relaxing in the sun after finishing an assignment a low obstacle situation. The frown, along with various other facial muscle movements, was measured by EMG. As expected, the eyebrows were drawn together significantly more when the subjects imagined situations involving an obstacle than when they imagined situations requiring no effort, even though all the imagined situations were pleasant ones.

This study provides the first experimental evidence for the hypothesis that facial movements that are components of emotional facial expressions reflect appraisals that are components of emotional experience. Other physical responses may also reflect appraisal components. Indeed, in the same study Smith found that heart rate differed significantly for high effort and low effort scenarios, and Scherer (1986) has presented evidence linking speech parameters to appraisals.

Obviously this research represents a very preliminary first step, and raises more questions than it answers. Students of emotion have generally assumed that certain combinations of facial elements tend to co-occur—that typically the facial expression of an emotion will show the common prototypical combination of elements rather than a partial or mixed pattern. The first question is, is this true? We may have assumed that these prototypical patterns are the most common ones because they are the ones we have studied. Early researchers, using less carefully selected photographs, found less evidence for basic recognizable emotions (cf Munn, 1940). Subjects in our experiments, unless we explicitly direct them to focus on instances when they felt a single, "pure" emotion, rarely do so. Usually they report feeling more than one emotion (Smith & Ellsworth, 1987; Ellsworth & Smith 1988a,b). Perhaps complete unblended facial expressions of emotion are relatively rare. The second question is, if it is true that certain facial elements tend to co-occur, why do they? Is it because they are biologically wired to co-occur, or because the appraisals tend to co-occur? (See Ortony & Turner, 1990 for an excellent discussion of why appraisals might tend to co-occur.)

Cultural patterns

A second line of questions goes as follows. If the appraisals correspond to facial movements, could the *appraisals* be universal components of emotion? Cultures may differ in the sorts of things that command attention; arouse basic positive or negative feelings, are believed to be caused by self, other, or no one; or are seen as obstacles. But if appraisals are universal components of emotion, we would predict that people in different cultures will feel angry when they believe that someone else has caused them trouble, though their beliefs about the kinds of trouble that are caused by other people, and even their definition of trouble, may vary. There is now some evidence for cross-cultural generality of some of the basic appraisals (Scherer, Wallbott & Summerfield, 1986; Mauro, Sato & Tucker, 1990).

Appraisal theories also suggest interesting hypotheses for exploring cultural diversity in emotions, not just cultural similarity. Suppose, for example, cultural world views differ in ideas about the forces that control human endeavor. Some cultures, such as our own, might emphasize human agency and individual enterprise, while others assign greater power to destiny or to supernatural powers less easily controlled by human efforts. Might we then predict differences in the socialization, the frequency, and even the experience, of anger and sorrow?

Individual patterns

Of course, cultures are not the only source of variation in the way human beings understand their environments. A perennial issue in research on emotions has been the range of individual variability within a single culture (typically our own). When faced with the same situation, different people often respond with different emotions. An obvious implication of the cognitive appraisal viewpoint is that people respond with different emotions because they appraise the situation differently. This general statement, of course, may be painfully self-evident, but appraisal theories go beyond the general statement to *specify* the differences in interpretation that produce the differences in emotions. An event may be seen as an obstacle by one person but not by another. Or people may differ in the amount of control they feel they have over events (cf Peterson & Seligman, 1987). If people habitually tend to favor some appraisals over others, differing in their "appraisal styles", we would predict that they would respond more readily and more frequently with the corresponding emotions. A person who characteristically sees her misfortunes as caused by bad luck or uncontrollable circumstances may be prone to depression, while one who characteristically attributes misfortune to other people's malice may be prone to aggression (cf Roseman, 1984; Wiener, 1985). Other individual differences may also affect a person's appraisals. Differences in self-concept are one major source of emotional differences. A person who is confident of her social skills will experience less uncertainty, and thus less fear, when faced with a large crowd of merrymakers than a person who is less confident. Differences in socialization can affect our taste in food, amusements, and other people, and thus our initial appraisal of a new exemplar as positive or negative.

EFFECTS OF EMOTION UPON COGNITION

Most of the work on cognitive appraisals and emotion has so far been concerned with the hypothesis that a given pattern of appraisals results in a particular, predictable emotion. This has been the working assumption; in fact, most of the work to date has been aimed at establishing the correlations between appraisal patterns and emotions in describing the domain of emotional experience. Nonetheless, the hypothetical sequence that has formed the basic working assumption of these endeavors is that appraisals cause the emotions. Studies using imagery (eg Smith, 1989) and vignettes have begun to examine the question of causality more directly, but there is still a great deal to be done along these lines.

Little attention has been devoted to exploring another possible causal sequence: the possibility that emotions influence future appraisals. Other researchers not associated with the cognitive appraisal perspective have studied the effects of emotion on cognition. Forgas and Bower (1987) review a number of studies showing that a generally positive or negative mood affects estimates of personal efficacy, judgments of political circumstances, and evaluations of one's own behavior in a social situation (see also Isen, 1984). Johnson and Tversky (1983) found that a negative mood brought on by reading newspaper reports of tragic events substantially increased people's estimates of the likelihood of other, unrelated catastrophes, while a positive mood decreased their likelihood estimates. This effect operated at a very general affective level: the surface similarity between the events in a newspaper story and the specific future risk evaluated did not affect subjects' estimates of the likelihood of the future risk. Reading about someone who was killed in a fire increased estimates of the likelihood of dying from cancer as much as it did estimates of dying from a fire or flood.

Work in this tradition has been limited both in the choice of emotional antecedents and in the choice of cognitive consequences. On the antecedent side, the "emotions" investigated are typically points on a simple positive–negative dimension; the experimenter compares a good, pleasant mood with a bad, unpleasant mood, occasionally adding a no-treatment control group to represent some intermediate point on the same dimension. On the consequence side, most of the influences that mood has been shown to exert on judgment can be characterized as simple optimism and pessimism.

A fundamental principle of appraisal theories is that different negative emotions (and, for that matter, different positive emotions) are quite dissimilar in their patterns of appraisal, suggesting that fear, sadness, and anger should affect future judgments in different ways. An emotion may affect people's judgments of new situations in ways that correspond to the appraisals that are most diagnostic of that emotion. For example, since the perception of agency has repeatedly been found to be important in differentiating among negative affective states (Ellsworth & Smith, 1988a; Roseman, 1984), one might predict that different negative emotions will result in different perceptions of the causes of subsequent events. Angry people should be prone to see other people as responsible, sad people to see the same events as caused by uncontrollable situational forces, guilty people to see themselves as responsible.

Some preliminary data (Keltner & Ellsworth, 1990) indicate that emotions can affect judgments in more specific ways than global optimism or pessimism, and in ways that are directly predictable from the appraisal model. In one study, we induced subjects to feel sad or angry by having them read detailed stories of a tragic or infuriating event. Then, following Johnson and Tversky (1983), we asked subjects to estimate the likelihood of various life events, some positive and some negative. Half of these events were described as the result of human agency ("Because of a dishonest salesman a new car you buy turns out to be a lemon"; "You meet your loved one through a friend"), while the other half were described in relatively impersonal terms ("Because of a factory problem a new car you buy turns out to be a lemon"; "You meet your loved one in a random encounter"). As predicted, compared to sad subjects, angry subjects rated events caused by other people as more likely and events caused by impersonal circumstances as less likely. It is especially striking that although all subjects were in a negative mood, the bias in estimates of agency affected perceptions of the likelihood of both positive and negative events.

In a second study, we predicted that when angry and sad people are confronted with a new situation that is ambiguous, allowing for several possible interpretations, the angry subjects would focus on the actions and intentions of other people and the sad subjects on situational causes. Anger and sadness were induced as in the previous study, we then gave the subjects a fairly long, complicated story and asked them to imagine themselves as the protagonist. In the story, the protagonist meets a wonderful new man (or woman if the subject was male), gushes about him to her room-mates, and invites him to a party.

When he finally arrives, he brings a date, the room-mates laugh, the man and his date seem upset, everyone keeps glancing at the embarrassed hostess, and all in all it is a social mess. Responsibility for this mess could be assigned to other people (eg the room-mates, the new man), to no one, or to oneself as protagonist. As expected, angry subjects were more likely than sad subjects to blame others and less likely to attribute the imbroglio to circumstances beyond anyone's control. (We attempted to run a guilt condition as well, but this failed.)

These results are quite preliminary, and do not yet provide unequivocal evidence for the effects of emotion on future cognitive appraisals. For one thing, the study needs to be replicated using an emotional induction that is less cognitive in order to avoid the problem that appraisals prime appraisals, with no causal role for the emotion.

Nonetheless, the results are encouraging. The idea that emotion exerts powerful effects on cognition is an ancient one, providing a central theme in literature ranging from great tragedies to innumerable self-help books. Scientifically the idea is also old, but it has remained fairly primitive. Most theory and research has argued either that emotions influence cognition by disrupting it (eg Claparède, 1928; Mandler, 1975) or that pleasant emotions lead to pleasant thoughts and unpleasant emotions lead to unpleasant thoughts. Both of these hypotheses are undoubtedly correct, at least some of the time, but even taken together they seem a bit thin for a century of research. Cognitive appraisal theories suggest new directions to follow in exploring the effects of emotions on cognition. We have begun to explore the agency dimension, but others—attention, perceived obstacle, certainty—may prove heuristic in generating new hypotheses as well.

THE SEQUENCING OF EMOTIONAL EXPERIENCE

Episodic sequencing

The commonsense, lay view of emotions, at least in this culture, is that they are immediate, holistic, subjective responses to arousing stimuli. When thwarted, we feel anger; when threatened, we feel fear. One of the earliest (and some would argue most pernicious) scientific theories of emotions explicitly took issue with this commonsense theory of sequencing. William James (1884, 1890) proposed that the exciting stimulus produced a specific pattern of autonomic arousal and muscular activity that either caused or defined the subjective experience of emotion. While the question "Which comes first, the feeling or the 'expression'?" has occupied researchers off and on for a century (James, 1884; Cannon, 1927; Tomkins, 1962; Laird, 1974; Tourangeau & Ellsworth, 1979; Winton, 1986), most of the discussions of this question have explicitly or implicitly assumed that the bodily response corresponding to a specific emotion has no time sequence of its own, nor does the subjective experience. The major disputes about the time course of an emotional episode have centred around the order of the central and peripheral components.

Appraisal theories put forward a different set of questions about an emotional episode. They suggest that full-blown emotions are not unitary, that not all of the components of the subjective experience, or of the peripheral response, emerge simultaneously. Some appraisals may be more immediate than others, suggesting that any given emotional experience may be broken down into a microsequence of events both centrally and peripherally. The existence of the general term "emotion" and the assumption that certain basic states such as fear, anger, joy, and sadness were prototypical examples of this general category may have led us unwittingly to assume more unitary experiences within each category and more similarity in the time sequence across categories than is justified. If appraisals are made sequentially, there may be much more variability in the states typically labelled "emotions" than previous researchers have considered.

Klaus Scherer (eg Scherer, 1984) has described some of the implications of the assumption that appraisals occur sequentially, and my own thinking follows very similar lines. According to this view, a possible sequence in the development of an emotion might be as follows.

First, something attracts the person's attention. This event is similar to Mandler's (1975) notion of an interruption. The arousal of attention is the first step in entering the emotional system; if nothing attracts or changes the focus of the person's attention, no emotion will be felt, or if the person was already experiencing an emotion, no new emotion will be felt. Scherer (1984) refers to arousal of attention as an evaluation of *novelty*. At this point the person may identify the arousing stimulus as uninteresting or inconsequential (the sudden noise was the dishwasher moving into a new cycle, the scream was part of a TV show) and no further progression towards a full-fledged emotional experience will occur. This is roughly the sort of process that Schachter and Singer (1962) posited for the subjects in their "informed" conditions; their attention was aroused in part by their own physiological arousal, but because they believed it was merely a side-effect of the drug they had taken, no emotion followed.

Before discounting or further appraising the eliciting stimulus, the person may experience startle or surprise. This view of surprise is common across many theories, not just appraisal theories (cf Tomkins, 1962, 1984). There is considerable controversy over whether surprise should be considered an emotion or not. It has a clear facial expression (Tomkins, 1962), which is recognizable cross-culturally, although not as readily as some other emotional expressions (Ekman, Sorenson & Friesen, 1969; Izard, 1971), but some theorists feel that *not enough has happened* for surprise to be considered an emotion: it is too reflex-like and primitive (Lazarus, 1982). It does not even have a valence, like other emotions (Ortony & Turner, 1990). It cannot last long without disappearing or turning into some other emotion. Appraisal theorists (and dimensional theorists in general) are less interested than other theorists in deciding which states are "really" emotions and which ones are not. In their view, surprise fits naturally into the sequence of emotional events at a very early stage (Scherer, 1984), and involves only one appraisal. The decision about whether surprise does or does not have enough in common with other emotions to deserve the label "emotion" is an arbitrary one.

Given that attention has been aroused, the next step in the sequence is a global response of positive or negative affect, a sense of pleasantness or unpleasantness. This may often occur simultaneously with the arousal of attention, as argued so persuasively by Zajonc (1980). In the case of basic sensory experiences— smells or tastes or walking out into a balmy spring day—the positive or negative response is probably immediate. Certainly there is strong evidence that a primitive positive or negative affective response *can* occur very early, even before other significant aspects of the stimulus (eg gender) can be identified (Murphy, 1990). In other cases, as when we meet a new person, it may be immediate, but it may not. We may instead feel uncertain, or vacillate between positive and negative views, or even feel fairly neutral. More complex stimuli may introduce a sense of "feeling emotional" before a clear-cut emotion emerges. For example, the news that East and West Germany were to be reunited may have elicited an immediate positive or negative response in some people, but other people may have responded, even immediately, with ambivalence or with undifferentiated excitement, sensing that this was emotionally relevant news but not immediately clear whether it was positive or negative.

If an immediate positive response occurs (and if we could stop the sequence then, or if there were no further developments), the person might say that she is feeling "good" or "happy". In general, the positive emotions seem to be less well differentiated than negative emotions (Ellsworth & Smith, 1988b), perhaps because the label happy can be applied to this fairly simple, immediate state. If the initial appraisal is negative, more is generally needed before the person can give the emotion one of the common emotion labels. The person may say she feels "unhappy" or "bad", meaning that she does not feel happy, but more is needed before she can say she feels angry, or sad, or frightened.

Zajonc (1980), as well as some appraisal theorists (eg Scherer, 1984), has argued that a definite pleasantness–unpleasantness response occurs at this early stage. Undoubtedly it often does, but I am arguing that this is not necessarily the case. The sequence of appraisals, once attention has been aroused, may be somewhat variable. Sometimes a sense of strong *uncertainty* may occur before a person feels positive or negative. Seeing a stranger walking up the driveway towards one's door may arouse strong curiosity (interest), which may turn to fear if a closer approach reveals an expression of hostility on the person; or pleasure, if it turns out not to be a stranger but a close friend; or anger, if a clipboard reveals that it is yet another door-to-door salesman.

These brief examples involve appraisals along other dimensions—appraisals of uncertainty, obstacle, and agency. The order in which the various appraisals take place may be quite variable depending on properties of the eliciting circumstances themselves and of the current state of mind (eg current goals) of the perceiver.

There are several implications of this point of view. One is that a substantial proportion of our emotional lives may be spent in emotional states that do not correspond to any of the prototypical "basic" emotions because we have not yet made all of the appraisals necessary to reach such a state (cf Stein & Levine, 1990). Being in one of these states may make some emotions more probable than others, in that some of the requisite appraisals have been made. Likewise, emotional responses to major life events with many implications are notoriously fluid (Parkes, 1972); the immediate emotion changes as the perceiver focuses on different aspects of the situation.

A second implication is that emotions may vary substantially in terms of their latencies. At least since Cannon's (1927) critique of the James–Lange theory of emotions, in which one of Cannon's arguments was that the autonomic nervous system responds too slowly to account for the immediate subjective experience of emotion, we have tended to assume that immediacy is a general characteristic of emotion, perhaps even criterial (cf Ekman, 1984). This assumption has distracted us, as researchers, from the possibility of slower sequences, or different sequences. Perhaps one of the reasons that the emotion of love has been ignored by many theorists is that it typically lacks the sudden onset implied by the commonly accepted view of emotion. Categorical theories which are based on the firing of discrete emotional programs make little allowance for differential latencies. Tomkins' theory allows differential latencies between emotions but does not easily accommodate the single emotion of anger developing quickly or gradually. One way to avoid this issue, of course, is to say that it is not anger (or fear, or sorrow) until the moment when the last step is taken and the program fires, or the last appraisal is definite. This may be a tidy answer but the question "What was it before that?" lingers in the air. A definitional answer simply distracts attention from a host of unanswered questions about sequence.

I have no doubt that many emotional experiences may be immediate and complete: in appraisal terms, all the appraisals are made in extremely rapid sequence and the subjective experience is much the same as we would expect if the underlying process were the firing of a complete program. But I also have no doubt that some emotional experiences follow other sequences. They may be slower. They may never get to an end state corresponding to one of the commonly recognized basic emotions. The person may remain uncertain about a key appraisal (eg What is responsible for my misfortune?) and so may remain indefinitely ambivalent. I believe it would be very useful for an understanding of emotion to turn our attention to emotional sequences that do not fit the standard theories. There are obvious cases where everything seems out of order. People who just barely avoid an automobile accident, for example, often report that the *behavior* (swerving to avoid the oncoming car) precedes *both* the appraisal and the emotion. People often seem to feel no affect at all for a brief period after hearing about some catastrophe. Eventually a theory of emotion must account for the exceptional cases as well as the rule, if it is the rule (cf Stein & Levine, 1990).

The view that appraisals, rather than whole emotions, are the basic units of affective processing not only suggests new questions about the sequencing of emotional experience, but also provides a new perspective on the traditional questions of sequence. From James (1884) to the Zajonc–Lazarus controversy (Zajonc, 1980, 1984; Lazarus, 1982), questions about the episodic sequence of emotional experience have provoked some of the most heated debates in the field. The three most commonly proposed sequences are:

1. The commonsense theory:

Stimulus→interpretation→affect→behavior

The commonsense theory could also be called the cognitive science theory (Ortony, Clore & Collins, 1988) and has been implied, if not explicitly stated, in most of the cognitive appraisal theories (Frijda, 1986; Roseman, 1984; Scherer, 1984; Wiener, 1985, Stein & Levine, 1989; Smith & Ellsworth, 1985). A person perceives (or evaluates or appraises or interprets) a stimulus and a subjective emotional experience results, followed by behavior.

2. The affective primacy theory:

Stimulus→affect→interpretation→behavior

This view was proposed by Wundt (1907) and revived in 1980 by Zajonc. In Zajonc's words, "it is entirely possible that the very first stage of the organism's reaction to stimuli and the very first elements in retrieval are affective. It is further possible that we can like something or be afraid of it before we know precisely what it is and perhaps even *without* knowing what it is" (Zajonc, 1980, p. 154; see also Murphy, 1990). The interpretation (sometimes, in this view, a justification) follows.

3. Motor feedback theories:

Stimulus→behavior→affect→interpretation

Here the visceral and motor response "follow directly the perception of the exciting fact" (James, 1890/1950, p. 449) and the awareness of the bodily changes is the emotion. The example of the near accident is a classic Jamesian sequence. Recent facial feedback theories (Tomkins, 1962; Izard, 1971; Laird, 1974) also assume this kind of sequence.

   Most of the proponents of these three sequences have put forward theories that are far more complex, and often qualified, than these simple schematic representations. Most of them have focused primarily on the first two stages after the eliciting event—interpretation preceding affect, affect preceding interpretation, or behavior preceding affect—and have been less clear about the last link (the role of behavior in the first two theories, the role of intepretation in the last). Also, considerable complexity is introduced when various definitions of "behavior" are considered—autonomic behavior, expressive (usually facial) behavior, or "instrumental" responses such as running away or striking a blow. I have obviously oversimplified all three points of view.

Nonetheless, many of the authors of these theories have themselves presented their ideas in strong, simple, provocative terms, introducing the complexities and qualifications only later, and this, I think, has led many readers, including many psychological researchers, to assume that interpretation, subjective experience, and possibly behavior are themselves somehow units. Thus the common view of the first theory is that *all* the interpretation must take place before *any* affect is felt, while in the second theory a complete emotional experience pops into existence before any interpretation takes place.

Appraisal theories, by breaking down the interpretation stage of the process into components, suggest that the stages implied by these theories are far too global. There is no reason to believe that a subjective sense of emotion must be delayed until *all* the appraisals have been made. Rather, the emotional experience develops over time in a rapid sequence of appraisals, bodily responses, and subjective changes. We have seen that individual appraisals can produce changes in facial expression (Smith, 1989) and we propose that they can produce changes in autonomic processes and affective experience as well. At the moment when the organism's attention is aroused, bodily changes take place (orienting response) and the organism *feels different* from the way it did before the event. When the organism senses that the stimulus is pleasant or unpleasant, the experience and the bodily responses change again. As each appraisal is made, the body and the affective experience change. The sequence may be so rapid as to be perceived as instantaneous or it may be considerably more drawn out. When all appraisals are clear, it may result in a "pure" emotion corresponding to one of the basic emotions proposed by the categorical theorists. When one or more appraisals are ambiguous, the person may say that she does not know what she is feeling, but would have no doubt that she is feeling "emotional". When one or more appraisals is variable, the person may vacillate among emotions. And, of course, the event itself may develop over time, so that initial appraisals are replaced by new ones.

In effect, this point of view allows the person to feel affect very early in the sequence, certainly as early as the initial assessment (or experience) of valence, possibly earlier. It also allows for some emotional states, such as guilt or anger, to depend on considerably more cognitive processing. Many of the debates among proponents of the time sequences outlined above are in fact debates about when in the sequence we are willing to say the person crosses the threshold into what we want to call an emotion. If emotions develop over time (even if very rapidly), then the answer to this question becomes somewhat arbitrary depending on the theorist's definition of emotion. In our view, feelings come first, and they also come last.

Ontogenetic sequencing

A further implication of appraisal theories is that if an organism lacks the cognitive capacity to make a particular appraisal, it will not feel emotions that depend on that appraisal. A newborn can feel a generalized distress (positive–negative appraisal), but cannot feel anger or sadness, which depend upon more sophisticated appraisals of agency. Scherer (1984) has proposed an ontogenetic sequence of the emergence of some of the basic emotions, based on his appraisal theory, and Stein and her colleagues (Stein & Levine, 1989, 1990) have done considerable work on appraisal–emotion relationships in older children. Further developmental work would be enormously useful for exploring hypotheses about whether the capacity for various appraisals is necessary for the experience of various emotions.

CONCLUDING REMARKS

Basically, this chapter has been a highly self-indulgent account of why I find my own theory, and others like it, so interesting. It has allowed me to discuss ideas and implications that I have barely begun to study empirically, and some that I have not studied at all, in the hope that they will be taken up and incorporated into other people's research, to be developed, revised, or refuted. I have not dealt with certain fundamental problems that emotions theorists must face, most notably the questions of unconscious emotions, vicarious emotions, and unconscious appraisals leading to conscious emotions. I have not claimed that emotion is impossible without appraisal. I have not even tried in this chapter to argue that the appraisal theories of emotion are true, but to argue that they are heuristic. They suggest lines of investigation that are not suggested by other theories, and they suggest that certain commonly held assumptions about emotions may need to be examined more closely. Because I wanted to put forward a wide range of implications, my treatment of each one of them has inevitably been superficial.

REFERENCES

Arnold, M. B. (1945). Physiological differentiation of emotional states. *Psychological Review*, **52**, 35–48.

Arnold, M. B. (1960). *Emotions and Personality, Vol. 1. Psychological Aspects*. New York: Columbia University Press.

Ax, A. F. (1953). The physiological differentiation between fear and anger in humans. *Psychosomatic Medicine*, **15**, 433–442.

Berthoff, A. (1990). Killer dichotomies: Reading in/reading out. In K. Ronald & H. Roshelly (Eds), *Farther Along: Transforming Dichotomies in Rhetoric and Composition*. Portsmouth, NH, Boynton/Cook-Heinemann.

Cannon, W. (1927). The James–Lange theory of emotion: A critical examination and an alternative theory. *American Journal of Psychology*, **39**, 106–124.

Claparède, E. (1928). Feelings and emotions. In M. L. Reymert (Ed.), *Feelings and Emotions: The Wittenberg Symposium*. Worcester, Mass: Clark University Press, pp. 124–139.

Darwin, C. (1872). *The Expression of the Emotions in Man and Animals*. London: John Murray.

Ekman, P. (1972). Universals and cultural differences in facial expressions of emotions *Nebraska Symposium on Motivation*, **19**, 207–283.

Ekman, P. (1984). Expression and the nature of emotion. In K. R. Scherer & P. Ekman (Eds), *Approaches to Emotion*. Hillsdale, NJ: Erlbaum.

Ekman, P., & Friesen, W. V. (1975). *Unmasking the Face*. Englewood Cliffs, NJ: Prentice-Hall.

Ekman, P., Friesen, W. V. & Ellsworth, P. C. (1972). *Emotion in the Human Face*. New York: Pergamon.

Ekman, P., Sorenson, E. R. & Friesen, W. V. (1969). Pan-cultural elements in facial displays of emotions. *Science*, **164**, 86–88.

Ellsworth, P. C. & Smith, C. A. (1988a). From appraisal to emotion: Differences among unpleasant feelings. *Motivation and Emotion*, **12**, 271–302.

Ellsworth, P. C. & Smith, C. A. (1988b). Shades of joy: Appraisals differentiating among positive emotions. *Emotion and Cognition*, **2**, 301–331.

Festinger, L. (1954). A theory of social comparison processes. *Human Relations*, **7**, 117–140.

Forgas, J. P., & Bower, G. H. (1987). Affect in social and personal judgments. In K. Fiedler & J. Forgas (Eds), *Affect, Cognition, and Social Behavior*. Toronto: Hogrefe International.

Frijda, N. H. (1986). *The Emotions*. Cambridge: Cambridge University Press.

Isen, A. (1984). Toward understanding the role of affect in cognition. In R. S. Wyer, Jr & T. K. Srull (Eds), *Handbook of Social Cognition*. Hillsdale, NJ: Erlbaum.

Izard, C. E. (1971). *The Face of Emotion*. New York: Appleton-Century-Crofts.

Izard, C. E. (1977) *Human Emotions*. New York: Plenum Press.

James, W. (1884). What is an emotion? *Mind*, **9**, 188–205.

James, W. (1890/1950). *The Principles of Psychology*, Vol. 2. New York: Dover Publications.

Johnson, E. J. & Tversky, A. (1983). Affect, generalization, and the perception of risk. *Journal of Personality and Social Psychology*, **45**, 20–31.

Keltner, D. & Ellsworth, P. C. (1990). Beyond simple pessimism: Effects of sadness and anger on social perception. Unpublished manuscript, University of Michigan.

Laird, J. D. (1974). Self-attribution of emotion: The effects of expressive behavior on the quality of emotional experience. *Journal of Personality and Social Psychology*, **29**, 475–486.

Landis, C. (1924). Studies of emotional reactions, II: General behavior and facial expression. *Journal of Comparative Psychology*, **4**, 447–509.

Lazarus, R. S. (1968). Emotions and adaptation: Conceptual and empirical relations. In W. J. Arnold (Ed.), *Nebraska Symposium on Motivation*. Lincoln: University of Nebraska Press, pp. 175–266.

Lazarus, R. S. (1982). Thoughts on the relations between emotion and cognition. *American Psychologist*, **37**, 1019–1024.

Lazarus, R. S., Kanner, A. D. & Folkman, S. (1980). Emotions: A cognitive–phenomenological analysis. In R. Plutchik & H. Kellerman (Eds), *Emotion: Theory, Research, and Experience*. New York: Academic Press 189–217.

Mandler, G. (1975) *Mind and Emotion*. New York: Wiley.

Mauro, R., Sato, K. & Tucker, J. (1990). A cross-cultural analysis of the cognitive dimensions of human emotion. Unpublished manuscript, University of Oregon.

Munn, N. L. (1940). The effect of knowledge of the situation upon judgment of emotion from facial expressions. *Journal of Abnormal and Social Psychology*, **35**, 324–338.

Murphy, S. T. (1990). The primacy of affect: Evidence and extension. Dissertation, University of Michigan Department of Psychology.

Ortony, A., Clore, G. L. & Collins, A. (1988). *The Cognitive Structure of Emotions*. Cambridge: Cambridge University Press.

Ortony, A. & Turner, T. J. (1990). What's basic about basic emotions? *Psychological Review*, **97**, 315–331.

Osgood, C. E. (1966). Dimensionality of the semantic space for communication via facial expressions. *Scandinavian Journal of Psychology*, **7**, 1–30.

Parkes, C. M. (1972). *Bereavement: Studies of Grief in Adult Life*. New York: International Universities Press.

Peterson, C. & Seligman, M. (1987). Explanatory style and illness. *Journal of Personality*, **55**, 237–265.

Plutchik, R. (1984). Emotions: A general psychoevolutionary theory. In K. R. Scherer & P. Ekman (Eds), *Approaches to Emotion*. Hillsdale, NJ: Erlbaum.

Roseman, I. (1984). Cognitive determinants of emotion: A structural theory. In P. Shaver (Ed.), *Review of Personality and Social Psychology. Vol. 5: Emotions, Relationships, and Health*. Beverley Hills: Sage, pp. 11–36.

Russell, J. A. (1980). A circumplex model of affect. *Journal of Personality and Social Psychology*, **39**, 1161–1178.

Schachter, S. & Singer, J. (1962). Cognitive, social and physiological determinants of emotional state. *Psychological Review*, **63**, 379–399.

Scherer, K. R. (1984). On the nature and function of emotions: A component process approach. In K. R. Scherer & P. Ekman (Eds), *Approaches to Emotion*. Hillsdale, NJ: Erlbaum, pp. 293–317.

Scherer, K. R. (1986). Vocal affect expression: A review and a model for future research. *Psychological Bulletin*, **99**, 143–165.

Scherer, K., Wallbott, H & Summerfield, A. (1986). *Experiencing Emotion: A Cross-Cultural Study*. New York: Cambridge University Press.

Schlosberg, H. (1954). Three dimensions of emotion. *Psychological Review*, **61**, 81–88.

Smith, C. A. (1989). Dimensions of appraisal and physiological response in emotion. *Journal of Personality and Social Psychology*, **56**, 339–353.

Smith, C. A. & Ellsworth, P. C. (1985). Patterns of cognitive appraisal in emotion. *Journal of Personality and Social Psychology*, **48**, 813–838.

Smith, C. A. & Ellsworth, P. C. (1987). Patterns of cognitive appraisal and emotional response related to taking an exam. *Journal of Personality and Social Psychology*, **52**, 475–488.

Stein, N. & Levine, L. L. (1989). Thinking about feelings: The development and organization of emotional knowledge. In R. E. Snow & M. Farr (Eds), *Aptitude, Learning, and Instruction: Cognition, Conation, and Affect*, Vol. 3. Hillsdale, NJ: Erlbaum, pp. 165–198.

Stein, N. & Levine, L. L. (1990). Making sense out of emotion: The representation and use of goal-structural knowledge. In N. L. Stein, B. Leventhal & T. Trabasso (Eds), *Psychological and Biological Approaches to Emotion*. Hillsdale, NJ: Erlbaum, pp. 45–73.

Tomkins, S. S. (1962). *Affect, Imagery, Consciousness: Vol. 1. The Positive Affects*. New York: Springer.

Tomkins, S. S. (1963). *Affect, Imagery, Consciousness: Vol. 2. The Negative Affects*. New York: Springer.

Tomkins, S. S. (1984). Affect theory. In K. R. Scherer & P. Ekman (Eds), *Approaches to Emotion*. Hillsdale, NJ: Erlbaum, pp. 163–196.

Tourangeau, R. & Ellsworth, P. C. (1979). The role of facial response in the experience of emotion. *Journal of Personality and Social Psychology*, **37**, 1519–1531.

Wiener, B. (1985). An attributional theory of achievement motivation and emotion. *Psychological Review*, **92**, 548–573.

Winton, W. M. (1986). The role of facial response in self-reports of emotion: A critique of Laird. *Journal of Personality and Social Psychology*, **50**, 808–812.

Woodworth, R. S. & Schlosberg, H. (1954). *Experimental Psychology* (rev. ed.). New York: Holt.

Wundt, W. (1907). *Outlines of Psychology*. Leipzig: Engelmann.
Young, P. T. (1943). *Emotion in Man and Animal*. New York: Wiley.
Zajonc, R. J. (1980). Thinking and feeling: Preferences need no inferences. *American Psychologist*, **35**, 151–175.
Zajonc, R. (1984). On the primacy of affect. *American Psychologist*, **39**, 117–123.

6 Identification of Emotions, Moods, and Personality via Diary Data

CAROL Z. MALATESTA-MAGAI
Long Island University, 1 University Plaza, Brooklyn, New York, NY 11291, USA

L. CLAYTON CULVER
New School for Social Research, 65 Fifth Avenue, New York, NY 10003, USA

A number of writers have noticed that emotions may be brief events or sustained over time and that the temporal aspects of feeling states bear a relation to social functioning and the organization of personality. When emotions are sustained beyond the original precipitating events they are described as "moods" (Ekman, 1984; Lewis & Michalson, 1983). When moods persist over longer periods of time and appear regularly in the repertoire, they are viewed as having significance for the personality. It is a common observation that individuals can be characterized by the dominance of a particular emotion. For example, an individual who is prone to display anger with great frequency is described as hostile, one prone to sadness as somber or depressed, one prone to contempt and disdain as supercilious. A number of terms have been used to describe this more enduring aspect of mood. Tomkins (1963) has described persisting moods as "monopolistic affect theories". Ekman (1984) refers to recurrent moods as personality traits. Malatesta (1990) uses the term "emotion biases". Lewis and Michalson (1983) refer to "enduring emotional states", Frijda (1986) to "habitual emotional attitudes". For these authors, as well as others, recurrent or enduring moods are viewed as systematic biases in personality.

It is clear that the temporal aspect of emotion is of central theoretical significance. Surprisingly, there has been little research documenting the temporal parameters of discrete emotions and their relation to social events or personality functioning (Frijda, 1986). In the present chapter we describe a method that can be employed to study emotions (fleeting or episodic events) and moods (sustained feeling states) in order to address a number of questions that are central to social and personality psychology, emotions theory, and clinical practice. First we briefly outline the areas of application and then specify the procedures for collecting and quantifying the relevant data.

APPLICATIONS IN THE FIELD OF EMOTIONS RESEARCH

There is now an extensive body of theory concerning the basic human emotions. Most emotions theorists specify a limited number of primary or fundamental

International Review of Studies on Emotion, Vol. 1. Edited by K. T. Strongman
©1991 John Wiley & Sons Ltd

emotions that are part of the basic human repertoire. Izard (1977), for example, has identified 10 primary emotions: joy, interest, surprise, anger, sadness, contempt, disgust, fear, guilt, and shame; each emotion is said to be characterized by a distinctive pattern of functional behavior, neurophysiology, expressive parameters, and phenomenology.⌐

Despite the advance in theory over the past several decades, there has been little documentation concerning the basic parameters of individual emotions with respect to their frequency, duration, and decay time (Frijda, 1986). The following questions have not yet been fully explored and would seem eminently researchable via the use of diary report. What is the typical decay function of various emotions? Do some emotions have a longer decay time than others? Does an "opponent process" (Solomon, 1980) effect operate with respect to emotions? If so, is this true of all emotions or only selected emotions? Are emotions experienced in relatively pure or blended form? Does this change over the life course? How do emotions covary? With respect to the latter, Izard (1972) has suggested a few prototypes of co-occurrence; but few data exist for the range of primary emotions.

APPLICATIONS IN THE FIELD OF SOCIAL PSYCHOLOGY

What are the social circumstances under which emotions tend to occur? Although certain investigators have described what appears to be a prototypical set of elicitors for the basic emotions (see Geppert & Heckhausen, in press), such lists tend to rely on interferences from evolutionary theory or are based on survey studies that ask informants to name common elicitors. A few enthnographic analyses exist but typically these do not address the entire range of primary emotions. There is very little in the way of sampling from ongoing experience.

We also know very little about the socialization of emotion. How do the behaviors of social agents affect feeling experiences of children and thus contribute to personality development and the ontogenesis of emotion traits? For example, Hoffman (1988) has suggested that discipline encounters between parents and children are repetitive, salient, emotionally charged events that conceivably have a profound impact on the character of a child's emotional development. Assumedly, power-assertive disciplinary techniques will leave a different emotional impact than will love-withdrawal techniques or induction techniques and result in different kinds of affective organization. Such differential organizations could be readily detected by the use of diary material.

APPLICATIONS IN THE FIELD OF PERSONALITY PSYCHOLOGY

Most affect theorists assume that emotions play a central role in the organization of personality (see Malatesta, 1990). This is true for many personality psychologists as well, although rarely are emotions given the explicit treatment found in the affect literature. In the context of personality tests, emotions are typically subsumed within one or two scales (Eysenck & Eysenck, 1985; McCrae & Costa, 1984) such as neuroticism or emotionality. Trait inventories exist for the individual emotions of anxiety (eg the Taylor Manifest Anxiety Scale) and hostility (eg the Cook Medley Hostility Scale derived from the MMPI); seldom is the entire range of emotions represented. An exception is Izard's (1972) Differential Emotions Scale, which yields state and trait ratings of 10 fundamental emotions based on ratings of 33 items. Ordinarily, however, this scale is administered to subjects at only one point in time.

The diary format introduced in the present report includes Izard's 10 affects and an intensity dimension but is designed to permit rapid and repeated sampling of experience so that fluctuations in affects and the covariance among affects can be tracked over time. Moreover, it includes other features that enhance its value for studying the relationship between situational events and fluctuations in mood states. As such, it is well suited to the evaluation of the prominence of various emotions within the personality with respect to other emotions and their permeability to social influence.

Of particular interest with respect to the foregoing is Silvan Tomkins' affect theory. Tomkins (1963) has hypothesized four different types of personality organization: (a) a monopolistic personality organization, in which a single emotion tends to dominate the affective life of the individual (as in the hostility of the type A behavior pattern); (b) an intrusion organization, in which a minor element in the general structure of personality intrudes and displaces a dominant affect under specific conditions (there may be a dominant affect and a "background" affect); (c) a competition type, where one emotion-based structural aspect of personality is in perpetual competition with others for the interpretation of information (as in the avoidant children of the attachment literature who appear to be organized around a fear/anger axis (Malatesta & Wilson, 1988); and (d) an integration type, where no single emotion is permitted to dominate the personality in a monopolistic way. Despite the great intuitive appeal of such a theory, there has been little research documenting the existence of such personality organizations.

APPLICATIONS IN THE FIELD OF CLINICAL PSYCHOLOGY

A diary of discrete emotions kept by a client can be a useful clinical adjunct. A client typically presents himself/herself to the therapist with some kind of "problems in living". The specifics are unknown, though some things can be assumed. The problems in living will almost assuredly involve emotion in an important way. Usually this emotion is referred to in general terms such as "anxiety" and is not specified beyond this gross level. The clinician will also usually be safe in guessing that the problem has continued for some time and involves some person–environment interaction. Finally, the clinician knows that the client will typically only be seen in the limited context of therapy, and information gathered here will be distorted by the demands of the context and the fallibility of memory.

A record of emotions experienced outside therapy in the day-to-day life of the client can be used to shed light on person–environment interactions and provide information as to the ways in which certain emotional patterns may be maintained over time through complex interactional sequences. The idea of an emotions diary is not new to clinical work. In rational–emotive therapy (Ellis, 1962; Walen, DiGiuseppe & Wessler, 1980) clients keep records which may include emotional states. Lewinsohn (1973) and others (Wolpe, 1973) in the behavioral tradition have had clients keep records of emotional states to keep track of improvement in emotions during treatment for depression.

While emotions diaries have been useful in past clinical work, this has at least two deficiencies. First, the work has been largely clinically derived and has therefore not taken into account current advances in the theory of emotions. In particular, most emotions diaries used in clinical work have been *ad hoc* to the client's immediate problem, such as depression (eg Burns, 1980), and have focused on a single dimension of emotion, such as sadness, or the positive versus negative valence of emotional state (McLean, Ogston & Grauer, 1973). This narrow emphasis on just one emotion or on basic hedonic tone is in sharp contrast to much contemporary emotions theory, which stresses a number of qualitatively different emotions and the interplay among them (Ekman & Oster, 1979; Izard, 1977). It is also contrary to clinical experience. The client experiences a rich emotional life far beyond the oversimplification of feeling good versus feeling bad (May & Yalom, 1984). Considering the client as merely more or less anxious or more or less depressed gets at the emotional life of the client at a gross, albeit practical level that leaves out too much that matters both within and outside the context of therapy. By introducing the broader range of discrete emotions hypothesized to be of significance by current psychological theory into the emotions diary, the clinician may add information useful in describing the richness of the client's emotional life.

In summary, the use of a diary-based, time-sampling method of ongoing emotional experiences has applicability to a wide domain of theoretical, research, and clinical interests. We now proceed to a description of the procedure for collecting and quantifying relevant data.

METHOD

Materials and procedure

A diary with individual pages corresponding to the number of time periods to be sampled is provided for the subject. At each sampling interval the subject indicates which of 10 primary emotions he/she is currently experiencing and with what degree of intensity. He/she then indicates how "typical" the time period sampled is. The diary entry can also include having the subject indicate what caused the emotion or emotions in question and the duration of the emotion. The 10 primary emotions rated are those identified by Izard *et al.* (1974) in their

Differential Emotions Scale (DES): happiness, surprise, sadness, interest, disgust, anger, guilt, shyness, fear, and contempt. These 10 emotion terms, as well as their everyday synonyms, are given the subject in a scaled format, in the following fashion:

Daily emotions diary

      Happy (joyful, glad):
      Intensity: low   high
                  1   2   3   4   5   6   7   8   9

      What do you believe caused this emotion? _____

Similar ratings follow for the other nine emotions. All 10 emotions are contained within a single diary page. At the very end of the page is a final question that asks the subject to rate (on a scale of 1–9) how typical the time just sampled is for the subject. The purpose of this rating is to yield a measure of the subject's insight into his or her emotional patterns. (A copy of the scale can be obtained from the authors.)

After several trials with the diary pages, subjects typically find that they can rate a whole diary page in 10–30 seconds. Therefore the procedure is not unduly taxing even if experience is sampled fairly often. The measure can be taken as frequently as dictated by the goals of the study or clinical need requires, and as tolerated by the subject.

Data analysis

Once all of the data have been collected, several summary statistics, graphs, and tables are used to characterize the emotional profile or changes in profile over time. The data are amenable to idiographic or nomothetic analysis. A $N=1$ case will be used to illustrate the usefulness of this methodology for theory, research, and clinical practice.

Detecting patterns

Two main types of patterns can be detected in the data with respect to particular emotions. Some emotions will be present continuously in the record and thus figure prominently in the individual's emotional experiences. Others will for the most part be absent and appear only episodically. For example, people, for the most part, do not feel disgusted for long periods of time, or at least one hopes that life is not that way. Such emotions occur only periodically and will appear as "spikes" in the record. These two patterns, continous and spiked, appear to correspond to the theoretical distinction between emotion traits and states (Ekman, 1984), dominant versus background affects (Malatesta, Fiore & Messina, 1987), and monopolistic versus intrusion affect theories (Tomkins, 1963), as described earlier.

Statistical approaches

Descriptive statistics

The pattern of each emotion, continuous or spiked, should be apparent via the standard battery of descriptive statistical methods. An emotion showing the continuous profile should conform to the following pattern. It should have a central tendency above zero, and all three measures of central tendency—mean, median, and mode—should generally agree as to where the central tendency is located. This is not to insist that all emotions are normally distributed (the relevant research has not yet been conducted), merely that one expects a single central tendency. The slope of the line between time points should be gentle, whether or not the slope is negative or positive. In contrast, an emotion showing the spiked profile should have measures of central tendency at about zero, a distribution that is not symmetrical about the mean (because the data can only vary above zero), and the slope of the line between most time points should be zero since most points will be rated as zero. When the emotion is greater than zero, one expects a highly positive slope followed by a highly negative slope as the emotion quickly rises from and quickly returns to zero.

Autocorrelation and time series analysis

In either pattern, continuous or spiked, there is an implicit assumption that the emotion has a natural decay function. Finding out just how long an emotion tends to last in any particular individual or group of individuals, its decay function, will require a slightly more complex analysis. The technique used is called autocorrelation and is commonly available from any statistical package that does time series analysis. The procedure involves Pearson correlations in which the paired points for the correlation are the emotion at one point and the emotion at some fixed time after the first point. The fixed jump in time is called a lag. Thus, a lag one autocorrelation involves pairs of a single emotion at: time 1, time 2; time 2, time 3; time 3, time 4; etc. A lag two involves: time 1, time 3; time 2, time 4; etc. In this way a set of correlations is computed. Each lagged correlation represents the degree that the data pairs vary from the mean together. A high positive lag one autocorrelation shows that the emotion tended to stay high after that time lag and suggests that the emotion tends to linger over time. The degree to which the autocorrelation stays large across increasing lags suggests a slower decay function for the emotion. A negative autocorrelation is less expected, but would suggest that the emotion at one point suppresses the emotion at some later point. This would be a kind of inhibition of the emotion by itself. In either case, the autocorrelations can be inspected to find out if they are greater than zero and, if so, how much time or lag is required before the autocorrelation returns to zero. One can even graph the autocorrelations with the magnitude of the correlation on the ordinate and the lag or time factor on the abscissa. This should make apparent how long it takes the emotion to decay. What a researcher or clinician considers as an autocorrelation greater than zero is a value judgment. Confidence intervals can be formed to help in the decision, but these require the standard assumptions of time series analysis which may not be met for many diaries. Problems may arise due to floor effects for the spiked emotions. These emotions should be considered carefully before trusting a moderate autocorrelation that suggests a pattern of decay. One expects that the spiked emotions should have a situation-specific rather than time-dependent pattern. Therefore, a large autocorrelation for a spiked emotion looks suspicious and should be inspected carefully. In general, one should only trust effects that are evident in the graph of the raw emotion across time rather than merely in summary statistics such as autocorrelation alone. Both techniques are valuable but should be used in conjunction with one another rather than independently.

Covariance

The third kind of quantitative data that may prove informative is the pattern of covariation across discrete emotions. Covariation between emotions can be most easily summarized by a correlation matrix computed between all possible pairs of emotions. Graphs can also be used to good advantage. A number of time series programs offer the opportunity to examine the profile of one emotion over time *vis à vis* the course of another or other emotions. By matching the abscissa between emotions on time, one can look at the tendency of one emotion to move with another at corresponding times. Again, neither technique should be used independently.

One may also wish to examine the pattern of correlations between the individual emotions and the subject's typicality ratings, as a measure of insight or self-awareness concerning emotions. A high positive correlation shows that the subject believes that the emotion is typical of his/her experiences. A large negative correlation shows that the subject believes that emotion is typically low for them. The sign of the correlation is due to the nature of the typicality rating, which is high for the more typical periods and low for less typical periods. To check how "insightful" the subject is one merely compares the information from the correlations with typicality and the data about the individual emotions. Was the emotion frequently present and therefore typical? If so, the correlation between that emotion and typicality should be at least moderately positive. If the emotion was generally infrequent for the total time considered or if the subject believes that the ratings were due to unusual circumstances, the correlation with typicality should be negative. One then checks to see if the individual emotion was either high or low across the total period sampled. A large mean and high relative frequency for values of the emotion greater than zero suggests that the emotion was typically high. A low mean and relative frequency for values of the emotion greater than zero suggests that the emotion was typically low. Close inspection of the relevant data is warranted.

In summary, there are four kinds of data that may be obtained through the co-examination of varous kinds of descriptive statistics applied to diary data: (a) an assessment of the individual or group's prevailing or dominant emotion (mood, personality trait); (b) an indication of how long the different emotions last (their respective decay functions); (c) a view as to how the various emotions covary; (d) an indication of the subject's level of insight. The preceding descriptors would yield information of importance to the personologist, affect theorist, and clinician. A social psychologist might be more interested in conducting a situation by person analysis, using the same descriptors but sampling and contrasting the profile of emotions in differing contexts.

AN EXTENDED ILLUSTRATIVE EXAMPLE

The foregoing can be illustrated by an extended single-subject analysis.

The data to be presented were collected as part of a semester project in a graduate-level psychology course. Although data were collected from several subjects, only one subject's data will be presented for illustrative purposes. The subject was a female, mid-thirties, who was not in psychotherapy. It was subsequently learned that the timing of the study coincided with the subject's being placed on a steroidal hormone treatment. At some point in the data collection she indicated this to the researchers. Inasmuch as she thought that the drug was affecting her mood states she wondered whether she should discontinue her participation in the study. She was told that she might continue or discontinue as she liked. The subject remained in the study for a month.

Twenty-seven days' worth of data form the corpus of our analysis. The subject rated her emotions on an hourly basis from 8.30 am until 8.30 pm during this period. In the following treatment we illustrate how various descriptive statistics can be used in conjunction with one another to make inferences about the emotional profile of an individual (or group) in terms of dominant or prevailing mood, decay function of various emotions, covariance of different emotions, and subject insight.

In the ensuing discussion, following Ekman (1984), we will distinguish between emotions as brief (episodic) events and moods as prevailing states. Some moods will seem more central in personality than others and so we make the following further distinction. We will refer to emotions that are both high in frequency and relative magnitude as dominant moods, and those that are high in frequency but relatively low in intensity as background moods. The term "affect" will be used as a more generic term to describe any emotional experience.

Table 6.1 displays the mean, median, mode, quartiles, SD, minimum, maximum, skewness, and slope for each of the 10 affects rated by the subject. Figure 6.1 provides a graphic representation of the means for each affect as they fluctuate on a daily basis. (A graph of the shyness/shame data is not given due to the presence of only one non-zero data point.) These data will serve as the starting point for our examination and discussion of the subject's affective profile.

Table 6.1. Descriptive statistics for emotions diary

Emotion	N of sample	Mean	Mode	First quartile	Median	Third quartile	Min.	Max.	SD	Skew
Interest	358	2.63	3.00	1.00	3.00	4.00	0.00	9.00	1.92	0.50
Happy	358	1.04	0.00	0.00	0.00	2.00	0.00	9.00	1.66	1.79
Surprise	358	0.09	0.00	0.00	0.00	0.00	0.00	7.00	0.54	7.93
Sad	358	1.15	0.00	0.00	0.00	2.00	0.00	8.00	1.52	1.51
Anger	358	0.10	0.00	0.00	0.00	0.00	0.00	3.00	0.47	4.86
Guilt	358	0.08	0.00	0.00	0.00	0.00	0.00	5.00	0.47	6.96
Contempt	358	0.04	0.00	0.00	0.00	0.00	0.00	3.00	0.30	7.31
Disgust	358	0.03	0.00	0.00	0.00	0.00	0.00	5.00	0.33	12.9
Fear	358	0.39	0.00	0.00	0.00	0.00	0.00	5.00	0.95	2.72
Shy	358	0.01	0.00	0.00	0.00	0.00	0.00	2.00	0.11	18.9

Moods

In order to explore which affects are more mood-like in nature and to distinguish between dominant and background moods, we need to examine the relative frequencies and intensity ratings of the various affects both overall and as they fluctuate over time. For this we need to evaluate whether particular affects show the spiked (episodic) or continuous (mood-like) pattern described above. It should be recalled that in the continuous pattern the affect's mean is greater than zero, whereas in the spiked pattern it is equal to zero.

In the present data there are three affects that clearly show the continuous pattern: interest, happiness, and sadness. Six affects show a clear spiked pattern: surprise, disgust, anger, guilt, shyness, and contempt. The remaining affect, fear, occupies a middle ground.

By inspection of Table 6.1 we can see that, of all the affects, interest has the highest mean rating for this subject, 2.63. The only other two affects that even approached the mean for interest were sadness at 1.15 and happiness at 1.04. One may infer then that the most dominant affect for the period studied was interest. However, it is also noted that sadness and happiness were present sufficiently frequently to be important for the subject. Inspection of the graphs of the affects across time (Figure 6.1) supports the above inference. Interest, sadness, and happiness were all frequently greater than zero and were often towards the upper range of the affect rating. All three affects had maximum values of eight or greater. Interest was the only affect out of all 10 that had a median greater than zero. The median for interest equaled three. This indicates that at least for 50% of the time periods sampled the subject was moderately or more than moderately interested.

Now note that there are still a greater number of intervals during which interest equals zero. For example, though interest is the dominant affect in that it was greater than zero quite frequently and had a higher mean than the other two,

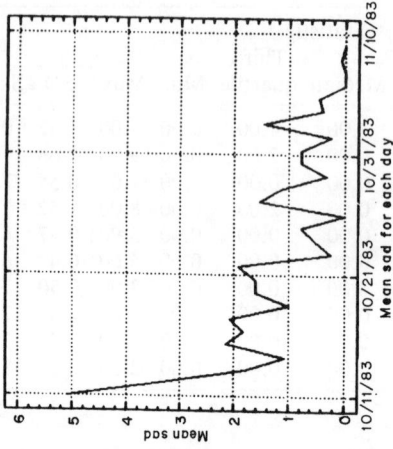

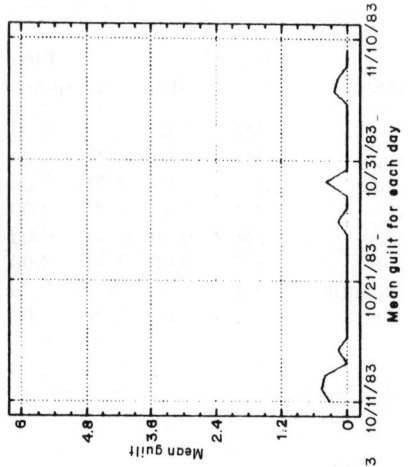

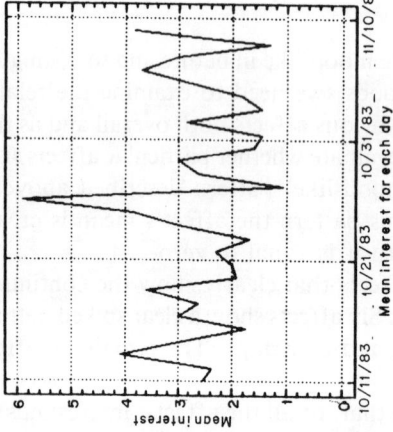

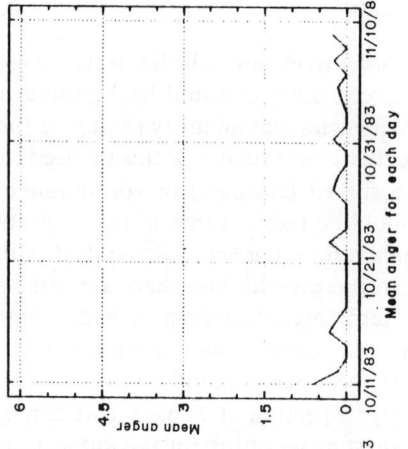

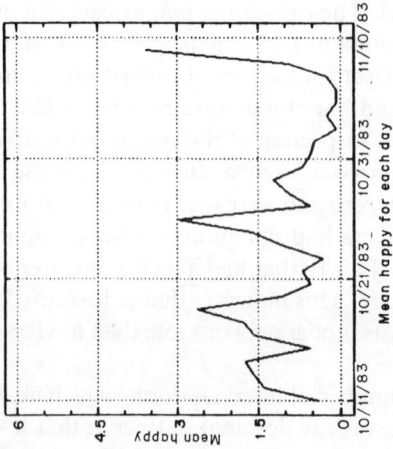

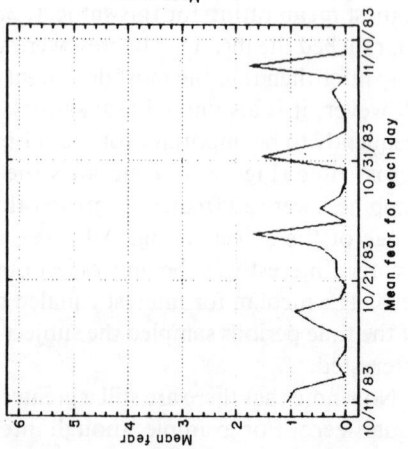

173

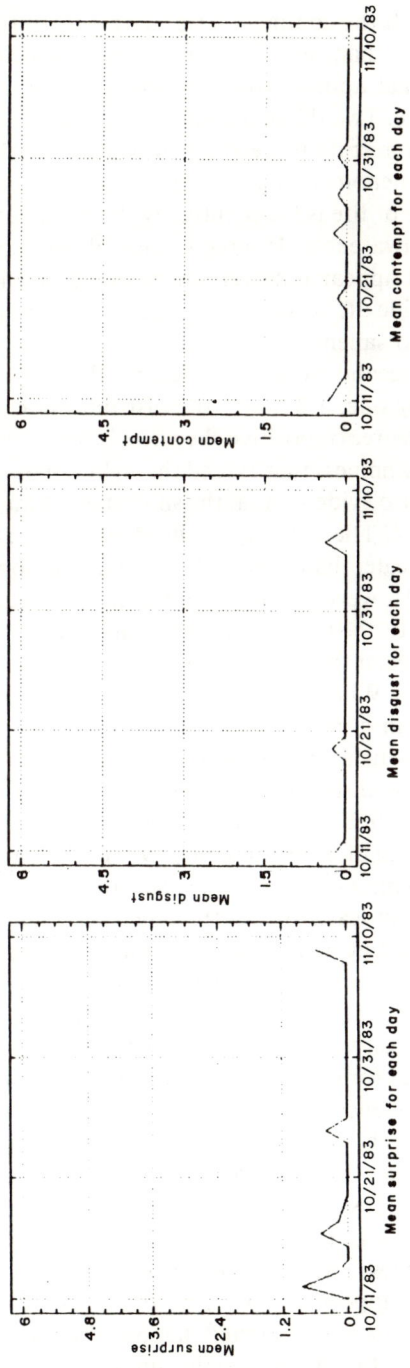

Figure 6.1. Time sequence plots for each of nine affects

interest equals zero 65% of the time if one restricts the data to 5.30 pm or earlier. It is only if one looks at the complete set of data—up until 8.30 pm—that one gets a median of greater than zero. These relative frequencies are to be expected from even an affect that appears to be mood-like. One is not aware of being interested all of the time. Two things are important to note here. First, the subject experienced life as interesting more frequently than anything else. Secondly, one should note the phenomenological importance of contrast. The moment-to-moment experience of life is highlighted by the reappearance of an emotion that has been out of awareness. If interest were always above zero, always in awareness, life would appear relatively more bland and less varied. It is the contrast of being outside of, versus being inside of, awareness that makes each affective experience so salient.

We turn now to the second mood-like affect for this subject—happiness. Here the mean is effectively one, 1.04, and the distribution of scores is positively skewed at 1.79. This degree of positive skewness is produced by the presence of very high ratings for happiness that extend the right tail of the distribution. The maximum of eight is also evidence that the subject was aware of a wide range of intensities of happiness. The upper quartile equaled 2.0, and 35% of the data points sampled were greater than zero. This percentage is approximately the same as that for interest. However, values tended to be higher for interest than happiness, as indicated by the fact that the upper quartile for interest was 4.0. Both emotions tend to be greater than zero and stay in the subject's awareness a great percentage of the time. Whether the two emotions tend to actually covary in time will be explored in a later section.

The third affect showing a continuous pattern in these data was sadness. Here the mean was 1.15. The distribution of scores was positively skewed at 1.51, and the maximum was 8.0. Even so, 51% of the data points were zero, indicating that the subject was aware of being sad about 49% of the time. The upper quartile was the same as for happy and was equivalent to about 2.0. It indicates that sadness was 2.0 or less at least 75% of the time. The point here is that sadness was experienced often, but when present it was most frequently experienced with a moderate degree of intensity. The moderate intensity of sadness is clearer if one compares it to the ratings for the most dominant emotion, interest. The upper quartile for interest was 4.0, ie two points higher than that for sadness, and 93.5% of the ratings for interest were less than 7.0. The higher upper quartile and lower relative frequency of ratings less than 7.0 for interest as compared with sadness suggests that the experience of sadness was frequent but more moderate in intensity than the most dominant emotion, interest. One might also note the similarity in intensity between sadness and happiness. For happiness, 83.9% of the data were less than or equaled 2.0, whereas 83.2% were less than or equaled 2.0 for sadness. At this gross level of inspection, the intensities of happiness and sadness appear similar. This similarity of intensity bears some further consideration. Is it to be expected that one should be sad about the same amount as one is happy? On the surface this similarity seems odd. It is doubtful that most people experience sadness about as frequently as happiness. It appears as though something were going on in the life of our subject to make her sad more frequently during the time period sampled. Inspection of the graph of sadness against day of the month suggests a situational (versus personality-based) explanation for the frequency of sadness. The graph has a clear negative slope, and by the end of the month has dropped from an intensity of 4–8 to an intensity of 1–2. Happiness, on the other hand, does not appear to have a slope, and stays at about the same frequency and intensity throughout the period sampled. Whatever the cause of the unusual intensity and frequency of sadness (and, by self-report, the steroidal hormones are implicated), the effect has dissipated by the end of the rating period.

If one is interested in personality description (for research or clinical purposes), it is this kind of oddity in the *pattern* of emotions that is especially provocative. In this particular case, we detected an anomaly via comparing and contrasting several different kinds of descriptive statistics. No single statistic was capable of capturing what was really going on in this individual's data. Suffice it to point out that a good rule of thumb is to start with general statistics such as means, modes, quartiles, skewness, and range, and proceed to examine more specific statistics such as percentiles to find out how the affects actually differ.

The spiked pattern

In general, affects that display a spiked profile will be easier to discuss than affects that show the continuous pattern. The relative infrequency of the spiked emotions indicates that there will simply be less variance to explain. Two issues should be considered in regard to the infrequency of the spiked emotions. The first concerns the salience or importance of the affects showing the spiked profile, and the second concerns how infrequent data may best be described statistically.

First, the infrequency of the experience of the spiked affects or episodic emotions should not lead one to the belief that they are unimportant. The fact that episodic emotions, by definition, are usually not in awareness admits conditions for very strong contrast effects. One can become somewhat inured to an emotion that is frequently inside awareness. This attenuation in the salience of an emotion is not likely to occur if the affect is rarely inside awareness. An infrequently occurring affect will be salient phenomenologically just as, on our graph, the spiked affect stands out against the longer periods in which the affect is absent. Thus, it may assume importance through contrast. It is also reasonable to assume that spikes of affect that have a higher intensity will be more important or salient. How one might best describe the spiked affect is the second issue.

The description of spiked affect engenders a statistical problem that is common to any dataset where the data are infrequent and are not normally distributed. The standard descriptive statistics that psychologists are familiar with, ie the mean, variance, and standard deviation, are adequate for describing data distributed normally. Other statistics become necessary when this is not the case.

Infrequent data such as those occurring in the case of the spiked pattern of affective event will typically fall into a distribution shape that is not that unfamiliar to psychologists—the "J" distribution. In the case of the spiked affects, the mode or upper point of the "J" will be at zero, reflecting the fact that the affect is not in awareness for the vast majority of time sampled. The lower end of the "J" represents those relatively infrequent periods when the affect is present. For the most part, the frequency of zeros is not informative beyond the fact that the emotion is out of awareness most of the time. The mean, mode, and median can be expected to be effectively zero and contain only the information that the emotion was generally out of awareness. On the other hand, the values greater than zero are informative. The intensity, frequency, and shape of spikes provide important data because of contrast effects and because one would like to make some kind of discrimination among spiked affects as to their relative importance.

In the present data, some of the affects that show a spiked pattern are so infrequent and so close to zero that there is little to say about them. For other emotions there is enough variance to indicate that the affect has importance due either to its relative frequency or to its intensity.

Disgust, shyness, and contempt are three affects that the subject almost never experienced. Across the time points sampled, disgust was experienced three times, shyness once, and contempt seven times. These affects appeared in roughly 2% or less of the periods sampled. It is possible that they were important at the period sampled, even very important. However, it is unlikely that these three affects play some vastly important role in the life of the subject. The relatively unimportant role these emotions play for the subject should not be taken as generalizable to all subjects. One can easily imagine an individual for whom contempt is the dominant posture towards the world, or for whom shyness is a consuming experience.

In the present data three other affects showed a spiked pattern—anger, surprise, and guilt. They were "on" or were greater than zero for 6% of the time or less. At this level of relative frequency it is difficult to say just what was important for the subject, but if one examines the frequency of the appearance of the emotion in the context of its intensity, a contrast may be argued for between the former and latter three emotions. If one uses the maximum as a measure of intensity of the affect, one finds the maxima five, two, three for disgust, shyness, and contempt respectively. The maxima for anger, surprise, and guilt were three, seven and five respectively. One might argue that shyness and contempt are both infrequent and low in intensity, and are thus of less importance. Why would disgust be unimportant, though, given its high maximum? Inspection of the data showed that disgust was greater than zero in only three of the times sampled and equaled six only once. The subject was intensely disgusted but it only happened once. It is hard to argue that an event so infrequent, albeit intense, has great importance in the subject's life. Compare the somewhat more frequent emotions of anger, surprise, and guilt to the three with so little variance. Anger does have a maximum of three, but it was greater than zero 16 times. This frequency is over twice the non-zero appearance of the most frequent affect in the first group. Contempt was greater than zero seven times. Without population parameters available it is impossible to make some probability estimate of the difference between anger and contempt. Nonetheless, a frequency of occurrence for one emotion that is over twice that for another suggests that a difference may exist. A similar argument can be made for the relative importance of surprise and guilt. Both emotions were greater than zero 11 times. Both emotions have high maxima. In the current data one would argue that anger, surprise, and guilt appear intensely enough and frequently enough to be of some importance in the life of the subject. Disgust, shyness, and contempt appear to be of lesser importance for reasons of lower intensity and infrequency. Infrequency should make one suspect the reliability of measurement, but it should not make one assume unimportance.

Most of the spiked emotions were very infrequent with the single exception of fear. Thus fear is somewhat unique and occupies a middle ground between the continuous affects that seem mood-like and the other spiked affects that appear related to environmental instigation. The other spiked emotions were low both in frequency and intensity. In contrast, fear is low but frequent. Of the several affects showing a spiked pattern, fear is the most frequent and only 79% of the data points equaled zero. Its maximum intensity was five, and its mode was zero. For the most part, when fear was experienced, it ranged between two and four. Fear was greater than four only seven times out of the 58 total of non-zero data points. The very frequency of the affect, though low in magnitude, indicates that something about the individual's personality or life circumstances makes her vulnerable to mild intrusions of anxiety. Thus, in the present subject's profile, interest and happiness are dominant moods, with fear or anxiety making occasional mild intrusions. Here, fear appears to be a "background affect" (Malatesta, Fiore & Messina, 1987), or "intrusion affect theory" (Tomkins, 1963).

Decay function of individual emotions

Once emotions are evoked, some dissipate fairly rapidly whereas others persist over time. This may be due to personality disposition or related to the natural decay function of different emotions. Different emotions might have different time courses due to their own distinctive phenomenological characteristics. For example, happiness may typically have a long decay function because the experience is pleasant and because individuals engage in activities to sustain positively toned experiences (Masters, in press). In the case of a negatively toned experience, the situation may be more variable depending on personality disposition. A particular individual may obsess about angry encounters and ignore occasions of anxiety, whereas another might spend more time ruminating about and sustaining an experience of contempt. Such ruminations may be at the service of deriving pleasure from negative experiences, as in the case of

178

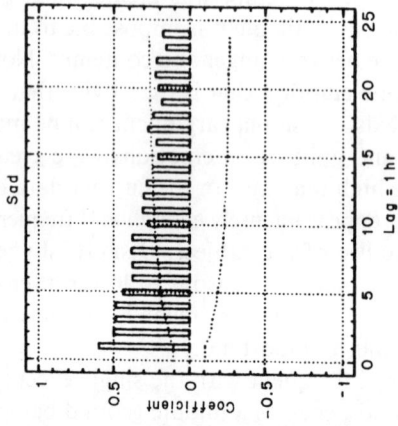

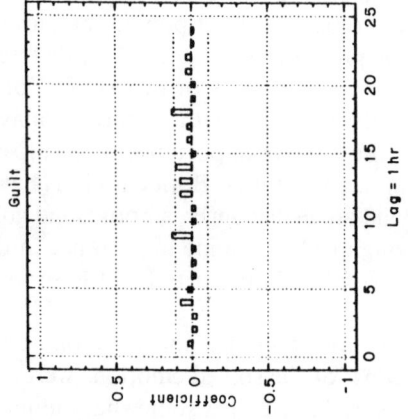

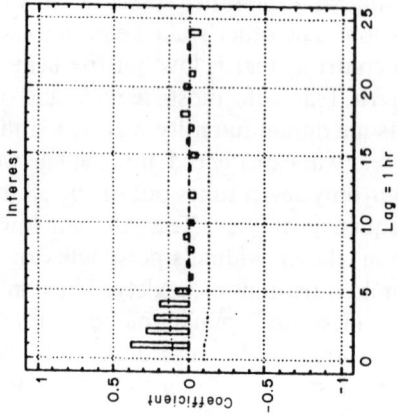

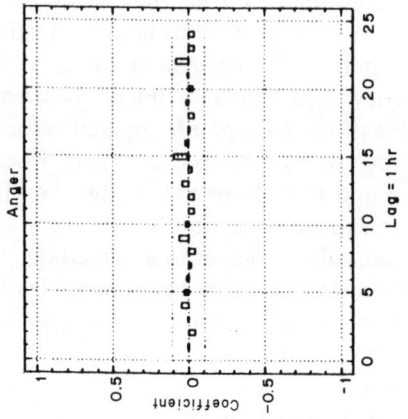

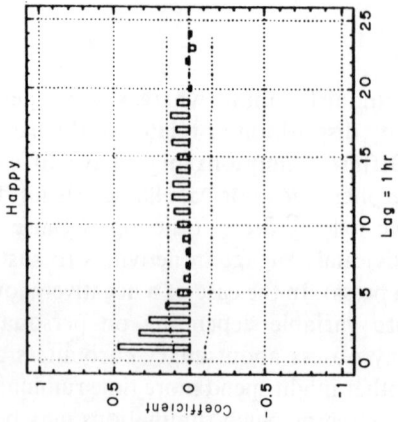

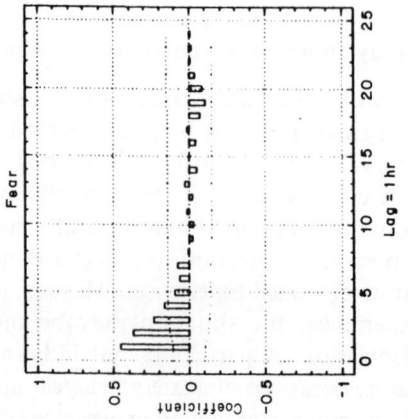

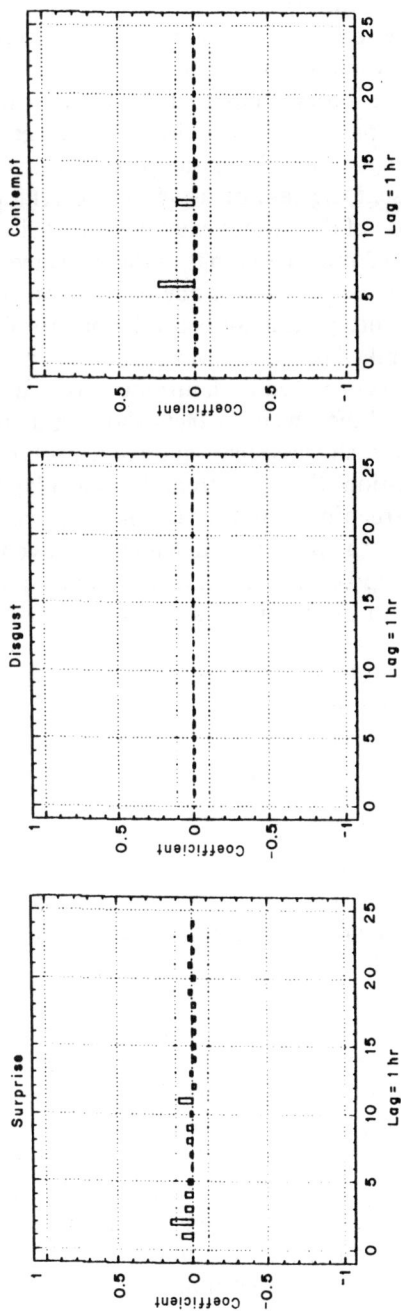

Figure 6.2. Estimated autocorrelations for each affect

negative–positive affect linkages acquired during development (Tomkins, 1963), or perhaps at the service of mastery.

Autocorrelation and time series analyses may be used to examine the decay function of emotions in individuals or in the general population. The principles of autocorrelation and time series analyses are similar; the latter is more appropriate for group data or in cases of individual subjects where the data are virtually without missing values. Since samples with missing data are so common, we chose to present the case of using autocorrelation descriptively to examine the decay function of the various emotions sampled without involving inferential statistics. Figure 6.2 provides graphs of the estimated autocorrelations for each affect (shyness/shame not shown due to one non-zero data point).

Part of the difficulty of interpreting autocorrelations for emotions derives from the definition of the spiked pattern. Given that an affect displays a spiked profile, one knows that it has occurred both infrequently and briefly, as in the case of the present data. Of the several affects showing a spiked profile (ie surprise, disgust, anger, guilt, shyness, fear, and contempt), only fear showed any evidence of autocorrelation. (In the current data each lag represented one hour.) Fear had an autocorrelation of 0.45 at lag one and was reduced to 0.23 by lag three. In other words, a spike of fear tended to have lingering effects three hours after the initial spike. Inspection of raw data supports the pattern of the autocorrelations. Most of the time fear has a rating of zero. However, when a spike appears, it tends to be followed by a rating that is greater than zero one or two times. Fear, although not extreme in the present subject, tended to linger in awareness three hours.

Of the remaining emotions to be discussed, happiness, sadness, and interest, two are positive and one negative. The lone negative emotion will be discussed first. Sadness may be likened to depressive affect in that clinical depression includes a low or sad mood as part of its clinical picture (Izard, 1972). It is important, though, not to equate a sad mood with clinical depression. One may be quite sad over a loss and still not be diagnosed as depressed. Autocorrelation alone is not sufficient information to differentiate normal sadness from clinical depression. Nonetheless, a lingering sadness is at least good evidence that emotion was important during the time period sampled or may be suggestive of a clinical depression. In the current data the autocorrelations are at maximum at lag one, $r = 0.60$, and decrease until about lag 15, $r = 0.21$. At around lag 15 the autocorrelations taper off but stay around 0.20. The minimum was 0.15. Inspection of the raw data supports the autocorrelations. Sadness tends to be greater than zero frequently and stay greater than zero for many hours. In many instances the sadness would continue across the break in the data for sleep, so that the subject reported sadness up until bedtime and again at the first hour the diary was recorded the next morning. It is important to recall earlier graphs showing that the pattern changed for the subject as the month progressed. In the early parts of the month the lag of 15 appears to be a good estimate of how long sadness lasted for our subject, but in the latter part ratings of sadness did not stay greater than zero for such a long time. In fact, during the latter part of the month sadness tends to linger only one or two hours at the most. This change suggests that the sadness is less a function of the personality than a response to some unique situation; in the present subject, incidental information obtained during the course of the study (that she had been placed on a steroidal hormone treatment) would seem to support this inference. Thus it is likely that the large autocorrelation noted above was due to a transient situation rather than related to something that was resident in the personality.

The contrast between autocorrelations that exhibit a pattern one might see as due to situational factors versus a more trait-like pattern can easily be seen by looking at the autocorrelations for the affect of interest. For this positive emotion the autocorrelations are at maximum for lag one, $r = 0.38$, and decrease to $r = 0.19$ by lag four. Interest tapered off more quickly than sadness, but the pattern stayed the same for the entire month sampled. The subject was as likely at the beginning of the month to stay interested for about four hours after an initial spike of interest as at the end of the month. This contrast was obvious from looking at the raw data of interest versus sadness.

The last affect to be discussed is happiness. Here the autocorrelations were at maximum for lag one, $r = 0.47$, and tapered off to 0.27 and 0.16 by lags three and four respectively. Again, the pattern of autocorrelations stayed the same across the month, suggesting a more trait-like emotion.

To summarize the section on autocorrelations, three comments are germane. First, one can expect that certain affects (often those displaying the spiked pattern) will exhibit little autocorrelation. This was true in the current data for surprise, disgust, anger, guilt, shyness, fear, and contempt. Secondly, one can get a rough idea of how long an affect tends to last for the subject by looking at the auto-correlations. Sadness tended to last for very long periods for our subject, around 15 hours, while both interest and happiness lasted around four hours. Thirdly, one should be sensitive to how consistent the autocorrelations are across the period sampled. If the pattern stays the same, one might infer that the pattern is more trait-like and will tend to remain the same. If the pattern changes, one might infer that there was a situational cause.

Covariance among emotions

It is, of course, possible for affects showing a spiked pattern to covary with another emotion. However, because the spiked pattern has, by definition, restricted variance, one expects that these affects will have fewer associations with other emotions. This held true for the current data. Table 6.2 displays the pattern of intercorrelations among the various affects. As indicated, those affects showing a spiked pattern either did not exhibit sample correlations greater than 0.20 or, if a correlation was greater than 0.20, the relationship was a spurious one based on a very few non-zero outliers. Inspection of the raw data did not reveal relationships involving affects showing a spiked pattern that were not picked up by

Table 6.2. Pattern of intercorrelations among emotions

	Happy	Surprise	Sad	Interest	Disgust	Anger	Guilt	Shy	Fear	Contempt	Typical
Happy	1.0000	0.2058	−0.2311	0.4393	−0.0222	−0.0531	−0.0823	0.0976	−0.0991	0.0042	0.5401
Surprise	0.2058	1.0000	0.0571	0.1306	−0.0158	0.0084	0.0133	0.2840	0.0207	0.1291	0.0776
Sad	−0.2311	0.0571	1.0000	−0.2793	0.0253	0.1341	0.1960	−0.0411	0.1086	0.1155	−0.3921
Interest	0.4393	0.1306	−0.2793	1.0000	−0.0524	−0.1493	−0.1393	0.0107	−0.1357	0.0081	0.7117
Disgust	−0.0222	−0.0158	0.0253	−0.0524	1.0000	−0.0188	−0.0149	−0.0048	0.0226	0.1593	0.0826
Anger	−0.0531	0.0084	0.1341	−0.1493	−0.0188	1.0000	0.0174	−0.0116	0.0208	0.1800	−0.0911
Guilt	−0.0823	0.0133	0.1960	−0.1393	−0.0149	0.0174	1.0000	−0.0092	−0.0281	−0.0242	−0.1195
Shy	0.0976	0.2840	−0.0411	0.0107	−0.0048	−0.0116	−0.0092	1.0000	−0.0217	−0.0077	−0.0083
Fear	−0.0991	0.0207	0.1086	−0.1357	0.0226	0.0208	−0.0281	−0.0217	1.0000	0.0678	−0.0637
Contempt	0.0042	0.1291	0.1155	0.0081	0.1593	0.1800	−0.0242	−0.0077	0.0678	1.0000	−0.0098
Typical	0.5401	0.0776	−0.3921	0.7117	0.0826	−0.0911	−0.1195	−0.0083	−0.0637	−0.0098	1.0000

the Pearson correlations. In other words, if an affect showing a spiked pattern changed from off to on or *vice versa*, the other affects did not tend to change with it. Not only do affects of the spiked variety tend to go on and off quickly by definition, but they also tend to do so alone. Those showing the spiked pattern tend to be independent of the other affects, at least in the present data. One would want to determine whether this is true in general or idiosyncratic to this individual.

For the affects showing the continuous profile, two patterns of covariation emerged. Happiness was correlated positively with interest, $r = 0.45$, and both happiness and interest were negatively related to sadness, $r = -0.23$ and $r = -0.28$, respectively. Here the data offer us nothing that is counterintuitive. Our subject tended to be happy and interested at the same time, and when happy and interested did not tend to be sad.

Assessment of insight

This last aspect may be of particular interest to those interested in clinical applications. Correlations between the typicality rating and both happiness, $r = 0.54$, and interest, $r = 0.71$, were both positive. The subject knew that these two emotions were frequent and thereby typical. There was also a negative correlation between typicality and sadness, $r = -0.39$. This is consistent with the inference drawn earlier that the lingering autocorrelation for sadness was situational. The subject viewed the degree of sadness as being unusual and rated typicality low when sadness was high. If the sadness were chronic and trait-like, the subject might not show the same degree of awareness, and discrepancies between the various measures taken would clearly identify this. Such discrepancies could be the focus of research or treatment issues in clinical practice.

DISCUSSION

This chapter presents a means of collecting, quantifying, and evaluating data relevant to emotion states. Such data are seen as having applicability to the fields of affect theory, social and personality psychology, and clinical research and practice.

An $N = 1$ sample was used to illustrate what the data might look like for any single subject. We demonstrated how four different kinds of information could be extracted from the data—the dominant or prevailing mood, decay function of various emotions, covariance of different emotions, and subject insight. Since the data evaluated were not group data, we have less to say about their meaning for affect theory. That is, we do not make the inference that these data can be generalized beyond the individual subject. It may be that any non-clinical sample would show a similar profile concerning the relative presence of positive and negative affect and the decay time and covariance among different emotions, but this remains a project for future research. Instead, for the present, all we are permitted is to make certain tentative statements about the subject from whom the data were drawn. Such single-subject analyses are particularly germane to personality and clinical issues as illustrated below.

In summarizing this subject's emotional profile we can begin to make inferences about personality, although, of course, we do so cautiously in light of the absence of cross-validation. Tentatively, at least, it would appear that if the month sampled were not an extraordinarily atypical sample of the subject's life, this is an individual whose affective engagement with life is primarily one of interest and happiness. Her dominant mood is interest, although there is a mild intrusion affect theory of fear. Sadness, which waned over time, appeared related to an atypical life circumstance. Other emotions such as anger, shyness, guilt, contempt, and disgust do not appear to form a prominent part of her personality. She appears to have good insight into her emotional life.

The dominance of positive affect in the subject's emotional profile and her level of insight is perhaps to be expected given that she is an actively engaged young woman who is not being seen for any kind of clinical problem. One can well imagine quite different profiles for various kinds of clinical disorder, the profiles undergoing change as a function of psychotherapy. The applications for clinical research and practice are self-evident.

With respect to personality theory it is interesting to note the presence of a mild intrusion theory (Tomkins, 1963) or background affect (Malatesta, Fiore & Messina, 1987) of fear in the present subject's data. It is our intuition that mild intrusion affect theories are typical of most normally functioning personalities, although the background affect may differ from one individual to another. We suspect that background affects are part of the idiosyncrasies of personality that make each individual unique and interesting. The phenomenon is worth exploring with an expanded sample size.

The present data also provided us with an example of the interaction between dispositional tendencies and environmental influences, permitting an examination of the kind of phenomena of interest to social psychologists. Although the subject experienced frequent, intense, and prolonged intervals of sadness during the first week of the study, the effect appeared to dissipate over time and was attributed to the waning influence of a pyschopharmacologic agent. We suspect that such patterns may obtain under a multitude of other circumstances, including the presence of certain challenging life events such as the illness of one's child or the prospect of retirement. Unlike other life event measures that assess general state or hedonic tone, for example degree of "stress" or "negative mood", the present method allows for a richer and more thoroughgoing examination of an individual's entire emotional response and the subtleties of the fluctuation of emotional states over time.

In concluding, it is worth mentioning an aspect of the diary method that was not explicitly treated in the present chapter, namely, the relationship between emotion and/or moods and environmental events and cognitive appraisals. Such data are potentially available. The diary format permits subjects to provide information as to events that precipitate or "cause" particular emotions as well as comment on their reactions. Of particular interest for the present case was the subject's comments to the experimenters regarding her experience of sadness during the earlier part of the study. She indicated that although the "feeling part" of her sadness was identical to other more naturally occurring occasions of sadness (ie low mood, psychomotor retardation, spells of weeping), in this instance the experience felt particularly strange because it was "contentless", ie had no location in life events or ruminations. Such an observation is of interest to the ongoing theoretical debate concerning the relation between emotion and cognition (Izard, Kagan & Zajonc, 1984) and would be worth exploring further.

REFERENCES

Beck, A. (1976). *Cognitive Therapy and the Emotional Disorders.* New York: International Universities Press.

Burns, D. (1980). *Feeling Good. The New Mood Therapy.* New York: Morrow.

Ekman, P. (1984). Expression and the nature of emotion. In K. Scherer & P. Ekman (Eds), *Approaches to Emotion.* Hillsdale, NJ: Erlbaum, pp. 329–343.

Ekman, P. & Oster, H. (1979). Facial expression of emotion. *Annual Review of Psychology*, **30**, 527–554.

Ellis, A. (1962). *Reason and Emotion in Psychotherapy.* New York: Lyle Stuart.

Eysenck, H. J. & Eysenck, M. W. (1985). *Personality and Individual Differences.* New York: Plenum.

Frijda, N. (1986). *The Emotions.* New York: Cambridge University Press.

Geppert, U. & Heckhausen, H. (in press). Ontogenese der emotionen. In K. R. Scherer (Ed.), *Enzyklopaedie der Psychologie*, Volume C/IV/3, *Psychologie der Emotion.* Toronto: Hogrefe-Verlag.

Hoffman, M. (1988). The socialization of emotion. Paper presented at the NICCHD Workshop on the Socialization of Emotion, Bethesda, MD.

Izard, C. E. (1972). *Patterns of Emotion: A New Analysis of Anxiety and Depression.* New York: Academic Press.

Izard, C. (1977). *Human Emotions.* New York: Plenum.

Izard, C., Dougherty, F., Bloxom, B. & Kotsch, W. (1974). The differential emotions scale: A method of measuring subjective experience of discrete emotions. Unpublished manuscript, Department of Psychology, Vanderbilt University.

Izard, C. E., Kagan, J. & Zajonc, R. B. (1984). *Emotions, Cognition, and Behavior.* New York: Cambridge University Press.

Lewinsohn, P. (1973). Clinical and theoretical aspects of depression. In K. Calhoun, H. Adams & K. Mitchell (Eds), *Innovative Treatment Methods of Psychopathology* New York: Wiley.

Lewis, M. & Michalson L. (1983). *Children's Emotions and Moods.* New York: Plenum.

Malatesta, C. Z. (1990). The role of emotions in the development and organization of personality. In R. A. Thompson (Ed.), *Socioemotional Development. Nebraska Symposium on Motivation*, Vol. 36. Lincoln: University of Nebraska Press.

Malatesta, C. Z., Fiore, M. & Messina, J. J. (1987). Affect, personality, and facial expressive characteristics of older people. *Psychology and Aging*, **2**, 64–69.

Malatesta, C. Z. & Wilson, A. (1988). Emotion/cognition interaction in personality development: A discrete emotions, functionalist analysis. *British Journal of Social Psychology*, **27**, 91–112.

Masters J. (in press). Strategies and mechanisms for the personal and social control of affect. In K. Dodge & J. Garber (Eds), *The Regulation and Disregulation of Affect.* New York: Cambridge University Press.

May, R. & Yalom, I. (1984). Existential psychotherapy. In R. J. Corsini (Ed.), *Current Psychotherapies*. Itasca, Illinois: Peacock.

McCrae, R. R. & Costa, P. T., Jr (1984) *Emerging Lives, Enduring Dispositions*. Boston, Mass: Little, Brown.

McLean, P., Ogston, K. & Grauer, L. (1973). Behavioral approach to the treatment of depression. *Journal of Behavior Therapy and Experimental Psychology*, **4**, 323–330.

Solomon, R. L. (1980). The opponent-process theory of acquired motivation: The costs of pleasure and the benefits of pain. *American Psychologist*, **35**, 691–713.

Tomkins, S. (1963). *Affect, Imagery, and Consciousness. Vol. II. The Negative Affects*. New York: Springer.

Walen, S., DiGiuseppe, R. & Wessler, R. (1980). *A Practitioner's Guide to Rational–Emotive Therapy*. New York: Oxford.

Wolpe, J. (1973). *The Practice of Behavior Therapy*. New York: Pergamon.

7 The Duration of Affective Phenomena or Emotions, Sentiments and Passions

NICO H. FRIJDA, BATJA MESQUITA,
JOEP SONNEMANS, STEPHANIE VAN GOOZEN
Department of Psychology, University of Amsterdam,
Weesperplein 8, NL-1018 XA Amsterdam, The Netherlands

What is the duration of emotions? How long do they last? Are they psychological events that take minutes, hours or days? The question may seem odd, since some emotions are short and others long. However, it becomes crucial when subjects are asked to recall instances of emotions. Many investigations use this approach to study emotions. In every such investigation a number of the reports describe emotions that go on for a long time. The reported instances show striking variations in duration and complexity. These varying durations and complexities raise the issue of the natural unit of analysis in the study of affective phenomena, and of the range of duration of these units.

The huge range of reported durations is indeed striking. In one of our studies (Sonnemans, 1990), subjects were asked to report on "an emotion they had had over the last week", and (among other things) to indicate its duration on a five-category scale. The distribution of responses is given in Table 7.1. The durations range over the available scale from five seconds to over one hour. Note that exactly half of the recalled instances were reported as having lasted for more than one hour. The same subjects were also asked to draw a graph on their PC screens of the course of their emotion over time, and to comment on different points on these graphs. Total durations were determined by subtracting the time of reported onset from that of return of the graphs to their baselines. These total durations range from under one minute to over one week. Their distribution is given in Table 7.2. The results accord with those of Scherer, Walbott and Summerfield (1986), who had their subjects recall an instance of fear, anger, joy and sadness and indicate "how long the feeling lasted". Durations ranged from less than five minutes (for fear) to several days (for sadness).

Recalled instances of emotions contain further striking, and in some respects puzzling, aspects. As can be seen from the data of Table 7.2, almost one quarter of the instances were said to have lasted for more than a day. In the Scherer *et al.* study this applied to 55% of the sadness instances and 29% of those of

International Review of Studies on Emotion, Vol. 1. Edited by K. T. Strongman
©1991 John Wiley & Sons Ltd

Table 7.1. Recalled durations of emotions

0–5 sec	0	0
5 sec–1 min	8	5
1–10 min	36	20
10 min–1 hr	48	25
More than one hour	93	50
Total	185	100

From Sonnemans, 1990

Table 7.2. Total durations in emotion graphs

Duration	Number	Percentage
< 1 min	5	3
1–10 min	16	8
10 min–1 hr	37	20
1–3 hr	38	20
3–6 hr	23	13
6–24 hr	22	12
1–3 days	25	14
3–7 days	15	6
> 1 week	4	2
Total	185	100

From Sonnemans, 1990

joy. Many of these emotions, then, were reported to have spanned interruptions due to sleep. The stories given illustrate this. A woman told about her anger after having been insulted, which lasted from when it happened in the evening till well into the next morning, after she woke up; a young girl related her sorrow when she began to live away from her parents and earlier surroundings, which she said lasted for about two months. We will give other examples later.

The second striking aspect of the self-reports is their complexity. Many of the reports mention more than one emotion, even when given as an instance of a particular emotion such as anger. Even then, they rarely report just that one emotion. Many reports of anger include moments of feeling hurt, hopelessness, and fear of retaliation, in addition to anger as such, and satisfaction about harm done to the opponent. Reports of grief often involve mention of despair, anger, and bewilderment, besides sorrow and distress; reports of jealousy involve distress, anger, and sheer anguish, besides what subjects label as pangs of jealousy. The girl who began to live by herself gave her story as an instance of sorrow, but it also contained feelings of loneliness and despair, and she further illustrated her sorrow by the joy felt when someone called her over the telephone. There often appears to exist a paradoxical relationship between an emotion and its description in terms of other emotions. It seems as if emotion labels are used by the subjects to characterize their emotion at some overall level, and also to characterize the constituents of that emotion or the responses which the overall emotion has induced. Such a paradoxical relationship appears to be the rule in the emotion reports. It has considerable practical implications for research. Many studies of emotion use reports on recalled emotion instances in the search for appraisals or other features characteristic of particular emotions (eg Frijda, Kuipers & Terschure, 1989; Shaver *et al.*, 1987; Smith & Ellsworth, 1985). The multiplicity of emotions within instances seriously obscures whatever correspondence between features and emotions exists.

One wonders, when faced with these complexities, about the appropriate units and levels of analysis in the description of emotion. Evidently, clarification is needed about the many aspects that enter into these spontaneous descriptions.

A third interesting feature of emotion reports is that they contain elements both with and without a definite time of occurrence. Some elements are of the form "X happened": "he insulted me", "I felt disgust" or "I was very angry". They refer to what Ryle (1949) called "occurrents". Other elements refer to conditions of indefinite duration, that have the form "X is..": "I consider him a dishonest person", "I have been angry with him ever since", "I am afraid of spiders", or "apartheid makes me furious". The majority of reports contain elements of both kinds. The emotion words as such can carry a temporally definite as well as indefinite meaning; they can refer to both occurrent and non-occurrent concepts. The non-occurrent statements or emotion word uses do not appear to refer to emotions but to what Ryle distinguished as "inclinations", which, according to Ryle, are dispositions rather than occurrents. It is not clear, though, what is the relationship between emotions and inclinations, nor, apart from their occurrence, what distinguishes them. Why are many occurrents and non-occurrents called by the same names? Why are they so often confused? Because that is indeed the case. Although current theorizing refuses to classify love and hate as emotions, for instance, the classical theories of emotion of Aristotle, Descartes and Spinoza did. This is still the common habit. "Love" and "hate" figure among the "prototypical" emotion words that naive subjects give rapidly and frequently when asked to write down all the emotion words they can think of. Fehr and Russell (1984) found love and hate to be among the 12 emotion words most frequently given in such a task by Canadian students. We found this held for "love" for Belgian, Dutch, English, Swiss and Italian students and sranang-speaking Surinam subjects, and for "hate" for English and Italian students (Mesquita & Fischer, 1990; Van Goozen & Frijda, in preparation).

In the present chapter, we analyze the various phenomena that are designated by emotion words but appear to differ in important respects. Collectively, we call these 'affective phenomena". We propose that affective phenomena can be usefully distinguished in terms of the following categories:

Emotions: activated or deactivated states of feeling, bearing upon a specified emotional object

Emotion episodes: states of emotional involvement with one emotional event

Sentiments: emotional dispositions with regard to a specified object
Passions: persistent goals for action of an emotional nature
Moods: more or less continuous feeling states, states of activation or
deactivation, or modes of appraisal, without specified object.

The concept of emotional object in these descriptions is to be taken in its philosophical sense: an emotional object is that person, thing or event that the emotion is about, in relation to which desires or aversions exist, and towards or away from which action is oriented. The term "bearing upon" is used to indicate the relationship, and fulfils the function of "intending" in the wider philosophical sense.

We will examine the structures of these different sorts of affective phenomena, the similarities that account for their being called by the same names, and their relationships. Our distinctions, and the terms we use, are not novel. We consider it useful, however, to give the various forms of affective phenomena renewed attention, and to analyze them in the light of current theorizing about emotions. Too often, we think, all affective phenomena of somewhat longer duration are assembled under the blanket heading of "mood" or the unilluminating ones of "attitude" or "personality". That practice hampers their closer analysis.

EMOTIONS

The word "emotion" is usually reserved for unpremeditated affective reactions to significant events; "an" emotion is a more or less unitary or elementary exemplar of such reactions. The problem is to define "an" emotion and, thus, the unit of analysis in describing emotions. The problem of defining "an" emotion is not straightforward. True enough, in their most prototypical form emotions are reactions with a fairly brisk onset that rise to a peak and subside thereafter. Their time course is given in Figure 7.1. However, although prototypical, this time course is not the only one, and it may not even be the most frequent. Emotions with true single peaks are probably relatively rare, and restricted to incidents such as when another car driver does not yield your right of way, or when a fierce-looking dog snaps at you. In the majority of instances in Sonnemans' (1990) study at least, the graphs do not show a single peak but a more or less extended plateau, with one or more peaks superimposed. Such is the course when the dog keeps barking at you, or when its unexpected bark has caused a real scare, or when the clash with the other driver has developed into a quarrel. It is probably the time course of any emotional incident of some true personal relevance. Sonnemans asked for reports on an intense emotion from the past year, in addition to emotions from the past week. When these reports are included in the data, 76 (34%) of the 222 graphs are found to show multiple peaks. An additional 48 (22%) subjects indicated the presence of multiple peaks in their checklists that computation on their graphs had not shown. Moreover, even the instances with single peaks do not all have the

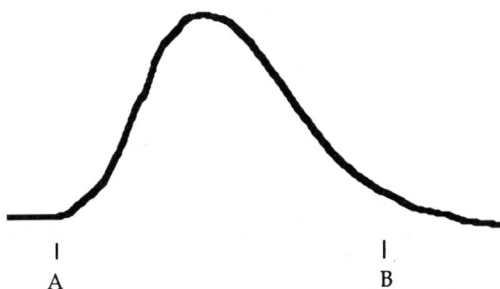

Figure 7.1. Single peak emotion

Figure 7.2. Common extended emotion

Table 7.3. Durations of single-peak emotions

<1 min	4
1–10 min	11
10 min–1 hr	21
1–3 hr	18
3–6 hr	8
6–24 h	12
1–3 days	11
3–7 days	5
>1 week	8
Total	98

From Sonnemans, 1990

character of Figure 7.1. Almost half of them lasted for three hours or more. Table 7.3 gives the distribution of the durations of single-peak responses, as read from the graphs.

The problem of defining the duration of "an" emotion is augmented because emotions are multicomponent phenomena (Scherer, 1984). Emotional reactions consist of several objective and subjective components that may each have different time courses. Tables 7.1 and 7.2, and the graphs, represent the course and duration of "felt overall intensity" (Frijda *et al.*, in press), which may not correspond to the individual components. We will therefore discuss these components and their temporal properties separately. The components will also serve as the framework for analyzing the other affective phenomena.

Expressive behavior

Spontaneous facial expressions are intrinsically linked to emotions as subjectively felt, in the sense of being dependable indications of the latter. The link between facial expression and felt emotion is often supposed to be virtually one-to-one; many discussions of emotion almost identify the two. Ekman (1984) suggested that duration as well as intensity of facial expression normally reflects that of emotional experience. The suggestion has been embraced by others (eg Oatley & Johnson-Laird, 1987).

How long do facial expressions last? Ekman (1984, p. 333) reports that ". . . the great majority of expressions of felt emotions last between ½ and 4 seconds, and those that are shorter or longer are mock or other kinds of false expressions". We do not know upon what data this conclusion is based. On the face of it, it seems implausible. It may apply to single expressive movements, as elicited by brief and unanticipated stimuli, or to the individual movements within a movement stream, such as the facial patterns that succeed one another in a person looking at a horrifying scene. However, most expressive movements are elements in continuous series of expressions of a similar type (say, frightened facial expressions, or laughs, or sobs) that occupy much longer periods of time. We are not familiar with time studies of such series. Incidental observation suggests, however, that ordinary bouts of laughter may last for up to 30 seconds; laughing fits when the subject is embarrassed or after vain efforts to suppress laughter may last for several minutes. Weeping bouts may well continue for 10 minutes or more.

Other types of expression, too, tend to occur in temporal series. Angry facial expressions follow one another for as long as the enraged harangues that they sometimes accompany, showing only variations in intensity over their course; such harangues again may last for 10 minutes or more. An angry scowl can be maintained during the entire period that a person is forced to listen to unjust or insulting talk, for instance. Expressions of sadness can persist for many hours when a person turns a grief-laden event over and over in her or his mind. Profound expressions of worry probably remain uninterrupted on the face of someone pacing up and down the corridor in front of the emergency ward in which a friend is undergoing surgery after an accident. In each of these cases it is unlikely that the same expression is maintained over the entire period. Expressions tend to wax and wane, and vary in their precise nature. However, they each remain items in a series, variations on a theme.

Moreover, many facial expressions can occur as elements in extended series of different expressions that are all, however, similar in meaning. Such series are composed of facial expressions, vocal behaviors, postures and locomotion patterns. The typical facial expression of fear (the facial expression consisting of Ekman & Friesen's (1975) facial action units 1, 2, 4, 5, 20 and 26) tends to be accompanied by movement arrest, head aversion, and a retreating movement of head and shoulders, or by movements towards a crouching posture (Frijda, 1956). All these items are similar in meaning, in that they can be understood as parts of a self-protective pattern. Similarly, in anger fierce facial expressions tend to accompany vigorous posture, a fierce tone of voice, and fierce words, all of which contribute to resisting or intimidating an offending agent. The total patterns may have quite different temporal characteristics from each of the composing elements.

Action readiness

Such sequences of behavior elements with a common meaning have led to the notion of action readiness. The various behavior elements in a pattern or series can all be understood as manifestations of a particular state of action readiness; that state of action readiness motivated them, may have preceded them, and can outlive them.

States of action readiness are meaningful inferences from the coherence in sequences of expressive behavior. By implication, states of action readiness may exist without being manifest in behavior, or they may be manifest only through minor signs such as voice inflections or absence of response where response would be expected. Whether they are manifest or not, they form important aspects of subjective emotional feeling. Self-reports mention them extensively: "I wished I were not there", "I could have killed him!", "I felt I wanted to disappear from view", "I wanted to do something but I didn't know what", "I felt like crying" are a few examples collected by Davitz (1969). Particular forms of action readiness are characteristic of particular emotions, such as the urge to self-protect for fear, the impulse to resist or hurt for anger, to draw near and inspect for curiosity, to get close to and possess for desire, to move, do things, dance, sing or shout for joy and elation. Correspondence between felt emotions and different forms of action readiness is generally close. Subjects systematically check the various states of action readiness as elements of their different emotions (Frijda, Kuipers & Terschure, 1989).

States of action readiness, as the concept is used here, have three properties that merit mention: their aim or intent (like self-protecting or resisting), their level and kind of activation, and what has been called their "control precedence". Control precedence defines what is meant by "action readiness". Emotional states of action readiness have, both subjectively and objectively, the characteristics of impulses or involuntary instigations that preempt action control and tend to override other actions and intrude upon the latter's execution. Control precedence applies not only to states of increased activation like anger, fear or desire, but also to diminished activation. Apathy in depression is not a matter of free choice but as imperative as the urge to fly at someone's throat in anger.

States of action readiness are manifestations of elementary emotion mechanisms. Certain states of action readiness can be considered to manifest central states of activation or deactivation of mechanisms for relational action ("action tendencies" for defense, approach, rejection, etc). In fact, emotional action tendencies are equivalent to what in ethology is called the activation of behavior systems; behavior systems are systems of behaviors with functionally equivalent aims that tend to co-occur under the same circumstances (Hinde, 1974). Other states of action readiness manifest the mechanisms of general behavioral activation and deactivation.

States of action readiness may emerge, wax and wane within a minute, but may also last for hours. An example of a state lasting for hours is taken from a self-report given by a subject as an instance of joy.

> Subject is a male Turkish immigrant, who succeeded in his examination as a driving instructor. "I was so happy, so happy. My joy just drowned out everything else. There was no room left to think anything else. As if the man who gave us our diplomas had done so from his own pocket. I thanked him a hundred times." Subject drinks something, then calls his mother. Then he goes home, is welcomed by his mother, who embraces him and tells him she had always thought he would pass, he had always succeeded in what he did. After dinner he goes into the coffee house to celebrate with his friends.

The joy, according to the subject, was manifest in feeling and the urge for expansive behavior. It continued at least until the end of his having had his drink, and probably without interruption until his celebration in the coffee house. The duration was from something like 11 am till 9 or 10 pm.

It is useful to make a distinction between strategic and tactical action readiness; the distinction was introduced by Lang (1988). Some felt or observable changes in readiness are strategic, in the sense that they serve the broad goals of furthering or countering interaction with the current situation. Other changes are tactical, in that they serve specific forms of furthering or countering interaction, such as flight or opposition. The difference is one of degree rather than kind but is useful for understanding the unspecific nature of some action readiness changes such as underlie the rather unspecific emotion labels like "excitement", "upset", or "dislike".

Whether strategic or tactical, action readiness with its feature of control precedence would seem to be the most distinctive feature of emotions generally. Arnold (1960) argued that the presence of some state of changed action readiness (including unreadiness) is what distinguishes emotions from mere affects. Many things are felt to be agreeable or disagreeable; hot chocolate can be felt to be delicious, and praise to be agreeable; stale beer and social rejection can be felt to be aversive. Yet, as long as they do not impel the subject to do something with or about them, or otherwise affect his or her tendencies to act, one would not say that they elicited an emotion. The presence of some change in action readiness with control precedence can be considered criterial for emotion.

It is plausible to infer from the self-reports that as long as a change in action readiness is felt, some emotion is felt; and as long as a particular form of action readiness is felt to be there, a particular emotion is felt to be there.

Appraisal

Much of what has been said about action readiness also applies to appraisal. Different emotional feelings consist to a large extent of different appraisals of the emotional event or its aftermath. Patterns of appraisal—of appraised valence, controllability, uncertainty, causal agency, and the like—form part of the major cues by which people identify their different emotions; emotional experiences derive their specificity, as feelings of anger, fear, jealousy, etc, to a large extent from the pattern of appraisal of the emotional object. The various emotion labels of a given language can be projected fairly precisely onto particular appraisal patterns (Ortony, Clore & Collins, 1988), and the way different emotions are labeled has been shown to correspond fairly closely to the occurrence of such patterns (Frijda, Kuipers & Terschure, 1989; Smith & Ellsworth, 1985).

In consequence, the duration of a particular emotion may be expected to correspond closely with the duration for which the event is appraised in a particular way. That duration may well be considerable. Many threats are felt as real, potentially uncontrollable events for as long as they are in force; the self-report of the driving instructor illustrated the continuous effective presence of a successful achievement appraisal. At the same time, does appraisal theory explain why emotions often change in the face of unchanging situations? Shifts in perception and cognitive elaboration may result in shifts in appraisal (Lazarus & Folkman, 1984). If in the confrontation with a frightening event attention shifts from the threat to the fact of its being caused by a responsible agent who might have avoided doing so, fear tends to give way to anger.

Appraisals are the product of processes in which perceived events are appraised as beneficial or harmful for the individual's concerns, and as whether or not they allow some way of dealing with the benefit or harm (Arnold, 1960; Frijda, 1986; Lazarus & Folkman, 1984; Ortony, Clore & Collins, 1988; Scherer, 1984). Whether or not an event is appraised as actually beneficial or harmful—that is, in an emotional way—probably depends upon factors like reality, urgency and proximity of the event, as sensed by the subject (Frijda, 1986; Ortony, Clore & Collins, 1988). Here again, appraisal persists for as long as attention is drawn to, or focused upon, the event being real, urgent and proximal.

Affect

The basic aspect of emotional feeling, the experience of pleasure or pain (Frijda, 1986), we will refer to as "affect" (in Frijda, 1986, affect was referred to as "feeling", between quotation marks). For many authors (eg Ortony, Clore &

Collins, 1988), positive or negative affect is the criterion for emotions; for almost all, it is one of the major criteria. The basic nature of affect follows from the fact that emotions and moods readily fall into the two classes pleasant and unpleasant, both when naive subjects classify terms (Russell, 1980) and upon analyses of co-occurrence in the use of emotion terms (Frijda, 1987). Affect, by definition, does not distinguish between different negative or positive emotions.

Affect may be considered a necessary component of emotions, but as we argued above, it is not a sufficient one. Affect of any strength would seem to be inextricably linked to action readiness at the strategic level, that is, to acceptance or rejection (Arnold, 1960; Frijda, Kuipers & Terschure, 1989). There exist, however, feelings that one would not classify as emotions, such as those evoked by mild sensory pleasure or displeasure, or by the thought of remote pleasant or unpleasant objects and circumstances, or as they occur in moods.

Physiological response

Physiological changes in response to emotional events form a relatively independent set of components of emotion. Actual physiological arousal is not a ubiquitous accompaniment of felt or manifest emotion. Correlations between physiological reactions ratings, behavioral assessments, and felt emotions tend to be low (Lader, 1975; Lang, 1977). Physiological responses have their own characteristic temporal properties, although few of these have been studied in great detail. Heart rate increases under acute prolonged stresses, for instance, tend to show steep peaks at the onset of stress that decrease to a little above baseline and a drop below baseline when stress is over. Different response systems manifest different latencies and decay times. For GSR, for instance, decay times to 50% of base level vary from one to 30 seconds (Edelberg, 1972). Physiological changes often extend in time beyond the emotional stimuli and beyond the emotional responses proper, due to restabilization processes. Inhibition of respiration during startle induces subsequent faster or deeper breathing to make up for the intake loss, for instance. Awareness of both may contribute to felt emotion duration.

The durations of felt bodily arousal and felt emotion are also relatively independent. Table 7.4 shows data from Sonnemans' (1990) study. On the whole, physiological arousal is felt only part of the time that the emotion is felt. In one quarter of the emotions, subjects reported no bodily arousal at all. Eleven per cent reported felt arousal for over one hour, which is considerably less than the 50% who, according to Table 7.1, reported emotion of that duration.

The pattern of felt bodily upset may contribute to the distinction between different emotions; certainly stable stereotypes concerning those patterns exist which perhaps derive from occasional actual experiences (Rimé, Philippot & Cisalmo, 1990).

Table 7.4. Durations of felt arousal

Duration	N	%
No bodily effects	48	26
0–5 sec	10	6
5 sec–1 min	30	16
1–10 min	49	26
10 min–1 hr	27	15
More than one hour	21	11

From Sonnemans, 1990

Goal formation and belief change

We mention two further components of emotional experience not frequently discussed in the emotion literature. One is closely tied to action readiness: the emergence of action goals. The other is closely tied to appraisal: temporary belief change. Both in a sense are consequences of emotions, in that they are motivated by current action readiness and appraisal respectively. Yet they form part of the emotion as experienced and may extend its felt duration.

First, action goals. States of action readiness, as we argued earlier, can be defined in terms of their aims, such as approach, self-protection, opposing interference, etc. Action readiness engenders expressive and other preprogrammed behaviors that in some way or other contribute to these aims. It may also, on occasion, engender explicit goals for achieving these aims by instrumental means. Fear may motivate the goal of seeking or constructing shelter, anger that of plotting revenge, and longing that of setting out to buy a railway ticket. Execution of these goals is not part of the emotions themselves but their emergence is. It complements the urges to protect, to oppose, to get closer, etc. Self-reports of emotions are often rich in mention of planned actions; the resulting actions are among the major grounds for attributing particular emotions to others in everyday interaction.

By "temporary belief changes" we mean the thoughts involving beliefs about persons or things that arise during emotions; "belief" here refers to a proposition with a truth value. These beliefs generalize aspects of the emotion appraisals or their implications. They extend these aspects over time, space or truth value. The beliefs are called temporary because they are part and parcel of the emotion: they last as long, and no longer, than the emotion does. When infatuated, people often think their loved one to be the most beautiful person in existence, and their feeling to be unprecedented and incapable of ending. When angry, people often feel that the antagonist not only has acted badly but is bad, and has always been, and that they will never get over the offense; they may be amazed to find such unexpected wickedness in that person. These beliefs, regardless of their own temporal content, may dissipate the very moment the emotion is over. They are the temporary beliefs that provide the reason for saying things one regrets when the emotion is gone, or that motivate one's apologetic smiles.

The unit of analysis

"An" emotion can be said to occur when a particular appraisal or state of action readiness occurs. Appraisal and action readiness are the major elements that constitute particular emotional feelings and that form the cues from which subjects take the names they give to their emotions. Signs of state action readiness, moreover provide a reasonably coherent segmentation of overt behavior. Most importantly, appraisal and action readiness provide an adequate level of analysis because they directly represent the basic emotion processes of transforming stimulus input into experience and of response mobilization. Therefore, the presence of a given kind of appraisal and/or given state of action readiness appears to define a meaningful unit of analysis. A particular emotion can be said to be present when a given state of appraisal and/or a given state of action readiness is present, and for as long as that is the case. When people report a succession of emotions, we suggest, they report a succession of appraisals and felt forms of action readiness.

Particular states of appraisal and action readiness may, as we argued, last for hours. Tables 7.1–7.3 suggest this, and although the durations include what we call "emotion episodes", they indicate the order of magnitude of the major segments of these episodes. The subjects' reports support this view; we gave some examples. It is no use, in our view, to label such more or less protracted responses and experiences as "moods" rather than emotions, since that would merely define the distinction between emotions and moods by these durations, and thus settle the duration issue by fiat. We come back to moods later.

Peripheral manifestations like facial expressions or physiological response appear to provide less satisfactory units of analysis. Contrary to the suggestions by Ekman (1984) and by Oatley and Johnson-Laird (1987), there are many reasons to reject the identification of expression duration and emotion duration. Facial expression is not an appropriate criterion for the presence of emotional experiences, or, rather, its absence is no good criticism for the absence of felt emotion. Facial expressions appear to be mere manifestations of the more basic processes of states of action readiness; these states may be present and felt without showing in expression, continue longer, and be common to varying expressions. Moreover, there is evidence that strong and articulate emotional experiences may occur without pronounced or specific facial expression, and not only because of control efforts. The deeper forms of happiness, for instance, probably do not translate themselves into laughter, or even smiling; who laughs or smiles during gratifying sexual union? The severest forms of distress and grief are generally held to be beyond tears; that, at least, has long been the opinion of writers on the subject. Montaigne (1580), for instance, quotes the often discussed story of king Psammetichus, who cried for an imprisoned servant but remained rigid upon news of his son having been killed. There is no evidence to contradict such observations. It is a plausible hypothesis that facial expressions are not just ubiquitous accompaniments to any emotional feeling but have a specific function in dealing with the environment. Most likely, they are parts of adaptive mechanisms that have determinants distinct from those of other emotion components. A similar argument can be advanced with respect to peripheral physiological responses. They form the "logistic support" of adaptive behavior but are, by that token, subservient to the mechanisms for that behavior.

It may be helpful, however, to make a distinction between acute emotions and emotions that are not acute, or less so. "Acute" is defined by the presence of distinctive expressive behavior, of pronounced physiological changes, or both. Acute emotions are the prototypical ones, which manifest the various emotion mechanisms to the full. Expressive behavior and distinct physiological changes, after all, are the most direct manifestations of action readiness. Were it not for expression control and expression thresholds, and the slow build-up of some emotions before they reach a stage of well-defined overt expression, the distinction might not be so meaningful. As things stand, it is more appropriate to distinguish between more or less acute phases within the occurrence of emotions. States of action readiness sometimes change in strength or nature, so as to lead to an acute phase; and after behavior terminates, the state of action readiness is not necessarily depleted. There is no information about the duration ranges of acute emotion phases.

The actual duration of emotion, of course, varies considerably. Little is known about its determinants. One possible determinant would be intensity. However, the correlation between felt emotion duration and self-report on other intensity parameters (including felt overall intensity) is weak (Frijda *et al.*, in press; Sonnemans, 1990). Another highly plausible determinant is the duration of the eliciting event and its aftermath. Many or most emotions are reactions to continuous distressing events, threats, adverse circumstances, confrontations with failure, companions and the presence of admirable objects.

Emotion durations seem to differ for different emotions. Some emotions typically take longer than others. Scherer, Walbott and Summerfield (1986), in their cross-cultural self-report study, found that fear rarely lasted longer than an hour (only 18% indicated a longer duration), and in a large number of cases less than five minutes. Anger lasted for more than a few minutes in the majority of cases, but rarely more than a few hours. Joy lasted for more than one hour in 78% of its instances; a similar figure applied to sadness. Fifty-five per cent of the instances of sadness lasted more than a day. The relative durations of several different emotions are consistent over various cultures (Scherer & Walbott, 1986). Several interpretations of these differences between emotions can be advanced, and are mentioned by Scherer *et al.* Different emotions may have different characteristic time courses. Also, the most common antecedent events of different emotions may have different durations. Sadness typically involves permanent loss of something significant, whereas fears can be caused by brief and passing events. Some emotions, like interest and fascination, by their very nature involve a tonic rather than phasic time course. They aim at the ongoing process of information uptake, as opposed to the end point aimed at in phasic emotions like fear or anger (Tan, in preparation).

There are indications that some emotions may have particular, built-in time courses, although most of the time these are obscured by regulation processes. The indications consist of the fact that some emotions, when intense, produce outbursts that develop regardless of the stimulus events and continue until spent. Dynamics of this sort are present in fits of laughter and weeping, and in outbursts of blind anger, panic and desire. Neither of these can be stopped at will by the subject once overt expression has been allowed to go beyond a certain point. Sometimes in blind anger, for instance, the actor in a frenzy continues stabbing his or her victim after the latter is motionless (Mergaree, 1966). Anger need not be very intense to have a sort of inertia: many people continue to shout and scold for some time after the antagonist has explained or apologized.

EMOTION EPISODES

More often than not, a particular event gives rise to a multiplicity of emotions that follow one another, blend into one another, and are felt by the subjects to constitute one emotion. An example is a story given as an experience of anxiety:

> Subject, female, had reasons to worry about the possibility of suffering from a serious infectious disease. She went for a medical test and had to come back two weeks later for the result. She felt worried and anxious. The day of the test result she felt nervous, tense and anxious, very afraid she had actually been infected, and reported feelings of despair. Tension mounted over the day. When entering the hospital she felt her heart pounding and her legs weak. Feelings peaked until the moment she was told that nothing was wrong, when tension fell abruptly. Her graph showed the gradual intensity increase, sharp peak and sharp drop.

A more complex example is the following story, given by a female subject as an instance of disgust:

> "One night I walked home from making a call in a phone booth. Two boys were leaning against a car, and one said to the other about me: 'tasty piece, that, I would like to get on top of her'. The remark almost made me vomit, it made me shiver. After coming home I became very, very angry, I felt it a dirty thing, so to humiliate someone I threw something across my room. That night I dreamt about girls carrying their sex parts in their face and I woke up feeling like one of those girls. . . . After an hour or so my feeling changed, though, I thought the boy who had made the remark just ridiculous, it made me laugh, and I felt above it. A little later I went out shopping, and that was the end of it." The intensity peak of the experience, as she drew it in her graph, was upon coming home. The laughter came after 10 hours, following which the graph went steeply down. Duration from beginning to end was 11 hours.

We will refer to such sequences as emotional episodes. We define an emotional episode as a continuous emotion sequence resulting from the more or less continuous impact of one given event or series of events. What subjects report in self-report studies like ours typically consists of emotional episodes.

There are two basic facts that the notion of emotional episode tries to catch. The first is the continuous felt emotional impact of one given event or of a series of events that are felt to constitute some sort of unity. The second is the multiplicity of emotions engendered by that one event or series of events. The subjects in our study could check a list of applicable emotion labels, regardless of the label they had given their self-report, and indicate the intensities on a 10-point scale. The girl whose report is given above checked anger 5, disgust 5, hatred 2. The multiplicity of emotions is further illustrated by the following example, given by the subject as an instance of anger:

> Subject, male, has helped his mother redesign her house; now he himself needs help in moving, mother has no time because she is busy and has her tennis appointments. Subject reports having been disappointed, quite sad, and angry. "I tried to explain to her her egoism and unreasonableness, but she didn't even hear me. When I still lived at home, quite disagreeable things happened, but this brings it to the boil. Now she really can go to hell, and I will never help her any more. When she didn't want to help me I was dumbfounded, and really didn't know what to say. I hated her."

The episode consists of the mother's initial refusal, her continuous refusal during the subject's explanations, and the latter's subsequent ruminations. Emotional arousal may be assumed to have been present during all that time. Several emotions were mentioned, and several others were also present. The subject checked the following emotions: anger 9, sadness 9, shame 9, contempt 8, disgust 10 (disappointment and frustration were not on the list).

Emotional episodes—episodes answering the above definition—do not necessarily contain a sequence of different emotions. One may properly apply the notion of emotional episode to the occurrence of just one emotion in different successive guises, when the subject successively focuses on different aspects of the emotional event and the emotion changes its coloring. The example of protracted joy, of the man who passed his examination as a driving instructor, may be classed as an emotional episode. Another example of an episode consisting of one kind of emotion varying over time was shown, last year, in the newsreels of people from Soweto, South Africa, watching on TV the release from prison of Nelson Mandela. Enraptured watching, smiling, sometimes bursting out in a shout of joy, sometimes covering the face with the hands, and looking up again with enraptured expression and tears on the cheeks, constituted one episode for each of the viewers. One might with justification call it one emotion, except when the focus is upon the changing admixtures, to the joy, the intent watching and being overcome.

The major point is that these episodes are not mere sequences or mixtures of individual emotions. The subjects treated each episode as one whole. They gave their stories as responses to the request for "an instance of . . ." fear, anger, sadness or joy, or whatever the precise request. The various emotions or the phases of one given emotion appear to hang together. What makes them hang together? What, if any, is the psychological property that constitutes an emotional episode, or calls for a psychological concept of that nature, over and beyond the presence of an event with continuous impact?

We think there are good reasons to consider episodes—certainly many episodes—as unitary psychological processes that on occasion may last for several days, or even longer. Experiences and responses during episodes vary in coherence; when coherent, however, at some level they form one response that waxes, gains one or more peaks or plateaus, and wanes gradually or abruptly. It is this response and its course of intensity over time that the subjects represent in their graphs. We will refer to such coherent response sequences as "emotion episodes", to distinguish them from sequences defined by continuous event impact only.

Coherence can occur at various levels. The basic unifying element that constitutes emotion episodes is the protracted transaction of the subject with a particular event or state of affairs. An emotion episode occurs when the subject tries to deal emotionally with that event or state of affairs. The episode begins when the event (or the first in a series of events) begins, and ends when the transaction is successfully completed or when the subject abandons acute efforts at meeting or solving it. Transactions involve a problem cycle presenting a continuous challenge. We use the word "transaction" in order to emphasize the elements of reciprocity between subject and event that are usually involved, as in a quarrel, a state of oppression, a developing love relationship, or cognitively even in a personal loss.

During transactions many things change, but one remains the same: the meaning of the event the transaction is about. Continuous over an episode is its core relational theme. This concept was recently introduced by Lazarus and Smith (1988). Different emotions, they say, correspond to different core relational themes; examples of such themes are threat, loss, offense, promise, and satisfaction. Each core relational theme implies a particular appraisal pattern of the kind described in the preceding section. It appears appropriate to slightly modify this view. A core relational theme implies a particular appraisal pattern, and hence emotion, to the extent that the subject takes full cognizance of the theme or is fully under its impact. That, however, is not always the case. Personal loss implies finality (the loss is forever) and uncontrollability (there is nothing one can do about it), but one may choose not to fully realize all the implications; however, the very effort is motivated by the loss. Threat leads to fear, but also to the joy that follows when the threat is over. Emotions switch according to the current appraisal—to anxiety or nervous preoccupation rather than sorrow in incompletely realized loss, and to joy in vanquished threat. Note that the joy after vanquished threat is a function of that threat; it is part of the transaction.

Further appraisal elements may remain constant over a transaction even when other elements vary. In the example of the insulted woman above, awareness of the insult remained constantly present and operative even when her feelings of being intruded upon varied and the wilfulness of the act was less focal in her thoughts. We will refer to the constant elements as "core appraisal". Core appraisal is a second element that may persist over episodes or parts of them, and contributes in constituting an emotion episode. This is particularly so because it is linked to further aspects. Affect is one of them. Forceful negative affect was continuously present in the subjects of both stories until the points of resolution in the events. Both represented episodes of misery until these points. Another enduring and uniting aspect in episodes is formed by action readiness at the strategic level. Action readiness for the situation at hand to continue to terminate, with its prominent property of control precedence, may persist throughout an episode. Many negative emotion episodes can be viewed as the occurrence of a forceful desire to terminate the situation which takes now this, now that shape, depending upon the fine grain of the events or their appraisal. Modes of activation may also persist for relatively long periods and over changes in specific emotions. The same excitement or active stance was present in the various emotions felt by the offended woman and the subject who was angry with his mother, as well as in the vivid, changing joy of the people watching Mandela's release. Activation and excitement as motivational concepts have their physiological counterparts, such as increased blood pressure or skin conductance level, and can likewise remain for extended periods.

What above all provides unity to an episode is the overall development of affect involvement. The various phases of involvement—rise, peaks, plateaux, decrease—are the life stages of one underlying process. Even when appraisal alters drastically and affect changes color, involvement provides coherence between the successive emotions; and when it dissipates, it is an overall process that does so. It is this overall process, above all that is represented in the graphs the subjects drew. The story of the woman at the beginning of this section again provides a clear illustration. Her disgust and anger mounted; the upset continued into her dream and emerged in the morning in her thoughts, and was rendered by a plateau of relatively high level in the graph. Her laughter initiated the decrease of that graph, and completed the excitement in the emotions of disgust and anger that went before. Similar considerations apply to the woman waiting for the outcome of her medical test. There is one curve over apprehension, expectancy, worry, anxiety, despair, and relief; it is, in fact, the characteristic curve of any suspense episode.

In a sense, then, an emotion episode constitutes "an emotion". It forms a unit not primarily because successive reactions occur to one event but because elementary, functional processes are manifest that possess continuity over time: affect involvement, strategic action readiness with control precedence. We have reserved the word "emotion" for particular states of fine-grained appraisal and of action readiness. There is justification, however, for the fact that many subjects do differently, and present episodes as instances of one given emotion like anger or joy. What is taken as "an emotion" depends upon the level of analysis, and both levels are meaningful as they each focus on elementary emotion processes.

This analysis solves the paradox of emotion labeling mentioned before. An episode is called by the emotion name corresponding to its core relational theme, while at the same time it manifests a sequence of different appraisals or states of action readiness. The states of action readiness and appraisal are in part called by the same, and in part by other, names. A given episode is called one of grief because personal loss exerts its continuing impact, and is felt to contain sorrow and anger as the loss is successively being suffered by and fought against and deep sadness when it is submitted to. Another given episode is called one of anger because one is the target of a blameworthy action, and it manifests the emotions of anger and joy as the protagonist is opposed and subsequently vanquished. An episode may be called one of jealousy because one feels the pain of being (or feeling) threatened by a third party in affections one considers oneself entitled to; and the painful event may generate the impulse of forcing change, which is anger, or submission to it, which is the state called suffering. The last example indicates the implications for the analysis of so-called complex emotions like jealousy or grief. They are not mixtures (Plutchik, 1980) or specifications (Johnson-Laird & Oatley, 1989) of hatred and sadness, but refer to the impact of given core relational themes that can give rise to various modes of action readiness and appraisal.

Episodes and emotions

Emotion episodes should not be considered as successions of individual emotions. The successive emotions are not independent and clearly separable responses. The structure of episodes can be described in several ways. One way is to say that in episodes the occurrence of individual emotions is facilitated by the current state of transactional engagement, affect involvement, strategic action readiness and activation. Another way is to say that affect involvement, etc, marshalls basic appraisal processes and action readiness dispositions which specify the moment-to-moment emotional state. Only under certain conditions do emotion mechanisms (that is, those of appraisal and action readiness) gain some independence in their development, which is when acute emotion phases emerge, the bouts of anger, sorrow, panic, that may occur within an episode.

The duration of emotional episodes

The present analysis also explains the other basic fact, that so many emotions are reported to have lasted for more than a day, and thus to have spanned interruptions. Table 7.2 shows that 22% of the subjects reported such long durations. Subjects indeed say that they were angry for days, or that they grieved for months, and that after sleep or diversion the emotion was felt to return or still be present. We do not think that these are figures of speech. The episode's continuity and coherence actually survive interruptions. The emotional event is found to be there upon awakening; the impact is still there. The self-report by the woman who overheard the insulting remark provided an illustration; so do almost all stories of grief upon loss. Also, aspects of action readiness may just remain continuously in force. The urgency of an emotion, its control precedence, by its very nature persists during interruptions in actual emotion manifestation. Control precedence was defined as readiness of a given action tendency to take control whenever circumstances permit, and which is in effect even while circumstances do not permit. The manifestations of action readiness may be overridden by sleep or diversion, but return to consciousness and actual operation thereafter. In the morning one finds oneself in the same hopeless apathy or restless agitation in which one went to bed. Often, in fact, action readiness is present even during sleep or diversion, in causing restless sleep and dreams or in forming a background of flatness or restlessness to the amusement caused by the diversion. Here, too, the woman's story illustrates the point.

The duration range of emotional episodes is difficult to judge. Its lower bound is arbitrary; the notion becomes meaningful whenever there is variation in appraisal or action readiness, and that may be a matter of minutes. For the upper bound, the only indication is what subjects report; that may not always refer to actual continuity. The longest duration mentioned in Sonnemans' study was two months. In a recent television interview, an ex-inmate of a German wartime torture center said "Fear? Yes, it felt like a strangling grip, day and night".

What determines the duration of episodes? The major factors, event importance and the duration of the emotion-eliciting event and its aftermath, have already been mentioned in the section on emotions. The aftermath is often the product of one's own emotional actions and the response of others. Anger persists when the antagonist fuels one's anger by her or his retorts, fear when the perpetrator of the threat takes advantage of one's fear by threatening more, and joy when one receives what one gives out. Often, the environment takes pains to keep emotional events alive by questions and conversation. An example of the influence of the action of others was present in the story of the Turkish driving instructor. His mother's welcome and admiration, and the celebration with his friends, extended the emotional episode. Another example is that of a male subject who made a 12-hour long holiday bus ride with his girl friend. Almost all the time she talked in a lively and friendly manner with another man. He was getting "all kinds of question marks in his head." Things got more difficult because his travelling companions started joking: "You better watch out."

There are other sources of episode extension. One is when the eliciting event sets up an unresolved intrapsychic or interpersonal conflict. Damage to one's self-esteem, and ambivalence towards a goal, may trigger off trains of deliberation and rumination each of which constitutes a further element in the episode. Impacts may come from the enduring conflict rather than from the precipitating event. Another source is the reinforcement provided by one's emotions, such as sympathy or subservience. Conversely, many factors contribute to the termination of transactions, and thus episodes; the factors have to do with adaptation, shifts in interest, emotion control and emotional processing (Rachman, 1980), and relinquishing of fruitless efforts. Discussion of these factors is far beyond the scope of this chapter.

SENTIMENTS

In the self-reports of emotion instances, emotion words were often used in a temporally indefinite sense. The self-reports also contain statements that, without mentioning emotion words, refer to emotional content of indefinite duration. We give two examples. The first report was provided as an instance of "when somebody has harmed you."

> S, an adult woman, had a relationship with a man who also had other relationships. On a particular occasion the man turned up with a venereal disease and suggested she was to blame. While dining out, the friend had said, "Gee, it's very unpleasant, but I probably have a venereal disease, and it's likely that it comes from you." S couldn't say a word, but thought: "I can't be hearing properly" and "One goes out for dinner for fun." Then she became amazed, disgusted, angry and excited. She went home and never told it to anybody until then. "The anger never went away." When people asked why they never saw her with her friend, she answered: "You'll never see me with him any more. I don't want to see him because he's a dishonest person." When asked how long it had continued to bother her, she answered: "Well, it remains there to bother you. It keeps pursuing you, more or less. Of course you meet people you like, but you have become distrustful." The event had happened six years ago, but she still felt angry.

In this story our concern is with the sentence "the anger never went away", and what comes after that: "he's a dishonest person", "it remains there to bother you. It keeps pursuing you, more or less." Dispositional states are expressed not merely in the emotion word but also in the perceptions that follow. The second story is by a male subject, about 25 years old, asked to recall an instance of anger.

> A newcomer in the band the subject plays in has spread the tale that S maligned the band and some of the individuals to others. The band believes it and is mad at S. S quits the band in anger. He feels "very very bad that my friends blindly

believed what was said about me." Later, the friends changed their view, but "that was too late. By then I had chilled altogether. Later on we did greet one another upon meeting, but that was all." "It completely went against my sense of friendship. I felt it could happen again at any moment. The relationship never became as it was before." S also talked to the newcomer. He denied everything, and said the group had misunderstood him. S shouted at him in anger, called him a moron, and told him that "as far as I'm concerned, I'm through with you." "I never saw him since."

The excerpt first describes a proper emotion then refers to an emotion episode in which he felt "very very bad". Emotion and episode then extend into a frozen relationship ("by then I had chilled altogether") and a feeling towards the newcomer that makes him shout in anger when the latter tries to apologize.

The various words and statements refer to something relatively enduring, the existence of an object (band, newcomer, friend) with a negative emotional value that came from having harmed the subject. That value caused emotions under particular circumstances: when the newcomer made excuses, or when people ask the woman why they never see her with her friend. It also led to negative feelings towards the objects whenever these were met or mentioned in conversation and to the rupture of the relationships. And it led to thoughts like "I felt it could happen again at any moment" and "he is a dishonest person". The disposition which involves this emotional value, the power to elicit emotions, affect, and avoidance behavior, the broken relationship, and the mentioned beliefs appear to persist indefinitely.

The structure of sentiments

We call these dispositions "sentiments", as they were called in the somewhat older literature, by Shand (1896), Murray (Murray & Morgan, 1945), and Arnold (1960) among others.[1] A sentiment we define as a disposition to respond emotionally to a certain object. The construct serves to explain the lasting effect of emotional events or episodes; it serves more generally to explain the emergence of emotions that are not warranted by an eliciting event *per se*. A sentiment is a disposition that turns innocuous encounters into emotionally laden ones. Affections and aversions towards individuals or groups are sentiments, and so are emotionally charged attitudes towards issues and political entities. Grudges, too, fall into this category, as do "preventive" jealousy (Van Sommers, 1988), which suspiciously watches a partner's every movement, and phobias, in which apparently innocuous objects like spiders or crowds elicit strong emotion.

Dispositions to respond emotionally to a particular object do not stand alone as aftereffects of emotions. They appear to be linked to other psychological phenomena that in some sense extend the emotional transaction in time. Sentiments might be defined in terms of any of these other phenomena or, alternatively, they can be conceptualized as dispositions with multiple components. We list the following.

1. Appraisal of the object in emotional terms. Emotions often result in attribution of emotionally relevant properties to the object, such as its threatening, despicable, infuriating, endearing or gratifying nature. It is conceived as possessing emotion-arousing potential even when not actually arousing emotions.

2. Affect arousal. The object is liked or disliked, accepted or rejected. This does not merely mean that emotions arise when the object is actually encountered, but that like and dislike are felt when the object is merely thought of. When speaking about the object of their sentiments, people experience feelings about it. They tend to go into the motions of mock affect. They speak of it in tones of rapture or revulsion, and mimic the corresponding facial expressions and gestures, like "Oh that man, he's horrible!!". Like and dislike refer to networks of feelings, evaluations, and a readiness or unreadiness to engage in interaction with the object. There are also cognitive aspects. Properties the values of which are consonant with the affect are accepted with less reserve than properties with a value opposite to the affect and they are more readily thought of, phenomena well known from attitude and prejudice research (Fiske & Taylor, 1984).

3. Motivation for actions to seek or avoid emotional confrontations, or to affect the sentiment object. A subject, a woman whose friend had betrayed a secret she had confided to her, called that friend over the telephone to abuse her; she kept having thoughts of doing so for several months after the event. She ignored the friend when she ran into her, and said when telling her story: "For me, she doesn't exist any longer!". Phobics generally try to prevent encounters with the phobic objects, and actually may do so to the extent that they may even be free of anxiety. Persons who feel their environment is unsafe avoid places they consider risky or restrict their freedom of movement in more general ways, which again may result in little actual fear. The result is the well-known discrepancy between professed fear sentiments and actual experiences of fearful incidents and victimship (of rape or other crimes; Van der Wurff, in preparation). Love, of course, leads to seeking the company of the object. Generally, sentiments are dispositions that motivate actions to decrease or promote the occurrence of relevant emotional events. These actions include not only proximity seeking and avoidance, but also instrumental actions such as helping or harming the relevant objects or more indirect ones like voting for parties that might effectuate the helping or harming. The evaluation of the object, in short, affects the conduct of life.

4. Existence of associational webs. Sentiments not only turn particular events into emotional encounters but charge many other events with meaning and seriousness (Allport, 1954). Sentiments spread their effects. The apology offered by the newcomer, in the musician's story, is an example: instead of an apology, it is felt as an additional offense. The spreading is also in time, as illustrated by the quotes from both preceding stories, "I felt it could happen again any moment" and "You have become distrustful". The following story illustrates the emergence of an associational web following emotional incidents.

Subject, female, about 60 years old, asked for an instance of an experience of shame, describes a situation that lasted during the whole of her marriage. The husband was an alcoholic. Each day, when shopping at the local market, she repeatedly felt ashamed on seeing her husband drinking in the bar, even early in the morning. She indicated that the feeling lasted "for years". Now he had died she still on occasion feels that shame when thinking of him or when shopping at the market.

5. Spontaneous emergence of thoughts about the object or events involving it. "It remains there to bother you", said the ill-used woman, "it keeps pursuing you, more or less." Affections often give rise to recurrent thoughts about the object and its well-being. The aftereffects of psychological traumas, which can be considered sentiments, include flashbacks of the traumatic event, sometimes triggered by fairly peripheral cues (Horowitz, 1976).

6. Presence of explicit beliefs. Most sentiments, like most attitudes, involve conscious beliefs about the nature and properties of the object that may or may not correspond to the reasons for the sentiment. The beliefs primarily concern the properties underlying the appraisal of the object.

The effect of these various phenomena is the prolongation of emotions into feelings, thoughts and motives that in several ways resemble them. The phenomena affect the conduct of life. Because of them, it is not quite appropriate to speak of sentiments as dispositions. Sentiments are manifest in several kinds of occurrents. One is aware of one's sentiments not merely through emotion, but also in conscious affect and thought.

Beliefs

Beliefs form an aspect of most sentiments. They merit some detailed attention because it is the fixity of these beliefs that gives sentiments their temporal stability.

The subjects' reports abound in expressions of altered beliefs triggered by the emotional incidents. An example occurred in the story of the woman whose man friend had a venereal disease and blamed her for it: "he is a dishonest person". The woman whose friend betrayed her secret said: "I want to have no dealings with someone like that". A man whose woman friend married another without announcing it to him in advance said: "one must not take every friendship seriously". We give some more examples below. A female subject, immigrant to the country, when asked to recall an instance of having done something that "gave you the feeling you wanted to disappear from view" produced the following story.

There is something that often drives me restless. I feel ashamed about it and it makes me sad. My husband's family only write to us when they need money. When they don't need money they may not write to us for years. One day we received a letter from my brother-in-law; by coincidence I picked it up and opened it. As usual they asked us to transfer money. I did not show the letter to my husband because it made me mad. Later I received a telegram that I did not show either. We therefore sent no money. Afterwards I found out that they really were hard put. When I received the telegram, I did not really believe it. But because I did not send money and kept my mouth shut, last year a son of theirs died. Now I blame myself and die from shame, I keep wondering if it would not have happened if we had sent money then. I blame myself and it is beyond description how ashamed I feel . . . I talked about it to nobody, not with my husband and children, let alone strangers. If I told them, nothing would be left of me in their eyes. I am deeply ashamed now, I tell you. I am a grown-up woman, I should not have done that. What I did does not correspond to me.

Another subject is a male student. He had been cheated by a female friend. While living with him, she had asked him to accommodate a friend of hers in his place, but after having moved out refused to help find a place for the friend when the subject himself had to move. He says: "That really is the limit. Such a thing I will never forgive. I'm very, very angry".

"What I did does not correspond to me" in the first story and "Such a thing I will never forgive" in the second involve beliefs. Although both are phrased in an episodic fashion, as incidents, their meanings are lexical.[2] They pertain to how the subject feels herself to be in the first, and how the friend is felt to be in the second. What makes these belief changes so interesting is that they involve a cognitive transformation, from the perception of an episode into the assertion of a truth. This cognitive transformation entails emotional transformations that are characteristic for many, if not all, sentiments.

We briefly discussed temporary belief changes in connection with emotions. Belief changes were defined as changes in beliefs about the nature of things. By this definition, their cognitive content is of a higher degree of generalization than that of the emotions that may be at their origin. Emotions are elicited by specific events appraised as such, and their cognitive content need involve no more than that. An insult is a blameworthy event, a frustration a disagreeable one, but that is all there is to it. Belief changes, however, lift such events onto a higher plane. An insult comes to be perceived as the act of a blameworthy person, a frustration is felt as an instance of how badly life treats you, and a friendly act is seen as the act of a sweet person. Acts lead to trait attributions, and the attributed entity rather than the event becomes the emotion's object. All this, as we indicated before, can happen in emotions and generate a temporary belief. When the attributions become fixed and survive the emotion, a sentiment is formed.

The transformation of the appraisal of an event into a belief about an object or person has an important consequence. Relations to objects or persons are different from those to events. The properties of persons are relevant to other concerns than the properties of the events in which persons were involved. By transforming event appraisal into a belief about a person, different concerns are drawn into the game. The emotional meaning of the object of a sentiment often rests upon other concerns than the emotional meaning of the event from which the sentiment took its birth. A subject started to hate her best friend who betrayed a secret, because "she was like a sister for me, and sisters don't do such things". The situation is clearest when the beliefs involve ideological transformation. An offense against one's feelings of self-esteem becomes an offense against the concern for decency in human interaction, or something of that sort. But the same concern shift can also be made without ideological transformation. When anger is transformed into hate and the perception of an evil deed into the perception of an evil person, the concern for physical integrity or for maintenance of self-esteem may yield to the concern for control over one's environment or for power equality.

Sentiments and attitudes

Evidently the notion of sentiment is close to that of attitude. The components enumerated are also found in analyses of attitudes (see Tesser & Shaffer, 1990). Sentiment and attitude, in fact, have often been treated alongside one another. Murray and Morgan (1945), as well as Asch (1952), were at some pains to explain their difference. Both felt it to be one of emphasis. Murray and Morgan pointed out that the notion of attitude has more cognitive and voluntary overtones; "attitudes" primarily suggests opinions, and one can change some attitudes at will. Asch defined sentiments as dispositions of a personal kind and attitudes as those one shares with others. The word "attitude" indeed arouses both kinds of association, which makes it less appropriate to designate the phenomena we are discussing; it feels discordant to call "love" an attitude. Although attitudes are usually defined in a tripartite way as having cognitive, behavioral, and emotional components, there do exist attitudes of a purely cognitive kind, or that involve positive or negative evaluations that would not give rise to emotions if the attitude object were met. Many people are against undue expansion of nuclear power plants, and like Coca Cola, but for few of them are these issues to get excited about. By contrast, the processes under discussion are primarily emotional. The object, by definition, is of emotional value to the subject. It tends to influence behavior by the actual emotions that the sentiment feeds or by anticipation of the emotions that it might feed. One could say that "sentiments" are those attitudes that involve truly emotional dispositions. In fact, sentiments, by definition, have those characteristics that, if applicable to an attitude, allow prediction of behavior; these characteristics include specificity (Ajzen & Fishbein, 1977), vested interest in the issue, temporal stability, affective–cognitive consistency, and accessibility (Fazio, 1986). In addition, sentiments may concern individual objects, which is not the way attitudes are generally conceived.

Nevertheless, when we try to sketch a plausible structure of sentiments in some detail, we find a tentative description that in many ways is indeed close to the description of attitudes by cognitive theorists like Fiske (1982) and Fazio (1986).

A sentiment, as we have said, is the construct invoked to explain the propensity of an object or class of objects to elicit emotions. That construct can be understood as a disposition to appraise the object as having certain emotionally meaningful properties. Structurally, a sentiment is an affective schema (Fiske, 1982) that links properties identifying the object to a given affective value and to beliefs that embody further appraisal features. It is an internal representation of these features. Such a disposition or schema mediates between earlier events and later dealings. It affects perception by adding elements to those actually presented by the object during those later dealings. An encounter with the object becomes an encounter with an emotionally charged event.

The appraisal features in sentiment schemas are structurally the same as those in emotions. This not only applies to the appraisal of positive or negative relevance, which accounts for affect, but also to the appraisals characteristic of different positive or negative emotions. Sentiments derive from schemas that invest the object with the potential of producing specific types of emotion-eliciting events. An angry sentiment (a sentiment that the subject calls "anger") is a disposition to appraise the object as a perpetrator of evil. A sentiment of fear is, among other things, a disposition to appraise the object as a potential or actual threat. A sentiment of hate is a disposition to appraise the object as capable of offending one's concerns or values. A guilty sentiment is a disposition to appraise the self as a person responsible for, and capable of, an evil act. One of the subjects who volunteered cooperation in a guilt-feeling study started her story as follows:

> Yeah, uh, I selected the following. I have, uh, there are so many things I feel guilty about. I had trouble choosing something, but I chose the guilt feeling I have about having gone to live with my boyfriend. That is now, let me see, 10 years ago. I had met my then boyfriend and we started living together quite soon. I told my parents nothing. I am very Christian, I was brought up an orthodox Protestant. That . . . well, I should tell only about the guilt feeling and not about the causes behind it, because I must admit tending to do that very strongly. (From Kroon, 1988)

Note the "many things" and the present tense of "the guilt feeling I have" about the event of 10 years ago. Even the last line hints at the self-accusatory appraisal tendency. Phobic anxieties similarly operate through appraisal propensities. For the spider phobic, spiders look threatening or weird. For the jealous person, every act of the partner is appraised as a potential infidelity. They are seen sooner than by other individuals and attract more attention (eg Watts *et al.*, 1986). In this sense it can be said that the individuals described are angry, guilt-ridden, afraid or jealous not only frequently but in a very real sense almost continuously. There is often an almost continuous readiness to perceive signals for the object or its ramifications, and for particular behaviors in relation to the object.

Of course, readiness for appraisal is not the same as appraisal. Sentiments are not emotions. The appraisal disposition defining a given sentiment is isomorphic to an emotional appraisal but not identical to it. The first relates to the latter as schema to perception. Similarly, the wary or suspicious feelings evoked by a corner that might contain a spider web or by an act that might mean interest in someone else are not emotions but relate to them as perceiving potentialities to perceiving actualities.

An important implication of this analysis of sentiments is their multidimensional nature. Sentiments are spoken of not merely as positive or negative, but as admiration, affection, jealousy, or love, and as anger, dislike, fear, guilt, indignation, and hate. This multidimensionality corresponds to the variety of behaviors sentiments typically lead to. These behaviors too are isomorphic to emotional behaviors. They involve seeking and accepting information about the object (about someone one admires), seeking proximity to and furthering the well-being of the object (of someone one loves), avoidance (of something one fears), obstructing, undoing, and harming the object (when one is angry or indignant about it or hates it). All these are actions matching the action tendencies of emotions.

Perhaps the most distinctive aspect of sentiments, and which sets them apart from attitudes in general, is that they constitute concerns. Concerns are defined as internal representations of preferred states that serve as standards against which actual states of the world are tested. People seek to achieve them and events may agree or disagree with them. Emotions arise when they are found to do so (Frijda, 1986). Sentiments include such representations, specified in terms of particular objects (elsewhere (Frijda, 1986) they have been called "surface concerns"). The preferred state in anxiety is that its object does not exist or may not be encountered; in love that the object should be close or sexually possessed, or that its existence should be enhanced, depending upon the kind of love (Scheler, 1923; Sternberg, 1986); in hate that its existence should be diminished (Scheler, 1923); etc. Often the preferred state consists of the occurrence or non-occurrence of particular emotions: fear of dogs consists of the representation that dogs elicit fear when encountered. From these representations spring the various preparatory and anticipatory actions (contact seeking, avoidance), even in the absence of actual emotions, and the other components of sentiments mentioned above.

The objects of concerns, or beliefs about them, involve a match or mismatch with the concerns. The existence of injustice and political oppression in a given country is an intolerable fact to that people's sympathizers; the well-being of a love object is a satisfying state of affairs for her or his lover. Affect is a result of these matches and mismatches. Implicit in sentiments, therefore, is the aim of amending mismatch or achieving or maintaining match. It is this constellation of concerns and match or mismatch that provides the emotional content of sentiments, because precisely the same constellation underlies emotions. But emotions arise when events provide the match or mismatch; sentiments exist because of one's knowledge of the sheer existence of the match and mismatch.

The preference for particular states involving the objects of sentiments derives from other, "deeper" concerns; sentiments are concerns of the second degree, so to speak. These other concerns were responsible for the occurrence of the emotions that may have been the sentiment's origin. One became angry (and remained so) because one's sense of friendship, or self-esteem, or trust in others (as in the above musician's case) was offended. Or one became happy (and fell in love) because a given person satisfied one's need for sex or for attachment. In consequence, emotions elicited by encounters with the objects of sentiments— the hate felt in meeting someone one hates, for instance, or the joy when the person one loves does well—have a two-step origin: they derive from the sentiment, which in turn derives from deeper concerns like the need for attachment.

Let us summarize. The effective dispositions called sentiments do have, in many respects, the structure of emotions. They carry modes of appraisal with them that are to a high degree isomorphic with appraisals in emotions. They lead to planned behavior that is of the same general nature as a corresponding emotion would motivate. And they involve the same concerns that underlie emotions. The major difference, of course, is that emotions are occurrents and sentiments are basically dispositions.

The kinship between emotions and sentiments explains the use of names common to varieties of both. As indicated, the sentiments of anger, fear, etc, involve the same appraisal structures as the emotions called by those names, and the planned behaviors have the same aims as the action tendencies of emotions. It will further be clear from the analysis that some words that are often considered emotion words most commonly refer to sentiments and not to emotions. This applies in particular to "love" and "hate". Love and hate refer to dispositions, with the properties indicated above. Both involve the disposition to act in ways consistent with the sentiments' aims, enhancing and diminishing the existence of the object. Both are concerns that give rise to emotions when events involving the objects represent core relational themes. Joy is aroused when that object is in fact enhanced or diminished, fear when there is threat to its existence or of its coming near, etc. Both love and hate spread associational webs over neutral objects so that the objects' handkerchiefs are cherished or their very names abhorred; indifferent acts are applauded or condemned. Both lead to seeking out their objects when absent, to join or to combat them, and to spontaneous thoughts about the objects' fate. All these phenomena are mentioned in descriptions and self-reports of people in love (eg Stendhal, 1820), and they can be observed in accounts of hate such as Hitler's *Mein Kampf*.

Emotions arising from sentiments

Sentiments lead to a multiplicity of emotions. As Shand (1922) expressed it: "a sentiment is a system of several emotion dispositions, having different conative tendencies, connected with a common object, and subordinated to a common end". Sentiments, like any other kind of concern, give rise to emotions under two general conditions. The first is the occurrence of an event that is relevant to satisfaction of that concern; the second is that of mere confrontation with the object of concern.

Events signalling concern relevance have been discussed already. Events are felt to be relevant to the satisfaction of a concern when they signal any of the core relational themes like promise, threat, loss, or interference. The variety of emotions follows from these themes according to general rules indicated in preceding sections. As regards the second kind of condition, mere confrontation, seeing or meeting the object of a concern at close quarters is the condition that leads to emotions of the class called "consummatory emotions" (Frijda, 1986) or "attraction emotions" (Ortony, Clore & Collins, 1988). Just as perceiving a fit object of sexual desire gives rise to an emotion of lust, confrontation with the object of a sentiment gives rise to emotions such as liking and aversion, admiration and contempt, and love and hate.

The words "love", "liking", "hatred", and "aversion", as we indicated, in most of their uses refer to sentiments and not emotions. However, the words can also be used for emotions, although in that case they are usually combined with modifiers denoting limited duration like "an upsurge of love", "a fit of hatred" or "a wave of aversion". The emotions have properties that correspond to those of emotions generally. The emotion of love is characterized by the appraisal of attractiveness or, more generally, by the feature of "never-too-much-to-be-close-to", and by the felt urge to be close to the object and to take care of it. The feeling of hate is characterized by the appraisal of an object of an evil, ill-intending nature, and by the action readiness for diminishing its existence. The action readiness in both emotions has the characteristics of an urge, with control precedence. That is what distinguishes the emotions of love and hate (or of liking and aversion) from sentiments with the same names. But as in the corresponding sentiments, the action is directed towards the objects as such, towards enhancing or diminishing their existence, and not towards furthering or terminating particular events. That is what distinguishes the emotions of love and hatred from those of, for instance, joy and anger.

Sentiments arising from emotions

In the preceding paragraphs we mainly discussed sentiments that originated from emotions and that continued the individual's affective preoccupations. Doubtless not all sentiments have this kind of origin. Love probably does not originate in joy and satisfaction but simultaneously with them.

Nevertheless, many sentiments do seem to be the aftermath of emotional incidents, the direct experiences as a source of effective attitudes emphasized by Fazio (1986). What precise direct experiences generate such sentiments? The conditions may be assumed to be those that in general lead to dispositional attributions, such as hedonic relevance (Jones & Davis, 1965). That is also clearly suggested by the interview materials, at least in regard to negative sentiments. In most cases the emotion seems to have precipitated an unresolved issue. The mismatch between actual conditions and some preferred state has remained, the emotion notwithstanding. Personal loss, having been slighted, and traumas often leave effects for indefinite periods. One is left alone and regrets one's lost companion; having been slighted often leaves a sting in the flesh of one's self-esteem that remains for a long time. Moreover, the new concerns that came into play because of the belief changes may strongly contribute to enduring mismatch and the establishment of a sentiment. The damage to one's vanity by having been slighted may pass more rapidly than the mismatch between one's desired self-image and one's actual self-image tainted by the subtle shift in power relationship due to the fact that one had to suffer the other's insult. A clear example of these workings of belief change is provided by the example of the woman who felt ashamed about having thrown away the letters of her relatives. She told her interviewer: "I am deeply ashamed now, I tell you. I am a grown-up woman. I should not have done that. What I did does not correspond to me". The discrepancy between the person she supposed herself to be and the person capable of such an act was there to stay.

It is not unlikely that such unresolved issues form precisely the reason why traumas have such long-lasting effects. The effects are sentiments because of the emotions triggered by stimuli resembling those belonging to the traumatic situation and by the associational webs surrounding them, and because of the motivations, avoidance in particular, established. One may venture the hypothesis that traumas have long-lasting effects to the extent that they have produced an enduring mismatch between the individual's concerns and actual conditions, as seen in his or her perception of the world or the self. After a traumatic event the world is not a safe place any longer; the woman quoted, whose friend had incurred a venereal disease and blamed her for it, indeed made a statement of that nature. A similar generalized appraisal has been described, in somewhat different words, as a causal factor in the effects of war trauma: one's basic trust in one's coping abilities, or the basic belief in one's invulnerability, has gone (Grinker & Spiegel, 1945). Sexual trama—sexual child abuse in particular— in a similar way tends to turn the world into a permanently unsafe place.

There are no doubt further conditions for the establishment of sentiments. One may be the sheer intensity or repetitiveness of emotional conditions. One learns to regard as dangerous or untrustworthy what has shown itself as deserving to be feared or distrusted, and to become fond of those who proved capable of providing satisfactions. Beyond that, the domain of the establishment of attachments and aversions is a complex one that we cannot go into.

PASSIONS

On occasion, emotions turn not into mere dispositions to react emotionally but, in addition, the aims of sentiments become long-term goals. Sometimes, people spend large amounts of time, effort and other resources to achieve emotional goals. The emotional nature of the goals is defined by their high standing in the individual's value system, their high priority with respect to goal competition, the high persistence shown in their pursuit, and the readiness to run high risks and pay high costs for their achievement. Structurally, their emotional nature is defined by their emotional content, to which we will return.

We call these goals "passions", thereby staying close to at least one of the accepted meanings of that term. Our material contains no clear examples; we have to draw these from other sources. One such example formed the substance of a recent criminal case in The Netherlands. On September 9, 1987, the vice president of the country's largest supermarket chain was kidnapped and a high ransom was asked. As a sign that the vice president was held, his left thumb was sent to a newspaper. Half of the ransom was paid; the kidnapper managed to get away with it without being caught. Then there was silence; no request for further ransom and no sign of the victim. Months later the kidnapper was traced and caught because he spent some of the marked ransom bills in a supermarket near his home. The kidnapped man had been killed in cold blood the day he was abducted; his thumb had been cut off at that time to serve as later proof that he was indeed held. The name of the murderer was Ferdi E.

Ferdi E was a 40-year-old engineer, married, with two children. After his arrest he told his story with frankness and in detail. He had selected the victim for the large amount of money that could be asked for ransom. He had carefully observed the man's habits and meticulously planned the assault (he had dragged the man from his car when he was setting out to drive to the dentist in the morning). Ferdi needed the money for the following reason. Five years earlier he had started a job creation firm, together with three other people. Two or three years later disagreements broke out; his colleagues did not support certain of his claims and his salary was decreased. He quit, filed suit twice, and both times lost. He felt slighted and humiliated, and had pondered revenge ever since. What exactly he was going to use the money for has not become clear, but it was meant to finance his revenge, involving plans to murder the three colleagues. His desire for revenge may be classified as a passion. It was a goal set up after an emotional incident. The goal was in force for about two years and motivated the use of considerable energy, attention, and meticulous planning. The goal derived its motivational force from the emotional charge of the humiliation and/or the prospect of retaliation. Yet, interestingly, everything was planned and done in cold blood and with a cold mind. Ferdi E was described in court as a man totally devoid of emotions. The way he had chatted with his victim and lunched with him in the lonely woods just before murdering him, his cutting off the victim's thumb for later use, as well as the detailed fashion in which he related these events to the police, attest to that diagnosis. Surprisingly, he declared himself shocked to hear that he was considered devoid of feeling; if that was true, he said, he had better be removed from society. The case presents a puzzling paradox. No acute emotions can be found in the story; to what extent an acute emotion was present at the time he was abandoned by his friends cannot be assessed from the available information, although testimony exists that no quarrel with his colleagues arose. Yet the motive that had been operative for several years can only be described in emotional terms.

The above is an example of a "cold" passion: as far as the available information goes, the goal was set and followed with little acute emotion. As an example of a "hotter" passion we may cite Hitler's hatred of Jews. We call it a passion because his hatred gave rise to self-initiated activities aimed at inciting others to this hatred, organizing intimidation raids, conceiving the idea of total destruction (in January 1939; Höhne, 1967) and ordering the actual execution of that total destruction (in the spring of 1941). We class it as a hot passion because of the violent emotions manifested when he spoke about the presumed role of the Jews in Bolshevist activity or the pollution of the German people; his paroxismatic outbursts, with foaming mouth, are well documented (Fest, 1973).

The word passion is more readily connected to less cruel goals. Biography gives descriptions of emotionally motivated life-long strivings to achieve the freedom of one's group; Gandhi, Martin Luther King and Mandela are cases in point. Then, of course, there are the erotic passions, some over shorter and others over longer time periods; Stendhal (1820) gives anecdotal details. The goals are sometimes self-sacrificing and sometimes not.

Passions are defined as high-priority goals with emotionally important outcomes. These outcomes are of the same nature as aimed at by emotional action tendencies and they involve correcting the same mismatches, or achieving the same matches, on the basis of the same concerns as underlie emotions. As with sentiments, they derive their emotional content from such constellations. And also as with sentiments, they derive their names, the same as those for emotions, from the precise nature of these mismatches or matches: anger, indignation, hatred, love, lust, desire, and the like. A passion of love is driven by the desire for proximity or enhancement of another's existence, just as the emotion of love is aroused by achievement of such proximity or enhancement; a passion of anger is driven by the awareness of uncorrected offense, which also characterizes the condition for the emotion of that name.

Passions too are best considered as dispositions, as are goals in general. They exist even when not pursued, as schemas to detect occasions for pursuance and upon such detection to turn into active goals that control behavior. The pursuits are abandoned when circumstances require it and taken up again when circumstances permit. When manifest as active goals they too are "temporary dispositions" that one can be acutely aware of but that dispose one to an often extensive class of actual behaviors. Also, they function as concerns. They form the basis for the whole gamut of emotions when progress towards their goal is threatened, obstructed, favored, failing, or successful; and they lead to "consummatory emotions"—the anger, pangs of love or lust, or satisfaction when situations embodying their mismatches or achieved matches are encountered.

Given the structure of a passion as defined, formidable scope and power are not among the characteristics; they are merely prototypical. What the concept singles out is the existence of goals of emotional value that are actively pursued over long periods of time.

What makes goals become passions? We do not know. Intensity of initial emotions may be one condition. But then intensity of emotion is a tricky, complex concept (see Frijda *et al.*, in press). The kind of intensity notion that is relevant here may well imply the passionate nature of the emotion rather than explain it. There are, of course, many high intensity infatuations or indignations that have few consequences beyond high autonomic arousal.

More likely, the source for passions has to be sought in the nature of the underlying concerns; it is in this sense in particular that emotions and passions appear closely related. In many instances, it seems, very basic and encompassing concerns are at stake. Such is probably the case with most consuming infatuations. Love passions (in this sense) probably arise from desires for ego–object fusion or far-reaching identification that have a very early origin in a developmental sense (Freud, 1927) and an inarticulate structure in a cognitive sense. The characteristic of basic and encompassing concerns also applies when an emotional goal is strongly supported by social norms that the individual adheres to and is committed to by standards of self-respect and social esteem. Passions of revenge in honor cultures would readily fall into this category. Revenges prescribed by the culture are often at the same time emotionally strongly engaging both as duties and as desires (Black-Michaud, 1975; Jacoby, 1983).

Ideological content is probably a further factor that engages basic, encompassing concerns such as self-esteem. Willingness to accept risks in pursuing a goal is likely to depend upon the suprapersonal values attached to that goal or to adherence to the goal. The latter addition is probably not tautological. There exist goals that one does not value highly but at the same time abandoning which would be inconceivable because of other concerns. Maintenance of self-respect is one of these concerns, and maybe the major one. We think of the extraordinary prolonged efforts occasionally spent on behalf of the welfare of others one does not particularly care about at the expense of the welfare of close relatives. Andre Brink's novel *A Dry White Season* provides a brilliant example. A white South African schoolteacher, not particularly interested in politics, is suddenly confronted with police brutality causing the death of his gardener's son and then of the gardener himself. He risks, and finally loses, his career, social position, marriage, and life, in trying to uncover and expose what had happened (the story is modeled after the Steve Biko case). One may venture that the real motive behind pursuing the goal is that one simply cannot afford to let the events pass by if one is to retain self-respect.

Situational factors also seem involved; namely, such factors as come under the heading of "commitment". Klinger (1975) is one of the few authors to have discussed the issue and used the term in this connection. All we can say in analyzing its possible processes is that they have to do with a basic acceptance of the emotional goal. An example may perhaps be found in André Gide's (1926) account of his discovery and acceptance of his homosexuality as involving an escape from previous emotional misery. A perhaps somewhat different condition for acceptance of an emotional goal—and therefore for the establishment of a passion—has to do with an act of will. That concept, of course, is totally hazy and undefined and we will not endeavor to develop theoretical notions about it. What we have in mind, however, is the mechanism behind the phenomenological process of the inspection of possible alternatives for action and their consequences and the consideration of the extent to which different courses of action agree with one's norms and self-image. In other words, commitment does not appear to be a passive process that just happens upon the waves of strong emotion. As we have said, strong emotions by themselves often pass by, leaving no more than an aftertaste. Prosocial passions generally would seem to require active choices of the nature alluded to. Extensive study of biographies is needed to give such a hypothesis some solidity, the main point being that this highly relevant domain of affective phenomena is in dire need of systematic attention.

MOODS

Finally, a few words on moods. We have discussed several types of affective structure that encompass longer durations than an hour or so: emotional episodes, sentiments and passions. To what extent are these just other names for what are generally called "moods"?

We have alluded already to our view that the concept of mood is often misused in studies on emotional phenomena. There is a tendency to subsume every low intensity emotional state of somewhat long duration under the label of mood. We consider this confusing.

There exist affective states of varying durations that have distinct emotional quality but that lack an object. These states are what, in everyday life, the word "mood" is usually employed for. This does not mean that the subject ignores their cause. One may know perfectly well what one's sad mood was caused by but the sad mood is still not felt to be "about" that event.

One way to describe moods is as feeling states that do not bear upon a particular object. Alternatively, moods can be described as appraisals of the world as a whole. In a depressed mood the world appears gray and empty in all its respects; there is nothing that diverts the eye or heart, and every task appears a burden. "Globality" is indeed the appraisal feature that has been shown to distinguish the experience of moods from that of emotions (Frijda, 1987). Moods can also be described in a third way: as states of action readiness not directed towards an object. Angry mood can be described as continuous felt readiness for antagonistic action towards whatever comes in sight; depressed mood can be described as apathy not felt as the complement of a particular loss.

Note that moods can be described in one further way: as states of lowered thresholds for particular emotions or of increased likelihood of such emotions. Angry mood can be seen as a state of lowered anger threshold. In this vein, Ryle (1949) and others interpret moods as dispositions. But that is not their only appropriate description. In the interval between angry emotions during angry moods, every object or event is appraised as a likely frustration or as possibly implying unfriendly intention and the readiness for rejection and backbiting is continuously present. Moods, in other words, are occurrents as well as dispositions; the opposition of these notions shows itself again to be false.

Moods are not necessarily states of low intensity feeling; many depressed moods are witness to that. They need not even lack feeling peaks. Depressed and elated moods can show strong variations in intensity, although it is true that the peaks are readily provided with objects, such as notions of one's worthlessness in depression or of rebirth in mania, and thus become emotions.

We have no information on the duration range of moods. Diffuse response tendencies and feeling states can certainly last for days. Judging from clinical evidence, they may last for months and perhaps years (Angst, 1973). It should be noted that moods, like episodes, may be in force without occupying center stage in experience. Depressed mood may tone down or qualify positive emotions without preventing their occurrence.

CONCLUSIONS

Several observations formed the starting-point of this investigation. One is the observation that the same emotion words are being used for psychological events of vastly different kinds and durations. Another is the paradox that emotion instances are sometimes described in terms of the occurrence of the same and other emotions. These observations, and the analysis of self-reports, have led us to distinguish five different kinds of affective phenomena: emotions, emotion episodes, sentiments, passions, and moods. Emotions are occurrent responses of a multicomponential nature. The features that appear most clearly to identify occurrence of a given emotion, and to distinguish it from a different or following one, are a specific mode of appraisal and of action readiness. Emotions may last for hours. Emotion episodes are identified by core relational themes and corresponding core appraisal, affect involvement and presence of *some* state of action readiness, particularly action readiness at the strategic level. Emotions as well as emotion episodes display the feature of control precedence: action readiness, whatever its nature, tends to control action and attention. Emotion episodes may last for days and perhaps even for weeks. Sentiments are basically dispositions to appraise a given object in a particular emotionally relevant way; they can be manifest in felt affect and in motivation to seek or avoid confrontations with their objects. They are identified by their object and the mode of appraisal of that object. Passions are long-term goals with emotional content and are identified by these goals. Both sentiments and passions may have

Table 7.5. Elements of emotion reports

Emotion
  Appraisal components
  Action readiness components
  Expressive behavior
  Physiological response
  Affect
  Temporary beliefs
  Actions and action goals

Episodes
  Concerns at stake
  Relational theme
  Core appraisal
  Activation features
  (Often) affect

Sentiments
  Beliefs
  Belief-based actions
  Ideological transformations

Passions
  Long-term goals

indefinite duration. Moods are identified by global appraisal or state of action readiness not bearing upon a specified object. Their duration range would appear to be up to months, or even longer.

The analysis indicates the relationships between the various forms of affective phenomena and explains why, to a large extent, they are called by the same names. They share appraisals and the match or mismatch between concerns and actual conditions from which the appraisals derive, be it as occurrent feelings or as dispositions and beliefs. They also share the aims of either action readiness or action goals.

There are practical sides to all this. The distinction of types of affective phenomena, and of their structural components, allows one to analyze emotion self-reports more completely and unambiguously. The analyses provide a schema for describing the content of such self-reports and for distinguishing the different levels—temporary responses, permanent beliefs, etc—of the various elements. We summarize the descriptive schema in Table 7.5. The distinction between emotions, episodes and sentiments, moreover, may help overcome certain problems in the systematic analysis of emotion structures, such as the confusion of appraisal features operative at different levels during emotion episodes.

Perhaps the present analysis may facilitate the integration of the affective phenomena other than emotions into the framework of current emotion theory. In any case, it may provide guidance on what components to expect and not to expect in the various sorts of reports one obtains when asking for "instances of emotions".

NOTES

1. In psychology the term has gone out of use. In sociology it is being used more commonly, although in a somewhat different sense from that used here; the same applies to "passion". Gordon (1981), for instance, uses the term sentiment to denote culturally shaped emotional relations to objects.
2. The distinction between episodic and lexical expressions was suggested to us by H. Verkuyl.

REFERENCES

Ajzen, I. & Fishbein, M. (1977). Attitude–behavior relations: a theoretical analysis and a review of empirical research. *Psychological Bulletin*, **84**, 888–918.

Allport, G. W. (1954). *The Nature of Prejudice*. Reading, Mass: Addison-Wesley.

Angst, J. (1973). The course of monopolar depression and bipolar psychosis. *Psychiatry, Neurology and Neurosurgery*, **76**, 489–500.

Arnold, M. B. (1960). *Emotion and Personality*. Vols I and II. New York: Columbia University Press.

Asch, S. E. (1952). *Social Psychology*. New York: Prentice-Hall.

Black-Michaud, J. (1975). *Feuding Societies*. Oxford: Blackwell.

Brink, A. (1979) *A Dry White Season*. London: W. H. Allen.

Davitz, J. R. (1969). *The Language of Emotion*. New York: Academic Press.

Edelberg, R. (1972). Electrical activity of the skin. Its measurements and uses in psychophysiology. In N. S. Greenfield & R. A. Sternbach (Eds), *Handbook of Psychophysiology*. New York: Holt, Rinehart and Winston, pp. 367–418.

Ekman, P. (1984). Expression and the nature of emotion. In K. Scherer & P. Ekman (Eds), *Approaches to Emotion*. Hillsdale, NJ: Erlbaum, pp. 319–344.

Ekman, P. & Friesen, W. V. (1975). *Unmasking the Face*. Englewood-Cliffs: Prentice Hall.

Fazio, R. (1986). How do attitudes guide behavior? In R. M. Sorrentiono & E. T. Higgins (Eds), *Handbook of Motivation and Cognition*. New York: Wiley, pp. 204–243.

Fehr, B. & Russell, J. A. (1984). Concept of emotion viewed from a prototype perspective. *Journal of Experimental Psychology: General Section*, **113**, 464–486.

Fest, J. C. (1973). *Hitler: Eine Biographie*. Berlin: Propyläen Verlag (1983).

Fiske, S. T. (1982). Schema-triggered affect: Applications to social perception. In M. S. Clark & S. T. Fiske (Eds), *Affect and Cognition: The 17th Annual Carnegie Symposium on Cognition*. Hillsdale: Erlbaum, pp. 55–78.

Fiske, S. T. & Taylor, S. E. (1984). *Social Cognition*. Reading, Mass: Addison-Wesley.

Freud, S. (1927). *Die Zukunft einer Illusion* (The future of an illusion), standard edn, Vol. XXI. London: Hogarth Press (1953).

Frijda, N. H. (1956). *De Betekenis van de Gelaatsexpressie*. Amsterdam: Van Oorschot.

Frijda, N. H. (1986). *The Emotions*. Cambridge: Cambridge University Press.

Frijda, N. H. (1987). Emotion, cognitive structure and action tendency. *Cognition and Emotion*, **1**, 115–144.

Frijda, N. H. (1988). Emotion and emotional expression. *Ricerche di Psicologia*, **3**, 5–33.

Frijda, N. H. (1989a). The function of emotional expression. In J. P. Forgas & J. M. Innes (Eds), *Recent Advances in Social Psychology: An International Perspective*. Amsterdam: Elsevier Science, pp. 205–217.

Frijda, N. H. (1989b). The different roles of cognitive variables in emotion. In A. F. Bennett & K. M. McConkey (Eds), *Cognition in Individual and Social Contexts*. Amsterdam: Elsevier Science, pp. 325–336.

Frijda, N. H., Kuipers, P. & Terschure, E. (1989). Relations between emotion, appraisal, and emotional action readiness. *Journal of Personality and Social Psychology*, **57**, 212–228.

Frijda, N. H., Ortony, A., Sonnemans, J. & Clore, G. (in press). The complexity of intensity. In M. Clark (Ed.), *Review of Personality and Social Psychology*.

Gide, A. (1926) *Si le Grain ne Meurt*. Paris: Gallimard.

Gordon, S. L. (1981). The sociology of sentiments and emotion. In M. Rosenberg & Ralph H. Turner (Eds), *Social Psychology: Sociological Perspectives*. New York: Basic Books, pp. 261–278.

Grinker, R. R. & Spiegel, J. P. (1945). *Men under Stress*. Philadelphia: Blakiston.

Hinde, R. A. (1974). *Biological Bases of Human Behavior*. New York: McGraw-Hill.

Höhne, H. (1967). *Der Orden unter dem Totenkopf. Die Geschichte der SS*. Gütersloh: Mohn Verlag.

Horowitz, M. J. (1976). *Stress Response Syndromes*. New York: Jason Aronson.

Izard, C. E. (1977). *Human Emotions*. New York: Plenum Press.

Jacoby, S. (1983). *Wild Justice*. New York: Harper and Row.

Johnson-Laird, P. N. & Oatley, K. (1989). The language of emotions: An analysis of a semantic field. *Cognition and Emotion*, **3**, 81–124.

Jones, E. E. & Davis, U. E. (1965). From acts to dispositions: The attribution process in person perception. In L. Berkowitz (Ed.), *Advances in Experimental Social Psychology*, Vol. 2, New York: Academic Press, pp. 219–266.

Klinger, E. (1975). The consequences of commitment and disengagement from incentives. *Psychological Review*, **82**, 1–25.

Kroon, R. M. (1988). *Aanleidingen en structuur van schuldgevoel*. Masters thesis, Psychology Department, Amsterdam University.

Lader, M. (1975). Psychophysiological parameters and methods. In L. Levi (Ed.), *Emotions: Their Parameters and Measurement*. New York: Raven Press, pp. 341–368.

Lang, P. J. (1977). Physiological assessment of anxiety and fear. In J. D. Cone & R. P. Hawkins (Eds), *Behavioral Assessment: New Directions in Clinical Psychology*. New York: Brunner/Mazel, pp. 178–195.

Lang, P. J. (1988). *The image of fear: Emotion and memory*. Invited address, Behavior Therapy World Congress, Edinburgh, Scotland, September 7, 1988.

Lazarus, R. S. & Folkman, S. (1984). *Stress, Appraisal and Coping*. New York: Springer.

Lazarus, R. S. & Smith, C. A. (1988). Knowledge and appraisal in the cognition–emotion relationship. *Cognition and Emotion*, **2**, 281–300.

Mandler, G. (1984). *Mind and Body: The Psychology of Emotion and Stress*. New York: Norton.

Mergaree, E. I. (1966). Undercontrolled and overcontrolled personality types in extreme antisocial aggression. *Psychological Monographs*, **80** (whole no. 613).

Mesquita, B. & Fischer, A. (1990). Gevoelens verwoord. *Tijdschrift voor Taal en Tekstwetenschap*, **9**, 97–111.

Montaigne, M. de (1580). *Essays I*. Paris: Gallimard, Ed. Folio (1965).

Morrow, G. R. & Labrum, A. H. (1978). The relationship between psychological and physiological measures of anxiety. *Psychosomatic Medicine*, **8**, 85–101.

Murray, H. A. & Morgan, C. D. (1945). A clinical study of sentiments: I. *Genetic Psychology Monographs*, **32**, 3–149.

Nowlis, V. (1970). Mood, behavior and experience. In M. B. Arnold (Ed.), *Feelings and Emotions. The Loyola Symposium*. New York: Academic Press, pp. 261–278.

Oatley, K. & Johnson-Laird, P. N. (1987). Towards a cognitive theory of emotions. *Cognition and Emotion*, **1**, 29–50.

Ortony, A., Clore, G. & Collins, A. (1988). *The Cognitive Structure of Emotions*. Cambridge: Cambridge University Press.

Parkes, C. M. (1972). *Bereavement: Studies of Grief in Adult Life*. New York: International Universities Press.

Plutchik, R. (1980). *Emotion: A Psychoevolutionary Synthesis.* New York: Harper & Row.
Rachman, S. (1980). Emotional processing. *Behavioral Research and Therapy*, **18**, 51–60.
Rimé, B., Philippot, P. & Cisalomo, D. (1990). Social schemata of peripheral changes in emotion. *Journal of Personality and Social Psychology*, **59**, 38–49.
Roseman, I. (1984). Cognitive determinants of emotion: A structural theory. In P. Shaver (Ed.), *Review of Personality and Social Psychology: Vol. 5. Emotions, Relationships, and Health.* Beverly Hills: Sage, pp. 11–36.
Russell, J. A. (1980). A circumplex model of affect. *Journal of Personality and Social Psychology*, **39**, 1161–1178.
Ryle, G. (1949). *The Concept of Mind.* London: Hutchinson.
Schachter, S. & Singer J. (1962). Cognitive, social and physiological determinants of emotional state. *Psychological Review*, **63**, 379–399.
Scheler, M. (1923). *Wesen und Formen der Sympathie.* Frankfurt (5e Edn. Schulte-Buhmke).
Scherer, K. R. (1984). Emotion as a multicomponent process: A model and some cross-cultural data. In P. Shaver (Ed.), *Review of Personality and Social Psychology*, Vol. 5. Beverly Hills: Sage, pp. 37–63.
Sherer, K. R. & Walbott, H. G. (1986). How universal and specific is emotional experience? Evidence from 27 countries on five continents. *Social Science Information*, **25**.
Scherer, K. R., Walbott, H. G. & Summerfield, A. B. (1986). *Experiencing Emotions: A Cross-Cultural Study.* Cambridge: Cambridge University Press.
Seligman, M. E. P. (1975). *Helplessness: On Depression, Development and Death.* San Francisco: Freeman.
Shand, A. F. (1896). Character and the emotions. *Mind*, **5**, 203–226.
Shand, A. F. (1922). The relations of complex and sentiment. III. *Journal of Psychology*, **13**, 123–129.
Shaver, P., Schwartz, J., Kirson, D. & O'Connor, C. (1987). Emotion knowledge: Further exploration of a prototype approach. *Journal of Personality and Social Behavior*, **52**, 1061–1086.
Smith, C. A. & Ellsworth, P. C. (1985). Patterns of cognitive appraisal in emotion. *Journal of Personality and Social Psychology*, **48**, 813–838.
Sonnemans, J. (1990). The structure and determinants of the intensity of emotions. Internal Report, Psychology Department, Psychonomics Section, Amsterdam University.
Stendhal, H. (1820). *De l'Amour.* Paris: Verda (1949).
Sternberg, R. J. (1986). A triangular theory of love. *Psychological Review*, **93**, 119–135.
Tan, E. (in preparation). *Psychological Affect Structure of Feature Films.*
Tesser, A. & Shaffer, D. R. (1990). Attitudes and attitude change. *Annual Review of Psychology*, **41**, 479–523.
Van der Wurff, A. (in preparation). *Onveiligheidsgevoelens in de woonomgeving.* PhD thesis, University of Nijmegen.
Van Goozen, S. & Frijda, N. H. (in preparation). Emotion words used in six European countries.
Van Sommers, P. (1988). *Jealousy.* Harmondsworth: Pelican.
Watts, F. N., McKenna, F. P., Sharrock, R. & Tresize, L. (1986). Colour naming of phobia related words. *British Journal of Psychology*, **77**, 97–108.

8 Gender in the Psychology of Emotion: A Selective Research Review

STEPHANIE A. SHIELDS
Department of Psychology, University of California, Davis, CA 95616, USA

In 1601 Thomas Wright presented a humoral theory of individual differences in *The Passions of the Minde*. Like others who undertook similar projects, he discussed differences between women and men. His list of women's emotional attributes included, on the positive side, inclinations to mercy and pity, piety and devotion, and less tendency to emotional incontinence than men. On the negative side were pride, envy, proclivity for slander, and inconstancy (Wright, 1601/1973, p. 74). The last, he believed, has the same source as the instability that characterizes the imprudence of young men who tend to "resolve rashly and performe rarely" (p. 76). Wright's list is interesting, not only because it diverges somewhat from contemporary gender stereotypes, but also because, at the same time as he engages in sweeping generalizations, this seventeenth-century writer understands that generalizations do not provide an invariant, comprehensive description of all men or all women. Humors, he notes, vary with age, physique, complexion, and "race,"[1] and so account for group similarities as well as individual variation from the norm: "because women have sundrie complexions, so they bee subject to sundry passions. Even as in like sorte, I could say of men; for some are more prone to one passion than an other" (p. 78).

Just as Wright was required to couch his "common sense" assertion about sex-related differences within cautions about the limits of those assertions, any late-twentieth-century attempt to list sex-related differences in emotion would require an even longer list of caveats and qualifications. Empirical studies of the relationship between gender and emotion have focused almost exclusively on the identification of sex-related differences. Analysis of emotions data by subject sex almost invariably fails to reveal stable or theoretically important gender differences. The list of small, unstable, and typically stereotype-consistent sex-related differences which this strategy yields has led many to conclude that gender is not particularly important to the study of the psychology of human emotion. Consequently, sociologists (eg Hochschild, 1983; Cancian, 1987) and anthropologists (eg Lutz, 1988a,b; Rosaldo, 1984; Abu-Loghoud, 1986) have taken the lead in investigating the link between gender and emotion.

In this chapter I will examine why the "sex-differences" approach has been fairly unproductive in the psychology of emotion, and discuss the need to distinguish between isolated sex-related differences and the pervasive influence

International Review of Studies on Emotion, Vol. 1. Edited by K. T. Strongman
©1991 John Wiley & Sons Ltd

of gender. First, however, a note on terminology is in order. Among psychologists who study gender, it is general practice to differentiate between the biologically based categories of female and male (sex) and the psychological features associated with biological states which involve social rather than biological categories (gender) (Unger, 1979; Deaux, 1985; Lorber, 1987). Thus, "sex" is used to refer to the physical fact of primary and secondary sex characteristics, "gender" to refer to a psychological and cultural construct. Gender is manifested in the public social world (as in culturally defined standards of sex-appropriate behavior) and within the individual's consciousness (as in one's identification of oneself as male or female).[2] In psychological research, gender (rather than sex) is usually the variable of interest, but the component or quality of "gender" that is of interest is not measured directly; instead, gender is inferred from subject sex. Subject sex is thus a "marker" for gender and obtained sex-related differences are interpreted as reflecting gender differences. Therefore, I will use "sex-related difference" to refer to the results of studies that report a comparison of subjects by sex and "gender difference" to refer to the inferences drawn from those results.

A distinction can be drawn between the aims and methods of what I will term a sex-differences model of research and research strategies that focus on gender-in-context. The sex-differences model (more properly the "sex-related differences" model) typically assesses quantitative differences between male and female research participants within a single research setting. When the obtained difference is statistically significant, there is a tendency to overinterpret it as a stable, fixed, and enduring trait which is often presumed to be biologically based (Unger, 1979; Jacklin, 1989). Dissatisfaction with an uninformed sex-differences approach to gender (and the accompanying reification of masculinity/femininity, eg Lewin, 1984a,b; Morawski, 1987) has been growing for some time.[3]

The most promising alternative research strategy is to view gender as it operates within the social context (eg Deaux & Major, 1987; Unger, 1988; West & Zimmerman, 1987). A gender-in-context perspective differs primarily from the sex-differences model by emphasizing the sensitivity of observed sex-related differences to social and cognitive aspects of the situation/environment (eg Deaux & Major, 1987; Unger, 1989). The emphasis shifts from a description of presumptively stable differences to an exploration of the variables that exaggerate or attenuate the occurrence of differences. Gender exerts an effect as an interaction among actor, observer, and situational variables, hence a gender-in-context perspective takes the position that research should not focus on *whether* differences exist but aim to identify the variables that exaggerate or attenuate these differences. Applying this strategy to the case of emotion, for example, results in replacing the question of whether women or men are more emotional with a strategy designed to identify the variables that differentially affect women's and men's judgments about their own or others' emotionality.

THE LIMITATIONS OF "SEX DIFFERENCES"

Jacklin (1981) discussed a number of limitations of the sex-differences research strategy, three of which stand out as having particular relevance to emotion research. (1) Because gender has largely been studied as a variable of empirical rather than theoretical significance, the level of analysis tends to be descriptive rather than explanatory, or *post hoc* rather than theory driven. (2) Research is largely guided by the assumption that sex-related differences should be invariant in form, stable over time, and biological in origin. (3) When sex is treated as a subject variable (as opposed to a stimulus variable), results vary inconsistently across experimental contexts. I would like briefly to consider each of these limitations as it bears on the psychology of emotion.

Post-hoc explanation

In her extensive and comprehensive review of gender differences in emotional development, Leslie Brody (1985) notes that investigation of gender has largely occurred outside of any organizing theoretical framework. Most of this work is not grounded in any theory of gender, but is rather like a catalog of loosely connected themes and particularistic findings. Rarely is gender *per se* of focal interest in emotions research; instead, statistical analyses for sex-related differences are undertaken in order to rule out (or serendipitously reveal) the importance of gender as a causal influence on the experiment's outcome (Manstead, in press). Add a publication bias towards statistically significant results, and the result is largely a literature of inconsistent conclusions.

Presumed biological origin

The sex-differences model, by virtue of being limited to assessment of the quantity of emotion expressed or reported, implies that psychologically relevant emotional phenomena (insofar as gender is concerned) should be viewed as fixed capacities of the individual. A sex-related difference in emotion-relevant behavior is therefore taken as an indication that one sex possesses "more" of a given emotional attribute. The sex-differences perspective regards "emotionality", for example, as a quantitatively fixed characteristic of the person, whereas a gender-centered analysis views emotionality as defined, at least in part, by the interpersonal negotiations that occur within particular contexts. The conceptual difference between the sex-differences and gender-in-context models of research is in whether the presumption is made that gender effects are due to stable traits and so ought to manifest *constancy* across contexts within individuals, or whether gender effects are better represented in dynamic, process terms and so ought to *vary predictably* across contexts. The emphasis is thus shifted from the actor's sex *per se* to the actor's beliefs (whether or not they can be verbally articulated) about what gender means within a situation.

The past two decades of gender research have seen the development of increasingly sophisticated views of the concept of gender. The explanatory limits of cataloging putative differences are widely recognized, as are the epistemological and broadly political consequences of adopting assumptions about the sources and social significance of gender differences and similarities (eg Crawford & Maracek, 1989; Hare-Mustin & Maracek, 1988; Morawski, 1987). Yet outside of this area of specialization it is still not uncommon to find that sex-related differences are inferred as being based in—and thereby explained by—subject sex. An example, published within the last few years in a prestigious social psychology journal, illustrates this widespread practice. In the experiment, women and men who reported fear of spiders were presented with a task in which they were to get as close as they could to a tarantula in a Plexiglass box. Dependent measures included proximity to spider, rate of approach to spider, self-report of fearfulness, and psychophysiological measures. The authors found sex-related differences on nearly all measures and then found that those differences were non-significant when women and men matched for phobia scores were compared. They also consistently found significant differences between high fearful and moderate fearful women. (None of the male participants scored as high as the high fearful women, so no comparable within-sex assessment of male subjects could be made.) On the basis of these findings the authors conclude that "these differences [in dependent measures] were due to a sex-linked difference in fear" (from the authors' abstract). The infelicitous wording suggests that the authors believe they have identified a gender difference that reflects a stable, biologically based trait. A more parsimonious interpretation would be that high fearful (phobic?) *individuals* respond differently to specific fear elicitors than do moderately fearful individuals, but this explanation was not considered in the paper.

Sex as a subject variable versus sex as a stimulus variable

Cataloging the differences between males and females is neither a good route to an explanation of gender nor does it yield a very reliable set of results. Sex as a subject variable is a now-you-see-it/now-you-don't phenomenon (Unger, 1981). Sex as a stimulus variable, however, exerts sometimes striking and often stable effects (Matlin, 1987).

Analyses of sex-related differences in the efficacy of various mood induction techniques is a good example of the instability of sex as a subject variable. In a pilot study of his original mood induction technique, Velten found a trend towards sex-related differences and so used females only in the final study (Lewis & Harder, 1988). Since then, others have reported significant differences (eg Strickland, Hale & Anderson, 1975) while others have not (eg Buchwald, Strack & Coyne, 1981), and still others find them only in interaction effects, such as interaction with experimenter (Lewis & Harder, 1988). The effects of mood on cognition have yielded similarly mixed results. Studies of the effects of mood on children's memory, for example, do not find consistent effects of sex of subject (eg Potts *et al.*, 1986; Masters, Ford & Arend, 1983; Barden *et al.*, 1985).

Sex as a stimulus variable, in contrast, yields more stable results. This is particularly true of stereotypes. In a series of studies, Birnbaum and her colleagues showed that beliefs about gendered emotion are learned by early childhood and persist in adulthood even when they conflict with other gender-related values. In one study, preschoolers as well as college students associated anger with males and happiness, sadness and fear with females (Birnbaum, Nosanchuk & Croll, 1980); in another, preschool children similarly associated angry statements with boys, happy statements with girls, and sad statements with neither sex (Birnbaum & Chemelski, 1984). Among working class parents and college students, males were associated with anger and females with sadness and fear (Birnbaum & Croll, 1984). The only difference between the groups was that the working class parents believed this difference was natural but the college students hoped that standards would change.

A SELECTIVE REVIEW

The following is not intended as a comprehensive review, but as a brief overview of three topical areas in which most of the gender-related research has been done: (a) understanding and application of emotion concepts (ie beliefs about emotion or specific emotions), including attributions regarding the causes and consequences of emotion; (b) encoding and decoding of facial expressions of emotion; (c) self-reports of experienced and expressed emotion. Other emotion-relevant topics (not discussed in this chapter) in which sex-related differences have been examined include clinical depression (Nolen-Hoeksema, 1987), intimate relationships (eg Gottman & Levenson, 1988), empathy (Eisenberg & Lennon, 1983), symptom sensitivity and reporting (Manstead, in press), and endocrine–aggression relationships (eg Jacklin, 1989).

Emotion concepts and attributions

Included in this general category of topics are studies which typically employ sex as a stimulus variable, particularly emotion-relevant stereotypes, and studies which typically employ sex as a subject variable, most of which focus on knowledge of the antecedents, constituents, and consequences of emotion episodes or specific emotions. The stability of findings when sex is a stimulus variable compared to the inconsistent results of sex as a subject variable is particularly pronounced.

Sex as a stimulus variable

In addition to Birnbaum's studies discussed above, other investigators have also demonstrated the robustness of emotion "master stereotypes", some of which are tacitly held (eg Shields & Koster, 1989). The expectation that women should and will display less socially negative affect is particularly pronounced. Undergraduates asked to imagine a female friend and a male friend in emotionally salient situations believed that female friends would experience more of all types of emotion and would express more socially valued positive emotion but that male friends would display more self-oriented, socially less desirable emotions (Johnson & Schulman, 1988). Women whose affective experience is described as highly negative are judged to be less likeable than men who are similarly described (Sommers, 1984). These values vary cross-nationally. Sommers and Kosmitski (1988) found different patterns in the United States and West Germany. For example German women report that rage need not be concealed whereas American women believe that it should be.

Fabes and Martin have thus far undertaken the most comprehensive study of gendered emotion stereotypes (Fabes, 1989). A study of preschoolers revealed that children's recall of images was affected by how well that image conformed to gender stereotypes (Martin *et al.*, 1990). Children were three times more likely to recall the sex of the person expressing an emotion incorrectly when the emotion was counterstereotypic (eg boy crying) than when it was stereotypic (eg boy angry). Interestingly, boys were more likely to distort than were girls and there was more distortion for boy targets than for girl targets. Furthermore, children were more likely to recall sex-consistent emotions as being more intense than sex-inconsistent emotions, even though pictures did not objectively differ in intensity of expression. A follow-up study measured the degree to which preschool children believe adults and children can experience stereotypic versus non-stereotypic emotions. Both boys and girls report that girls and women can sometimes get angry, but that boys and men (in particular) are unlikely to experience sadness. On the basis of these results, Fabes suggests that children's stereotypes about emotions are based primarily on their extreme beliefs about males rather than their beliefs about emotions. That is, young children's stereotypes about emotions may reflect the rigidity of their typing for males, with typing for females being more flexible: moms can get angry but dads can't get sad.

Fabes and Martin (1990a,b) have also compared adults' gendered emotion stereotypes as they are related to the age of the target. They find that sex of target by age of target interactions vary predictably with the emotion rated and whether capacity for experience, control, or expression of the emotion is rated. Their results suggest that adults' gender–emotion stereotypes are based on the belief that males do not show what they feel and that this exaggerated discrepancy between felt emotion and expressed emotion is largely a phenomenon of adolescence and adulthood that is emotion-specific. For example, the experience of sadness is believed to be similar for both sexes across ages, while expression is believed to decrease significantly as control increases, especially for males. When specific problematic negative emotions are considered, female targets are perceived to experience and express emotions related to internalized defenses (guilt, anxiety, depression) and males externalized defenses (hate).

Sex as a subject variable

In studies of emotion concepts that employ sex as a subject variable, a very different picture of gendered emotion emerges. The large majority of studies that report an analysis for sex-related differences find none for adults (eg Heise & Thomas, 1989; Clark & Teasdale, 1985; Shields, 1984; Lubin, Rinck & Collins, 1986) or for children (eg Covell & Abramovitch, 1988; Thompson, 1989). When differences do occur it is usually within a context that makes gender salient, such as asking subjects to imagine emotion scenarios that highlight social roles or relationships. For example, Egerton (1988) examined accounts of anger and weeping episodes that subjects provided while imagining themselves in the emotion-evoking scenario. Most notable of the sex-related differences obtained for the two types of emotion scenario was women's greater reported conflict about the anger episode (descriptions of the anger as effective, but upsetting and costly) and men's more frequent use of "passion schemas" (representations of the anger as externally caused and uncontrollable) for the anger episode.

Differences are also likely to be found when subjects have an opportunity to introduce the social or interpersonal aspects of emotion's context into their responses. Carlson and Carlson (1984) asked subjects to write scripts about excitement, fear, joy, and shame. Women used interpersonal themes for all emotions, while men used interpersonal themes only for joy and shame. O'Leary and Smith (1988) examined beliefs about what causes would lead to the experience of each of 10 emotions and found that women were more likely to attribute emotions to relational or internal sources, men to external stimuli. In these and other studies that report sex-related differences, interpersonal aspects of the situation appear to have been more salient for women research participants (eg Brabeck & Weisgerber, 1988).

Results in studies with children are very similar to those employing adults. Strayer (1986), for example, interviewed four–five and seven–eight year old children regarding their beliefs about the antecedents of particular emotions. Girls mentioned more interpersonal themes as instigators of emotion than did boys. Trepanier-Street and Romatowski (1986) looked at stories written by girls and boys (grades 1 and 2, 3 and 4, and 5 and 6) and found that children used more emotion statements with reference to their own sex than the other sex. Older children ascribed more emotion statements to characters than did younger children and this was especially true of the oldest group of girls. Feshbach and Hoffman (1978) interviewed kindergarten, second, third, fourth, and sixth graders of diverse ethnic backgrounds regarding situations that children believe elicit several emotions. The only significant sex-related difference they found was in the tendency for girls to describe emotions as occurring within family and social contexts, while boys were more self-oriented, manifesting greater preoccupations with possessions, competence, and autonomy.

The special significance of the social and interpersonal aspects of emotion's context for gender is particularly striking in Saarni's studies of the acquisition

display rules. Although she finds no sex-related differences
ledge about effective display rules and the conditions for
1979, 1989), sex-related differences in *performance* occur,
older children (Saarni, 1984; Cole, 1986). In one study, for
, children in three age groups (6–7, 10–11, and 13–14 years of age) were
interviewed regarding their beliefs about emotional dissembling (Saarni, 1988).
A few sex-related differences emerged, primarily because the oldest girls were
unique in several of their beliefs. Specifically, they reported that dissembling
works and that they value honest expression of emotion to peers. They also
used more complex reasoning in explaining the relationship between felt and
expressed emotion.

The general pattern of these results suggests that the interpersonal causes and
consequences of emotion may be more salient to girls and women. However,
it is impossible on the basis of available research to separate the "uncensored"
on-line reaction that constitutes a gender-based conceptual system from the more
self-conscious knowledge of the "gender-correct" response. This is not to suggest
that research participants' reports are based on self-presentation concerns, but
rather that they may be the non-deliberative reflection of a deeply ingrained
gender belief system. Until research is designed directly to sort out the relationship
of these two (or other) variables contributing to this apparent gender difference,
no conclusion about the "real" basis of the performance difference is possible.

Encoding and decoding expression

The great majority of this research has dealt with the processes involved in
producing (spontaneous or posed) and judging others' facial expressions of
emotion. Of all emotions research it is in this area that the most consistent
performance differences between male and female subjects occur. Some studies
report women as better at decoding posed or spontaneous expressions (eg
Kirouac & Dore, 1985; Sogon & Izard, 1987) or at encoding (eg Haviland &
Lieberman, 1990; Wagner, MacDonald & Manstead, 1986; Noller & Gallois,
1986; Gallois & Callan, 1986). The rare studies that find men more accurate
at encoding or decoding find greater accuracy for anger (Rotter & Rotter, 1988;
Wagner, MacDonald & Manstead, 1986; Walbott, 1988), but this effect is related
to cultural background (McAndrew, 1986).

The most extensive reviews and evaluations of this literature have been provided
by Judith Hall (1978, 1984, 1987). Her most comprehensive review of the
literature concluded that females are better at decoding non-verbal cues, at
recognizing faces, and at expressing emotions via non-verbal communication
than are males. Females also have more expressive faces, smile more (except,
apparently, children), gaze more, receive more gaze (adults at least), employ
smaller approach distances when observed unobtrusively, and are approached
closer by others. Women use body movements and positions that appear to be
less restless, less expansive, more involved, more expressive, and more self-

conscious than men do. Finally, they emit fewer speech errors and filled pauses. (1984, p. 143)

The size of most of these differences is moderate, and meta-analyses have since suggested that a very small portion of the variance accounted for overall is attributable to subject sex (Hall, 1987). This certainly suggests that characteristics of the experimental situation may be moderating the effects of subject sex. Hall (1987), in fact, notes an important mitigating factor in interpreting these data: the contexts in which expressive behavior is measured tend to be settings in which there are demand characteristics for gender-appropriate behavior. She observes that laboratory studies, conducted largely with college students in contexts that imply or encourage conversation with strangers, ''are probably marked by strong implicit demands to be nice, by self-consciousness, and by social anxiety in the presence of strange experimenters and fellow subjects'' (Hall, 1987, p. 183).

The signal complexity that is possible when affective channels carry a message different from that expressed linguistically suggests the possibility for a richer, more complex medium of communication (Hall, Mroz & Braunwald, 1983; Halberstadt, Hayes & Pike, 1988). Skilled communicators take advantage of the fact that humans can simultaneously ''multiplex'' as senders *and* as receivers of communications. The capacity to smile while conveying negative messages need not simply be a deceptive device but can be used as a strategy for maintaining the positive affective side of the relationship while negotiating conflicting goals. von Salisch (1988) examined children's patterns of smiling during structured quarrels in the social psychology laboratory. Like Hall and Halberstadt (1986), she found a weak and non-significant tendency for higher smiling frequency (''genuine'' smiling as opposed to social smiling) in girls. Much more striking, however, was the interaction between gender and closeness of friendship: girls who were close friends smiled significantly more and had a higher proportion of synchronous smiles than boys who were close friends. Boys were generally more distant in their communication style. They expressed comparatively few reproaches, smiled significantly fewer genuine smiles and showed more non-verbal signs indicating tension or unrest (eg lip bites, wiggling in their chairs). That complex affective communications may have a relationship-building outcome is suggested in the way adult men and women talk about their friendships. Women (in the United States and New Zealand) report that they are more intimate and emotional in their same-sex friendships than do men; men report deriving more emotional support from friendships with women than with men (Aukett, Ritchie & Mill, 1988).

Reported experience and expressiveness

To obtain information about the subjective component of emotion we must rely largely on self-report measures. This technique is not inherently flawed; unfortunately, however, self-report measures are often poorly constructed, inappropriately employed, or grossly misinterpreted. Because self-report reflects belief, it is important to keep in mind that subjects' notions of what "ought" to be true or is "typically" true can be the foundation of the response, particularly when they are asked to make aggregate retrospective self-assessments. When concurrent or highly specific accounts are obtained, the subject's report is better able to reflect beliefs about ongoing experience or factual occurrences. Studies of mood and the menstrual cycle illustrate this point. Global retrospective reports, which are heavily influenced by beliefs about what "ought" to occur or what is "typical", tend to yield "classic" patterns of mood variation over the cycle, whereas concurrent diaries or daily mood checklists show no such pattern (eg Parlee, 1973; Slade, 1984). McFarlane, Martin and Williams (1988), for example, obtained daily mood self-ratings for undergraduates for an extended period (70 days). Mood for both sexes varied as a function of day of the week and mood was equally stable over time for women and men. The concept of emotion, which is larded with stereotypes and tacit beliefs, may be particularly sensitive to different methods of obtaining self-report.

Self-report frequently yields sex-related differences whether subjects are asked about the experience and expression of emotion generally or about specific emotions. The difference typically takes the form of women reporting greater frequency or intensity of the emotion in question (eg Balswick & Avertt, 1977). One notable exception to this pattern is anger. Allen and Haccoun (1976) used a questionnaire method to obtain self-reports about experiencing, expressing, and valuing anger, fear, joy, and sadness in a small sample of college students. Women reported more expression of all four emotions and greater intensity of experience for all emotions except anger, for which there was no difference in women's and men's reports. Allen and Haccoun's finding that women and men report similar intensities of anger has been observed by several other investigators. Averill (1983) obtained college students' self-reports concerning anger episodes. He found no sex-related differences in frequency, intensity, expression, or causes of anger. Stoner and Spencer (1987), using the Anger Expression Scale (Spielberger, Johnson & Jacobs, 1982) found no difference between women's and men's reports about feelings or expressions of anger in 21–83 year old midwestern adults. Spielberger and his colleagues had originally found differences in a high-school sample, with males reporting more unexpressed anger. Janisse, Edguer and Dyck (1986), also using Spielberger's scale, found that type A males gave higher ratings of state anger, more vivid anger imagery, and lower perceived self-control ratings than type B males or either type A or B females. Burrowes and Halberstadt (1987) obtained self-ratings on a question-naire regarding the expression and experience of anger in social situations from college students and non-student adults. A subset of their sample was also rated on expressivity via a brief questionnaire given to a friend or family member. These investigators found no significant sex-related differences on any measure.

Laboratory manipulations of anger tend to be equally effective for subjects of both sexes, although Frodi (1978) noted that verbalization of reactions to and feelings towards a research partner who had provoked the subject's anger tended to have different consequences for each sex. Women instructed to write down their thoughts downplayed anger and aggression, whereas men "tended to preoccupy themselves with thoughts of anger or 'stirring themselves up'" (p. 347). When these men were given an opportunity to retaliate (via delivery of noxious sounds), they delivered sounds of significantly greater intensity than did men who had not been instructed to ruminate on the event.

Research participants' reports about their own experience and expressive behavior reflect their understanding of cultural and personal values and their beliefs about their own behavior, and it is not typically possible to discern the extent to which norms and self-observation each contribute to that report. For example, Malatesta and Kalnok (1984) surveyed non-student adults in three age groups and found that men were more likely to agree with the belief that men should conceal their feelings, but when reporting on their own behavior, it was women rather than men who reported more inhibition of emotional expression. Sex-related differences in self-report tend to be consistent with emotion stereotypes, as if some comparison of oneself to an emotional standard is operative in generating a response: "I must be emotional, after all I'm a woman" or "I must be inexpressive, after all I'm a man". The link between people's beliefs about emotion as gendered and their own conceptualization of gender role is further demonstrated in a study that grouped subjects on the basis of gender role self-concept (Ganong & Coleman, 1985). College students completed a measure of gender role self-concept (Bem Sex-Role Inventory; BSRI) and a self-report measure of emotional expressiveness. "Androgynous" students—those rating themselves as possessing a high degree of both "masculine" and "feminine" characteristics on the BSRI—rated themselves as most expressive. "Masculine" students—those rating themselves as possessing a high degree of "masculine" characteristics only—rated themselves as least expressive. Gender role self-concept appears to play a significant role in emotion-related self-evaluation processes and perhaps can explain why sex-related differences in self-report do not occur for anger (a "masculine" emotion) but are routinely obtained for "emotionality" (Deiner, Sandvik & Larsen, 1985; Flett et al., 1986; Kircaldy, 1984), other individual emotions (eg Stapley & Haviland, 1989), and emotion-related behaviors such as empathy (Eisenberg & Lennon, 1983; Strayer, 1989).

Tacit beliefs about the relationship between emotion and gender account for many of the differences obtained in self-report studies, and these beliefs may play a prominent role in how the individual regulates his or her emotional life vis-à-vis others. In the course of developing an Emotional Self-Disclosure Scale, Snell, Miller and Belk (1988) found that reported tendency to disclose emotion to another was a function of the personal characteristics of the disclosure recipient as well as the sex of the speaker. Both women and men were less willing (and about equally so) to discuss their emotions with men friends than women friends, and women were more willing to disclose a variety of emotions to women friends and spouses/lovers than were men. Among college students, women and men hold different expectations about the likelihood that they would express particular emotions and the kinds of reactions that others would have to their expressions (eg Dosser, Balswick & Halverson, 1983). Like adults, children also seem to have gender-based beliefs about their own expressiveness and others' responses to it. Fuchs and Thelen (1988) reported that less positive expectancies and lower likelihood of expression were particularly pronounced for older boys (grade 6 compared to grades 1 and 4). These explicitly held beliefs are reflected in conversational content outside of the laboratory. Shimanoff (1983) found that in natural conversation between friends, college student women and men talked equally about emotion, although men used more affect words and talked more about their own emotions when they were in opposite-sex dyads. Sex of conversation partner did not affect the emotive references of women conversationalists.

Strategies for studying the psychology of gender and emotion

This brief and selective review suggests that the greatest effect of gender lies less in what each sex knows about emotion than in what each sex is likely to do with that knowledge, particularly in contexts in which gender is salient. A discrepancy between knowledge and practice has been observed for other behaviors that are gender-coded. For example, boys' and girls' knowledge about babies and caregiving is equivalent (Fogel & Melson, 1986), but by age four boys and girls respond quite differently when instructed to "take care of" an infant (Berman, 1987). Furthermore, by age 10, girls have acquired a caregiving "script" that they employ while caregiving, whether or not the script matches the particular needs of the baby (Berman, 1987). The effect is particularly pronounced when instructions to subjects make gendered standards of behavior salient, that is, when the research participant's response may wholly or in part be influenced by his or her sense of what is "correct" or "desirable" behavior. For example, sex-related differences in adults' avowed attraction to infants are exaggerated when self-reports are obtained in public, mixed-sex setting and attenuated when the self-report is private and anonymous (Berman, 1980).

A recurring theme in this review is the robust effect of sex as a stimulus variable. There is clear evidence that beliefs about gender and emotionality influence interactions between infants and caregivers and other adults' communication with the infant. A number of investigators have shown that babies' emotional displays are differentially evaluated solely on the basis of sex. Haviland (1977) had judges rate the expressions of babies in segments of videotape. Some judges were told the correct sex of the infant, others were told that the baby was of the other sex, and still other judges were asked to guess the baby's sex. Babies believed to be boys were seen as expressing fear, anger, and distress much more often than those who were believed to be girls; those believed to be girls were seen as joyful more often than boys. Condry and Condry (1976) similarly found that subjects who saw a child labeled as a boy displaying an ambiguous negative response interpreted the response as anger, while those who saw the same videotape with the child labeled a girl saw the emotion as fear. Even the earliest interactions with the caregiver are characterized by the caregiver's differential responsiveness to the specific emotional expressions of female and male infants (Haviland & Malatesta, 1981; Malatesta & Haviland, 1982).

While the research participant's susceptibility to a gender-based "response bias" adds horrifying complexity to research design, it at least offers a point of origin for the development of testable explanations of apparently ephemeral effects of gender. Paradoxically, instead of demonstrating the insignificance of gender effects in emotions research, it shows how powerfully a tacitly held standard can deploy its effects. It also makes clear the boundaries for generalizing from effects observed within a single measurement context. To infer anything about gender, comparisons of male and female subjects must include consideration of the measurement context as a variable. Such a strategy is exemplified in Hall and Halberstadt's (1986) examination of the conditions of social smiling in adults. To test the extent to which situational variables moderate sex-related differences in smiling frequency, they blind-rated several dimensions of situations (face-to-face involvement, situational friendliness, social tension, and relative status) in which subjects' expressive behavior had been observed. They found that in situations characterized by a friendly tone, inspiring more nervousness, or involving face-to-face involvement women smiled significantly more frequently than men; the individual's relative status in the situation was unrelated to smiling frequency. Another example can be drawn from Gottman and Levenson's (1988) longitudinal investigation of marital interaction, which has revealed some striking and apparently stable sex-related differences. A complete model will require examining how the effect of subject sex is moderated by the role relationship and context. For example, do lesbian or gay male couples show the same behavioral asymmetry and physiological patterning that Gottman and Levenson find in heterosexual couples? Are prototypes of the married couple pattern found in non-intimate heterosexual or same-sex relationships based on role-governed power inequities (eg boss–worker) or on equality (eg close co-workers)?

The effects of beliefs about gender are sufficiently consistent and powerful to deserve greater attention in emotions research. A key set of questions revolves around the relationship between the constructs of expressiveness (variation in behavioral tempo) and emotionality, constructs which are generally conflated in emotion theories.[4] Buck (cited in Hall, 1984) defines facial expressiveness in terms of "breakpoints", that is, the observer's judgment that something meaningful has happened on the face of the expressor. If expressiveness can be conceptualized as a communication, what, then, is "emotionality"? Is it conceptually, expressively, or experientially distinct from the occurrence of specific emotions? For example, to what extent is emotionality inferred by observers in the *absence* of FACS and MAX-codable expressions? More specifically, to what extent is the expectation that different kinds of emotions are expressed by males and females based on actual differences in their expression?

In conclusion, a "gendered" approach to the study of human emotion brings to light assumptions about the operation of emotion in social life. Saarni (1989, p. 182) proposes that "Emotional development occurs *because* we exist within interpersonal systems". To this we can add the proposition that, within these interpersonal systems, sex (as a stimulus variable) serves as one of the most powerful regulators of emotional transactions.

NOTES

1. For the seventeenth-century writer "races" were Italians, Germans, Jews, Spaniards, etc. Like Wright, I must qualify the generalizations that I make in this chapter by noting that they are largely based on the North American research literature. Gender as a social variable is, of course, moderated by class, ethnicity, and historical era.
2. By distinguishing between "sex" and "gender", the phenomena referenced by sex/gender labels are more clearly identified. For example, "gender role" is a more accurate term than "sex role" to apply to a culture's expectations regarding sex-appropriate behaviors, beliefs and attitudes. "Core gender identity", one's identification of oneself as male or female, clearly refers to the individual's beliefs about identity rather than genital appearance alone. The sex/gender distinction is not meant to imply that an independent reality can be or ought to be ascribed to each; rather, the semantic distinction is explicitly concerned with furthering theory development and increasing the conceptual sophistication of empirical research. To adopt the sex/gender distinction is neither to suggest that one is derivative of the other nor that the two are necessarily causally linked. Some continue to use the terms sex and gender interchangeably (eg Maccoby, 1988). For a discussion of the analogy between sex/gender and the biological and cultural manifestations of emotion see Shields (1990).
3. See, for example, Hare-Mustin and Maracek's (1988) analysis of the intellectual consequences of models that emphasize sex differences or sex similarities.
4. Recently, Halberstadt (in press) has developed a model of socialization of expressiveness within the family that successfully disembeds these two constructs.

REFERENCES

Abu-Lughod, L. (1986). Honor and the sentiments of loss in a Bedouin society. *American Ethnologist*, **12**, 245–261.
Allen, J. G. & Haccoun, D. M. (1976). Sex differences in emotionality: A multidimensional approach. *Human Relations*, **29**(8), 711–722.
Aukett, R., Ritchie, J. & Mill, K. (1988). Gender differences in friendship patterns. *Sex Roles*, **19**(1/2), 57–66.
Averill, J. R. (1983). Studies on anger and aggression: Implications for theories of emotion. *American Psychologist*, **38**(11), 1145–1160.
Balswick, J. & Avertt, C. P. (1977). Differences in expressiveness: Gender, interpersonal orientation, and perceived parental expressiveness as contributing factors. *Journal of Marriage and the Family*, **39**, 121–127.
Barden, R. C., Garber, J., Lieman, B., Ford, M. & Masters, J. C. (1985). Factors governing the effective remediation of negative affect and its cognitive and behavioral consequences. *Journal of Personality and Social Psychology*, **49**, 1040–1053.

Berman, P. W. (1980). Are women more responsive than men to the young? A review of developmental and situational variables. *Psychological Bulletin*, **88**, 668–695.

Berman, P. (1987). Children caring for babies: Age and sex differences in response to infant signals and to the social context. In N. Eisenberg (Ed.), *Topics in Developmental Psychology*. New York: Wiley, pp. 141–164.

Birnbaum, D. W. & Chemelski, B. E. (1984). Preschoolers' inferences about gender and emotion: The mediation of emotionality stereotypes. *Sex Roles*, **10**(7/8), 505–511.

Birnbaum, D. W. & Croll, W. L. (1984). The etiology of children's stereotypes about sex differences in emotionality. *Sex Roles*, **10**(9/10), 677–691.

Birnbaum, D. W., Nosanchuk, T. A. & Croll, W. L. (1980). Children's stereotypes about sex differences in emotionality. *Sex Roles*, **6**(3), 435–443.

Brabeck, M. M. & Weisgerber, K. (1988). Responses to the Challenger tragedy: Subtle and significant gender differences. *Sex Roles*, **19**(9/10), 639–650.

Brody, L. (1985). Gender differences in emotional development: A review of theories and research. *Journal of Personality*, **53**(2), 102–149.

Buchwald, A., Strack, S. & Coyne, J. (1981). Demand characteristics and the Velten mood induction procedure. *Journal of Consulting and Clinical Psychology*, **49**, 478–479.

Burrowes, B. D. & Halberstadt, A. G. (1987). Self- and family-expressiveness styles in the experience and expression of anger. *Journal of Nonverbal Behavior*, **11**(4), 254–268.

Cancian, F. (1987). *Love in America: Gender and Self-Development*. New York: Cambridge University Press.

Carlson, L. & Carlson, R. (1984). Affect and psychological magnification: Derivations from Tomkins' script theory. *Journal of Personality*, **52**(1), 36–45.

Clark, D. M. & Teasdale, J. D. (1985). Constraints on the effects of mood on memory. *Journal of Personality and Social Psychology*, **48**(6), 1595–1608.

Cole, P. M. (1986). Children's spontaneous control of facial expression. *Child Development*, **57**, 1309–1321.

Condry, J. C. & Condry, S. (1976). Sex differences: A study of the eye of the beholder. *Child Development*, **47**, 812–819.

Covell, K. & Abramovitch, R. (1988). Children's understanding of maternal anger: Age and source of anger differences. *Merrill-Palmer Quarterly*, **34**(4), 353–368.

Crawford, M. & Maracek, J. (1989). Psychology reconstructs the female: 1971–1988. *Psychology of Women Quarterly*, **13**(2), 147–165.

Deaux, K. (1985). Sex and gender. *Annual Review of Psychology*, **36**, 49–82.

Deaux, K. & Major, B. (1987). Putting gender into context: An interactive model of gender-related behavior. *Psychological Review*, **94**(3), 369–389.

Deiner, E., Sandvik, E. & Larsen, R. J. (1985). Age and sex effects for emotional intensity. *Developmental Psychology*, **21**(3), 542–546.

Dosser, D. A., Balswick, J. O. & Halverson, C. F. (1983). Situational context of emotional expressiveness. *Journal of Counseling Psychology*, **30**, 375–387.

Egerton, M. (1988). Passionate women and passionate men: Sex differences in accounting for angry and weeping episodes. *British Journal of Social Psychology*, **27**, 51–66.

Eisenberg, N. & Lennon, R. (1983). Sex differences in empathy and related capacities. *Psychological Bulletin*, **94**, 100–131.

Fabes, R. (1989, May). Stereotypes of emotionality. Paper presented at the Nags Head Conference on Sex and Gender, Nags Head, NC.

Fabes, R. A. & Martin, C. L. (1990a). Gender and age stereotypes of emotionality. Paper presented at the meeting of the American Psychological Society, Dallas, Texas.

Fabes, R. A. & Martin, C. L. (1990b). Gender stereotypes of problematic negative emotions. Submitted for publication.

Feshbach, N. D. & Hoffman, M. A. (1978). Sex differences in children's reports of emotion-arousing situations. In D. McGuinnes (Chair), Sex differences: Commotion, motion, or emotion: Psychological gender differences. Symposium conducted at the meeting of the Western Psychological Association, San Francisco, California.

Flett, G. L., Boase, P., McAndrews, M. P., Pliner, P. & Blankstein, K. R. (1986). Affect intensity and the appraisal emotion. *Journal of Research in Personality*, **20**, 447–459.

Fogel, A. & Melson, G. F. (1986). *Origins of Nurturance: Developmental, Biological, and Cultural Perspectives on Caregiving*. Hillsdale, NJ: Erlbaum.

Frodi, A. (1978). Experiential and physiological responses associated with anger and aggression in women and men. *Journal of Research in Personality*, **12**, 335–349.

Fuchs, D. & Thelen, M. H. (1988). Children's expected interpersonal consequences of communicating their affective state and reported likelihood of expression. *Child Development*, **59**, 1314–1322.

Ganong, L. H. & Coleman, M. (1985). Sex, sex roles, and emotional expressiveness. *The Journal of Genetic Psychology*, **146**(3), 405–411.

Gallois, C. & Callan, V. J. (1986). Decoding emotional messages: Influence of ethnicity, sex, message type, and channel. *Journal of Personality and Social Psychology*, **51**(4), 755–762.

Gottman, J. M. & Levenson, R. W. (1988). The social psychophysiology of marriage. In P. Noller & M. A. Fitzpatrick (Eds), *Perspectives on Marital Interactions*. San Diego: College Hill Press, pp. 182–200.

Halberstadt, A. G. (in press). The ecology of expressiveness: Family socialization in particular and model in general. In R. S. Feldman & B. Rimé (Eds), *Fundamentals in Nonverbal Behavior*. New York: Cambridge University Press.

Halberstadt, A. G., Hayes, C. W. & Pike, K. M. (1988). Gender and gender role differences in smiling and communication consistency. *Sex Roles*, **19**(9/10), 589–603.

Hall, J. A. (1978). Gender effects in decoding nonverbal cues. *Psychological Bulletin*, **85**(4), 845–857.

Hall, J. A. (1984). *Nonverbal Sex Differences: Communication Accuracy and Expressive Style*. Baltimore, Md: Johns Hopkins University Press.

Hall, J. A. (1987). On explaining gender differences: The case of nonverbal communication. In P. Shaver & C. Hendrick (Eds), *Sex and Gender, Volume 7: Review of Personality and Social Psychology*. Beverly Hills, Ca: Sage, pp. 177–200.

Hall, J. A. & Halberstadt, A. G. (1986). Smiling and gazing. In J. S. Hyde & M. C. Linn (Eds), *The Psychology of Gender: Advances Through Meta-Analysis*. Baltimore, Md: Johns Hopkins University Press.

Hall, J. A., Mroz, B. J. & Braunwald, K. G. (1983). Expressions of affect and locus of control. *Journal of Personality and Social Psychology*, **45**, 156–162.

Hare-Mustin, R. T. & Maracek, J. (1988). The meaning of difference: Gender theory, postmodernism, and psychology. *American Psychologist*, **43**(6), 455–464.

Haviland, J. M. (1977). Sex-related pragmatics in infant non-verbal communication. *Journal of Communication*, **27**, 80–84.

Haviland, J. M. & Lieberman, M. S. (1983). Individual factors relating encoding and decoding of facial affect: Gender and personality. Unpublished manuscript.

Haviland, J. M. & Malatesta, C. Z. (1981). Fallacies, facts and fantasies: A description of the development of sex differences in nonverbal signals. In C. Mayo & N. Henley (Eds), *Gender and Nonverbal Behavior*. New York: Springer.

Heise, D. R. & Thomas, L. (1989). Predicting impressions created by combinations of emotion and social identity. *Social Psychology Quarterly*, **52**, 141–148.

Hochschild, A. R. (1983). *The Managed Heart*. Berkeley, Ca: University of California Press.

Jacklin, C. N. (1981). Methodological issues in the study of sex-related differences. *Developmental Review*, **1**, 266–273.

Jacklin, C. N. (1989). Female and male: Issues of gender. *American Psychologist*, **44**(2), 127–133.

Janisse, M. P., Edguer, N. & Dyck, D. G. (1986). Type A behavior, anger expression, and reactions to anger imagery. *Motivation and Emotion*, **10**(4), 371–386.

Johnson, J. T. & Shulman, G. A. (1988). More alike than meets the eye: Perceived gender differences in subjective experience and its display. *Sex Roles*, **19**(1/2), 67–79.

Kirkcaldy, B. D. (1984). The interrelationship between state and trait variables. *Personal and Individual Differences*, **5**(2), 141–149.

Kirouac, G. & Dore, F. Y. (1985). Accuracy of the judgment of facial expression of emotions as a function of sex and level of education. *Journal of Nonverbal Behavior*, **9**(1), 3–7.

Krokoff, L. J. (1987). The correlates of negative affect in marriage: An exploratory study of gender differences. *Journal of Family Issues*, **8**(1), 111–135.

Lewin, M. (1984a). "Rather worse than folly?" Psychology measures femininity and masculinity, 1: From Terman and Miles to the Guilfords. In M. Lewin (Ed.), *In the Shadow of the Past: Psychology Portrays the Sexes*. New York: Columbia University Press, pp. 155–178.

Lewin, M. (1984b). Psychology measures femininity and masculinity, 2: From "13 gay men" to the instrumental–expressive distinction. In M. Lewin (Ed.), *In the Shadow of the Past: Psychology Portrays the Sexes*. New York: Columbia University Press, pp. 179–204.

Lewis, S. J. & Harder, D. W. (1988). Velten's mood induction technique: "Real" change and the effects of personality and sex on affect state. *Journal of Clinical Psychology*, **44**(3), 441–444.

Lorber, J. (1987). From the editor. *Gender & Society*, **1**, 123–124.

Lubin, B., Rinck, C. M. & Collins, J. F. (1986). Intensity ratings of mood adjectives as a function of gender and age group. *Journal of Social and Clinical Psychology*, **4**(2), 244–247.

Lutz, C. (1988a). Engendered emotion: Gender, power and the rhetoric of emotional control in American discourse. Paper presented for the workshop Accounts of Human Nature, Windsor, England.

Lutz, C. (1988b). *Unnatural Emotions: Everyday Sentiments on a Micronesian Atoll and Their Challenge to Western Theory*. Chicago: Univeristy of Chicago Press.

Maccoby, E. F. (1988). Gender as a social category. *Developmental Psychology*, **24**(6), 755–765.

Malatesta, C. Z. & Haviland, J. M. (1982). Learning display rules: The socialization of emotion expression in infancy. *Child Development*, **53**, 991–1003.

Malatesta, C. Z. & Kalnok, M. (1984). Emotional experience in younger and older adults. *Journal of Gerontology*, **39**(3), 301–308.

Manstead, A. S. R. (in press). Gender differences in emotion. In M. A. Gale & M. W. Eysenck (Eds), *Handbook of Individual Differences: Biological Perspectives*. Chichester: Wiley.

Martin, C. L., Fabes, R. A., Eisenbud, L., Karbon, M. M. & Rose, H. A. (1990). Boys don't cry: Children's distortions of others' emotions. Paper presented at the meeting of the Southwestern Society for Research in Human Development, Tempe, Arizona.

Masters, J. C., Ford, M. E. & Arend, R. A. (1983). Children's strategies for controlling affective responses to aversive social experience. *Motivation and Emotion*, **7**, 103–116.

Matlin, M. W. (1987). *The Psychology of Women*. New York: Holt, Rinehart & Winston.

McAndrew, F. T. (1986). A cross-cultural study of recognition thresholds for facial expressions of emotion. *Journal of Cross-Cultural Psychology*, **17**(2), 211–224.

McFarlane, J., Martin, C. L. & Williams, T. M. (1988). Mood fluctuations: Women versus men and menstrual versus other cycles. *Psychology of Women Quarterly*, **12**, 201–223.

Morawski, J. G. (1987). The troubled quest for masculinity, femininity and androgyny. In P. Shaver & C. Hendrick (Eds), *Sex and Gender, Volume 7: Review of Personality and Social Psychology*. Beverly Hills, Ca: Sage, pp. 44–69.

Nolen-Hoeksema, S. (1987). Sex differences in unipolar depression: Evidence and theory. *Psychological Bulletin*, **101**(2), 259–282.

Noller, P. and Gallois, C. (1986). Sending emotional messages in marriage: Non-verbal behaviour, sex and communication clarity. *British Journal of Social Psychology*, **25**, 287–297.

O'Leary, V. E. & Smith, D. (1988). Sex makes a difference: Attributions for emotional cause. In D. Smith (Chair), Two different worlds: Women, men, and emotion. American Psychological Association Convention, Atlanta, Georgia.

Parlee, M. B. (1973). The premenstrual syndrome. *Psychological Bulletin*, **83**, 454–465.

Potts, R., Morse, M., Felleman, E. & Masters, J. C. (1986). Children's emotions and memory for affective narrative content. *Motivation and Emotion*, **10**(1), 39–57.

Rosaldo, M. (1984). Toward an anthropology of self and feeling. In R. Shweder & R. Levine (Eds), *Culture Theory: Essays on Mind, Self, and Emotion*. New York: Cambridge University Press.

Rotter, N. G. & Rotter, G. S. (1988) Sex differences in the encoding and decoding of negative facial emotions. *Journal of Nonverbal Behavior*, **12**(2), 139–148.

Saarni, C. (1979). Children's understanding of display rules for expressive behavior. *Developmental Psychology*, **15**, 424–429.

Saarni, C. (1984). An observational study of children's attempt to monitor their expressive behavior. *Child Development*, **55**, 1504–1513.

Saarni, C. (1988). Children's understanding of the interpersonal consequences of dissemblance of nonverbal emotional–expressive behavior. *Journal of Nonverbal Behavior*, **12**(4), 275–294.

Saarni, C. (1989). Children's understanding of strategic control of emotional expression in social transactions. In C. Saarni & P. L. Harris (Eds), *Children's Understanding of Emotion*. Cambridge: Cambridge University Press, pp. 181–208.

Shields, S. A. (1984). Distinguishing between emotion and nonemotion: Judgements about experience. *Motivation and Emotion*, **8**, 355–369.

Shields, S. A. (1990). Conceptualizing the biology–culture relationship in emotion: an analogy with gender. *Cognition and Emotion*, **4**, 359–374

Shields, S. A. & Koster, B. A. (1989). Emotional stereotyping of parents in child rearing manuals, 1915–1980. *Social Psychology Quarterly*, **52**, 44–55.

Shimanoff, S. B. (1983). The role of gender in linguistic references to emotive states. *Communication Quarterly*, **30**(3), 174–179.

Slade, P. (1984). Premenstrual emotional changes in normal women: Fact or fiction? *Journal of Psychosomatic Research*, **28**, 1–7.

Snell, Jr, W. E., Miller, R. S. & Belk, S. S. (1988). Development of the emotional self-disclosure scale. *Sex Roles*, **18**(1/2), 59–73.

Sogon, S. & Izard, C. E. (1987). Sex differences in emotion recognition by observing body movements: A case of American students. *Japanese Psychological Research*, **29**(2), 89–93.

Sommers, S. (1984). Reported emotions and conventions of emotionality among college students. *Journal of Personality and Social Psychology*, **46**(1), 207–215.

Sommers, S. & Kosmitski, C. (1988). Emotion and social context: An American–German comparison. *British Journal of Social Psychology*, **27**, 35–49.

Spielberger, C. D., Johnson, E. H. & Jacobs, C. A. (1982). *Anger Expression Scale Manual*. Tampa, Fl: Human Resources Institute, University of South Florida.

Stapley, J. C. & Haviland, J. M. (1989). Beyond depression: Gender differences in normal adolescents' emotional experiences. *Sex Roles*, **20**(5/6), 295–308.

Stoner, S. B. & Spencer, W. B. (1987). Age and gender differences with the anger expression scale. *Educational and Psychological Measurement*, **47**(2), 487–492.

Strayer, J. (1986). Children's attributions regarding the situational determinants of emotion in self and others. *Developmental Psychology*, **22**(5), 649–654.

Strayer, J. (1989). What children know and feel in response to witnessing affective events. In C. Saarni & P. L. Harris (Eds), *Children's Understanding of Emotion*. Cambridge: Cambridge University Press, pp. 259–289.

Strickland, B. R., Hale, D. W. & Anderson, L. K. (1975). Effect of induced mood states on activity and self report affect. *Journal of Consulting and Clinical Psychology*, **43**, 57.

Thompson, R. A. (1989). Causal attributions and children's emotional understanding. In C. Saarni & P. L. Harris (Eds), *Children's Understanding of Emotion*. Cambridge: Cambridge University Press, pp. 117–150.

Trepanier-Street, M. L. & Romatowski, J. A. (1986). Sex and age differences in children's creative writing. *Journal of Humanistic Education and Development*, **25**(1), 18–27.

Unger, R. K. (1979). Toward a redefinition of sex and gender. *American Psychologist*, **34**(11), 1085–1094.

Unger, R. K. (1981). Sex as a social reality: Field and laboratory research. *Psychology of Women Quarterly*, **5**, 645–653.

Unger, R. K. (1988). Psychological, feminist, and personal epistemology: Transcending contradiction. In M. M. Gergen (Ed.), *Feminist Thought and the Structure of Knowledge*. New York: New York University Press, pp. 124–141.

Unger, R. K. (1989). Sex, gender, and epistemology. In M. Crawford, M. Gentry (Eds), *Gender and Thought: Psychological Perspectives*. New York: Springer-Verlag, pp. 17–35.

von Salisch, M. (1988). Girls' and boys' ways of arguing with a friend. Paper presented at the Third European Conference on Developmental Psychology, Budapest, Hungary.

Wagner, H. L., MacDonald, C. J. & Manstead, A. S. R. (1986). Communication of individual emotions by spontaneous facial expressions. *Journal of Personality and Social Psychology*, **50**(4), 737–743.

Wallbott, H. G. (1988). Big girls don't frown, big boys don't cry—gender differences of professional actors in communicating emotion via facial expression. *Journal of Nonverbal Behavior*, **12**(2), 98–106.

West, C. & Zimmerman, D. H. (1987). Doing gender. *Gender & Society*, **1**, 125–151.

Wright, T. (1973/1601). *The Passions of the Minde*. New York: Verlag.

9 Emotion and Health: Towards an Integrative Approach

ROBERT J. ROBINSON
*Department of Psychology, Stanford University, Stanford, California,
CA 94305-2130, USA*

JAMES W. PENNEBAKER
*Department of Psychology, Southern Methodist University, Dallas,
Texas 75275, USA*

> *My life is in the hands of any rascal who chooses to annoy me*
> Dr John Hunter, 1723–1793 (in Jenkins, 1978, p. 544)

Our culture has evolved a set of contradictory beliefs about the links between emotion and health. Most of us, for example, agree that it is unhealthy always to keep unpleasant emotions locked up inside ourselves. At the same time, many of us think that people who chronically express anger or other negative emotions are prone to heart attacks and other health problems. Alternatively, we may believe that an optimistic outlook is healthy and, at the same time, think someone who is too cheerful is probably repressing unhealthy emotions. Depending on the newspaper that we may be reading at the moment, we are told that emotions cause, are caused by, or are independent of health and illness. This confusion is reflected in our popular culture, as revealed by sayings such as "get it off your chest" and "nothing like a good cry to make you feel better" which exhort us to unburden ourselves of our negative emotions and which hint at the fact that we may thereby improve our psychological state. On the other side we have the "cowboys don't cry" and "when the going gets tough, the tough get going" mind-sets, which instruct us that it is both unseemly and non-productive (and possibly harmful) to display emotion, particularly distress. Such cultural ambivalence is shared by the psychological community. A cursory glance at recent research suggests that there are strong research findings that support all sides of this controversy.

One of the central problems in studying the links between emotion and health is in disentangling a variety of seemingly contradictory theories and approaches. As will be discussed, the apparent disarray within the emotion world reflects the diverse methodological training and theoretical focus of emotion researchers. The concept of emotion has very different meanings for a neuroscientist interested in brief and highly specific psychological events than it does for a personality researcher who studies chronic mood states.

International Review of Studies on Emotion, Vol. 1. Edited by K. T. Strongman
©1991 John Wiley & Sons Ltd

The purpose of this chapter is to explore the empirical links between emotion, emotional expression, and health. We begin with a discussion of the definition and time course of emotion. As will be seen, the relation between emotion and physiological activity depends on the way emotion is conceptualized. By considering the different definitions of emotion, we can better understand how the various beliefs concerning emotion, emotional expression, and health have evolved. Within any given horizontal level of analysis for research, the links between emotion and health are reasonably predictable and understandable. Between horizontal levels, however, the relationships between emotion and biological processes are often contradictory. We conclude the chapter by suggesting that researchers attempt to develop more vertical theories of emotion. That is, in understanding how emotions influence health, it is important to consider the brain activity, autonomic nervous system responses, hormonal changes, and long-term personality processes. As a possible model of such a vertical approach, the present findings from recent work on emotional inhibition and health are discussed in some detail.

WHEN EMOTIONS OCCUR: THE INVESTIGATOR PROBLEM

Imagine the following scene.[1] You are car-pooling to work in morning traffic. You are sitting in the passenger seat in the front of the car, and the traffic is moving swiftly. The road you are on has just changed from being a highway to a major suburban road and there is a sidewalk on which pedestrians are walking. You happen to glance to your right at the very instant a businessman steps onto the pedestrian crossing, right in front of the car ahead of yours. There is a moment of wild incongruity, the sight of a person walking steadily in front of a car which is bearing down on him. All of a sudden, the rhythm of movement is completely altered. You hear a metallic thud and see the pedestrian tossed in the air like a collection of rags, rotating incredibly fast, head over heels. He flies into the air, passing over the car which struck him and across the path of your vehicle, striking the road just outside your vehicle. You hear an awful soft and liquid sound as he hits the ground. As you swivel your head to look further, you see him seem to lift his head slightly for an instant then it sags down, and in that moment your car turns a bend in the road and the scene is cut off.

From the time you saw the pedestrian step off the curb to the time you lost sight of him less than two seconds have elapsed, although that familiar "slow-motion" action was operating on everything you saw. You work your mouth for what seems like an eternity, but which is again probably less than two seconds, and begin to blurt out what you have just witnessed. Incredibly, no one else in the car, including the driver, saw the incident.[2]

Try to imagine your emotions at various points as the events unfolded. How did you feel when you realized that the pedestrian was about to be struck by the car? When you heard the thud and saw him fly into the air? When you saw him hit the ground? When you tried to convince your friends of what you had seen? Later that day? Now, several years later? Obviously, these questions are asking about emotions which are related to events with a time-lag of microseconds to seconds, minutes, hours, and years. This raises the question: what is the link between events, emotions and physiological activity? Where is the emotion? What is the link between the event and the various outcome measures? How long does the emotion last? What might be the links between viewing this scene and long-term health changes? And what about individual differences? How much would your responses to the event be similar to others?

As should be apparent, the answers to these questions depend on the time unit, the measure of emotion, and the person or organism under investigation. In this section, we briefly examine how scientists from four different perspectives would evaluate your reactions to witnessing this scene. The definition of the mind–body problem, it seems, is highly dependent on the investigator's measurement of physiological processes and their relevant time units. Indeed, in this chapter we wish to make an even stronger claim, viz that the link between emotion and health is anything but clear or well understood, and a great deal of this is due to the fact that practitioners in this field consist of a diverse array of subspecialities, many of which are interested in very different time-frames, physiological processes, and health outcomes. We suggest that there are at least four major temporal classifications of investigators in this area, and by way of background we will look briefly at each.

THE NEUROSCIENTIST'S EMOTION: WHEN MILLISECONDS COUNT

Walter Cannon (1929) was the first to point to the role of the brain in the experience of emotion. In his view, primary emotions such as fear and anger were triggered almost immediately following an emotion-eliciting stimulus. In the pedestrian accident scenario, Cannon would have argued that your perception of emotion would begin as soon as the visual information had been crudely processed and registered in your cortex and limbic system: a matter of milliseconds. Thus, fractions of a second after you saw the pedestrian in the obviously endangered position in the road, messages would have begun flashing through your brain that this was a highly unusual sight.

Since Cannon's initial publication, an important and often ignored body of literature has arisen that points to the immediacy of emotion as it stems from the central nervous system. In both animal and human research, direct electrical stimulation of various brain regions in the limbic system, medial forebrain bundle, and elsewhere produces the manifestation, and in humans the subjective experience, of immediate and profound pleasure, misery, anger, frustration, and fear (eg Heath, 1964). In these cases, no peripheral feedback (as demanded by William James, 1890) or situational information (as posited by cognitive labeling theorists) is necessary for the emotional experience.

More recently, studies relying on electroencephalography (EEG) point to the close contiguity between the perception of a stimulus and the beginnings of an emotional response. Perhaps best known are studies that examine evoked-related potentials, or ERPs. In this research, biological reactions corresponding with the perception of novel or emotion-evoking stimuli are detected within 300 ms of the presentation of stimuli (eg Coles, 1989). Presumably, this central nervous system neural activity signals the beginning of later (and slower) biological changes that are eventually detected in autonomic nervous system activity. Thus it is clear that in 300 ms the observer of the pedestrian accident would not have a coherent thought about the situation, yet a fairly well-developed biological response would be under way.

As can be seen in Figure 9.1, the neuroscientist will define emotion as occurring in very close contiguity to the eliciting stimulus. Bodily changes and feedback would be considered irrelevant or, at best, secondary. In addition, assumptions about physiological specificity and emotion (ie the specificity hypothesis) would not be of particular interest or relevant to the study of emotion. Among the popularly held emotion theories, then, the neuroscientific community would have no alternative but to endorse Cannon's centralist emotion theory.

THE PSYCHOPHYSIOLOGIST'S EMOTION: THE FOUR-SECOND RULE

In an outstanding article on the psychophysiology of emotion, Robert Levenson (1988) posits that emotions last from 0.5 to 4 s. Indeed, most autonomic nervous systems, and even somatic nervous system activity, peak during this brief time period following an emotional stimulus. We know, for example, that when people hear a loud and unexpected noise, there will be a change in facial

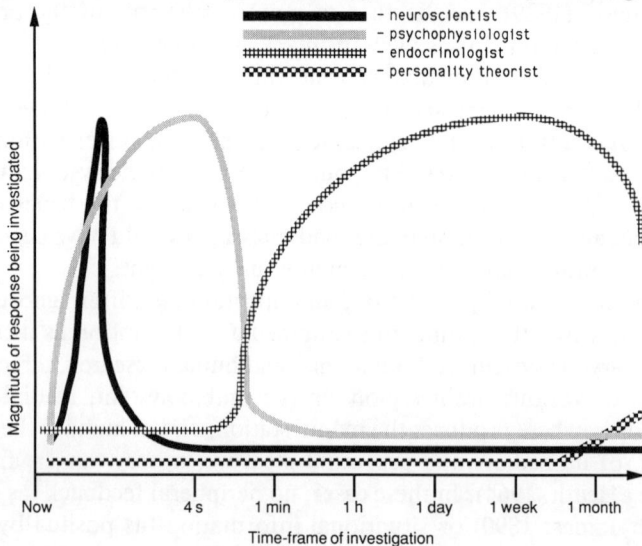

Figure 9.1. Time-frame of events for investigators

expression within 500 ms (Ekman, 1984). Within 1–2 s after the noise, measurable changes in cardiovascular activity (eg elevation of heart rate, stroke volume of the heart, and cardiovascular tone) occur. Other sympathetic nervous system changes, such as electrodermal activity, typically peak within 2–4 s after the noise (see Cacioppo, Petty & Tessinary, 1990, for a review of each of these systems).

The physiology of the peripheral nervous system is, of course, delayed relative to the activity of the central nervous system. Harking back to seeing the pedestrian struck by the car, the event must be processed in several brain regions before the hypothalamus stimulates the direct action of the sympathetic system. Any feedback from the body to conscious systems will be delayed. By adopting the four-second rule, the emotion theory of William James both makes sense and is supportable. This model is also intuitively appealing. Most people find it very difficult to describe a response or emotion that occurs within 0.5 s of a stimulus event, but the period of 0.5–4 s after a stimulus is a familiar time, when the first, raw, emotions are recognizable and usable to most of us. This period covers the event sequence in our accident from about the time the pedestrian was struck to the time verbalizations were attempted to convey the information about the incident. In that period, an observer (and this will vary greatly by individual) might have passed through mild surprise, alarm, fear, horror, and a sense of shock, and at the end of the period will be actively and consciously attempting to make useful decisions about what to do next.

THE ENDOCRINOLOGIST'S EMOTION: MINUTES, HOURS, MAYBE DAYS

Within medicine, the field of psychosomatics have been shaped by researchers interested in the relation between psychological events and hormonal changes. In 1953 Hans Selye (1976) was one of the first investigators to discover that when individuals are confronted by stressors, a number of significant, albeit slower, physiological changes occur. The endocrine, or glandular/hormonal system is controlled in large part by the pituitary gland, which, in turn, is under control of the hypothalamus. In Selye's view, the shock of seeing the pedestrian struck by the car would cause the release of minute amounts of hormones from the hypothalamus, which would stimulate the pituitary gland (corticotrophin-releasing factor, or CRF). The pituitary gland would then manufacture and release its own hormones to various glands throughout the body that could variously influence glucose regulation and inflammation (adrenal gland), immune function (thymus gland), and so forth. Although these changes might be initiated several seconds after the emotion-eliciting event, they may take hours or days to return to normal. It is important to note that emotion-induced biological changes can have direct and indirect effects on all the major biological systems of the body.

The cardiovascular system

Today, the cardiovascular system is implicated in more premature deaths in industrialized countries than any other physiological system, and is probably the most studied part of all human physiology. Emotions mediate several of the key indicators for possible CHD and other symptoms. In particular, anger, anxiety, fear, and various other emotionally distressed states have been implicated in elevated rates of heartbeat and blood pressure. It has long been known that emotions will affect cardiovascular indices. Thus in examining the heart rate and stroke volume of subjects in anxiety- versus hostility-provoking situations, Ax (1953) noted that the two emotions produced clearly distinguishable reactions in the two indices. Adsett, Schottstaedt and Wolf (1962) showed that stressful interviews can increase heart rate. Since this early work, there has been such an avalanche of evidence that today it is common knowledge among the lay population that strong emotions like anxiety, anger, and fear can drive up indices like blood pressure or heart rate (for reviews, see articles by Matthews *et al.*, 1986; Joesoef *et al.*, 1989; Dembroski *et al.*, 1989).

The gastrointestinal tract

Many of our phrases which we use to indicate emotional distress involve the gastrointestinal tract. Cannon (1929) observed that various digestive secretions in cats were suspended in threatening situations—we now know that this is true of humans as well. This is probably an adaptive response, in that we rush blood to our muscles and away from our stomach in threatening situations, as well as undergoing several other physical changes which make us better prepared for physical confrontation with an enemy. In more extensive classic demonstrations, Wolf and Wolff (1947) investigated the secretions, motor activity, blood flow, and temperature of the stomach lining under various conditions. They discovered close links to psychological and emotional factors, which moderated the physical activity in highly complex and somewhat unpredictable ways. Signs like the color of the stomach-lining, amount and acidity of bile, amount of saliva, and speed of digestion appear to be powerfully moderated by emotional states. The largest body of research dealing with this system concerns the various kinds of ulcers and the role of psychological factors in exacerbating or alleviating them (Kirsner, 1968; Whitehead & Schuster, 1985). Psychophysiological phenomena have also been noted for conditions such as irritable bowel syndrome (Welgan, Meshkinpour & Hoehler, 1985) and nausea and vomiting (Stunkard *et al.*, 1985).

The adrenal system and catecholamines

In recent years, rapid advances have been made in our understanding of the links between emotional states and the activity of the endocrine system. Of particular importance to health psychologists are the activities of the adrenal, thyroid, and pituitary glands. The endocrine system is primarily hormonal, and its normal functioning is critical for growth, sex drive, repair of cuts and bruises, the overcoming of infection, our state of arousal, and our emotions. Preparation for fight or flight is mediated by the secretion of epinephrine (also called adrenalin), which is controlled directly by the autonomic nervous system and, within the blood, indirectly via epinephrine secreted by the adrenal medulla. Frankenhaeuser, Sterky and Jarpe (1962) documented that neuroendocrine secretions (called catecholamines) were highly correlated with the amount of subjective stress and the intensity of other emotions reported by subjects (see also Lovallo et al., 1990). In another emotional realm, Board, Wadeson and Persky (1957) noted elevated catecholamine levels for depressed subjects. Indeed, an area of great philosophical and practical importance is the extent to which psychological and emotional states are caused by chemical imbalances and to what extent emotions change the body chemicals. For a more in-depth discussion of these issues, see Schaffer and Baum, (1984), Leedy and Wilson, (1985), Fredrikson, Sundin and Frankenhaeuser (1985), and Dabbs et al. (1987).

The immune system

Immune functioning is a critical survival issue for humans. Daily, our lives depend on our body's ability to screen out and destroy noxious substances, microbes, viruses, parasites, infections, and diseased or damaged cells. When immune functioning fails, we become vulnerable to a variety of health problems. Immunocompetence, or the ability of the immune system to deal with foreign bodies, infections, etc, is influenced by various lifestyle habits such as smoking, alcohol, and caffeine, as well as broader psychological and emotional factors (Kiecolt-Glaser et al., 1984; Persky, Kempthorne-Rawson & Shekelle, 1987; Kemeny et al., 1989).

Using mice, Sakakabara (1966) found that a stressor, in the form of a bright flashing light, resulted in more and faster tumor growth than for control animals. In humans, Locke et al. (1978) found that natural killer cells were present in the lowest numbers under conditions of high personal stress as caused by significant changes in life circumstances. In terms of personal factors, there have for many years been theories suggesting certain personalities may be more prone to certain diseases, such as cancer (LeShan, 1959). Although clear-cut evidence for the existence of a stable and disease-prone personality remains controversial, it seems clear that individuals exhibiting a tendency towards certain persistent emotional or mood states have systematically superior or inferior immunocompetence. Thus, Levy et al. (1985) illustrated that apathy, depression, and fatigue predicted lowered natural killer cell activity among women with breast cancer (also, Levy et al., 1988; Evans et al., 1988).

Whereas early findings in the psychosomatic literature focused on chronic changes within the cardiovascular system (eg various catecholamines, hypertension, constriction of the coronary arteries) and systems affected by specific diseases such as cancer (eg mortality rates, survival times), more recent work has been examining the specific action of the immune system. From the ground-breaking studies of Ader (eg 1981) up to more recent work such as Kiecolt-Glaser and Glaser (1988) and Levy et al. (1985), the findings from the new field of psychoneuro-immunology have demonstrated that immune functioning can be enhanced or compromised for hours, days, or even weeks following stressors of differing magnitudes.

THE PERSONALITY THEORIST'S EMOTIONS: YEARS, MAYBE DECADES

The fourth time-frame to be considered is that of the personality theorists. These researchers approach the emotion–health link from the broadest temporal perspective. Most agree that individuals differ in their proclivities to experience and to report different emotions. The research reviewed to this point has been concerned with transient emotions, which, when induced in a laboratory setting, last anywhere from a few seconds to a few minutes at most. Within such a time-frame, the physiological responses of the body may well serve a specific purpose, for example preparing the individual for physical exertion by pumping epinephrine into the blood, suspending digestion of food and saliva production, and rushing more blood to the muscles. However, when such arousal continues over hours, days, and perhaps months and years, it is possible for negative physical results to occur.

The personality approach linking emotions and health has its roots in the science of the ancient Greeks. They believed that individuals who had an excess of blood, phlegm, or yellow or black bile would display the dominant character-istics of being chronically sanguine, choleric, phlegmatic, or melancholic.[3] More recently, researchers have begun to distinguish an assortment of emotion-related personality types that are correlated with disease outcomes. Although dozens of individual-difference strategies have evolved, we briefly discuss personality–disease links associated with anger, positive and negative emotions, and the suppression of emotion.

Anger-related personalities

Over two decades ago the beginnings of a special partnership between medicine and psychology emerged. Two cardiologists, Howard Friedman and Ray Rosenman (eg 1976), popularized the link between the type A personality style and coronary heart disease (CHD). Controlling for various risk factors, it was discovered that the hard-driving, competitive and hostile type As were more than twice as prone to CHD as their more easy-going type B counterparts (Rosenman et al., 1975).[4] Although the type A literature originally described the individual as suffering from a hurry sickness, later research began to point a finger towards the role of anger and hostility as the noxious component of the type A syndrome (Glass, 1977; Dembroski *et al.*, 1978; Chesney & Rosenman, 1985). Today, the role of anger and the manner in which it is expressed or inhibited appears to be central in the etiology of many diseases.

Typically, much of the research continues to link both type A and anger or hostility with various physiological indices. Thus, Weidner *et al.* (1987) report a close interrelationship between type A and hostility scores, and elevated blood lipids in adults. Lundberg *et al.* (1989) have reported elevated cholesterol levels for angry/hostile type As versus other type As and type Bs. Williams *et al.* (1980) reported far more coronary arteriosclerosis among adults scoring high on the type A scale, and within the type A subjects, a greater percentage (70% vs 48%) of those displaying elevated scores on the hostility scale of the MMPI had signs of arteriosclerosis.

Other research has concentrated on hostility and anger without invoking the role of type A. A particularly promising development in this direction employs inventories designed to measure hostility, such as the Cook–Medley Hostility scale (Cook & Medley, 1954). High hostility scores have been associated with lower survival rates in lawyers over a 30-year period (Barefoot *et al.*, 1989) and greater cardiovascular reactivity to stress (Weidner *et al.*, 1989).

Even anger *per se* has proven to be a somewhat elusive correlate of heart disease. Research has diverged according to anger suppression versus anger expression (Spielberger, 1980; Spielberger *et al.*, 1985). While traditional type A research has indicated a link between anger expression and CHD, other work suggests that anger suppression may be tied to a greater predisposition to certain kinds of cancer. The exact role of anger and its various manifestations and its links to health remain complex.

The robustness of the type A phenomenon led to the domination of type A research in the health psychology literature. Also, the link to CHD, the major killer in western society, made this the obvious issue to investigate further. Coupled to this, the fact that anger is a reasonably easily identifiable emotion and is quite simple to induce under controlled conditions, as opposed to more complex and subtle emotions such as envy or ennui, has meant that most of the research has, until quite recently, been concentrated in this area.

In conducting a meta-analysis of the type A literature, Booth-Kewley and Friedman (1987) have clearly illustrated that the individual suffering from hurry sickness is representing only one kind of CHD-prone behavior syndrome. CHD seems also to be strongly linked to depression, as well as anger and hostility. They conclude that "the picture . . . revealed . . . is not one of a hurried impatient workaholic but instead of a person with one or more negative emotions" (1987, p. 343). Today, it seems that the type A personality is descriptive of a process of specific anger as well as a more diffuse negativity rather than being the definitive psychological disease syndrome behind CHD.

Individual differences related to negative and positive emotions

The research on anger or hostility and health has usually been based on the assumption that highly specific anger-related emotions cause health problems. Another tradition within the personality realm assumes that people who display generalized negative emotions or moods are at risk for a variety of health problems. Conversely, individuals who are optimistic or chronically happy are posited to be healthy. As intuitively appealing as these ideas are, the evidence to support them is controversial at best.

One uncontested point is that individuals who have chronically high levels of negative moods and are pessimistic about life are more likely to report greater levels of distress and minor health problems (Costa & McCrae, 1987; Pennebaker, 1983; Watson & Pennebaker, 1989). Those individuals who are labeled as high in negative affect, or NA, tend to experience negative, distressing emotions consistently over time. Behaviorally, high NAs appear as depressed, anxious, complaining, and insecure.

The construct of NA can be viewed as a central component to a variety of popular individual-difference measures (Watson & Clark, 1984). Among scales that are predominantly NA markers are those such as the Taylor Manifest Anxiety Scale (Taylor, 1953), Byrne's Repression/Sensitization Scale (Byrne, 1961), Scheier, Weintraub and Carver's (1986) Life Orientation Test (a measure of dispositional optimism/pessimism), Cohen's Perceived Stress Scale (Cohen, Kamarck & Mermelstein, 1983), Kobasa's (1979) measurement of hardiness (a portion of which is determined by low scores on an anxiety scale), and other scales that tap neuroticism, anxiety, and mild depression.

Of particular interest is that NA markers such as these appear to be strongly related to perceived or self-reported distress and physical symptoms but only weakly correlated with objective health measures. In other words, individual differences that tap health complaints may not be related to true health outcomes at all. In a large survey, Watson and Pennebaker (1989) were unable to find significant correlations between NA measures and biological dysfunction or pathology, fitness and lifestyle, health-related visits/absences, and overall mortality. What NA was significantly correlated with was health complaint scales. Thus NA appears to predict symptom reporting but not actual pathology. Considering anxious university students during finals week, Taylor (1989) notes: "people may mistake symptoms associated with their mood disorder for legitimate medical problems and thus seek a physician's care because they think it is appropriate to do so" (p. 234). This kind of phenomenon suggests that NA is likely to remain a nuisance variable in health research and emphasizes the importance of including health data from several different sources when conducting research.

That NA markers may be unrelated to true physical ailments does not bode well for health psychology research that relies exclusively on self-report measures. It further suggests that personality approaches to health psychology that tap people's proclivities to report general negative or positive moods may not be strongly correlated with health outcomes.

Inhibition versus expression of emotion as an individual difference

An alternative approach to searching for which emotions may be most strongly linked to health problems is to consider the nature of emotional expression. That is, are people who fail to express the emotions they feel more prone to health problems than those who openly express their feelings? Recent work dealing with emotional inhibition suggests that the answer may be yes.

Recently, researchers have suggested that traits related to emotion inhibition, such as repression (Weinberger, 1989), may be causally implicated in a variety of health problems. Individuals scoring high on various measures of constraint or inhibition appear not to recognize their own affective reactions, and deny experiencing negative affect or affect-related arousal even when physiological measures clearly indicate arousal (Weinberger, Schwartz & Davidson, 1979; Davidson, 1988). Such individuals report low anxiety scores, but score in the top third of defensiveness measures such as the Marlowe–Crowne Social Desirability Scale (Crowne & Marlowe, 1960). These people seem to have erased the borderline between what we should feel and do feel (Horney, 1950).

An interesting development within the emotion suppression literature has been research linking an inhibited personality trait with cancer. The cancer-prone personality style, sometimes referred to as the type C individual, scores high on measures that tap mood suppression of various types. Temoshok and her colleagues (Temoshok & Heller, 1981; Temoshok et al., 1985) specifically defined the type C personality as a group of traits characterized by emotional constraint, particularly in the face of stress, or a hopeless–helpless personality with depressive tendencies. In research on women with breast cancer, Greer and Morris (1975) reported a greater likelihod of cancer among women scoring high on anger suppression. Greer's follow-ups (Greer, Morris & Pettingale, 1979; Greer, 1981) have shown that of those women with cancer, those who exhibited a "fighting spirit" had a far lower mortality rate than those who stoically accepted their condition or who became depressed. Depression can also, it seems, be predictive—Shekelle et al. (1981) reported that over a 17-year period, elevated depression scores on the MMPI were associated with a twofold increase in cancer mortality (Appel, Holroyd & Gorkin, 1983).

It has been argued that life stressors may be mediated by sharing the experiences or discussing the events with other people (Jourard, 1971; Derlega, 1984). Thus, those individuals scoring high on inhibition measures would be at greater risk for negative health consequences, particularly following major traumas. In this regard, research has revealed that those individuals who discussed the sudden death of a spouse were healthier and less preoccupied with the trauma a year later, compared to those people who did not discuss the events (Pennebaker & O'Heeron, 1984). Childhood traumas which were never discussed appear to be associated in adulthood with a host of ailments from hypertension to cancer, influenza and diarrhea (Pennebaker & Susman, 1988).

A disease-prone personality?

There is a certain appeal in subscribing to the belief that specific emotions are related to specific diseases: that anger causes heart disease and emotion suppression results in cancer. In recent years, however, it has become increasingly clear that emotion–disease specificity models are limited in their explanatory power. In an extensive meta-analysis, Friedman and Booth-Kewley (1987) selected five major psychosomatic illnesses, asthma, headaches, ulcers, arthritis and heart disease, and investigated whether a concept such as a disease-prone personality in fact had any scientific viability. They concluded that a constellation of personality variables could in fact be identified, viz depression, anger/ hostility, anxiety, and in certain cases extraversion. The evidence for all of these was, however, weak except in the case of CHD.

On a broader level, we must appreciate the different levels of analysis involved in the emotion–health link. A disease-prone personality, if it exists at all, will only account for a small percentage of the total variance of correlations between emotions and health. This is due, in part, to the processes studied by the neuroscientists, psychophysiologists, and endocrinologists. For a personality-based approach to be successful, it should consider the findings from each of the horizontal perspectives in emotion research.

TOWARDS MORE VERTICAL THEORIES OF EMOTION AND HEALTH

It is now fashionable for review papers in health psychology to call for more integrative approaches to health and disease. One solution that many writers have adopted is to create horrifyingly complex "box models" with dozens of boxes attached to one another with arrows pointing in all directions. Rather than present a new array of boxes, we would simply like to implore researchers to consider the various levels of analysis inherent in our understanding of the emotion–disease link. In this final section, we briefly summarize a case study of vertical research from our own laboratories on the relationship between inhibition and illness. We then point to the value of this approach in addressing several recurring emotion-related issues in health psychology.

The case of inhibition and confrontation

For the last several years, Pennebaker and his colleagues have been developing a general model of inhibition and psychosomatic disorders. The inhibition model is vertical in the sense that it attempts to isolate the social, personality, and even neural and biochemical correlates of coping with traumatic experience (eg Pennebaker, 1989). According to the model, the inhibition of ongoing thoughts, feelings, and behaviors is associated with physiological work. In the short run, we can measure this work by changes in brain wave activity and autonomic nervous system action. Over time, the work of inhibition serves as a cumulative stressor—much the way that Selye (1976) discusses stress—which can serve to exacerbate disease processes. One of the primary examples of inhibition in daily life occurs when people face a trauma that they are unable to discuss with others. Indeed, they have to actively hold back from telling others about their own personally significant experiences. Accordingly, if we force people to psychologically confront these experiences by writing or talking about them (ie disinhibition), we see immediate reductions in autonomic nervous system activity as well as improvements in health.

A model such as this can be difficult to test and evaluate because it crosses so many levels of analysis. Nevertheless, multiple experiments have tended to support the various components. Using college students, we have employed a confession paradigm wherein experimental subjects write about their deepest thoughts and feelings concerning the most upsetting or traumatic experiences of their entire lives (eg Pennebaker & Beall, 1986). Over the subsequent school year, it was found that those subjects who disclosed upsetting experiences (as opposed to those who had been asked to write about relatively innocuous subjects) exhibited better health as measured by a lower number of visits to the health center (Pennebaker, Colder & Sharp, 1990; Pennebaker, Kiecolt-Glaser & Glaser, 1988).

A critical aspect of this process appears to be that in transforming the memories of the traumas from repressed thoughts into written, structured language, the subjects gain both perspective on the incidents and insight into themselves and the past. The issue of insight reoccurs constantly in interviews with subjects, and failure to consider this may be one of the reasons that classical catharsis fell short. Interestingly, brain wave analysis while people disclose suggests that the linking of emotions and thoughts requires the integration of information from different brain regions (Pennebaker, 1989).

The connection between inhibition and health appears to be directly linked to the immune system. Inhibition of traumas and negative affect appears to cause an increased level of internal arousal which adversely affects immunocompetence. Pennebaker, Kiecolt-Glaser and Glaser (1988) discovered that after a writing paradigm such as the one described above, subjects exhibited improved immune functioning as compared to before the experiment. Further, this improvement was greatest in those individuals who had written about issues that they had previously never discussed. Other physiological indices also appear to be related to inhibition, such as skin conductance levels (SCL). Pennebaker, Hughes and O'Heeron (1987) observed a significant drop in SCL for those subjects who disclosed traumatic events.

The inhibition approach is only one of a small but growing group of vertical theories in health psychology. In addition to examining the autonomic and immune mechanisms, it also addresses some of the psychological and personality processes at work. Like an overstuffed cupboard, the mind constantly threatens to burst open and reveal the painful emotions. Holding back the creaking doors is a stressor which causes arousal and elevated physiological markers such as SCL, and ultimately compromises immunocompetence, resulting in a greater susceptibility to illnesses and disease. Confronting the trauma or negative affect releases the tension and reduces the physiological arousal, allowing the body's defenses to operate more effectively. Additionally, defensiveness and self-control appear to be implicated in heart disease as measured by increased LDL–cholesterol levels for individuals showing elevated scores on these dimensions (Muller, 1989). Although inhibition does not explain all or even most physical problems, the specific nature of this process appears to be strongly implicated in the two major killers facing industrialized nations today—cardiovascular disease and cancer—and must be worthy of close future scrutiny.

The specificity–generality debate

Nowhere is the failure to consider multiple levels of analysis in the emotion-health world so glaring as in the debate surrounding the specificity of emotion and physiological activity. As mentioned earlier, Selye's (1976) general adaptation syndrome asserts that physiological arousal is a non-specific response of the body to a stressor. Conceptually, therefore, the mechanism which causes arousal is always the same, differing only in degree, be the stressor a mugger lunging out of an alleyway or grief for the death of a loved one. Although there is some significant evidence to support this contention in the literature, we suggest, based on the evidence already reviewed, that the body's response is indeed specific to different emotional states.

By definition, if we are to see any links between emotion and health, we must define emotion broadly. For emotion—however it is defined or measured—to influence health it must last long enough to influence the major organ systems either directly (in some pathogenic way) or indirectly (eg by affecting health-related behavior). This can be accomplished in at least three general ways. First, specific emotions can irritate specific organ systems. Over time, the emotions produce sufficient wear and tear on the body to result in specific health problems. The question as to whether this actually happens or not is what is usually meant by the specificity debate. A second approach that is predominant in health psychology is more cognitive. According to research on cognitive styles, the particular outlook or belief systems held by the individual can influence both the emotions that people experience and the health-related behaviors that they exhibit. The cognitive styles approach, then, assumes that emotions and health covary but may not necessarily be causal. Thirdly, the expression/inhibition debate focuses on the relative health costs and benefits of repressing or expressing particular emotions.

Regarding evidence supporting the concept of generality of response, significant support is to be found within the area of social psychology. Schachter and Singer (1962) conducted a classic experiment in which they injected subjects with either epinephrine or a placebo, and either briefed subjects on the likely effects of the injection, deceived them, or led them to believe there would be no effects at all. While ostensibly waiting for the task to begin, subjects were paired with a confederate of the experimenter, who exhibited an elaborate set of behaviors indicating either (in different conditions) euphoria or anger. While all subjects who had received epinephrine were considerably more aroused than those who had received the placebo (as measured by heart rate, palpitations, and tremors), the self-reports of the experiences of the subjects varied greatly. Subjects who had been misinformed or who were ignorant of the effects of the injection were much more likely to report feeling euphoric or angry than those subjects who understood that their symptoms were consistent with effects of the injection or those who were given the placebo injection. The fact that a simple parasympathetic arousal could be misinterpreted as either anger or euphoria was seen as strong evidence to suggest that there is a general arousal mechanism in the body, and that specific emotions do not produce significantly different patterns of this arousal.

More recent research has, however, pointed to evidence supporting a specificity argument. Some authors have suggested that different emotions are associated with distinguishable autonomic nervous system activity (Ekman, Levenson & Friesen, 1983). Zajonc, Murphy and Inglehart (1989) have argued that different facial expressions cause microchanges in blood supply and temperature to different parts of the brain, bringing about the appropriate affective state to accompany the facial representation of that emotion. As technology has improved, it has become easier to discern distinct patterns of both physical and brain activity in response to different subjective emotional states.

The specificity–generality debate will probably never be fully resolved, since there are different levels of analyses—at least the same four levels as exist for the investigation of emotion. In this regard, we can imagine the debate having a different answer within each of these four time-frames. For the neuropsychologist and psychophysiologist, there is little problem: clear and specific physiological processes are associated within these short time periods with various emotional states. For the endocrinologist group, some doubt must exist—"arousal" *per se* appears to lower immune functioning, and although this may be more associated with certain emotions than others, the links are quite unclear. The most interesting controversy is within the personality domain, and involves whether there is a general "disease-prone" personality (see above) or more specific disorders related to distinct personality styles or type. Anger is a good example: Type A and its offshoots, hostility and aggression, have been widely implicated in cardiovascular disease. Yet, the closer one looks at this issue, the harder it is to pin one emotion or emotional style to a specific physical problem.

FUTURE DIRECTIONS FOR EMOTION AND HEALTH

As long as CHD and cancer remain major killers in our society, they will be a topic worthy of future research. The ways in which affect, particularly anger and hostility, increase CHD morbidity rates must be investigated and ways to combat the syndrome developed. At this time we know enough to conclude that anger and hostility probably do significantly increase proneness to CHD, via a reduced ability to metabolize cholesterol (Muller, 1989) and increased blood pressure and heart beat (Melamed, 1987). Regarding cancer (and other diseases which implicate immune function, such as AIDS), the role of emotion and its impact on the immune system has already been extensively reviewed, while old-fashioned but recently revamped and depressing social phenomena such as unemployment have been shown to lower immune functioning in women (Arnetz *et al.*, 1987). Derogatis (1986) notes that there is an increasing emphasis on the psychological aspects of cancer, while Appel, Holroyd and Gorkin (1983) see emotion as both friend and foe in the fight against cancer, with depression being the enemy and anger directed against the disease as a possible savior.

Following the change in emphasis of research on emotion and health from a focus on transient feelings to long-term moods and personality, the question becomes more and more one of identifying at-risk individuals. Controversial findings suggest that personality may be far more hereditary than was ever previously suspected (Tellegen *et al.* 1988); if so, this will have significant implications for the ways in which the interaction of disease of emotion are conceptualized. If individuals arrive in this world with a fairly predetermined personality structure (at least with regard to the "big three" affective personality dimensions, viz NA, positive affect, and inhibition), then future researchers will have to concern themselves with ways of helping people deal with or neutralize the toxic components of their personalities, just as we all have to learn to live with whatever physical characteristics we inherit.

The field of health psychology is broadly interested in the links between emotion, physiology, and health. This strength is also its weakness. The field is quite broad, drawing on researchers who represent different levels of analysis—from neuroscientists to personality theorists. All invoke terms such as emotion and stress, even though they refer to completely different concepts depending on the investigator's training. This leads to very different research results from the various fields regarding the role of emotion in health and the specificity of physical outcomes associated with various emotional states.

The differing approaches to emotion become primarily important when we begin to move in the direction of health. Changes in health usually reflect long-term changes—often involving multiple organ systems. To understand the links between emotion and health, we must adopt a relatively broad strategy that considers a wide window of time. This is not to dismiss the neuropsychologists' or the psychophysiologists' contributions. Rather, it is critical to extrapolate their findings to longer-term biological changes. For these reasons, the personality perspective appears to have a crucial role in coming work in this area, particularly the effect of inhibition/openness on health outcomes.

NOTES

1. This incident was observed, exactly as described here, by the first author as a college undergraduate on the way to school one morning.
2. We never did establish what had happened to that individual. The newspapers never reported the accident, and, after several days had passed, the incident had receded into a background memory.
3. Interestingly, the ancients were also quick to relate personality to disease. Roman physician Galen (AD 200) noted that melancholic women were at greater risk of cancer than sanguine women (Goldfarb, Driesen & Cole, 1967).
4. In their book *Type A Behavior and Your Heart* (1976), Friedman and Rosenman describe first crystalizing their theory when the chairs in their waiting-room were reupholstered and the workperson commented that only the fronts of the seats were worn, as if all the patients had literally been sitting on the edge of their seats!

Requests for reprints should be sent to the second author.

REFERENCES

Ader, R. (1981). *Psychoneuroimmunology*. New York: Academic Press.
Adsett, C. A., Schottstaedt, W. W. & Wolf, S. G. (1962). Changes in coronary blood flow and other hemodynamic indicators induced by stressful interviews. *Psychosomatic Medicine*, **24**, 331–336.
Appel, M. A., Holroyd, K. A. & Gorkin, L. (1983). Anger and the etiology and progression of physical illness. In L. Temoshok, C. Van Dyke & L. S. Zegans (Eds), *Emotions in Health and Illness: Theoretical and Research Foundations*. New York: Grune & Stratton, pp. 73–87.
Arnetz, B. B., Wasserman, J., Petrini, B., Brenner, S. O., Levi, L., Eneroth, P., Salovaara, H., Hjelm, R., Salovaara, L., Theorell, T. & Petterson, I. L. (1987). Immune function in unemployed women. *Psychosomatic Medicine*, **49**, 3–12.
Ax, A. F. (1953). The physiological differentiation between fear and anger in humans. *Psychosomatic Medicine*, **15**, 433–442.
Barefoot, J. C., Dodge, K. A., Peterson, B. L., Dahlstrom, W. G. & Williams, R. B., Jr (1989). The Cook–Medley hostility scale: Item content and ability to predict survival. *Psychosomatic Medicine*, **51**, 46–57.
Board, F., Wadeson, R. & Persky, H. (1957). Depressive affect and endocrine functions. *Archives on Neurology and Psychiatry*, **78**, 612.
Booth-Kewley, S. & Friedman, H. S. (1987). Psychological predictors of heart disease: A quantitative review. *Psychological Bulletin*, **101**, 343–362.
Byrne, D. (1961). The repression–sensitization scale: Rationale, reliability, and validity. *Journal of Personality*, **29**, 334–349.
Cacioppo, J., Petty, R. & Tessinary, L. (1990). *Handbook of Psychophysiological Measurement*. New York: Cambridge University Press.
Cannon, W. B. (1929). *Bodily Changes in Pain, Hunger, Fear and Rage*. Boston: Branford.
Chesney, M. A. & Rosenman, R. H. (Eds) (1985). *Anger and Hostility in Cardiovascular and Behavioral Diseases*. New York: Hemisphere.

Cohen, S., Kamarck, T. & Mermelstein, R. (1983). A global measure of perceived stress. *Journal of Health and Social Behavior*, **24**, 385–396.

Coles, M. G. H. (1989). Modern mind–brain reading: Psychophysiology, physiology, and cognition. *Pyschophysiology*, **26**, 251–269.

Cook, W. W. & Medley, D. M. (1954). Proposed hostility and pharisaic virtue scales for the MMPI. *Journal of Applied Psychology*, **38**, 414–418.

Costa, P. T. & McCrae, R. R. (1987). Neuroticism, somatic complaints, and disease: Is the bark worse than the bite? *Journal of Personality*, **55**, 299–316.

Crowne, D. P. & Marlowe, D. (1960). A new scale of social desirability independent of psychopathology. *Journal of Consulting Psychology*, **24**, 349–354.

Dabbs, J. M., Frady, R. L., Carr, T. S. & Besch, N. F. (1987). Saliva testosterone and criminal violence in young adult prison inmates. *Psychosomatic Medicine*, **49**, 174–182.

Davidson, M. L. (1988). *Distinguishing repressive defensiveness from impression management*. Unpublished doctoral dissertation, Stanford University.

Dembroski, T. M., MacDougall, J. M., Costa, P. T. & Grandits, G. A. (1989). Components of hostility as predictors of sudden death and myocardial infarction in the multiple risk factor invention trial. *Psychosomatic Medicine*, **51**, 514–522.

Dembroski, T. M., Weiss, S. M., Shields, J. L., Haynes, S. G. & Feinleib, M. (Eds) (1978). *Coronary-Prone Behavior*. New York: Springer-Verlag.

Derlega, V. (1984). Self-disclosure and intimate relationships. In V. Derlega (Ed.), *Communication, Intimacy, and Close Relationships*. Orlando: Academic Press, pp. 1–9.

Derogatis, L. R. (1986). Psychology in cancer medicine: A perspective and overview. *Journal of Consulting and Clinical Psychology*, **54**, 632–638.

Ekman, P. (1984). Expression and the nature of emotion. In K. Scherer & P. Ekman (Eds), *Approaches to Emotion*. Hillsdale, New Jersey: Erlbaum.

Ekman, P., Levenson, R. W. & Friesen, W. V. (1983). Autonomic nervous system activity distinguishes among emotions. *Science*, **221**, 1208–1210.

Evans, D. L., McCartney, C. F., Haggerty, J. J. *et al.* (1988). Treatment of depression in cancer patients is associated with better life adapation: A pilot study. *Psychosomatic Medicine*, **50**, 72–76.

Frankenhaeuser, M., Sterky, K. & Jarpe, G. (1962). Psycho-physiological relations in habituation to gravitational stress. *Perceptual and Motor Skills*, **15**, 63.

Fredrikson, M., Sundin, O. & Frankenhaeuser, M. (1985). Cortisol excretion during the defense reaction in humans. *Psychosomatic Medicine*, **47**, 313–319.

Friedman, H. S. & Booth-Kewley, S. (1987). The "disease-prone personality": A meta-analytic view of the construct. *American Psychologist*, **42**, 539–555.

Friedman, M. & Rosenman, R. H. (1976). *Type A Behavior and Your Heart*. London: Wildwood.

Glass, D. C. (1977). Stress, behavior patterns, and coronary disease. *American Scientist*, **65**, 177–187.

Goldfarb, C., Driesen, J. & Cole, D. (1967). Psychophysiologic aspects of malignancy. *American Journal of Psychiatry*, **123**, 1545–1552.

Greer, S. (1981). *Psychological response to breast cancer and eight-year outcome*. Paper presented at the 89th Annual Convention of the American Psychological Association, August 25, Los Angeles.

Greer, S. & Morris, T. (1975). Psychological attributes of women who develop breast cancer. *Journal of Psychosomatic Research*, **19**, 147–153.

Greer, S., Morris, T. & Pettingale, K. W. (1979). Psychological responses to breast cancer: Effect on outcome. *Lancet*, **2**, 785–787.

Heath, R. G. (1964). Pleasure response of human subject to direct stimulation of the brain: Physiologic and psychodynamic considerations. In R. G. Heath (Ed.), *The Role of Pleasure in Behavior*. New York: Hoeber.

Horney, K. (1950). *Neurosis and Human Growth*. New York: W. W. Norton.
James, W. (1890). *The Principles of Psychology*. New York: Holt.
Jenkins, C. D. (1978). Behavioral risk factors in coronary artery disease. *Annual Review of Medicine*, **29**, 543–562.
Joesoef, M. R., Wetterhall, S. F., DeStefano, F., Stroup, N. E. & Fronek, A. (1989). The association of peripheral arterial disease with hostility in a young, healthy veteran population. *Psychosomatic Medicine*, **51**, 285–289.
Jourard, S. M. (1971). *The Transparent Self*. New York: Van-Nostrand Reinhold.
Kemeny, M. E., Cohen, F., Zegans, L. S. & Conant, M. A. (1989). Psychological and immunological predictors of genital herpes recurrence. *Psychosomatic Medicine*, **51**, 195–208.
Kiecolt-Glaser, J. K., Garner, W., Speicher, C., Penn, G. M., Holliday, J. & Glaser, R. (1984). Psychosocial modifiers of immunocompetence in medical students. *Psychosomatic Medicine*, **46**, 7–14.
Kiecolt-Glaser, J. K. & Glaser, R. (1988). Psychological influences on immunity: Implications for AIDS. *American Psychologist*, **43**, 892–898.
Kirsner, J. B. (1968). Peptic ulcer: A review of the current literature on various clinical aspects. *Gastroenterology*, **54**, 610–618.
Kobasa, S. C. (1979). Stressful life events, personality and health: An inquiry into hardiness. *Journal of Personality and Social Psychology*, **39**, 1–11.
Leedy, M. G. & Wilson, M. S. (1985). Testosterone and cortisol levels in crewmen of US Air Force fighter and cargo planes. *Psychosomatic Medicine*, **47**, 333–338.
LeShan, L. L. (1959). Psychological states as factors in the development of malignant disease: A critical review. *Journal of the National Cancer Institute*, **29**, 1–18.
Levenson, R. W. (1988). Emotion and the autonomic nervous system: A prospectus for research on autonomic specificity. In H. L. Wagner (Ed.), *Social Psychophysiology and Emotion: Theory and Clinical Applications*. New York: Wiley, pp. 17–42.
Levy, S. M., Herberman, R. B., Maluish, A. M., Schlien, B. & Lippman, M. (1985). Prognostic risk assessment in primary breast cancer by behavioral and immunological parameters. *Health Psychology*, **4**, 99–113.
Levy, S. M., Lee, J., Bagley, C. & Lippman, M. (1988). Survival hazards analysis in first recurrent breast cancer patients: Seven-year follow-up. *Psychosomatic Medicine*, **50**, 520–528.
Locke, S. E., Hurst, M. W., Williams, R. M. & Heisel, I. S. (1978). *The influence of psychosocial factors on human cell-mediated immune function*. Paper presented at the Meeting of the American Psychosomatic Society, Washington, DC.
Lovallo, W. R., Pincomb, G. A., Brackett, D. J. & Wilson, M. F. (1990). Heart rate reactivity as a predictor of neuroendocrine responses to aversive and appetite challenges. *Psychosomatic Medicine*, **52**, 17–26.
Lundberg, U., Hedman, M., Melin, B. & Frankenhaueser, M. (1989). Type A behavior in healthy males and females as related to physiological reactivity and blood lipids. *Psychosomatic Medicine*, **51**, 113–122.
Matthews, K. A., Weiss, S. M., Detre, T., Demdroski, T. M., Falkner, B., Manuck, S. B. & Williams, R. B. (1986). *Handbook of Stress, Reactivity, and Cardiovascular Disease*. New York: Wiley.
Melamed, S. (1987). Emotional reactivity and elevated blood pressure. *Psychosomatic Medicine*, **49**, 217–225.
Muller, K. L. (1989). *Relations between social–emotional adjustment styles and lipoprotein metabolism*. Unpublished doctoral dissertation, Stanford University.
Pennebaker, J. W. (1983). Implicit psychophysiology: Effects of common beliefs and idiosyncratic physiological responses on symptom reporting. *Journal of Personality*, **51**, 468–496.

Pennebaker, J. W. (1989). Confession, inhibition and disease. In L. Berkowitz (Ed.), *Advances in Experimental Social Psychology*, Vol. 22. New York: Academic Press, pp. 211–244.

Pennebaker, J. W. P. & Beall, S. K. (1986). Confronting a traumatic event: Toward an understanding of inhibition and disease. *Journal of Abnormal Psychology*, **95**, 274–281.

Pennebaker, J. W., Colder, M. & Sharp, L. K. (1990). Accelerating the coping process. Southern Methodist University. *Journal of Personality and Social Psychology*, **58**, 528–537.

Pennebaker, J. W., Hughes, C. & O'Heeron, R. C. (1987). The psychophysiology of confession: Linking inhibitory and psychosomatic processes. *Journal of Personality and Social Psychology*, **52**, 781–793.

Pennebaker, J. W., Kiecolt-Glaser, J. K. & Glaser, R. (1988). Disclosure of traumas and immune function: Health implications for psychotherapy. *Journal of Consulting and Clinical Psychology*, **56**, 239–245.

Pennebaker, J. W. & O'Heeron, R. C. (1984). Confiding in others and illness rates in spouses of suicide and accidental death victims. *Journal of Abnormal Psychology*, **93**, 473–476.

Pennebaker, J. W. & Susman, J. R. (1988). Disclosure of traumas and psychosomatic processes. *Social Science and Medicine*, **26**, 327–332.

Persky, V. W., Kempthorne-Rawson, J. & Shekelle, R. B. (1987). Personality and the risk of cancer: 20-year follow-up of the Western Electric Study. *Psychosomatic Medicine*, **49**, 435–449.

Rosenman, R. H., Brand, R. J., Jenkins, C. D., Friedman, M., Strauss, R. & Wurm, M. (1975). Coronary heart disease in the Western Collaborative Group Study: Final follow-up experience of 8½ years. *Journal of American Medical Association*, **233**, 872–877.

Sakakabara, T. (1966). Effects of brightness or darkness on carcinogenesis. *Nagoya Shiritsj Daigaku Igakkai Sasshi*, **19**, 525–547.

Schachter, S. & Singer, J. E. (1962). Cognitive, social, and physiological determinants of emotional state. *Psychology Review*, **69**, 379–399.

Schaffer, M. A. & Baum, A. (1984). Adrenal cortical response to stress at Three Mile Island. *Psychosomatic Medicine*, **46**, 227–238.

Scheier, M. F., Weintraub, J. K. & Carver, C. S. (1986). Coping with stress: Divergent strategies of optimists and pessimists. *Journal of Personality and Social Psychology*, **51**, 1257–1264.

Selye, H. (1976). *The Stress of Life*. New York: McGraw-Hill.

Shekelle, R. B., Raynor, W. J., Ostfeld, A. M., Garron, D. C., Bieliauskas, L. A., Liu, S. C., Maliza, S. C. & Paul, O. (1981). Psychological depression and 17-year risk of death from cancer. *Psychosomatic Medicine*, **43**, 117–125.

Spielberger, C. D. (1980). *Preliminary Manual for the State–Trait Anger Scale (STAS)*. Tampa, Florida: University of South Florida.

Speilberger, C. D., Johnson, E. H., Russel, S. F., Crane, R. J., Jacobs, G. A. & Worden, T. I. (1985). The experience and expression of anger: Construction and validation of an anger expression scale. In M. A. Chesney & R. H. Rosenman (Eds), *Anger and Hostility in Cardiovascular and Behavioral Diseases*. New York: Hemisphere, pp. 5–30.

Stunkard, A., Foster, G., Glassman, J. & Rosato, E. (1985). Retrospective exaggeration of symptoms: Vomiting after gastric surgery for obesity. *Psychosomatic Medicine*, **47**, 150–155.

Taylor, J. (1953). A personality scale of manifest anxiety. *Journal of Abnormal and Social Psychology*, **48**, 285–290.

Taylor, S. E. (1989). *Health Psychology*. New York: Random House.

Tellegen, A., Lykken, D. T., Bouchard, T. J., Wilcox, K. J., Segal, N. L. & Rich, S. (1988). Personality similarity in twins reared apart and together. *Journal of Personality and Social Psychology*, **54**, 1031–1039.

Temoshok, L. & Heller, B. (1981). *Stress and Type "C" versus epidemiological risk factors in melanoma*. Paper presented at the 89th Annual Convention of the American Psychological Association, August 25, Los Angeles.

Temoshok, L., Heller, B. W., Sagebiel, R. W., Blois, M. S., Sweet, D. M., DiClemente, R. J. & Gold, M. L. (1985). The relationship of psychosocial factors prognostic indicators in cutaneous malignant melanoma. *Journal of Psychosomatic Research*, **29**, 139–153.

Watson, D. & Clark, L. A. (1984). Negative affectivity: The disposition to experience aversive emotional states. *Psychological Bulletin*, **96**, 465–490.

Watson, D. & Pennebaker, J. W. (1989). Health complaints, stress, and distress: Exploring the central role of negative affectivity. *Psychological Review*, **96**, 234–254.

Weidner, G., Friend, R., Ficarrotto, T. J. & Mendell, N. R. (1989). Hostility and cardiovascular reactivity to stress in women and men. *Psychosomatic Medicine*, **51**, 36–45.

Weidner, G., Sexton, G., McLellarn, R., Connors, S. L. & Matarazzo, J. D. (1987). The role of Type A behavior and hostility in an evaluation of plasma lipids in adult women and men. *Psychosomatic Medicine*, **49**, 136–145.

Weinberger, D. A. (1989). The construct validity of the repressive coping style. In J. L. Singer (Ed.). *Repression and Dissociation: Defense Mechanisms and Personality Styles*. Chicago: University of Chicago Press.

Weinberger, D. A., Schwartz, G. E. & Davidson, R. J. (1979). Low-anxious, high-anxious, and repressive coping styles: Psychometric patterns and behavioral and physiological responses to stress. *Journal of Abnormal Psychology*, **88**, 369–380.

Welgan, P., Meshkinpour, H. & Hoehler, F. (1985). The effect of stress on colon motor and electrical activity in irritable bowel syndrome. *Psychosomatic Medicine*, **47**, 139–149.

Whitehead, W. E. & Schuster, M. M. (1985). *Gastrointestinal Disorders: Behavioral and Physiological Basis for Treatment*. New York: Academic Press.

Williams, R. B., Haney, T. L., Lee, K. L., Kong, Y. H., Blumenthal, J. A. & Whalen, R. E. (1980). Type A behavior, hostility, and coronary atherosclerosis. *Psychosomatic Medicine*, **42**, 539–549.

Wolf, S. & Wolff, H. G. (1947). *Human Gastric Function*. New York: Oxford.

Zajonc, R. B., Murphy, S. T. & Inglehart, M. (1989). Feeling and facial efference: Implications of the vascular theory of emotion. *Psychological Review*, **96**, 395–416.

10 Emotional Creativity

JAMES R. AVERILL

CAROL THOMAS-KNOWLES
*Department of Psychology, University of Massachusetts, Amherst,
MA 01003, USA*

The juxtaposition of the terms "emotional" and "creativity" in the title of this chapter might seem incongruous, even self-contradictory. According to popular stereotypes and some scientific theories, emotions are biologically primitive and relatively fixed responses over which we have little control; creativity, by contrast, calls for flexibility, openness, and deliberation. In a similar vein, emotions are typically viewed as non-cognitive and divorced from higher thought processes; creativity, on the other hand, is highly prized as the epitome of intellectual accomplishment.

In fact, however, emotional creativity is ubiquitous. Its prevalence, however, is masked by stereotypes such as those noted above. For example, cross-cultural variations in emotions are well documented (Heelas, 1986; Levy, 1984; Lutz, 1988; Needham, 1981; Rosaldo, 1980). Such variations could not occur if emotions were as immutable as is often presumed. Emotional innovation and change are also common within cultures. The history of romantic love offers a good example (Averill, 1985; Beigel, 1951; deRougemont, 1949); so, too, does accidie, a kind of religious sloth that flourished during the Middle Ages but that now is a prime candidate for the "endangered emotions list" (Harré & Finlay-Jones, 1986).

Individual emotional development also involves innovation and change. Thus, falling romantically in love for the first time can be a creative experience. More seasoned observers may view the episode as commonplace, even clumsy, but for the person involved it is a unique and wondrous affair.

The typical reply to examples such as the above is that they simply represent variations on a small number of underlying themes. The *real* ("basic", "fundamental") emotions are there all along, unchanging and immutable—across cultures, across historical epochs, and across the individual lifespan.

If this reply were valid, the possibilities for emotional creativity would be severely limited. To borrow an analogy from Plutchik (1980), emotional creativity would be like mixing primary colors to obtain the various hues of the spectrum. We prefer a different analogy. Emotions are more like paintings than color mixtures. Paintings have form as well as substance. They are a product of the artist's inner vision, a meaning imposed on the world, and they admit

International Review of Studies on Emotion, Vol. 1. Edited by K. T. Strongman
©1991 John Wiley & Sons Ltd

of endless possibilities. Needless to say, not all paintings are original or creative. Conformity to established standards is as common in art as in any other field. But although most paintings may be grouped into genres or categories based on commonalities in origin and style (eg cubism, expressionism, surrealism), no category is more basic or fundamental than another.

To conclude this brief introduction, we define emotional creativity as follows:

> Emotional creativity is the development of emotional syndromes that are novel, effective, and authentic.

The key concepts in this definition (emotional syndrome, novelty, effectiveness, and authenticity) are discussed in the next two sections: in the first, we propose a general framework for the analysis of emotional syndromes, one that illustrates not only the possibility of emotional creativity, but its near inevitability; and in the second, we examine the criteria for evaluating a response as creative (novelty, effectiveness, and authenticity). In subsequent sections, we present

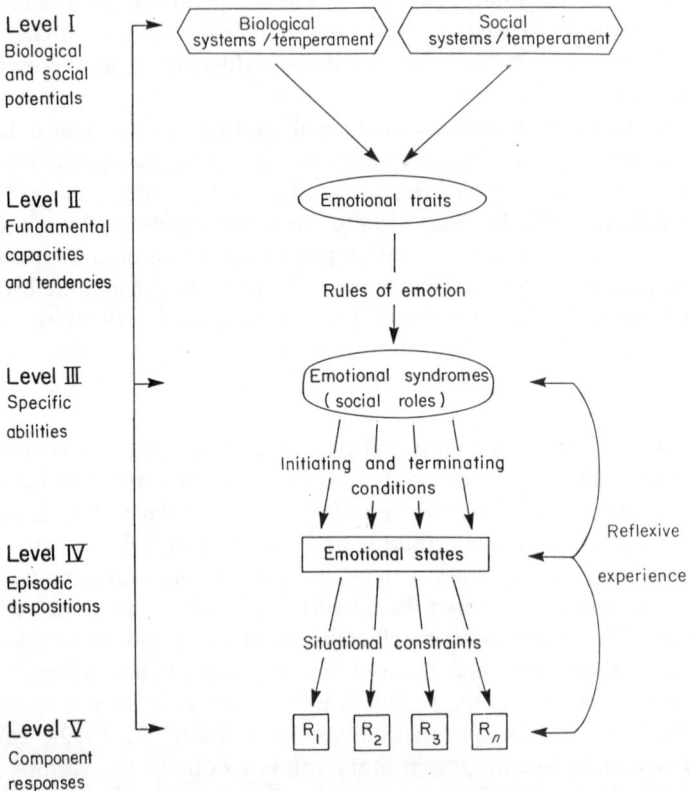

Figure 10.1. A framework for the interpretation of emotional behavior. (Reproduced by permission from Averill, 1988)

the results of an exploratory study designed to validate the construct of emotional creativity in conventional psychometric terms; and, based on the results of that study, we offer a sketch of the emotionally creative person.

HOW IS EMOTIONAL CREATIVITY POSSIBLE?

When we speak in the abstract of anger, love, fear, grief, etc, we are referring to emotional syndromes. As an abstraction, an emotional syndrome is a theoretical entity. It is like a concise conceptual map of the responses that tend to occur when a person is in an emotional state. A syndrome, however, is not like an ordinary map, that is, one which describes but does not alter the terrain it represents. A syndrome is more like an architect's blueprint—it is a "prescriptive description". The syndrome of anger, for example, not only describes but also helps determine the behavior of a person in an angry state.

Emotional creativity, as our definition indicates, involves the development of new and different emotional syndromes. Therefore, to understand how emotional creativity is possible, we must have a framework for understanding the origins and consequenes of emotional syndromes. Such a framework is presented in Figure 10.1. Five levels of organization are depicted in the figure; emotional syndromes are at the midpoint (level III). The levels above the midpoint (I and II) concern the biological, social, and psychological origins of emotional syndromes; the levels below the midpoint (IV and V) concern the ways emotional syndromes become manifested in behavior. The interconnected arrows at the left of Figure 10.1 indicate that intermediate levels of organization can sometimes be bypassed or short-circuited. The looped arrows on the right of the figure relate to the subjective experience of emotion (feelings), about which we will have more to say shortly.

Level I

An individual's biological and social potentials represent the origins of behavior at the most general or abstract level of organization. Biological potentials are the genotype, ie the genetic endowment drawn from the gene pool of the species. Social potentials may be defined analogously. During socialization, the individual is endowed with the potential for certain behaviors, drawn from the total repertoire of behaviors available to members of the society. No two persons have exactly the same biological or social potentials. This fact helps account for some of the individual differences in emotional behavior, but it is only a beginning.

Level II

Biological and social potentials interact to form, at the next lower level of organization, a person's fundamental capacities and tendencies. This is the first level of organization that can be measured directly. It represents the "source traits" of personality theory. Intelligence, as measured by IQ tests, is a good example. Creativity as a personality trait would also be defined at this level, as would the capacity to react in an emotional fashion (temperamental traits).

Level III

A distinction can be drawn between the capacity to respond (level II), discussed above, and the ability to respond (level III). Consider, for example, a person who has the genetic endowment for intellectual achievement, and who has been raised in a social environment that encourages intellectual activity; such a person might have the capacity to be a good mathematician. However, before the person would have the ability to solve calculus problems, say, he or she would have to acquire the rules and skills relevant to calculus. That is to say, abilities are rule-constituted, capacities are not, or at least not to the same degree.

Emotional syndromes can best be conceptualized at the level of specific abilities (Averill, 1988, 1991). Before people are able to become angry, hopeful, or whatever, they must acquire the rules relevant to the particular emotion. To return to an analogy used earlier, rules of emotion form the blueprints according to which emotional syndromes are constructed; when internalized, the rules help constitute the cognitive schemas without which there would be no ability to respond. The fact that emotional syndromes are rule-constituted is what makes emotional creativity possible. Change the rules and you change the emotion.

Level IV

Given the ability to engage in a particular emotional syndrome, such as anger, appropriate initiating conditions may result in the activation of an emotional state. An emotional state is not an occurrent or ongoing reaction. Rather, it is a relatively short-term, reversible disposition to respond in a manner consistent with the emotional syndrome (Averill, 1991).

Level V

The most concrete or specific level of organization comprises the component responses that a person might (or might not) exhibit during an emotional state, depending upon constraints imposed by the situation. These component responses normally include cognitive appraisals, physiological changes, expressive reactions, instrumental acts (including verbal behavior), and subjective experiences.

In pursuit of the tangible, theorists have tended to identify emotional syndromes closely with component responses, such as autonomic reactions and facial expressions. That, we believe, is a category mistake (Ryle, 1949); it treats variables belonging to one logical category (level V, Figure 10.1) as though they belonged to another (level III). We emphasize this point because it has particular implications for emotional creativity. Too close an identification of emotional syndromes with response variables can easily mislead. For example, the fact that certain facial expressions are universal (Ekman, 1984; Izard, 1977) is not, by itself, evidence for a corresponding set of universal ("basic", "fundamental") emotional syndromes. To make the example more specific, the fact that some facial displays are universally recognized as aggressive does not mean that anger is universal—unless anger as an emotional syndrome is inappropriately identified with aggressive behavior (Averill, 1982).

The subjective experience of emotion

Of all the types of component responses, none has been more consistently identified with emotional syndromes than subjective experience. Emotions are sometimes equated with "raw feelings", perhaps reflecting proprioceptive feedback from peripheral responses (eg the James–Lange theory and its various offshoots) or changes in the state of central neural mechanism (Oatley & Johnson-Laird, 1987). Such a view, if correct, would place severe limitations on emotional creativity. There are only so many ways that a person can "see red"; if emotional feelings were analogous, there would be only a few ways a person could feel angry or joyful or whatever.

In Figure 10.1, emotional feelings are depicted as involving a feedback loop connecting component responses (level V) to emotional states (level IV) and emotional syndromes (level III). That is, cues from bodily responses (including central neural states) are combined with information from the environment to further guide behavior, in accordance with the rules that help constitute emotional syndromes. Stated differently, emotional feelings are not simple experiences *sui generis*; rather, they are determined by the same rules that help constitute emotional syndromes.

Rules of emotion

Social rules or norms occupy a central place in the above analysis and hence deserve brief elaboration. Three types of rules can be distinguished: constitutive, regulative, and procedural (Averill, 1984, 1991). Strictly speaking, the distinction between these three types of rules does not represent a true trichotomy. Any given rule may have constitutive, regulative, and procedural aspects, albeit to varying degrees. For expository purposes, however, it is convenient to treat these three aspects as though they were separate classes of rules.

Consider a game such as chess. Some rules (eg with regard to the way the various pieces may be moved) help *constitute* the game as a game of chess, as opposed, say, to a game of checkers. Other rules (eg stipulating the time between moves) help *regulate* how the game is played on any given occasion. The third class of rules—*procedural rules*—help determine the quality of play. A chess-playing computer program, for example, consists primarily of procedural rules (heuristic algorithms).

Emotional syndromes are both constituted and regulated by rules, and they require appropriate heuristics for skilled enactment. Take the case of anger (Averill, 1982). If a constitutive rule is broken, the response will not be considered *real* anger but perhaps some other kind of emotion—envy, for example, or, if the violation is sufficiently extreme, a neurotic syndrome. By contrast, if a regulative rule is violated, the response may be recognized as anger but it will be considered inappropriate or illegitimate. Finally, if a procedural rule is broken, the response may be accepted as appropriate anger but its expression deemed clumsy or inept.

Constitutive rules are the most relevant to emotional creativity. All theorists recognize that emotions are regulated by rules, and that emotions can be enacted skilfully or clumsily. The idea that emotions are also constituted by rules is not so widely accepted. The more common view is that emotions are rather direct reflections of biological potentials—regulated but not constituted by social rules.

Even Hochschild (1983), who has done much to underscore the importance of emotion rules, implies that behind the institutionally enforced cheerfulness of an airline stewardess, or the anger of a bill collector, there exist feelings that are more authentic or "true" than others, and from which we may become "estranged". What is the origin of these "true feelings"? That is a question addressed by Morgan and Averill (in press). One possibility is that true feelings represent what we are as a biological organism. Hochschild (1983) rejects such an organismic view as "limited" (p. 28). Another possibility is that "true feelings" originate in social institutions but at an earlier point in time (childhood, perhaps). But that possibility would not confer on them the kind of authenticity Hochschild seeks. She therefore equivocates, but ultimately comes down on the side of biology:

> Emotion . . . is a biologically given sense, and our most important one. Like other senses—hearing, touch, and smell—it is a means by which we know about our relation to the world, and it is therefore crucial for the survival of human beings in group life. (p. 219)

We come down on the side of society. People consider true those feelings that are congruent with their fundamental values, and values are primarily a reflection of our social and not our biological heritage (Morgan & Averill, in press).

This is not the place to debate the relative importance of nature versus nurture in the determination of emotional syndromes and associated feelings. However, two further points deserve brief mention.

First, most of the evidence cited in favor of the innateness of basic emotions actually deals with biological potentials (eg towards aggression, attachment, avoidance, and the like—level I, Figure 10.1). Our concern is with specific emotional syndromes, such as anger, fear, and love (level III, Figure 10.1).

Secondly, as Figure 10.1 also indicates, there is no contradiction in saying that emotions are determined in part by biological potentials and that they are also constituted by rules. To further emphasize this point, an analogy may be made with language. Human beings as a species have a strong biological potential for language. However, any specific language (English, say, or Chinese) is constituted by social rules—the grammar of the language. Similarly, human beings may have a biological potential for aggression, but whether that potential becomes actualized in anger or in some other syndrome, or whether it becomes actualized at all, is a matter of social norms and rules.

We emphasize these points because, to the extent that emotional syndromes are constituted by rules, they are subject to innovation and change—not just superficially, but fundamentally. However, not every change deserves to be called "creative".

CREATIVITY

After a period of relative neglect, creativity is once again becoming a topic of considerable research and speculation (Amabile, 1983; Glover, Ronning & Reynolds, 1989; Richards et al., 1988; Sternberg, 1988; Wallace & Gruber, 1989). Two topics are of particular relevance to emotional creativity: first, the criteria for evaluating a response as creative; and, secondly, the stages in the creative process.

Criteria for evaluating a response as creative

To a certain extent, creativity is domain specific. For example, with few exceptions (eg Leonardo da Vinci), great scientists are not great artists, and *vice versa*. This specificity reflects, in part, the time and energy required to become proficient in a given field; and, in part, it reflects lower-order skills unique to a field (eg a musician requires motor coordination that a mathematician does not). But in addition to such specificities, there also are commonalities that cut across different domains of creative activity. These commonalities are reflected in three main criteria for evaluating a response as creative: novelty, effectiveness, and authenticity.

Novelty

The most frequently cited criterion for a creative response is that it should be, to some extent, new, different, or unusual. This criterion is so often taken for granted that relevant qualifications are sometimes overlooked. For one thing, not every novel response is creative. We must distinguish the creative from the bizarre, the merely eccentric, the random. For another thing, not every creative response is novel. As will be discussed shortly, authenticity can sometimes displace novelty as the hallmark of creativity.

Effectiveness

To be considered creative, a response must be of some potential benefit or value to the individual or society. This is what we mean by "effectiveness". In most instances, the evaluation of effectiveness is relatively straightforward, but that is not always the case. "Effectiveness" is a relative concept. What is effective in one context may be ineffective in another and what is effective in the short run may be detrimental in the long run, and *vice versa*. Even extraordinary scientific achievements and major works of art are sometimes recognized only after a change in circumstance or with the wisdom of hindsight. Galileo was arrested for his discoveries; van Gogh died a pauper; and Stravinsky was jeered at the *première* of Le Sacre du Printemps. Emotional innovation is especially likely to be disturbing to the individual and/or disruptive to society, at least in the short run. Thus, the effectiveness of an emotionally creative response must take into account more than the joys and sorrows of the moment; it must also consider the potential long-term benefit or harm to the individual and the group.

Authenticity

This third criterion might also be labeled "originality", except that the latter term is often confused with novelty. The difference between authenticity (originality) and novelty is well expressed by Arnheim (1966):

> The creative individual has no desire to get away from what is normal and ordinary for the purpose of being different. He is not striving to relinquish the object but to penetrate it according to his own criterion of what looks true. . . . The desire to be different for the sake of difference is harmful, and the urge to evade the given condition derives from a pathological state of affairs inherent either in the situation . . . or in the person, as in the "escape mechanism" of neurotics, attributed to artists by the Freudians. Faced with the pregnant sight of reality, the truly creative person does not move away from it but toward and into it. (p. 299)

A creative response should reflect in some fashion the individual's own values and beliefs about the world. Authenticity sometimes requires that a person stand alone, against social custom and the expectation of friends and family. But not always. People are sometimes more authentic – and in this respect, more creative – when they conform than when they diverge from social expectations, provided they have adopted those expectations as their own. Too often, authenticity is sacrificed in a vain and superficial attempt to be different.

Stages in the creative process

Creativity does not occur suddenly, without prior preparation. The creative response typically unfolds in stages, often over an extended period of time. Wallas (1926) has broken the entire sequence into four stages: preparation, incubation, illumination, and verification. Preparation is, for the most part, a deliberate process in which a solution (eg to a mathematical problem, or a musical score) is sought. If a solution occurs, the remaining stages may be short-circuited. More commonly, the initial efforts end in frustration, and the problem is put aside for a time (from a few minutes to years). This is the stage of incubation. Eventually, perhaps under the influence of some environmental stimulus, a solution suddenly appears in a "flash of insight". The validity or appropriateness of the insight must then be verified. The following account by the French mathematician Poincare (1908/1952) dramatically illustrates these stages in the creative process:

> For fifteen days I strove to prove that there could not be any functions like those I have since called Fuchsian functions. I was then very ignorant; every day I seated myself at my work table, stayed an hour or two, tried a great number of combinations and reached no results. One evening, contrary to my custom, I drank black coffee and could not sleep. Ideas rose in crowds; I felt them collide until pairs interlocked, so to speak, making a stable combination. By the next morning I had established the existence of a class of Fuchsian functions, those which come from the hypergeometric series; I had only to write out the results, which took but a few hours. (p. 36)

Of the four stages of the creative process outlined by Wallas, the first (preparation) and the last (verification) are the most amenable to observation and assessment. The second stage (incubation) occurs largely outside of awareness, and the third stage (illumination) is often momentary.

We have already discussed the criteria by which a creative response may be verified, namely, novelty, effectiveness, and authenticity. The following remarks, therefore, concern the first or preparatory stage.

For any given task, preparation may be brief. For example, Coleridge (1816/1952) reported that he wrote the poem *Kubla Khan* upon waking from a dream. However, as Weisberg (1986) has documented, this and other famous examples of sudden inspiration without preparation involve more myth than fact. Evidence suggests that Coleridge had previously written a poem on the same theme, and that he might even have fabricated the story of *Kubla Khan*'s composition for personal aggrandizement. But be that as it may, Coleridge was an accomplished poet who had spent many years in preparation, perhaps not to write this particular poem but to write poetry in general. It has been estimated that roughly 10 years of concentrated effort are required before an individual is capable of truly creative accomplishments within a given field (Hayes, 1981). It follows that one way to assess the creative potential of an individual is to assess the time and effort that have been devoted to preparation.

The following diagram provides a brief summary of the creative process and the criteria relevant to its evaluation:

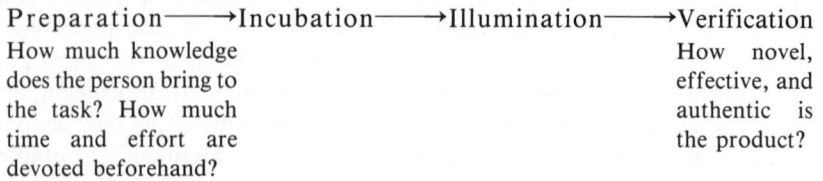

Preparation———→Incubation———→Illumination———→Verification
How much knowledge   How   novel,
does the person bring to   effective, and
the task? How much   authentic   is
time and effort are   the product?
devoted beforehand?

Thus far, our discussion has been largely theoretical. In the next section, we present the results of an exploratory study (Thomas, 1989) designed to assess individual differences in emotional creativity and to examine the similarities and differences between emotional and cognitive creativity.

EMOTIONAL CREATIVITY: A PSYCHOMETRIC STUDY

The primary purpose of this study was to establish emotional creativity as a valid domain of psychological inquiry. To this end, three tests of emotional creativity were developed. Relations between these tests and corresponding measures of cognitive creativity were examined. Some similarities were expected between emotional and cognitive creativity, but also some differences. Specifically, it was predicted that emotional creativity would be differentially related to the capacity to respond in an emotionally adaptive manner, and that cognitive creativity would be differentially related to intellectual achievement.

Subjects

Subjects were 100 undergraduate students (48 male, 52 female) at the University of Massachusetts, Amherst. They ranged in age from 18 to 56 (mean age = 20.0). Subjects were recruited from a variety of psychology courses. For participating they were paid a small remuneration and/or received credit towards their course requirements. Four categories of behavior were assessed: emotional creativity, cognitive creativity, emotional capacity, and cognitive capacity.

Emotional creativity

The three measures of emotional creativity developed specifically for this study were the Emotional Creativity Inventory, the Emotional Triads Test, and the Emotional Consequences Test. It should perhaps be emphasized at the outset that these tests were not developed for applied use, but only to help validate a construct—emotional creativity.

Emotional Creativity Inventory

This test was designed to provide a self-report estimate of emotional creativity in everyday settings. Items focused on the first (preparation) and last (verification) stages of the creative process. More specifically, the preparatory items assessed the tendency of subjects to think about and devote attention to their emotional lives, and the verification items assessed the novelty, effectiveness, and authenticity of the emotions. The following examples illustrate each type of item:

I. *Preparation stage*
I think about past emotional experiences to help me cope with a current emotional problem.
II. *Verification stage*
Novelty. I like art, music, dance, and paintings that arouse new and unusual emotional reactions.

Effectiveness. I can vary my emotions effectively to fit the situation.

Authenticity. My emotional reactions do not reflect who I really am. (Reversed)

Each of the 32 items was rated on a nine-point scale from 0 to 8; the total score could thus range from 0 to 256. The actual range was 75–242, with a mean of 165.52. Coefficient alpha for the 32-item scale was 0.89 for the total sample of 100 subjects. This indicates a high degree of reliability, at least over the short term. (Coefficient alpha represents an estimate of the correlation of a test with a hypothetical alternate form having the same number of items—see Cronbach, 1951.)

Emotional Triads Test

This test required subjects to write stories that integrated incongruent emotions into single, unified experiences. Four sets of emotional triads were selected: serene/bewildered/impulsive; affectionate/disgusted/hopeful; lonely/angry/joyful; and embarrassed/jealous/amused. The terms in each triad are located approximately 120 degrees apart on Plutchik's (1980, p. 170) emotion circle, indicating a high degree of incongruence.

Research by Harrington (1975) and Amabile (1983) suggests that creativity is enhanced by explicit instructions to be "creative". Subjects in the present study were therefore told to be as creative as possible in writing their stories and not to worry about spelling, grammar, or style. It was also emphasized that the three emotions should be integrated into a unitary experience and not described as separate (eg sequential) events.

The four stories were scored on a scale from 1 to 5 for novelty, effectiveness (adaptiveness), authenticity, integration, and creativity. The nature of the first three ratings (novelty, effectiveness, and authenticity) has already been described. "Integration" refers to the extent that the three emotions were combined to form a unitary experience. The "creativity" rating represents an overall assessment of the story, taking into account the other four dimensions as well as any other factors that might seem relevant to the judges.

To illustrate, the following story involving the triad "serene, bewildered, and impulsive" was given a high rating for creativity:

> The clouds are few, the sky is clear. I'm at the top of the cliff. It's real peaceful up here. Suddenly, I want to jump, I don't know why, I just want to. Calmly, I look down at what would be my unquestioned doom. It looks so peaceful; warm and friendly. But why, why do I want to dive into the hands of the grim reaper? What does this mean? I hesitate, then motion to jump, something strange pulls me back. It is the peacefulness of the cliff. I can't destroy that peacefulness. The wind feels like velvet against my skin as I slowly walk away and shake my head. Why?

By contrast, the following story was rated low in creativity:

> I am sitting in a field with high grass, alone with no one visible for as far as the eye can see. I am serene. But I am also bewildered when I discover I do not know where I am nor how I got there. I impulsively and frantically run in every direction looking for any sign of human life. After running for about five minutes, and after working up a great sweat, I come across a Coke machine. I buy myself a Coke and subsequently drink it while contemplating my insane-like actions.

The two authors served as judges. Analyses were conducted using the mean of the judges' ratings on each dimension. Because the creativity rating was highly correlated with a combined score consisting of the first four dimensions ($r = 0.93$), the creativity score alone was used to represent emotional creativity as measured by the Emotional Triads Test. The interjudge reliability for this score was 0.71. The total score summed over the four items (triads) could range from 4 to 20. The actual range was 4 to 16, with a mean of 9.95. Coefficient alpha for the four-item test was 0.66.

Emotional Consequences Test

This test was modified from one of the Torrance (1962) Tests of Creative Thinking. Subjects were asked to list as many consequences as possible for each of four impossible situations. The test differed from the original Torrance version in that each item described a situation of an emotional nature. The four items were: what would be the consequences (a) if people fell in love with a different person every other day? (b) if people could detect every emotion that others were feeling? (c) if people could only experience positive emotions in the morning and negative emotions in the afternoon? and (d) if whenever people fell in love, they developed a terrible odor that became worse as their love got stronger?

The scoring technique developed by Torrance (1974) was modified for evaluating the responses. Each item was given a flexibility score, indicating the number of different categories used, and a fluency score, indicating the number of relevant, non-repeated ideas expressed within categories. A high flexibility score thus reflects the ability to shift from one category of thought to another. A high fluency score, by contrast, reflects the ability to elaborate on, or give numerous examples of, ideas within categories. All the responses to an item also were rated as a unit on a five-point scale for creativity. This rating reflects primarily the overall novelty and perspicacity of the ideas presented.

The following are examples of responses to the item: what would be the consequences if people could only experience positive emotions in the morning and negative emotions in the afternoon?

Good: The sign on the door of the local mental health clinic would say:
   Office hours: Morning—Mania
         Afternoon—Depression
         Bipolar patients may visit twice daily
Poor: There would be fights in the afternoon

A typical subject provided from three to 10 responses (some good, some poor) to each of the four items (impossible situations).

A number of suggestions have been made for obtaining a single, derived score for the consequences test (Torrance, 1974). Based on preliminary analyses of the present data, a derived score was obtained by multiplying the flexibility score by the creativity rating for each item (situation) and then summing over the four items. (The flexibility score, it will be recalled, is the number of distinct categories into which responses fell [mean $= 4.72$ categories per item]; the creativity rating is a summary judgment of the uniqueness and insightfulness of the responses taken as a whole.) The derived score for the four-item test ranged from 13 to 124, with a mean of 57.70. Coefficient alpha was 0.71.

Emotional creativity composite score

The Emotional Triads Test and the Emotional Consequences Test are both "performance" measures and hence methodologically distinct from the Emotional Creativity Inventory, a self-report measure. The correlation between the two performance tests was 0.31 ($p < 0.01$, one-tailed test). In order to obtain a broader measure of performance, these two tests were combined (following conversion to z-scores). Coefficient alpha for the eight-item composite score was 0.68 for the entire sample.

Cognitive creativity

Cognitive creativity was measured in two ways: a Cognitive Creativity Inventory and a Cognitive Consequences Test.

Cognitive Creativity Inventory

This test was based on research by Sternberg (1985). He reported lists of items that represent people's implicit theories or conceptions of creativity, intelligence, and wisdom. Starting with Sternberg's creativity descriptors, but eliminating any with an explicitly emotional content, we constructed a 30-item self-report inventory of cognitive creativity to parallel the Emotional Creativity Inventory. The total score on this test could range from 0 to 240. The actual range was 78 to 162, with a mean of 114.73. Coefficient alpha for the inventory was 0.81.

Cognitive Consequences Test

This test consisted of four items taken directly from the Torrance (1962) Tests of Creative Thinking: what would be the consequences (a) if human beings could become invisible at will? (b) if a hole could be bored through the earth? (c) if the language of birds and animals could be understood by human beings? and (d) if human beings could live forever on earth? Responses were evaluated in the same manner as the Emotional Consequences Test described above, and a derived score (the product of the flexibility and creativity measures) was calculated. The derived score for the four-item test ranged from 10 to 136, with a mean of 61.35. Coefficient alpha was 0.69.

Measures of emotional capacity

It was hypothesized that emotionally creative people would experience more intense or vivid emotions than their less creative counterparts, and that they would be better able to communicate their emotions to others. To test these hypotheses, two measures of emotional capacity were obtained: the Affect Intensity Measure (AIM) and the Affective Communication Test (ACT).

Affect Intensity Measure (AIM)

This self-report inventory assesses the emotional intensity with which people react to typical life events, both positive and negative (Larsen, 1983; Larsen & Diener, 1987). The scale consists of 40 items, each rated on a six-point scale (0–5).

Although it was predicted that emotionally creative people would experience emotions more intensely than others, that prediction must be tempered by the fact that emotional creativity is not simply emotional reactivity. The emotionally creative response should be novel, effective, and authentic, not simply intense

Table 10.2. Correlations of the Emotional and Cognitive Consequences Tests with the Emotional and Cognitive Creativity Inventories

Self-report inventory	Emotional Consequences Test	Cognitive Consequences Test	Significance of the difference[a] T_2	p
Emotional Creativity Inventory				
Females	0.33**	0.09	2.18	0.05
Males	0.27*	0.22	0.43	NS
Total	0.35***	0.17*	2.31	0.05
Cognitive Creativity Inventory				
Females	0.24*	0.28*	−0.36	NS
Males	0.32*	0.38**	−0.53	NS
Total	0.28**	0.33***	−0.64	NS

[a]Significance levels are based on Steiger's (1980) T_2 statistic for the difference between two dependent correlations, one-tailed test. (T_2 has a t distribution with $df = N - 3$.) Comparisons also were made between corresponding correlations within columns; the results are discussed in the text.
Note: Females, $N = 58$; males, $N = 42$.
*$p \leq 0.05$; **$p \leq 0.01$; ***$p \leq 0.001$; one-tailed.

Consequences Test (0.17). The difference between these two correlations is statistically significant ($p < 0.05$). Similarly, the Cognitive Creativity Inventory was more highly correlated with the Cognitive Consequences Test (0.33) than with the Emotional Consequences Test (0.28). In this case, however, the difference is not statistically significant.

The same pattern of results is evident if one examines the columns of Table 10.2. Thus, the Emotional Consequences Test was more highly correlated with the Emotional Creativity Inventory (0.35, total sample) than with the Cognitive Creativity Inventory (0.28), and the Cognitive Consequences Test was more highly correlated with the Cognitive Creativity Inventory (0.33) than with the Emotional Creativity Inventory (0.17). In the latter case, the difference between the correlations is statistically significant ($T_2 = 1.97$, $df = 97$, $p < 0.05$, one-tailed).

In summary, on the basis of the tests developed for this study, there appears to be considerable overlap between the domains of emotional and cognitive creativity. For reasons already discussed, such overlap is to be expected. But the two domains of creativity are also distinguishable, as evidenced by the fact that the within-domain correlations are generally larger than the between-domain correlations (and in several instances, significantly so).

Differential predictive validity

It was hypothesized that emotional creativity would be differentially related to effective (functional) emotional reactivity, and that cognitive creativity would be differentially related to intellectual capacities and academic achievement. Data relevant to the first part of this hypothesis are presented in Table 10.3.

Note first that both the Emotional *and* the Cognitive Creativity Inventories were more highly correlated with the functional than with the dysfunctional

Table 10.3. Correlations of the Emotional and Cognitive Creativity Inventories with emotional capacities

Emotional capacities	Emotional Creativity Inventory	Cognitive Creativity Inventory	Significance of the difference[a]	
			T_2	p
Affect Intensity Measure				
Functional subscale				
Females	0.47***	0.13	2.75	0.01
Males	0.58***	0.38*	1.89	0.05
Total	0.58***	0.24*	4.24	0.001
Dysfunctional subscale				
Females	0.20	−0.15	−2.65	0.01
Males	0.23	−0.06	2.42	0.05
Total	0.32***	−0.09	4.70	0.001
Affective Communication Test				
Females	0.34**	0.49***	−1.23	NS
Males	0.55***	0.32*	2.15	0.05
Total	0.47***	0.42***	0.59	NS

[a]Significance levels are based on Steiger's (1980) T_2 statistic for the difference between two dependent correlations, one-tailed test. Comparisons also were made between corresponding correlations within columns; the results are discussed in the text.
Note: Females, $N = 58$; males, $N = 42$.
*$p \leq 0.05$; **$p \leq 0.01$; ***$p \leq 0.001$; two-tailed.

subscales of the AIM. Significance levels for these contrasts are not presented in Table 10.3, but all are significant at least at the 0.05 level of confidence. To illustrate, if one reads down the first column of Table 10.3 it can be seen that, for the total sample, the Emotional Creativity Inventory correlated 0.58 with the functional subscale of the AIM but only 0.32 with the dysfunctional subscale ($T_2 = 3.52$, $df = 97$, $p < 0.001$, one-tailed).

Reading across the rows of Table 10.3, it can be seen that, as predicted, the Emotional Creativity Inventory was more highly correlated with the AIM (both subscales) than was the Cognitive Creativity Inventory. The differences are all significant at least at the < 0.05 level of confidence.

The data for the Affective Communication Test (ACT) are presented in the bottom portion of Table 10.3. In this case, the hypothesis was confirmed for the males but not for the females. That is, only the males showed a significantly higher correlation between the Emotional Creativity Inventory and the ACT than between the Cognitive Creativity Inventory and the ACT (0.55 vs 0.32, $p < 0.05$).

Table 10.4 compares the correlations between the Emotional and Cognitive Creativity Inventories and the measures of scholastic aptitude (SAT scores) and academic achievement (grade point average). For the SAT mathematical section, the results are in the predicted direction, and all (females, males, and total sample) are statistically significant. For the SAT verbal scores, the results for the males reached statistical significance in the predicted direction, but not the results for the females or the entire sample.

Table 10.4. Correlations of the Emotional and Cognitive Creativity Inventories with cognitive capacities and achievement

Cognitive capacities	Emotional Creativity Inventory	Cognitive Creativity Inventory	Significance of the difference[a] T_2	p
SAT—mathematics section				
Females ($N = 53$)	− 0.23	0.08	− 2.22	0.05
Males ($N = 40$)	− 0.02	0.26	− 2.30	0.05
Total ($N = 93$)	− 0.21*	0.13	− 3.61	0.001
SAT—verbal section				
Females ($N = 53$)	0.01	− 0.03	0.28	NS
Males ($N = 40$)	0.03	0.36*	− 2.83	0.01
Total ($N = 93$)	0.04	0.17	− 1.40	NS
GPA				
Females ($N = 57$)	0.06	0.02	0.28	NS
Males ($N = 41$)	0.40**	0.41**	− 0.09	NS
Total ($N = 98$)	0.26**	0.21*	0.52	NS

[a]Significance levels are based on Steiger's (1980) T_2 statistic for the difference between two dependent correlations, one-tailed test.
*$p \leq 0.05$; **$p \leq 0.01$; ***$p \leq 0.001$; two-tailed.

Looking now at the bottom portion of Table 10.4, both emotional and cognitive creativity predicted academic achievement (GPA) about equally well. Although contrary to hypothesis, this result is not entirely unexpected. Success in coursework depends on motivational and temperamental factors as well as intellectual capacities.

Altogether, the results presented in Tables 10.3 and 10.4 provide satisfactory evidence that emotional and cognitive creativity, as measured by the self-report inventories, can be differentiated in terms of their respective relationships to emotional and intellectual capacities and achievements. Similar analyses were conducted using the Emotional and Cognitive Consequences Tests. The results were generally consistent with those reported in Tables 10.3 and 10.4, but they were of smaller magnitude and not statistically significant.

Some researchers (eg Barron & Harrington, 1981; Sternberg, 1985) maintain that self-report measures provide more accurate assessments of creative capacities than the kind of performance tests (such as the Consequences Test) used in the present study; other investigators disagree (eg Amabile, 1983; Torrance, 1962). Each type of measure undoubtedly has its advantages and limitations. In this study, at least, the self-report measures (Emotional and Cognitive Creativity Inventories) provided the most consistent (statistically significant) results. However, the performance measures, especially the Triads Test, were particularly useful in another way, as will be discussed next.

CHARACTERISTICS OF THE
EMOTIONALLY CREATIVE PERSON

A composite creativity score, it may be recalled, was obtained by combining scores from the Emotional Triads and the Emotional Consequences Tests. Based on this composite score, two groups of subjects were formed. A high-creativity group was composed of subjects whose composite scores fell above the median, and a low-creativity group was composed of subjects whose composite scores fell below the median. A series of t-tests was then conducted on the items of the Emotional Creativity Inventory. The items that distinguished the high- from the low-creativity group are presented in Table 10.5. Over half of the items of the Emotional Creativity Inventory (18 out of 32) reached "significance" at $p < 0.15$ level of confidence (one-tailed).

Earlier, we distinguished two stages of the creative process as most amenable to assessment, namely, preparation and verification. We further enumerated

Table 10.5. Items from the Emotional Creativity Inventory that distinguished high-creative from low-creative subjects, as determined by their responses to the Emotional Consequences and Triads Tests

Significance level	Item
$p < 0.01$	
1.	I am an emotionally sensitive person
2.	I am interested in the emotional aspects of my life
3.	My emotional life is important to me
4.	I like art, poetry, music, dance, and paintings that arouse new and unusual emotional reactions
$p < 0.05$	
5.	I am good at expressing my emotions
6.	When I have a strong emotional reaction, I search for reasons for my feelings
7.	I sometimes feel that I am having an appropriate emotional reaction to a situation, even though my friends do not understand my feelings
8.	I think about how my emotional reactions will affect other people
9.	I communicate my emotions well
10.	I am sensitive to the emotional experiences of others
$p < 0.10$	
11.	I think about and try to understand my emotional reactions
12.	I think about past emotional experiences to help me cope with a current emotional problem
13.	I sometimes experience a variety of different emotions at the same time
14.	I am unable to experience deep emotions (Reversed)
15.	I am able to communicate my feelings effectively
$p < 0.15$	
16.	I am in touch with my feelings
17.	My emotional reactions do not reflect who I really am (Reversed)
18.	I often react to situations in ways that others would not, but they usually understand and respect my feelings

Note: Significance levels are based on t-tests, $df = 98$, one-tailed probabilities.

three criteria for the verification of an emotionally creative response—novelty, effectiveness, and authenticity. These distinctions were based on an analysis of the creative process and its evaluation; however, as the items listed in Table 10.5 indicate, they also reflect personal characteristics of creative persons.

Specifically, emotionally creative persons place a good deal of importance and value on their emotions; they try to understand their emotional reactions, and they use that understanding to cope with new situations (preparation). According to their self-statements, highly creative persons also are able to generate uncommon emotional responses; indeed, they enjoy situations in which unusual emotions might be elicited (novelty). Emotionally creative persons also are sensitive to how their own emotions may affect others; they communicate their emotions well; and others respect their feelings, even when those feelings are out of the ordinary (effectiveness). Finally, emotionally creative persons describe their emotions as "deep", that is, as reflecting who they "really are" (authenticity).

The above description is, of course, constrained by the nature of the items included in the Emotional Creativity Inventory. To supplement this description, a qualitative analysis was made of the 400 stories subjects wrote in response to the Triads Test. Emotional responses are particularly revealing of the self (Epstein, 1983). In this respect, the Triads Test can be treated as a projective measure of personality.

The exploratory nature of these analyses precluded any serious attempt at quantification. However, seven features seemed to stand out as readily identifiable characteristics of the emotionally creative person. We will illustrate these features with verbatim quotes from some of the more creative stories. But before presenting these results, a possible confounding factor should be mentioned, namely, verbal fluency. For the most part, the more creative stories were longer and better written than the less creative stories. Moreover, the correlations between scores on the Triads Test and the SAT verbal scores were 0.36 for males and 0.29 for females, both statistically significant ($ps < 0.05$).

Some common variance is to be expected between verbal fluency and emotional creativity. Language is one of the primary vehicles for the codification and transmission of emotional rules (Averill, 1980, 1990). Facility with language should therefore be associated with emotional creativity; and, conversely, emotional creativity should find expression in language, as well as in other forms of behavior. All good poetry, Wordsworth (1805/1952) remarked, "is the spontaneous overflow of powerful feelings: it takes its origin from emotion recollected in tranquility" (p. 84).

Most of the episodes described by subjects in response to the Triads Test were at least partially recollected. In many instances, the lack of articulation that marked the less creative stories appeared to reflect impoverished emotional experiences rather than a lack of verbal ability. Stated conversely, subjects who had richer experiences provided richer descriptions. We elaborate on this point in the first feature discussed below.

1. *Emotionally creative persons are better able to integrate and express their emotions in symbolic form*

> Driving on never to return—I wish. Another family fight, my typical reaction, get in the car and take off. Riding into the summer night air, mild and damp, makes me glad to be in motion, the breeze coming through the windows produces sensations of joy.—I'm angry as I was chased out of my own home. Things will be humid, intense, and static upon my return. And I'm lonely as I drive alone with my broodings, angry that it is I who must go into the night.—I'm better off this way. The air is so pleasant in the form of a breeze. It's a lonely feeling yet so peaceful it brings its own joy—and so I run in cycles until these cycles wear me down and I yield to my weariness and head for home. (Lonely/angry/joyful)

In attempting the integration of incongruent emotions required by the Emotional Triads Test, emotionally creative persons often relied on symbols as a means to express feelings that were not easily articulated. In the above example, driving through the damp night air is a source of both loneliness and joy; metaphorically, it also reflects the conflict-ridden atmosphere at home ("humid, intense, and static"). The metaphor of cycles is also a recurring theme, both implicit and explicit. The story as a whole depicts an episode that is part of a cycle ("another family fight"). Within the story, another cycle unfolds: "driving on never to return"—but he does return, having "run in cycles" until worn down.

Goldstein (1983) suggests that only through symbolism can people express their innermost feelings. We would go further. Symbols are not simply a means of expressing preformed experiences. Through symbols (and the symbols need not always be verbal) people can mold and transform—in a word, create—experiences that may then be expressed in a variety of ways, symbolic and otherwise.

2. *Emotionally creative persons make more complex appraisals, take into account a greater range of stimuli, and are less likely to reach premature conclusions*

> The woods are so peaceful and quiet. A great place to think out problems. Just why does she have to be sick anyway? What is going to happen to her? I don't know what to think anymore. I feel myself sinking into the peacefulness and longing of the woods. How I love to spend time here relaxing, being myself, thinking. Yet, there is this longing deep in my heart just to run to her and tell her how special she is to me. Just let my feelings open up and spill out. No more hiding and wondering and guessing. But, is that what would be best for her? The woods are telling me to go; she needs to hear all that, they say. I don't want to leave this protective peace, though, I am not ready yet. Just let me sit in its arms and think. No, tomorrow may not give me this chance. (Serene/bewildered/impulsive)

The greater complexity of emotional appraisals was one of the most obvious features distinguishing the creative from the non-creative stories. In the non-creative stories, subjects tended to focus almost exclusively on themselves. When other aspects of the incident were attended to, emphasis was placed on the hedonic value of the situation for the subject, and the episode was brought to a rapid conclusion. In the creative responses, by contrast, various aspects of the situation (including the potential reactions of others) were given meaningful interpretation, and the conclusion of the episode was often left open to new possibilities.

The appraisals of the emotionally creative person seem to be related to a phenomenon observed in creative problem-solving. Performance on cognitive creativity tasks has been found to be positively correlated with overinclusion, the tendency to attend to a greater amount of information than necessary to solve a problem (Barron & Harrington, 1981). Although some of the information may appear to be trivial or even irrelevant, attention to such details may yield fresh insight into the problem at hand. Similarly, it is reasonable to assume that a more novel and effective emotional response would be generated by greater and more careful consideration of eliciting events.

3. Emotionally creative persons are deeply involved in exploring the meaning of their emotional experiences

Auditioning for community music theatre productions is always quite an experience. I have such incredible respect for many of the people involved, yet at times I must laugh to myself and wonder if they know that I can sometimes see right through them. Oh, to have the talent that I might be admired as I admire them, but always my performance is fatally flawed, although they say "good job" or worse, "thank you, we'll be in touch". To dance, to sing, to fly through the stars without lying awake until dawn repeating and repeating in my mind every obvious falter. I shall never, not ever, have what it takes. And I pause. In a moment of what I hope is honest reflection, I hope I am honestly laughing at myself. (Embarrassed/jealous/amused)

Although the moment of creative insight—like the moment of emotional reaction—is often depicted as spontaneous and beyond control, creative responses, whether cognitive or emotional, are largely dependent on background knowledge and experience. It may be recalled that prior preparation was one of the criteria used in construction of the Emotional Creativity Inventory; it was not, however, an explicit criterion used in rating the responses to the Triads Test. Nevertheless, as the above example illustrates, emotionally creative persons devote time and energy to understanding their emotions; they are honest about their feelings; and they consider the possible consequences of their behavior.

4. Emotionally creative persons give thoughtful consideration to the feelings and behavior of others

While working at the city's home for mentally disturbed children, I find myself drawn to a particular little girl named Anne. She is autistic, yet somewhere beneath those thin feathered curls, I know lies a smart, affectionate person. I feel myself drawn to her, like a big sister, and I watch every day for signs that she is starting to respond. After lunch, she gets sick, and can only sit there in her own vomit.

I must clean it up. It's not pleasant, she smells. As I clean her, I take special care to wash her hair. I know that some day she will be a beauty. (Affectionate/disgusted/hopeful)

Emotional experiences are self-centered almost by definition. That is, emotional appraisals, contrast to more objective judgments, interpret events in relation to the individual's own needs and goals (Arnold, 1960; Lazarus, 1966). To a certain extent, emotionally creative persons are able to "decenter" their experiences and accommodate the needs and goals of others. This decentering is facilitated by the greater use of symbolization, to which we have already referred. Symbolization allows emotionally creative persons to reflect upon the meaning of their experiences within a broader, more encompassing context.

5. *Emotionally creative persons are less bound by preestablished personal or social standards, and they are more tolerant of conflicting traits in themselves and others*

How did he think this up from his position? My brother won't admit his lies even when the family tells him we know he's lying. He's a dropout, a chronic liar, and he's working in a 24-hour foodmart. It's my niece's birthday, and he got her a windup toy pig. She pushed her new dolls aside and grabbed the pig. You wind it up and it moves and squeals. To watch her play with it and to think of him—he's a genius.—I watch the pig and I'm disgusted with him for his inability to organize his life, but he's his own person.—I'm hopeful that something will sweep him out of the dimestore and into the spotlight he deserves—he's an actor, you know. (Affectionate/disgusted/hopeful)

It is one thing to recognize the feelings of others, it is another to afford some legitimacy to those feelings when they go against one's own or society's values. Emotionally creative persons do not rigidly impose their own standards on others. In the above story, the woman begins by expressing strong disapproval of her brother's behavior. On further reflection, however, she recognizes that he is a "genius" in his own way. She thus displays the capacity to accommodate two conflicting assessments simultaneously. She vacillates between these assessments, without relinquishing one for the other.

In terms of cognitive style, creative persons have been described as having a tolerance, or even a preference for inconsistency or conflict with regard to perceptions and concepts (Arieti, 1976). The importance of this characteristic for creative achievement in general is illustrated by Kuhn's (1970) assertion that important scientific advances result from the tension between two incompatible modes of thought. But perhaps most relevant to the above example is Barron and Harrington's (1981) finding that creative persons have the ability to accommodate conflicting traits within their self-concepts. In terms of emotional creativity, it appears that conflicting traits in other persons are also tolerated with compassion.

6. Emotionally creative persons experience the less prototypical features of even standard emotions

> I am at my mother's funeral. She has died after a long illness and now, after all those years of suffering, the pain is gone. I am standing amidst a group of people, all of whom I can easily and quickly imagine being with my mother at some point in time. It seems odd that she is not visually present in the room with us. And I wonder how I should act now in front of these people—how do they know me, and what do they associate me with? My mother? The poor daughter of a dead mother? Or should I feel strong and bold now? Now that it is over, I can be anyone I want to be. (Serene/bewildered/impulsive)

Not every emotion is equally susceptible to innovation and change. Grief is a good example of one that is less malleable. Many of the reactions following bereavement are biologically based, although even in the case of grief, biology allows ample room for cultural and individual variation (Averill, 1979). From reading the responses to the Triads Test, it is apparent that emotionally creative persons are not only able to fashion unusual emotions; they also experience the less prototypical features of more standard emotions, such as grief. In the above story, for example, the young woman finds serenity at her mother's funeral. She is also bewildered, but not for the reasons one might suppose. She imagines the other mourners interacting with her mother, and it strikes her as odd that her mother is not "visually" present in the scene. She also wonders how the mourners regard her and how she should act in front of them. She is obviously unclear about her role as a grieving daughter. But it is not just her behavior that is uncertain. She also does not know quite how to feel; sad, depressed, relieved, strong, bold, or liberated. The sense of freedom and enthusiasm expressed in the last sentence of the story seems especially contrary to our usual conceptions of grief. For the emotionally creative person, however, bereavement can be an opportunity for growth and change, as well as for despondency and despair (Marris, 1975).

This brings us to the last characteristic of emotionally creative persons as revealed in their responses to the Triads Test.

7. Emotionally creative persons find challenge where others see threat

> "It's my turn to see what I can see, I hope you'll understand, this time's just for me." I sing out loud to the black night sky and the yellow glowing silhouette of Boston across the bay. I strongly throw pebble after pebble into the night black harbor almost hypnotized and unaware of what goes on in my mind. I'm all alone, I think. Just me and the woods and the water and no one. And a tear escapes. I wipe it away angrily and stand up. I am alone, by myself, with myself, and for myself. I don't need him. I don't need them. Any of them at all. I have me. I can do anything I want and not be tied to them and their routines. Who needs them, not me I shout at the empty sky. I can do it all, all by myself. I'll show them, I'll tell them! But who will I tell—who will care? (Lone/angry/joyful)

"Necessity is the mother of invention." This old adage is as true in the emotional as in the intellectual domain. If a situation is sufficiently demanding, creativity is to an extent forced upon us. But most situations are not so extreme. The possibility exists for alternative appraisals—threat or challenge (Lazarus, 1966; Lazarus & Folkman, 1984). The emotionally creative person is more likely to choose the latter.

For a person to find challenge where others see threat presumes some degree of self-confidence or perceived self-efficacy (Bandura, 1986). Again, we note the importance of prior preparation and understanding. Emotional creativity, no less than creativity in other domains, does not simply happen. It is an achievement, born of struggle and forethought.

Picasso once remarked, "Every act of creation is first of all an act of destruction" (quoted in May, 1975, p. 63). What is destroyed in emotional creativity? Often, customary values, established relationships, and familiar ways of responding. The challenge is too great for many. Not having prepared, they lack the resources and self-confidence to be emotionally creative.

CONCLUDING OBSERVATIONS

We began this chapter by noting some incompatibilities between the concepts of emotion and creativity. We conclude by noting some similarities. In a letter to a friend, Dostoyevsky gave the following description of the creative process:

> If you wish—he [the author or poet] is not the creator; life is—the powerful essence of life, the living and essential God, putting his strength in many distinct creations at various places, and most of all in the great heart and in the strong poet . . . (quoted in Weisberg, 1986, p. 117)

Change a few words and this quotation by Dostoyevsky could be used to describe the emotions, which to many theorists are "the powerful essence of life" put in us by Nature, if not by God.

We do not mean to gloss over the important distinctions that exist in the everyday connotations of the words "emotional" and "creative". Under most circumstances, these concepts belong to different "language games", that is, to the social microcosms in which words attain meaning (Wittgenstein, 1953). In a court of law, a person accused of a crime might well plead, "I couldn't help it, I was overcome by emotion". It would be odd indeed, however, to hear a person who is about to be awarded the Nobel prize for science or literature proclaim, "I couldn't help it, I was overcome by creativity". But as first-hand accounts of creative achievements often indicate (see Ghiselin, 1952), both assertions could be equally true—and equally false.

One purpose of this chapter has been to change, or at least to broaden, the ways we talk about emotions. Such a change in discourse would have ramifications both upwards, to the way emotional syndromes are understood and constituted, and downwards, to the way they are experienced and expressed. The old language games still have their place, but their limitations can no longer be ignored. The world is changing rapidly, largely due to human invention. Possible nuclear holocaust is perhaps the most dramatic, and hence the most frequently mentioned, threat facing humankind. However, it is probably not the most likely. Less dramatic but more relentless are the threats posed by an ever-burgeoning population, by medical technology that prolongs life at terrible costs in social resources and personal dignity, and by the steady erosion of our natural environment. If we are going to meet these threats as challenges and ultimately prevail, new ways of feeling as well as thinking will be required. Emotional creativity may be demanded of us, not simply as a theoretical exercise, but as a practical necessity.

ACKNOWLEDGMENTS

Parts of this chapter are based on a Masters thesis by the second author (Thomas, 1989). Thanks are due to Drs Icek Aizen, Susan Fiske, and Ronnie Janoff-Bulman for their contributions to the project as members of the thesis committee. We would also like to express our appreciation to Drs Elma Nunley and John Knowles for sharing their insights on many aspects of emotional creativity.

REFERENCES

Amabile, T. M. (1983). *The Social Psychology of Creativity*. New York: Springer-Verlag.

Arieti, S. (1976). *Creativity: the Magic Synthesis*. New York: Basic Books.

Arnheim, R. (1966). *Toward a Psychology of Art*. Berkeley: University of California Press.

Arnold, B. (1960). *Emotion and Personality* (2 vols). New York: Columbia University Press.

Averill, J. R. (1979). The functions of grief. In C. Izard (Ed.), *Emotions in Personality and Psychopathology*. New York: Plenum, pp. 339–368.

Averill, J. R. (1980). On the paucity of positive emotions. In K. R. Blankstein, P. Pliner & J. Polivy (Eds), *Assessment and Modification of Emotional Behavior*. New York: Plenum Press, pp. 7–45.

Averill, J. R. (1982). *Anger and Aggression: An Essay on Emotion*. New York: Springer-Verlag.

Averill, J. R. (1984). The acquisition of emotions during adulthood. In C. Z. Malatesta & C. E. Izard (Eds), *Emotion in Adult Development*. Beverly Hills, California: Sage, pp. 23–43.

Averill, J. R. (1985). The social construction of emotion: With special reference to love. In K. Gergen & K. Davis (Eds), *The Social Construction of the Person*. New York: Springer-Verlag, pp. 90–109.

Averill, J. R. (1988). Disorders of emotion. *Journal of Social and Clinical Psychology*, 6, 247–268.

Averill, J. R. (1990). Inner feelings, works of the flesh, the beast within, diseases of the mind, driving force, and putting on a show: Six metaphors of emotion and their theoretical extensions. In D. E. Leary (Ed.), *Metaphors in the History of Psychology*. New York: Cambridge University Press, pp. 104–132.

Averill, J. R. (1991). Emotions as episodic dispositions, cognitive schemas, and transitory social roles: Steps toward an integrated theory of emotion. In D. Ozer, J. M. Healy & A. J. Stewart (Eds), *Perspectives in Personality*, Vol. 3a. London: Jessica Kingsley, Publishers, pp. 137–165.

Bandura, A. (1986). *Social Foundations of Thought and Action: A Social Cognitive Theory*. Englewood Cliffs, NJ: Prentice-Hall.

Barron, F. & Harrington, D. M. (1981). Creativity, intelligence, and personality. *Annual Review of Psychology*, **32**, 439–476.

Beigel, H. G. (1951). Romantic love. *American Sociological Review*, **16**, 327–335.

Coleridge, S. T. (1952). Prefatory note to Kubla Khan. In B. Ghiselin (Ed.), *The Creative Process*. Berkeley: University of California Press (original work published 1816).

Cronbach, L. J. (1951). Coefficient alpha and the internal structure of tests. *Psychometrica*, **16**: 297–334.

Crown, D. P. & Marlowe, D. (1964). *The Approval Motive*. New York: Wiley.

deRougemont, D. (1940). *Love in the Western World*. New York: Harcourt.

Ekman, P. (1984). Expression and the nature of emotion. In K. Scherer & P. Ekman (Eds), *Approaches to Emotion*. Hillsdale, NJ: Erlbaum, pp. 319–343.

Epstein, S. (1983). A research paradigm for the study of personality and emotions. In M. M. Page (Ed.), *Personality—Current Theory & Research: 1982 Nebraska Symposium on Motivation*. Lincoln: University of Nebraska Press, pp. 91–154.

Friedman, H. S., Prince, L. M., Riggio, R. E. & DiMatteo, M. R. (1980). Understanding and assessing nonverbal expressiveness. The Affective Communication Test. *Journal of Personality and Social Psychology*, **39**, 333–351.

Ghiselin, B. (Ed.) (1952). *The Creative Process*. Berkeley: University of California Press.

Glover, J. A., Ronning, R. R. & Reynolds, C. R. (Eds) (1989). *Handbook of Creativity*. New York: Plenum.

Goldstein, M. I. (1983). The production of metaphor in poetry therapy as a means of achieving insight. *Arts in Psychotherapy*, **10**, 167–173.

Harré, R. & Finlay-Jones, R. (1986). Emotion talk across times. In R. Harré (Ed.), *The Social Construction of Emotions*. Oxford: Basil Blackwell, pp. 220–233.

Harrington, D. M. (1975). Effects of explicit instructions to "be creative" on the psychological meaning of divergent thinking test scores. *Journal of Personality*, **43**, 434–454.

Hayes, J. R. (1981). *The Complete Problem Solver*. Philadelphia: Franklin Institute Press.

Heelas, P. (1986). Emotion talk across cultures. In R. Harré (Ed.), *The Social Construction of Emotions*. Oxford: Basil Blackwell, pp. 234–266.

Hochschild, A. R. (1983). *The Managed Heart: Commercialization of Human Feeling*. Berkeley: University of California Press.

Izard, C. E. (1977). *Human Emotions*. New York: Plenum.

Kuhn, T. (1970). *The Structure of Scientific Revolutions*, 2nd edn. Chicago: The University of Chicago Press.

Larsen, R. J. (1983). *Manual for the affect intensity measure*. Unpublished manuscript, University of Illinois at Urbana-Champaign.

Larsen, R. J. & Diener, E. (1987). Emotional response intensity as an individual difference characteristic. *Journal of Research in Personality*, **21**, 1–39.

Lazarus, R. S. (1966). *Psychological Stress and the Coping Process*. New York: McGraw-Hill.

Lazarus, R. S. & Folkman, S. (1984). *Stress, Appraisal and Coping*. New York: Springer.

Levy, R. I. (1984). The emotions in comparative perspective. In K. R. Scherer & P. Ekman (Eds), *Approaches to Emotion*. Hillsdale, NJ: Erlbaum, pp. 397–412.

Lutz, C. A. (1988). *Unnatural Emotions: Everyday Sentiments on a Micronesian Atoll and Their Challenge to Western Theory*. Chicago: University of Chicago Press.

Mandler, G. (1984). *Mind and Body*. New York: Norton.

Marris, P. (1975). *Loss and Change*. Garden City, NY: Anchor Books.

May, R. (1975). *The Courage to Create*. New York: Norton.

Morgan, C. & Averill, J. R. (in press). True feelings, the self, and authenticity: A psychosocial perspective. In D. D. Franks & V. Gecas (Eds), *Social Perspectives on Emotion*, Vol. 1. Greenwich, CT: JAI Press.

Needham, R. (1981). Inner states as universals: Skeptical reflections on human nature. In P. Heelas & A. Lock (Eds), *Indigenous Psychologies*. New York: Academic Press, pp. 65–78.

Oatley, K. & Johnson-Laird, P. N. (1987). Towards a cognitive theory of emotions. *Cognition and Emotion*, 1, 29–50.

Plutchik, R. (1980). *Emotion: A Psychoevolutionary Synthesis*. New York: Harper & Row.

Poincare, H. (1952). Mathematical creation. In B. Ghiselin (Ed.), *The Creative Process*. Berkeley: University of California Press (original work published 1908).

Richards, R., Kinney, D. K., Benet, M. & Merzel, A. P. C. (1988). Assessing everyday creativity: Characteristics of the Lifetime Creativity Scales and validation with three large samples. *Journal of Personality and Social Psychology*, 54, 476–485.

Rosaldo, M. Z. (1980). *Knowledge and Passion: Ilongot Notions of Self and Social Life*. Cambridge: Cambridge University Press.

Ryle, G. (1949). *The Concept of Mind*. London: Hutchinson.

Shields, S. A. (1987). Women, men, and the dilemma of emotion. In P. Shaver & C. Hendrick (Eds), *Review of Personality & Social Psychology. Vol. 7. Sex and Gender*. Beverly Hills: Sage, pp. 229–250.

Solomon, R. C. (1976). *The Passions*. Garden City, NY: Doubleday Anchor.

Steiger, J. H. (1980). Tests for comparing elements of a correlation matrix. *Psychological Bulletin*, 87, 245–251.

Sternberg, R. J. (1985). Implicit theories of intelligence, creativity, and wisdom. *Journal of Personality and Social Psychology*, 49, 607–627.

Sternberg, R. J. (Ed.) (1988). *The Nature of Creativity*. Cambridge: Cambridge University Press.

Thomas, C. E. (1989). *Emotional creativity: A social constructivist perspective*. Unpublished Masters thesis, University of Massachusetts, Amherst.

Torrance, E. P. (1962). *Guiding Creative Talent*. Englewood Cliffs, NJ: Prentice-Hall.

Torrance, E. P. (1974). *The Torrance Tests of Creative Thinking: Norms-Technical Manual*. Lexington, Mass: Personnel Press.

Wallace, D. B. & Gruber, H. E. (Eds) (1989). *Creative People at Work*. New York: Oxford University Press.

Wallas, G. (1926). *The Art of Thought*. New York: Harcourt, Brace.

Weisberg, R. W. (1986). *Creativity: Genius and Other Myths*. New York: W. H. Freeman.

Wittgenstein, L. (1953). *Philosophical Investigations*. Oxford: Basil Blackwell & Mott.

Wordsworth, W. (1952). Preface to second edition of lyrical ballads. In B. Ghiselin (Ed.), *The Creative Process*. Berkeley: University of California Press (original work published 1805).

11 An Introduction to the Sociology of Emotions

THEODORE D. KEMPER
Department of Sociology, St John's University, Jamaica, NY 11432 USA

At an international, interdisciplinary meeting on emotions a few years ago, I spoke to a plenary session on the topic, "What psychologists, psychophysiologists, and sociologists have to talk to each other about". I proposed that a complete theory of emotions required an integrated set of understandings about body, psyche, and society, and that a dialogue must take place between practitioners in these areas in order to enable such a theory to be constructed. In the question period, one psychologist vigorously attacked my position, maintaining that any putative social basis for emotions could be reduced to psychology, thus the sociological contribution was extraneous. A more sympathetic psychologist commented to me privately that it was too bad that I had been so stoutly attacked when, after all, he said, "You are only trying to help us".

Two hubrises do not a humility make, but they do illustrate what is at the core of a good deal of the difficulty in many psychologists' misapprehensions about the respective places of sociology and psychology in the study of emotions. The first respondent to my talk essentially affirmed that sociology has no place, since all is psychology in the final analysis. The second respondent essentially affirmed that sociology does have a place, but it was only a tail, or perhaps a toenail, of the dog.

My hope is to show here that the sociological role in the study of emotions is not reducible to the psychological, and, further, that emotions cannot be disarticulated like canine anatomy, but rather comprise a human experience that is rooted in our evolutionary nature, which is ineluctably social. That makes the work of all the disciplines that examine emotions—psychophysiology, endocrinology, psychology, sociology, anthropology, at a minimum—not pieces of a dog, but, rather, *equal* partners in the effort to understand our common topic. Any other viewpoint is intellectually dim and ultimately self-defeating.

To make stark (and to oversimplify) the differences between a psychological and a sociological approach to emotions, it can be said that for the most part psychologists study emotions as a property of generic human beings, while sociologists study emotions as a property of socially specific people, alive in a particular time, living a particular culture in particular circumstances. For the most part, those circumstances are socially determined. Psychological accounts

International Review of Studies on Emotion, Vol. 1. Edited by K. T. Strongman
©1991 John Wiley & Sons Ltd

of emotion often convey the sense of Aristotelian essences, properties of the species across time and space. By contrast, sociological accounts reflect, to some degree, the biography of an age, a culture, and a location in a social structure, whether of social class, gender, ethnicity, occupation, or other social differentia.

In psychology, the human subject is a relatively fixed quantum, structured in major part by physiological properties that impose certain limits on cognitive, behavioral, and emotional degrees of freedom. In sociology, the subject is a relatively free agent—at least if he/she thinks so—but is subject more to the shaping of nurture than of nature. Emblematic of this difference in the cognitive domain, Piaget (1948, 1977) speaks of stages of maturation in mental and moral development, while sociologists examine socialization contents that are specific to social class, ethnicity, gender, and other categories that socially construct specific outlooks and perceptions. No less in the domain of emotions, the sociological emphasis is on the socially derived elements, formulated as history, or culture, or social structure. This places the person/organism in a context that is more than the occasion of the emotion, but is rather its inspiration. Indeed, the sociological understanding of emotion is that while it is indubitably experienced by discrete individuals, it is a collective property of sorts, whether dyadic or societal in scope. If this is hard to appreciate, it can perhaps be made more palatable by reflecting that a recollection of, let us say, a Euclidean theorem to solve a geometry problem is no simple property of an individual, but rather participation in a culture where Euclid's theorems make sense. There is no legerdemain here. A culture that lacks Euclid does not process its territorial claims or practice logic by Euclidean methods.

Sociologists are centrally interested in context, for that is as much the source and field of emotion as the hypothalamus or the autonomic nervous system. As to why the latter two should be privileged in the study of emotion and the former not, this has less to do with the rational organization of our understanding of how to study emotion than with the (non-Euclidean) territorial claims of professions that thrive on what they see as invidious differences. Indeed, psychologist James Averill (1974) has traced the history of the physiological metaphor that guides the study of emotions in much of psychology and has challenged its validity. (It is possible to take issue with Averill as perhaps having gone too far (Kemper, 1987a).) Though it might seem that sociologists too would necessarily support that challenge, they can be differentiated into those who deny or ignore the physiological grounds of emotion and those who see an opportunity in a unified field theory, so to speak, that combines even so distant a reach as that between sociology and psychophysiology.

Ultimately, as at least some psychologists acknowledge, a complete theory of emotions must accommodate not only interior cognitive and autonomic processes, but also exterior social and cultural processes that evoke particular emotions in particular contexts and enable us to focus our attention on them as phenomena worthy of study. Without their social settings, emotions remain in a state of ambiguity. In another context, George Santayana said:

The attempt to speak without speaking any particular language is not more hopeless than the attempt to have a religion that shall be no religion in particular. (From *The Life of Reason: Reason in Religion*, cited in White, 1955, p. 58)

Mutatis mutandis, there are no emotions that are purely internal or context-free—this is parallel to Wittgenstein's (1981) rejection of the possibility of private language—hence there are no emotions not rooted in a historically specific environment as a functional adaptation to it, as a beneficial or noxious response to it, or as a contributor to the maintenance of it. Just how the environment accomplishes its end of the transaction in any of the above senses is one locus of sociological inquiry into emotions. Another is how emotions undergird the possibility of society and social life in the first place. Most psychologists have ignored this part of the emotions domain, but it is one of the major contributions of sociologists to knowledge about emotions. In many instances sociologists address issues that are only one step removed from standard psychological concerns. The boundary between the disciplines is extremely permeable.

I will proceed here by providing first a brief historical introduction to sociological concern with emotion. This should make it clear that a sociology of emotions is neither outlandish nor without substance. What should emerge clearly is that the thinkers who founded sociology in the late nineteenth and early twentieth centuries employed emotions as central elements in their work. Their views on emotion are still vital theoretically and provide a foundation for the modern work on emotions, which began sporadically in the 1950s but was launched across a broad front in the 1970s.

Since the 1970s there has been an efflorescence of sociological concern with emotions, parallel in its way to the upsurge of interest in emotions in other disciplines. The *Zeitgeist*, marked by a disillusion with high technology, bureaucracy, and big institutions in all domains, has turned attention to the nearer phenomenon of the self. Turner (1976) has spoken of the movement away from the "institutional" towards the "real" self. The former is marked by status and role identities that have a locus in conventional groups and social structures and in the kinds of normative controls that subordinate the self to social purposes. By contrast, the real self is relatively deinstitutionalized, less committed to conventional groups and organizations, and skeptical about the sacredness of social norms. The needs of the individual are deemed more worthy of attention than those of the group. The real self is not only a cognitive, but an affective entity. Emotion is thus the vanguard personality process of our age, as reason was in the eighteenth century and the will in the nineteenth.

The modern sociology of emotions is no monolithic enterprise. And in this there is both some opportunity and some cause for regret. Among any set of N sociologists of emotions, it seems almost as if there were $N+1$ opinions as to what the problems are and how to think about them. There is more likely to be theory than research, as Thoits (1989) has noted, although research is beginning to emerge (see special issue of *Social Psychology Quarterly* 1989, volume 52, number 1). Just as in psychology there are perhaps a dozen distinct theories and approaches to emotion (for example see Plutchik & Kellerman, 1980, 1983, 1985), in sociology too there are diverse avenues into the field. It is not likely these will coalesce into a single comprehensive theory until the diversity of psychological approaches is also brought under the umbrella of a single paradigm. This may finally occur not so much because of the logical or empirical refinements of existing theories, but because a daimon of coalescence in society, or globally, acts as inspiration in all areas of social life, including science. In this respect, every age gets the science it deserves.

Notwithstanding the many routes into the sociology of emotions, there is one major axis of difference, namely, between those who study emotions from the perspective of social structure and those who study emotions from the perspective of culture. This will constitute an organizing principle for the discussion of the modern sociology of emotions below. Regardless of which of these two possibilities informs the work, it is noteworthy that a great deal of the sociological address to emotions overlaps or is contiguous with what one or more psychologists is doing. Thus, as neighbors, psychologists and sociologists may stand to gain more from taking each other seriously than from succumbing, as Freud (1917/1957, p. 199) marvelously put it, to the "narcissism of minor differences".

THE CLASSICAL SOCIOLOGY OF EMOTIONS

Sociologists are not just latecomers to the study of emotions. The nineteenth and early twentieth century makers of modern sociology—Karl Marx, Max Weber, and Emile Durkheim—accorded emotions a central place in their analyses of the major social forces of modernity, or of society itself. Remarkably, although emotions were not specifically their topic, which was the macro-world of capitalism, or the workings of the Protestant ethic within capitalism, or the fundamental significance of religion in society, it is striking that these big questions could not be pondered without a treatment of emotions.

Marx

Marx is perhaps the preeminent sociologist by virtue of the technical detail and comprehensiveness of his theories and of their active political pursuit for more than a century worldwide. Notwithstanding the barrenness of some of Marx's conclusions, and the frequent political, economic, and social failures attendant on their implementation (1989 was the remarkable watershed year in this regard), Marx provided important hypotheses not only about how human hopes can be mobilized to work for the attainment of Utopian dreams, but also about how social organization and social structure determine emotions in masses of people. The central emotions here are alienation and class consciousness.

Marx (1842–44/1971) adapted the concept of alienation from the philosopher Georg Friedrich Hegel, who had reflected on the somewhat tragic fate of human energy and effort, which, once crystallized in objects, exist separately from the individual who made them, and in this sense are alienated from the maker. Marx transformed Hegel's philosophical concept into a historically specific effect of particular social class and economic and political conditions. This led him to several specific forms of alienation.

First was the fundamental psychic experience of workers in capitalism, the feeling of chagrin, bitterness, and resentment of those who lose possession of the product of their labor to another—the capitalist—who did not labor to produce it. According to Marx, this was the fundamental emotional consequence of the separation of the one who had labored to produce an item from what was produced. In practical terms, divorcing the producer from his product led ultimately to a state of "immiseration", a condition of so mean an existence that life itself was threatened. Indeed, in early capitalism working-class deprivation was a monstrous political and social scandal. Even the bourgeoisie, whose comforts depended on the process by which workers were alienated from their products, were shocked by its full extent when they became aware of it (Ure, 1835/1967; Engels, 1845/1958).

A second form of alienation was experienced in the boredom and mental numbingness of mechanized and highly divided tasks in the early factories of the industrial revolution by contrast with what Marx assumed to be the prideful investment of self in craft work or even the challenges of the farmer's lot. A third form of alienation was specified in the experience of rote work, inhumanly paced by machines and severed from any opportunity for creative investment of mind or energy. Charlie Chaplin captured some of this hilariously in the opening scenes of his movie 'Modern Times'.

Yet a fourth type of alienation was the emotional isolation of individuals from each other: workers from owners and workers from each other, since they competed with their fellows for jobs. This was the crucial breakdown of community, which is the sense of belonging to a meaningful social unit where one is received as a worthy member given adequate regard. The result was to drive individuals inwards towards privatization and the family, the only group on which one could rely for emotional support and warmth. The interesting latent consequence here was to make the family an outsized source of emotional security, a hotbed of emotions that otherwise had no place to flower. Freud created a theory, a therapy, and a philosophy on the model of the bourgeois family and those who emulated its forms (see Poster, 1978, for a critique of the universality of Freud's analysis of the emotional life of the family).

In an effort to translate Marx's concepts of alienation into modern social psychological language and to provide measurable dimensions, Seeman (1959) proposed that Marx's discussion of alienation contained five elements: powerlessness, or the feeling of anxiety and anger that one's fate is in the hands of others; meaninglessness, or the sense of perplexity over the value and significance of one's efforts (at work or elsewhere); self-estrangement, or the sense of a gap between one's authentic (real) self and the conduct required of one by social forces; isolation, or the sense of longing for connection with others in a world in which most others are felt to be only enemies or competitors; and normlessness, or a sense of aimlessness and goallessness of one's existence.

Need humanity suffer these emotional strains indefinitely? According to Marx (Marx & Engels, 1848/1959), the coming to consciousness by workers that their deprived state need not continue, that there was a class of owners of the means of production who could be replaced, would lead inevitably, in Marx's more or less determinist view, to feelings of solidarity among the oppressed and, as a consequence, to revolution and a succeeding idyll of comparative human harmony. From the anger, depression, and despair of alienated existence in capitalism, humanity would achieve emotional contentment in socialism.

Even if one rejects entirely Marx's indictment of capitalism, it would be mistaken to overlook the contribution here to emotion theory: specifically, for Marx, emotions are not merely inner properties of individuals contained by the envelope of the organism. They can both be products of social forces and, in the aggregate, unleash social forces in turn. Certain forms of social organization—relations of ownership and of property—and certain forms of the social organization of production—extreme division of labor, deskilling and the routinizing of tasks—determine to a significant extent the emotions of persons involved in such systems of production. Ultimately, production itself is threatened, since alienated workers are careless and unconcerned (Blauner, 1964; US Congress, 1972). No student of modern industrial society fails to appreciate the extent to which Marx's critique of capitalism via the concept of alienation and the supposed solution via class consciousness and revolution have affected the course of capitalist societies and all of modern world history. In fact, by a choice piece of irony, in the advanced capitalist societies, Marx may have invalidated Marxism by raising the specter of the consequences of not heeding his critique. The welfare state concept that is the foundation of institutional social responsibility today in all modern societies, with Japan as the major lingering exception, flows directly from this critique. Though seldom viewed from this vantage point, Marx's theory of the social production of emotions is central to an understanding of modern societies.

Weber

It is by now almost cliché to cite the notion that Max Weber can be understood best as debating with the ghost of Marx. What is not cliché is that at least some pivotal elements of that debate are cast in terms of emotion. Perhaps Weber's (1904–05/1958) best known work is his *Protestant Ethic and the Spirit of Capitalism*. Here Weber most clearly engaged Marx in an intellectual battle of the Titans over who possessed the better key to the understanding of some of the fundamental principles of the organization of institutions in contemporary society.

The specific arena of the contest, determined by Marx, was capitalism. According to Marx, the economic infrastructure of the social organization of production—the details of private property, the conditions of labor, the ownership of the product—determined other social forms in society, the so-called superstructure—the political and juridical systems, the religious and aesthetic codes and practices, scientific development, even the structure and values of the family. As a general formula, Marx (Marx & Engels, 1848/1959, p. 26) declared: "The ruling ideas of each age have ever been the ideas of its ruling class". In sum, the material conditions of production determine ideas and their forms of expression in any society.

Indeed, Marx's analysis of the social conditioning of ideas has inspired the development of one of the most active subfields in present-day sociology, namely, the sociology of knowledge. A fundamental premise is that ideas are fostered and held not only because of their factual validity, but also because they serve ideological purposes. A common example is a belief in racial and gender differences in intellectual ability by those who are institutional beneficiaries of existing racial and gender barriers. Ideas thus become weapons in social struggles and though passionately believed are often little more than rationalizations for existing social practices.

Weber sought to show that in a crucial instance Marx's idea about the dominance of social organization in the determination of ideas could more or less be stood on its head. Just as Marx had marshaled the forces of revolution via emotions, Weber too saw emotion as the core experience that was able to change the localistic and small-reach economies of the fifteenth and sixteenth centuries into world-transforming entrepreneurial capitalism. As Weber saw it, the source of the crucial emotion was a religious doctrine, namely Calvinism, which preached so deterministic and bleak a vision of human salvation that, in Weber's eyes, it necessarily yielded emotions that led to an entirely unintended set of consequences, namely, the undergirding ethos of modern capitalism.

Calvin averred that salvation in the religious sense was determined long before any individual was born. Some few, the elect, were chosen for eternal grace while most others were consigned to eternal damnation. What one did in one's life did not matter, one's fate was predestined. Unbeknownst, one could be of the company of the saved while one's spouse or children or parents could be of the company of the damned, or *vice versa*.

Except for some religious fundamentalists for whom hellfire is not simply a metaphor, the Calvinist doctrine is today regarded by most people with disbelief or simply laughed at. Students often ask, "How could anyone have believed that?" This is said with no regard for those beliefs of the present that will inspire the same question in students of a later age. But in the precincts of Geneva and in other places of Calvinist hegemony or influence, no question was more important than the fate of one's soul.

At this point, says Weber, the crisis of concern transmuted into an anxiety so powerful that it led to a wholly unexpected development. Under the pressure of the emotion released by doctrinal stringency, many Calvinists struggled to find a certainty against their despair. They found it in a self-inspired optimistic formula: perhaps, just perhaps, by obeying in scrupulous detail God's every wish and commandment, some sign of God's grace might be forced to reveal itself. Moreover, quite in the face of the unrelenting harshness of the doctrine of predestination, conformity and religious observance might yet alter the unalterable. How to do this? Weber argued that other of the Reformationist tenets showed that the best way to follow God's will was in the undertakings of everyday life. By simply following one's *Beruf* or vocation—whether as humble bread baker, dutiful bootmaker, honest merchant—one would be doing God's work. Indeed, in human work, one followed God. And from this proceeded an irony. If one did one's daily work diligently, honestly, scrupulously, one was likely to attain worldly success. If one read the profits of success as possible signs of God's grace, how much more grace might be enticed by multiplying those profits through even more diligent, honest and scrupulous workmanship? Reinvestment of profits, as opposed to their sumptuary expenditure and display, thus emerged as the principal feature of entrepreneurial capitalism and as a practical solution to a profound religious dilemma. Indeed, it became quasi-religious doctrine to practice economic activity in a certain way—the capitalist way. Calvinism, a central feature of the Protestant ethic, thus gave rise in Weber's view to those economic ideas that constituted the spirit of capitalism.

According to Weber (1904–05/1958), the spirit of capitalism that arose from the emotional tensions of Calvinists was well reflected in the proverbs and apothegms of Benjamin Franklin's *Necessary Hints to Those That Would Be Rich* and *Advice to a Young Tradesman*: "Time is money"; "Money is of the prolific, generating nature. Money can beget money"; "The good paymaster is lord of another man's purse"; "The sound of your hammer at five in the morning, or eight at night, heard by a creditor, makes him easy six months longer". All this and more like it would have failed to develop had the early believers accepted Calvin's teachings with passive equanimity rather than with the anxious desperation Weber indicates.

Thus, while Marx located the source of ideas in the workings of the economic aspects of social organization, Weber found the source of a fundamental economic idea in emotionally mediated religious doctrine. Importantly for how sociology as a field and the sociological approach to emotions developed, Marx can be understood as a theorist who espoused social structure, or the arrangement of social positions and their standing on power and status, as the crucial independent variable, while Weber can be understood as espousing culture, or the content of ideas, values, norms, and other symbolically mediated elements. This difference still divides the field today and also penetrates the sociological study of emotions, as will be seen below. Although the emotional pivoting central to Weber's thesis about the spirit of capitalism is not his only contribution to the sociology of emotions, it must suffice for this presentation.

(There is, in addition, the work on charisma as a source of political legitimation; the ideas of affective and *Wertrational* or value-mediated action; and the role of priesthoods in mobilizing, rationalizing, and containing religious enthusiasm. In Collins' (1974, p. 171) trenchant phrase, priests "control the means of emotional production". An understanding of Weber's most rationality-oriented concept, namely bureaucracy, requires some insight also into the emotional grounds that make it possible for the supposedly emotion-free bureaucratic structure to work (see Kemper & Birenbaum, 1987).)

Durkheim

Emile Durkheim (1912/1965), the last of the great triad of founding figures in sociology, also debated with the spirit of Marx as well as with the ultra-rationalists of the late nineteenth century. Marx had relegated religion to the category of superstition and to a working-class anodyne—an opiate against the pain of their existence under capitalism. In the succeeding socialist society, putatively set up on just principles, religion would be superfluous. In this intellectual climate, shared by many who were not Marxists, Durkheim sought to analyze the religious question. He reasoned that if he examined the most primitive form of religion, the least intellectually elaborated by dogma and other rationalized doctrine, he would be able to discern the fundamental elements of religion and perhaps tell from these what it contributed to any society. Durkheim settled on the religious practices of Australian aborigines, about whom there was a relative plentitude of ethnographic material at the time.

First, Durkheim distinguished between the everyday world and special occasions when everyday practices were suspended and different conduct, supported by transcendental sanctions, was enjoined. These were, respectively, the domains of the profane and the sacred. Durkheim then argued that the sacred was demarcated not only by conduct, but also in time and space and in the objects that required veneration. The latter were the emblematic totems of the clan—animals, birds, or fish, with whom there was, in primitive mental structure, some sense of kinship, and who contained also the spirit of the clan's founders and ancestors. Thus, worship of these totems was a matter of the clan's worshipping itself, and this was one of Durkheim's most original conclusions: in worshipping the gods or other transcendental entities of religion, a group was engaged in the worship of society itself. For only society stood over and above the individual, giving a sense of something "exterior and constraining".

But Durkheim saw that worship itself, to be personally and socially effective, necessarily generated emotions. Periodically the relatively small bands that constituted the clan would assemble to engage in night-long rituals of frenzied dancing, sexual congress, rhythmic chanting and other activities marked by heightened arousal. The profane world was suspended while all participated in the very different world of the sacred. In these sessions of extraordinary emotional arousal, individuals felt themselves to be in the grip of forces larger than themselves, giving the feeling that there was a reality over and above one's individual consciousness. But what was the source of their perception of a supraindividual reality except the activities of the group itself? The power and force of group life thus appeared to individuals as exterior to them, and, because it was not identified with the group and its activities, came to be seen as emanating from an extrahuman source.

Durkheim argued that these rituals—indeed all ritual—magnified and intensified any shared emotion in the participants. This is an early version of Zajonc's (1965) description of social facilitation, where crowding stimulates adrenocortical secretions that underlie arousal, which in turn enhances dominant responses. For Durkheim, the dominant response was the emotion, and the copresence and coparticipation of others in the ritual performance acted as a multiplier effect on the passions already felt in the sacred moment. A powerful psychological consequence is to bind together those who have had their emotions thus augmented in a feeling of solidarity. Indeed, if the popular American billboard and magazine slogan of the 1950s and 60s—"Those who pray together stay together"—actually refers to something efficacious, it can best be understood in the light of Durkheim's insight. It means not that those who share a common faith in a set of religious ideals are prone to remain united, but rather that prayer as a ritual behavior intensifies the common emotions of those who practice it together, and that this elicits the further feeling of solidarity among them.

If we now reflect on what the sacred is in Durkheim's view, we see that ritual and the emotions it arouses are central to the constitution of society. Those who pray together indeed make a community that shares a feeling of connectedness. Society itself, then, is at bottom only possible because of the emotions that its ritual practices generate in its members. These practices need not be grand displays marked by either pageantry or frenzy. Even relative quiet, as Quaker practice shows, can unite through the enhancement of a common emotion. Sadness too can be as much a source of unity as exuberance, and this deserves special comment. Durkheim noted that among many groups a supreme time of ritual enactment occurs on the occasion of death. The loss of a member of the group entails funerary rites during which kin, as well as those who are more peripheral, gather to mourn. There is a coming together and a closeness that is structurally identical with the periodic convening of aborigine clan members, described above. The results, said Durkheim, are similar: an emotional effervescence through the sharing of a common feeling, even if it be sadness, a sense of the strengthening of the self through the sense of unity with others who are one's allies, and, even in the face of death, a renewed interest in life. Thus, social ritual, because it literally brings people together, enhances emotion, which evokes an overarching sentiment that unites those who share the original emotion.

We see then that the progenitors of modern sociology treated emotion as theoretically central. They set some of the important guidelines for how emotions are viewed in present-day sociological analysis and they provided more than a few research leads on how emotions function in social life—both the social conditions that release emotions and the consequences for social life when emotions are released.

THE MODERN SOCIOLOGY OF EMOTIONS

Despite some differences between classical and modern themes and topics in the sociological treatment of emotions, present-day sociologists have retained a central element of the classical inheritance, namely, the guiding idea that, as with many other aspects of human conduct—perceptions, ideas, behaviors—emotions are socially constituted. This means several things to sociologists. First, the source of many emotions is the social transaction that preceded their occurrence. To understand why certain emotions are experienced at all, we must look primarily at prior incidents of social relations. These may even be prior simply in the anticipation of their occurrence. An imaginative projection of future interaction is as capable of evoking emotion as the actual interaction itself.

Secondly, there is a normative component to emotions, and individuals are responsive enough to it to make efforts to change their emotions when they find themselves out of tune with the prevailing normative order. This means that while interaction outcomes determine emotions in the first instance, social fiat can determine them in the final instance. In this way, social regulation of emotion leads to a certain uniformity of emotional presentation.

Thirdly, over long historical periods emotion options and the normative requirement for them change. This means that emotions, at least as yoked to certain social contexts and situations, are subject to change as new relational practices and their accompanying mental constructions make older emotional expression personally and socially dysfunctional.

These ideas ought not to be alien to psychologists of emotion. At a minimum, they raise the venerable and always important question that is central to all inquiry in the human sciences, namely, nature versus nurture. Because of the physiological nexus between psyche and soma, psychologists of emotion frequently assume the nature side of the debate. But the evidence from studies of human culture, and of differences between social classes and other societal groupings, should at least allow the old question to be rephrased as: how much nature, how much nurture. If psychologists most often prefer to assume the side of nature, sociologists prefer to assume the side of nurture. But there is, it must be recognized, an important complementarity in this.

The fundamental theorem in the sociological study of emotions is that emotions are socially constituted. This does not mean that all occasions of emotion are social or socially framed, but that human emotions are overwhelmingly so. What might the exceptions be? Hypothalamic or autonomic pathology may initiate or exacerbate emotions without social intervention, for example Tourette syndrome. Victims of that condition become unaccountably (in the social sense) anxious and depressed, often use scatological language, and engage in other similarly untoward and socially unprovoked conduct (Licamele and Goldberg, 1988). Yet, even in this condition, the disease presents itself in the forbidden conduct of the surrounding culture. The scatological language is a cultural vehicle for the expression of anger, and the expressed grounds of anger are relevant to the prevailing social structure. Only the inner trigger does not appear to be under social or cultural control. But is not this a rare occurrence?

Another apparently non-social cause of emotion is found in a variety of psychopathologies, from neurotic personality disorder to schizophrenia. Individuals experience what are called irrational anxieties, antipathies, phobias, rages, disgusts, and the like, that do not appear to be associated sensibly with behavior by others in the given context. It should be apparent that while there may be either wilful or unintentional misinterpretation of others' behavior, the resulting emotions are derived from what are conceived to be the prevailing social relations. For example, A is momentarily distracted and fails to acknowledge B's presence, and B takes this as an insult. The frame of interpretation, even if misguided, is still social. Though the reading is flawed and the emotion falsely founded, the interpretive logic still falls within the social model where social relations as experienced by the actor instigate emotions.

Finally, there are the occasions of emotion that have no evident social reference at all: the joy and awe of a splendid mountain vista or other natural display, the irritation at a dead battery in the car, the sadness on a dreary day, and so on. It could be argued—and, as we will see below, it has been by George Herbert Mead—that though these are not human contexts, they are nonetheless social. The scene, the event, the object over which the emotion is aroused is in some sense an "other" who either "gives" us something valuable—the beautiful vista—or "takes" something away—the energy of the battery—or provides a source of contagion—the gloomy day. Although these examples may seem to strain the limits of the social, the extension needs to be considered on its merits. What is proposed here is a way of looking at the total environment as if it were a responsive organism towards which we initiate activity and which responds or initiates activity towards us. Certain outcomes of these initiations and responses will involve emotions. Thus a social paradigm extended to nature, objects, and so forth may usefully apply. In fact, to give it its full due, the social is as powerful a framework for understanding emotion as any thus far proposed.

Two major sociological traditions converge on the social constitution of emotions, but in somewhat different ways. In one, emotions are directly activated by social relations between the participant actors. There is insult and anger; threat and fear; praise and pride; wrong and guilt; and so on. Fundamentally, from this point of view, actors occupy certain social locations and from these they must deal with other actors in other social locations. In the relational exchanges between the actors, emotions are instigated. Formally, this is the social structural approach in the sociology of emotions, and derives from the type of analysis initiated by Marx (described above) in which social locations and their attendant social relations determine action, thought, and feeling.

By contrast, there is the cultural approach, which looks mainly to social regulations of emotions through normative specification—happy at weddings; sad at funerals; sobriety at the office; tenderness in intimacy; and so on; or to the availability and dissemination of other materials that augment or inhibit knowledge, attitudes, and motives. The important difference from the social structural approach is in the emphasis of the analysis. Culturally oriented sociologists of emotions do not so much reject the determination of emotions by social structure in the immediate instance, but choose to look beyond this to the way culture may interpose itself to regulate those emotions, so that they become something else from what they were at first. That is, above and beyond direct elicitation of emotions by structures of social relations, cultural pressures force emotions in directions they might not otherwise take. Perhaps the classic discussion of how culture attempts to regulate emotions that social relations inaugurate is Freud's (1930) *Civilization and its Discontents*. There, Freud examined the tension between emotions (anger and lust) that were aroused in the course of social interaction, and the social regulation of those emotions for the sake of "civilization". Emotions that are structurally initiated are thus often suppressed, repressed, sublimated, or otherwise deflected; hence, for many, culture has the final say.

Given that the social structural and the cultural approaches look to different sources for emotions, the two views have sometimes crossed swords, frequently under the rubrics of "positivism" and "social constructionism", respectively (Kemper, 1981, 1983; Hochschild, 1983a; Hunsaker, 1983; Franks, 1989). However, with respect to the larger issue of whether the social determines emotions, both are in agreement. Each has some distinct contributions to make to our total understanding, and they will be discussed in turn.

Social structural approaches

One group of sociologists contends that individuals experience a large class of emotions directly from their involvement in social relations or through the occupancy of certain social positions that expose them to certain kinds of social relations (Goffman, 1967; Collins, 1975, 1981, 1990; Kemper, 1978, 1981, 1990b; Heise, 1979, 1988; Smith-Lovin, 1988, 1990). Several paths have been taken here and different investigators have approached the task with somewhat different social conditions in mind. It is all the more encouraging that they have converged to a significant degree on what kinds of social relations produce which emotions.

Erving Goffman (1967) was among the first of the modern sociologists of emotions, initiating his efforts well before others turned their attention to emotions. He located one of the fundamental contexts of social relations in conversation or talk. He was concerned not with semantics or meaning, but with the formal aspects of talk, and found there a cosmos of emotional potential. Basically, he took his lead from Durkheim (discussed above), who spoke of the enhancement of emotion in the presence of others engaged in ritual activity, and the emergence of a sense of unity among those sharing the same emotions in the context of the sacred. By enlarging the scope of the sacred, Goffman enormously extended Durkheim's insight into the domain of the profane. Most of social life is of a prosaic, everyday nature. Notwithstanding, it takes place, according to Goffman, in a ritual context. The temple of the ordinary for Goffman is conversation.

Simple, commonplace conversation is fraught with emotional high drama. The reason we are so often ignorant of this is that, usually, things go off so well. But successful conversation is a mini-ritual in which the participants take certain parts in order to make the conversation flow and proceed to its desired end. Using the analogy of music, the parts are not scripted as in transcribed orchestral parts, but rather follow the improvisational options of jazz. Of course, jazz is also rule-governed. Social actors, like jazz musicians, must know when to take their turn and when to give it up, how long a turn should be, and what silence means.

A conversation, then, may be banal but that is only its surface. In fact, it is an accomplishment that is successfully brought off only through the cooperative, sensitive performance of the participants. It is, in Goffman's metaphor, a "dramaturgical" occasion. The emotional result of playing one's part well, and of others also playing their parts well, is one of deep satisfaction. Indeed, few activities give more satisfaction than good conversation.

More than two centuries ago Samuel Johnson put it thus: "That is the happiest conversation where there is no competition, no vanity, but a calm, quiet exchange of sentiments" (Boswell's *Life of Johnson*, cited in Evans, 1968, p. 127). In good conversation, each participant has a sense of self-realization, of participation in a drama in which one's own role is accorded its full due, something not unlike one's wholehearted acceptance and satisfaction in authentically participating in a religious performance where one bears a ritual responsibility. Indeed, there is a virtually sacred quality to conversation. What makes this so is that conversations put on display some extremely sacred objects, namely, the self of each participant. In conversation, the self is either accorded a due reverence by the acts of one's coparticipants or violated and denied by them.

Goffman proposed that every actor in conversation proffers a "line" about him or herself that is his or her relevant persona as far as other participants are concerned. One is a doctor who has just returned from Asia, or a $100-million-a-day bond trader, or a believer in a new form of faith healing, or whatever. If one lives up to the expectations that accompany the line one has presented about oneself—the self that one wants others to find credible and creditable—then one feels confident and assured. One has been confirmed in a fundamental claim. But if one fails to live up to the line one has claimed, other emotions emerge: embarrassment, shamefacedness, chagrin. The actor has "lost face" by the discreditable performance. Unless the actor has poise, which Goffman defines as the ability to conceal embarrassment even when there is occasion for it, the conversational encounter falters (Goffman, 1967).

Of course, others must sustain the line one claims. According to Goffman, there is a general unspoken conspiracy to do so by virtue of the emotional identification of each participant with the others. Everyone's reputation, and all selves, are on the line, so to speak, and there is a tacit agreement to help each other along, to accept each other's self-presentation without expressing too much skepticism about it, and to avoid overrecognition of gaffes and *faux pas*. Otherwise, the delicate web of connectedness that is sustained in the conversation is severed, and the occasion disintegrates. Remarkably, the failure of one produces embarrassment in others, for in conversation, dependencies are so articulated that another's failure to sustain his or her line is also everyone's failure to enable him or her to succeed in doing so. Thus every conversational move is fraught with emotional potential, whether positive or negative, whether one's own or another's. Anger, pride, anguish, confidence, embarrassment, guilt, gratitude—all these are potential emotional accompaniments of conversation as a social form, forgetting now the substantive content, that is, what the talk is about. Rather, it is the "forms of talk" (Goffman, 1981) that make the emotion.

Goffman's sensitive apprehension of the landscape of ordinary talk reveals how even the most prosaic instances of social interaction are emotionally engaged. And while Goffman examined talk as an ordered process that requires cooperation so as to make it possible, he did not push on to a formal analysis of social relations. Even as talk can be examined as an "order", all other actions can be examined as an order too. Prominence or precedence in talk is not merely opportune or structured by task requirements but also structured by how actors are located in formal precedence orders. Collins (1975, 1981) and Hochschild (1983b) have examined this issue through the lens of stratification.

One of the major organizing principles of society is its system of distributing rewards and punishments and its hierarchy of power and control. Together, these constitute the system of stratification. Few aspects of individual fate escape its effects. Weber (1922/1968) referred to stratification as the distribution of life chances, and it literally is this. Longevity, physical and mental health, aspirations, opportunities, tastes, recreations and diversions, sexual practices, politics, aesthetics, communal participation, linguistic style, and on and on. Virtually no aspect of conduct or functioning escapes the impress of stratification, whether of one's class of origin or one's class of aspiration or destination. If so many life processes are caught up in stratification, it is no wonder that emotions are too.

Modeling on Weber (1922/1968), Collins (1971, 1975, 1990) takes what is called a conflict view of stratification, namely, that there is a pervasive competitive struggle among all groups for a fatter share of the benefits and power that define one's stratification location. With specific reference to American society, workers and owners, whites and blacks, Protestants, Catholics, and Jews, male and female, young and old, etc, compete for advantage. According to Collins, the main arena of modern conflict is in the organizations where most of society's work is done, social status is obtained, and wealth is earned. Here the stratification system is crystallized into those who give orders and those who are required to take them. According to Collins, this is the major structural axis of differentiation for all of the millions in society who are involved in work. This almost daily exposure to stratificational reality also disposes major aspects of one's emotional fate.

According to Collins, order-givers are mainly secure, confident, and charged with emotional energy. This is because they stand at the head of organizational coalitions that will support their legitimate orders and punish recalcitrants. They give orders in the name of the organization, and thus sense the power resources of the organization behind them. Their orders are in the service of organizational goals and, given their position, their contribution to those goals is likely to be recognized.

Continuing in the tradition established by Goffman (1967), Collins examined the emotions of order-givers and order-takers through the lens of a Durkheimian analysis of ritual. Durkheim (1915/1965) had proposed that a fundamental source of social solidarity is found in ceremonial co-enactments of people who are otherwise geographically separated. As Collins has elaborated this, people come together face to face, focus on a common topic, experience a common emotion, and through the augmenting social facilitation of this behavior, share even stronger emotions, not the least of which is the sense of solidarity with others in the ritual occasion.

In modern organizations, too, Collins proposes, social occasions are essentially formatted in a ritual manner. The content, here, is less important than that all shall play their ritually correct roles. The order-givers (or bosses or managers) display their social value by providing information, critically evaluating the performances of others, speaking rousingly about policies and future operations, and so forth. The order-takers, *per contra*, are the objects of the order-givers' attention. It is they who are provided information, evaluated, addressed with intent to arouse them (as Henry V did in Shakespeare's play: "Once more, unto the breach dear friends, once more").

According to Collins, order-givers are the focus of the organizational ritual, hence they themselves are most aroused by it, and are most likely to cleave emotionally to the symbols of the organization they represent. Indeed, they are symbols or totems of it themselves. This helps to produce the feelings of security, confidence, energy. In contrast, those who are the objects of the ceremony, the order-takers, must endure resentment, indifference, boredom—alienation in Marx's word—during the public occasions when they are in the presence of the order-givers. Subsequently, when they are "backstage", in Goffman's (1959) term, they can tell of their apathy, anger, depression.

In Collins' view, these are direct effects of social structure. Order-giving and order-taking social relations evoke these emotions without intermediate cultural input, for example cultural ideologies that pervade order-giving and order-taking classes, that is, what one is supposed to feel. This is not to say that such ideologies have not been tried. Order-givers are frequently socialized to feel superior and "right" in their positions of command. Elite schooling, cultural differentiations enunciated at the family table, and explicit training provide this legitimacy for them (Mills, 1956; Cookson & Persell, 1985). Indeed, one of the subtlest forms of this pattern is found in the concept of *noblesse oblige*, which, Goffman (1967) has pointed out, underscores the superiority of the one who acts upon it even as the action appears to negate that superiority.

Order-takers, on the other hand, are also aroused to their alienated feelings directly by the experience of order-taking. Yet they too may be additionally aroused or damped in their feelings by cultural prescriptions. Ideologies of submission and rationalization of everyone's due have been utilized in many societies to pacify those who might otherwise be discontented with their lot. It is this, called "false consciousness", according to Marxists, that has delayed socialist revolutions in advanced industrial societies.

Hochschild (1983b) too examined some structural conditions of labor in organizations that foster emotions, particularly among those whose work is to provide service. In an exemplary study of airline flight attendants, Hochschild discovered that these personnel often found themselves in an emotional dilemma. Owing to the expectations of passengers in a situation of high time-and-space constraints, or passengers' impolite, drunken, or harassing conduct, a good many negative emotions were naturally generated in the flight attendants: anger, disgust, contempt. But employment as a service person prohibited the expression of these emotions, lest passengers be offended and switch to other airlines for future flights. According to some of these attendants, the experience of constantly suppressing their true feelings left them emotionally "numb". In situations where they might release their true feelings—even, it is suggested, in sexual encounters—there was some withholding of feeling, supposedly owing to the frequent practice of doing so in their job.

Hochschild generalized the issue of emotional containment to the service economy as a whole. Particularly striking is that the larger proportion of such jobs is held by women. In conformity with the general pattern of women containing anger in relations with males (Henley, 1977; Lerner, 1977), there is the additional requirement of containing anger, along with other disturbing emotions, as a requirement of one's work.

Kemper (1973, 1978; Kemper & Collins, 1990) has tried to generalize the dimensions of social structure for the purpose of understanding emotions. Collins' designation of a major axis of stratification in terms of order-giving and order-taking was a major step towards formalizing the nomenclature of social structure. But a more general and comprehensive approach to formalization is possible. Indeed, once such a formulation is available it makes possible a systematic derivation of the emotional consequences of social relations across the spectrum of social structural conditions. One of the main issues has been the specification of the kinds of social relations or social positions, that is, social structures, that evoke particular emotions.

Drawing on a large body of factor analytic descriptions of social interaction, Kemper (1973, 1978, 1987b; Kemper & Collins, 1990) proposed that social relations and the structures they constituted could be adequately represented in two orthogonal dimensions. One of these entailed relations of dominance and control, in which one actor is able to obtain compliance from another actor who does not wish to comply. This is the dimension of *power* in social structures and social relations. Processually it involves applying noxious stimuli or depriving another of usual or expected benefits—or threatening to do these. Noxious stimuli include the infliction of physical or psychic pain, restriction of freedom of movement, high-intensity communications such as shouts and screams, fierce looks, and so forth. Deprivations include simple denial of access to goods and services the other has a right to or deserves, withdrawal of emotional warmth or love, snubs, ignoring one another, insults and humiliations, and so forth.

It should be apparent that in psychological terms power entails either the infliction of punishment or the withdrawal of reward. While psychological interest in these is mainly restricted to the experience of the focal person who is being punished or rewarded, sociological interest is mainly in the relationship in which punishments and rewards are distributed between the actors. Thus, one of the central patterns of social arrangements entails power relations between human actors, or between organized collectivities and their members. In modern societies, the state in relation to its citizens is the prime example of a social structure of power. Sociologically, the state is understood to be the ultimate source of coercion in society, often legitimately so, in which case we speak of authority; when it is without authority, we speak of naked power. At the middle levels of social organization, between micro and macro levels, most power is centered in organizations, as Collins (1975) has specified, and is distributed between the order-givers and order-takers. In interpersonal relations too, power, the ability (or the effort) to coerce another to do what he or she does not want to do, is a major feature. Rarely are individuals able to avoid the power incursions of others, though they may adequately defend against them; nor are they able often to resist employing power when it seems advantageous to do so, or when they are in the grip of anger or even fear. Indeed, power is a feature of all human social relations—in states, communities, organizations, families, between any two individuals.

If power is so general, it seems to reflect a Hobbesian world in which violence and brutishness contribute to making life for many both nasty and sometimes short. Indeed, it was against such calamitous prospects that Hobbes saw the supposed social contract by which a civil society surrendered power to a sovereign who would be charged with protecting it from the depredations of those who could muster high power and who had no compunctions about using it.

But there is a second dimension of social relations that the Hobbesian theory does not contemplate, namely, one that entails relations of voluntary compliance, where actors provide benefits, goods, services, regard, approval, acceptance to another willingly, without coercion or the threat of it. This is the dimension of status-accord, or *status* (in brief). It is the ground of true social solidarity or community. Structurally, actors share or aspire to share common group membership with those to whom they give status. At its ultimate, the giving of status is love (Kemper, 1978). In psychological terms, the language of status relations is the language of rewards, through either the removal of noxious stimuli or the incrementing of what is felt as pleasant and desirable. Again, the sociological focus is on the relationship, namely, what passes between one actor and another and what thus constitutes the bond between them.

According to a large body of supporting evidence (aggregated in Kemper & Collins, 1990), the power and status dimensions constitute the main framework for relations between human actors. This means that from a social perspective, emotions are instituted by outcomes of social relations in power and status terms. With these concepts in mind, Kemper (1978) reviewed a large body of experimental studies of emotion conducted mainly by psychologists and found that the instigating contexts, usually the "treatment" conditions, could be understood as social contexts of power and status relations. A consistent set of results relating power and status outcomes to emotions was seen to emerge from them.

For a sense of how this works, it is important to see that a relatively simple model of social relational outcomes suffices for the analysis. Every relational exchange takes place along the dimensions of power and status. For each actor the outcomes can be: an increase in power and/or status, a decline, or no change in these. This produces 12 possible outcomes (two actors × two dimensions × three results), but only four of these will actually occur, namely, a power and status outcome for each actor. Emotions will flow from these.

In the power dimension, the available evidence suggests (see Kemper, 1978; Kemper & Collins, 1990 for details) that if one actor loses power or the other actor gains it, the emotional outcome is some degree of fear or anxiety. If one actor gains power and/or the other actor loses it, the emotional outcome is likely to be a sense of security. In the status domain the outcomes are slightly more complex. If an actor gains status, he is likely to feel contented, satisfied, happy. If an actor loses status, the emotional outcome depends on the felt sense of agency: who was ultimately responsible for the status loss. If the other is held culpable, the emotional result is anger. If self is held culpable, the emotional result is shame, or more seriously depression if the actor feels that the situation is irremediable.

When the situation is one in which the focal actor gives status to the other, we may expect satisfaction and contentment in the focal actor. When he or she withholds or withdraws status from the other, several emotional outcomes are possible. If the other actor is deemed responsible (he or she "deserves" this treatment), the result is likely to be satisfaction of a self-righteous kind. If the other actor was not responsible (he or she does not "deserve" the treatment), then two emotions are possible, either singly or jointly. If the focal actor deems that he or she did not live up to his or her character standing, that is, the amount of status which he is generally credited by others as deserving, he or she will feel shame. On the other hand, if the focal actor concentrates on the harm or hurt he or she did to the other, guilt is likely to ensue. In the instance of shame, the actor recognizes that he or she has acted so as not to deserve the status he or she has been accorded. In the case of guilt, the actor recognizes that he or she has used an excess of power against the other.

Some aspects of emotion also follow from anticipations that are either confirmed or disconfirmed by subsequent interaction. Thus the actor who anticipated losing power, but did not, should feel especially secure. The actor who did not anticipate receiving status, but receives it, is likely to feel especially pleased. In general, discomfirmations of expectations tend to exert a multiplier effect on the emotions that would ordinarily be felt from the power–status outcome in the situation.

By way of introduction to the last social structural approach to emotions to be presented here, it is useful to know that among the bodies of evidence supporting the power–status framework of social relations is the set of results derived from work on the semantic differential (Osgood, Suci & Tannenbaum, 1957). The method attempts to arrive at fundamental meanings of objects by evaluating them on a set of bipolar scales. In much replicated work across many objects, and cross-culturally as well (Osgood, May & Miron, 1975), the scales reduce to three underlying concepts; evaluation (E), potency (P), and activity (A). The first two closely parallel the status and power factors respectively.

The activity factor falls outside the power–status relational framework, since it does not touch on relational behavior as such. It has been associated with level of emotional arousal (Lutz, 1981) or with Collins' concept of "emotional energy" (Collins, 1981; Kemper & Collins, 1990). In a multidimensional scale analysis of emotion terms obtained from a Southwest Pacific culture, Lutz (1981) found only two factors, strongly approximating the power and status dimensions. She argued that the arousal dimension frequently found in analyses of emotion may be simply an add-on of the western cultural tradition.

In a unique form of social structural analysis, Heise and his colleagues (Heise, 1979; Smith-Lovin & Heise, 1988), build on the semantic differential version of power–status analysis in a methodologically sophisticated, mathematically based effort to predict emotions. The work is also unique in that it combines cultural judgments with social structural analysis. The particular shape of Heise's approach derives most immediately from the work of Gollub (Gollub, 1968; Gollub & Rossman, 1973), who developed a mathematical–statistical method by which to predict impressions of events from a combination of judgments about objects before an event in which they were involved, and about the event. For example, after obtaining separate good–bad evaluations of such objects as man, kicks, child, Gollub created equations to predict the evaluation of the man in the event, a man kicks a child. (See Smith-Lovin, 1990, for a succinct description of Gollub's work and its application to Heise's.)

Heise has launched a research program that has sought to understand emotions from similar types of evaluations of objects separately and then in compound event situations. It goes by the name of affect control theory (ACT). The theory is based on a dictionary of language terms for identities, behaviors, emotions, etc., that have been evaluated by semantic differential. In accordance with the results of this method, each word in the dictionary has a score on each of the three SD dimensions, namely, evaluation (E), or how good–bad the item is, potency (P), or how strong–weak it is, and activity (A), or how active–passive it is. Ignoring now the activity dimension, Heise's predictions of emotions are derived from essentially the same conceptual matrix as Kemper's. Activity, which has sometimes been joined with potency in Heise's (1969) work, finds no place in Kemper's formulation. Notwithstanding the presence of the additional dimension, Heise's predictions of emotions are quite close to what is obtained from Kemper's theory (Averett & Heise, 1988).

The basic notion behind ACT is that individuals behave out of a homeostatic need to maintain their fundamental identity. If behavior deviates too far from one's sense of identity, some reparative action needs to be taken to return the self to a comfortable sense of itself. Behavior ordinarily conforms to fundamental identity, but on occasion it does not. It therefore reveals a transient identity that differs from the fundamental one. For example, a parent may ordinarily be kind and thoughtful to his or her child. Thus behavior conforms to the cultural notion of the parent identity. But occasionally, the parent's behavior is out of line with the fundamental identity of parent, for example he or she is tired or overburdened and acts indifferently or cruelly to the child. The transient identity of parent who is cruel is now in conflict with the fundamental identity of (good) parent. A discrepancy between the basic identity and the transient identity produces an emotion, and from this flows some of the motivation to restore one's fundamental identity. Which emotion it will be depends on the type and degree of discrepancy. We see here the basic social structural approach in which actors experience emotions on the basis of their relations with others.

Through regressing criterion emotion terms on the EPA values of behavior and identity terms in the dictionary, Heise has generated a series of parameters for equations to predict emotions for a wide variety of situations and discrepancies of identity from fundamental identity. Averett and Heise (1988) undertook to predict both qualitatively and quantitatively which emotions might result from different types of interactions. For example, if a father serves a son, father's emotions were predicted to be relieved, contented, pleased, while son's emotions were amused, euphoric, lighthearted. If a judge sentences a gangster, the judge's emotions were predicted to be contented, relieved, proud, while the gangster's emotions were uneasy, awestruck. Several emotions are usually generated by ACT because they have approximately equal EPA values in the prediction equation. When there are discrepancies between basic and transient identity, the usual case is for the individual to recapture his or her basic identity by some reparative act. Failing this, basic identity suffers a change: "Maybe I'm not as bright, moral, careful, etc, as I thought". It is also possible in Heise's model for the social environment, observing the discrepancy and the accompanying emotion, to reidentify the individual.

Heise (1989) has examined a complex set of instances in which an individual is observed to perform an act and reveal a variety of emotions. Reidentifications of the focal actor by observers are predicted in line with the emotions manifested to the observer. Furthermore, the method allows reidentifications of the focal actor according to the emotions manifested by the social object of the focal actor's action. For example, Heise examined the effects of displaying different emotions on judgments of the fundamental identity man when he has kissed a woman. If he is cheerful, he is reidentified as a gentleman, pal, or mate, identities that gain significantly in E or status but with some decline in P or power. On the other hand, if he kisses and manifests disgust, he is reidentified at a much lower E or status level, although his P or power remains unchanged. If the kisser displays nervousness, the reidentification shows him to be lower in both P and E.

The flexibility and suppleness of the ACT model is such that it easily allows judgments of the man now based not on his emotions but on the woman's. If she is cheerful, he is upwardly evaluated in both P and E. On the other hand, if she is disgusted, he loses in E but gains in P. (It is noteworthy that this is exactly what we would expect from Kemper's model, in which the situation described is one of the man exercising power over the woman, while he is downgraded in status for having done so.) If the woman shows nervousness, the man shows a similar loss of E and a gain in P.

Heise's method also allows for a distinction between emotions and moods (Averett & Heise, 1988). If an event occurs that is discrepant from fundamental identity, for example, father ignores son, father is likely to feel unhappy, according to predictions from ACT. The theory now predicts that father will act to compensate for the behavior of ignoring the son by becoming especially attentive. This action would restore the father's fundamental identity, which is a cultural object that normatively does not ignore a son. Thus, emotion which arises in the situation of transient departure of behavior from fundamental identity gives rise to action opposite to what might be intuitively expected of a father who is unhappy.

But, by contrast with the father who is unhappy (a transient state), there is the unhappy father. Here the fundamental identity comprises both the social position and the emotion. Heise defines this as a mood. According to ACT, moods give rise to consistent behavior, for example the unhappy father might neglect or attack the son (Averett & Heise, 1988).

Sociologists of emotion who use the social structural approach are usually concerned with predicting emotions from the social relations in which actors are engaged. This ordinarily assumes that there is a natural (or pancultural) universal emotional response to certain kinds of social relations. For example, insult naturally or universally evokes an anger response. One of the most important differences between the social structural and the cultural orientation to emotions is in whether this assumption is correct.

Kemper (1990b) has argued that culture is indeed powerful and may in fact override the natural response in given contexts, but this is often obtained at a price. Once again Freud (1930) provided a useful model here in *Civilization and its Discontents*. Although aggression and lust were normally understandable responses to certain social conditions, the requirements of an orderly, irenic society did not permit them to be expressed. This meant that they were repressed, and for Freud it meant also a significant source of neurosis. Thus, civilization does not come without a price. Among present-day sociologists, Hochschild has pointed in the same direction. In her study of airline flight attendants, she found that attendants claimed to suffer from emotional numbness, even frigidity, putatively due to the extreme control they were required to exercise over their emotions in the course of their work. Anger, fear, disgust, disdain, contempt instigated by the untoward or unruly conduct of passengers were necessarily suppressed as part of the airline's commercial strategy to keep customers happy. The point here is that while social regulation may divert emotion from its natural channel, it is usually at some cost, and the cost itself may be a warped emotion.

Culture

In social structural analysis, emotions result from the direct enactment of one's social position. For example, in Collins' analysis, the order-giver feels easy, confident, secure in transmitting commands that he then sees order-takers obeying, while the latter feel uneasy, insecure, resentful at what they often see as their enforced obedience, over which they have little choice. Or in Kemper's analysis, the use of power usually produces fear in its object; according status, satisfaction; withdrawal of status, anger; and so forth. Each structural condition of relationship produces its associated emotion.

By contrast with this direct social constitution of emotions, cultural analysis interposes an additional consideration. This is the normative social definition of situations and the rules that are laid down for the emotions it is appropriate to feel in them. These "feeling rules" (Hochschild, 1979) are parallel to the rules that Ekman, Friesen and Ellsworth (1972) proposed were present in every culture to define and regulate the expression of emotion. In cultural analysis, one looks not at the social position and its direct emotional effects, but rather at the rules that govern the range of possible meanings and knowledge that can be invoked about the situation and its applicable emotion. Culture thus constructs emotions by providing a convention for feeling, a guidebook for what is legitimate in the circumstance, with sanctions provided for not feeling what is prescribed. Hochschild (1979, 1983b), Thoits (1985, 1990), and Gordon

(1981, 1990) have examined emotions from this perspective, focusing on their management, that is, in what circumstances, and how, actors bring their feelings into line with what is normatively prescribed.

Culturally oriented sociologists of emotion are also concerned with the way emotions help to maintain social order, or, what is equivalent, make for social control. Guilt and shame are two emotions that are especially significant here because they can be experienced not only on account of how one has acted towards or in the presence of others, but also on account of how one feels, especially if it is discrepant from what the culture determines one should feel. Shott (1979) and Scheff (1988) are especially interested in the way these emotions contribute to social order.

Prior even to specific rules governing emotions are overarching cultural motifs and bodies of knowledge that endorse certain emotional emphases, or make them possible in the first place. For example, western achievement motivation has no place in a Buddhist society, while Buddhist quietism is out of place in a western nation. This kind of analysis points towards the sociology of knowledge as a source of understanding about emotions in a society in a given age. McCarthy (1989) and Perinbanayagam (1989) offer views from this perspective.

As might be expected, the cultural approach to the sociology of emotions is especially appealing to cognitive and idealist viewpoints. These assign a leading role to mental processes in the determination of emotions, and are quite close in fundamental intent to the very popular cognitive approach in psychology as espoused, for example, by Arnold (1960), Lazarus and his colleagues (Lazarus, 1984; Lazarus, Averill & Opton, 1970), and Mandler (1975). However, sociologists of emotions do not find their inspiration in these works. Rather, they derive their position from symbolic interactionism, an approach that psychologists might more easily endorse (though they ignore it) than sociologists, who might more easily ignore it (though they frequently endorse it).

Symbolic interactionism

Although sociologists ordinarily are theoretically indifferent to the cognitive processes of actors, one school of sociological discourse, symbolic interactionism, actually requires close attention to these. Symbolic interactionism stands with those groups in psychology that reject behaviorism, the notion that actors simply respond to stimuli. Rather, they say, a stimulus is itself a construction by the actor, and any response to it is mediated by a process of interpretation in which the actor indicates to him or herself the meaning of the stimulus object for a potential course of action. Symbolic interactionism derives from the pragmatic school of American philosophy, among whose leading figures were John Dewey and William James. Through its interest in the material world and in social problems, this school separated itself from the airy domains of European philosophical idealism, but some of its offshoots ended up in idealism notwithstanding. The pathway back was through reasoning that in order to come as close as possible to the human actors who were experiencing a particular social condition, one had to try to get into their position and feel the experience as they did. Idealism in the sense intended here signifies the fundamental importance of ideas and cognition, particularly those belonging to the actor in the situation being investigated. This requires getting the (scientific) observer into the interpretive processes of the thinking and feeling subject. Indeed, the only valid world to which theoretical understanding can be applied is the one reported by the subject. A clarion call of this approach was the dictum of W. I. Thomas (Thomas & Thomas, 1928, p. 720): "If men define situations as real, they are real in their consequences". Bishop Berkeley could not have been more pleased.

This view is also quite close to what is known as the "emic" as opposed to the "etic" approach in cultural anthropology (Pike, 1967; Pelto, 1970). In the former, the field observer tries to apprehend the stimulus world as the native culture does, refraining as much as possible from imposing his or her own categories of analysis on the situation. By contrast, in the etic approach the observer imports his or her cultural categories in viewing the local system. To come full circle, in psychology, parallel meanings and research programs have distinguished the idiographic and nomothetic approaches (Allport, 1968; Campbell, 1970; Denzin, 1978).

Across the spectrum of the social sciences, we can see a common axial division between those who espouse the social structural, etic, nomothetic approaches on the one hand, and those who favor the cultural, emic, idiographic approaches on the other. In a fascinating speculation, Colomy and Barchas (1984) have suggested that the appeal of each of these polarities may be related to the differentiation between cerebral hemisphere functions. The more linear, logical, left-hemisphere-dominant type of personality is likely to prefer the social structural, etc., approach, while the more integrative, gestaltist, right-hemisphere-dominant personality is likely to prefer the cultural, etc., approach. Whether there is any validity in this is a matter for evidence to determine. That it partitions sociologists of emotions is evident.

The earliest expositor of the ideas of the cultural school was George Herbert Mead (1934), a pragmatist philosopher who, like William James, was strongly interested in psychology. His initial thrust was at the notion of psychophysical parallelism proposed by Wundt, namely, that the world that provided the stimulus for the physical processes of the brain simultaneously stamped its impress on consciousness or mind, thus giving it its content and thereby offering a bridge between mind and brain. In particular, Mead (pp. 49–50, emphasis added) argued, Wundt's approach could not explain how, in a social context, "a responding organism [could] get or experience the same idea or physical correlate of any given gesture that the other organism making this gesture has. The difficulty is that Wundt presupposes *selves* as antecedent to the social process in order to explain communication within that process, whereas, on the contrary, selves must be accounted for in terms of the social process, and in terms of communication. . . . Wundt's analysis of communication presupposes the existence of minds that are able to communicate, and this existence remains an inexplicable mystery on his [psychophysical parallelist] basis''.

Per contra, Mead proposed that mind was a product of social interaction. Thinking, said Mead, was an internal rehearsal of social interaction. The process of thinking involves a subject with a need or goal that requires the cooperative contribution of another actor. In order to obtain that contribution, the subject must reflect, or "think", how to get it. In the projected scenario, this involves proactions by the self that will elicit the desired responses from the other. The crucial question, said Mead, was how to determine what proactions would yield the proper responses. In his most original contribution, Mead proposed that after some amount of interaction with another actor, we have the capacity to call up in ourselves the likely reaction of that actor to proactive moves of our own. This ability is not based on some preexisting quality of mind, but rather necessarily depends on previous interaction with the other person, or with yet others who have reacted the way he or she would. Thus, when a proactive move comes to mind, it evokes (in an importantly physical way) the response of the other. It is the desired response. The proactive move is now launched in reality. Or, in a failed scenario, a proactive move comes to mind. It calls up in the self the response of the other. It is *not* the desired response. Thus, this move is not launched and the actor must recycle to consider another potential move, again calling up the other's possible response to it, and so on, until a satisfactory proaction–reaction sequence is attained.

In this construction, thinking is actually a recapitulation of social interaction projected into the future. Thus, without the prior social interaction with the other that could be rehearsed mentally, mind, in the sense of having the ability to rehearse social interaction, is not possible. Curiously, although the possibilities for a science of mind are abundant here, they have not been exploited either by psychologists, whose proper domain they would be, or by sociologists, who accept Mead's model of mind and take the work in other directions. A recent exception is the work of Collins (1989), who hypothesized with unusual specificity the content of mind. Given Collins' social framework for emotions, that content consists substantially of the interactions, both past and anticipated, that are precursors to the emotional outcomes.

Having set down a model of the thinking process, Mead went on to explain the self more or less in the same manner. However, here he differentiated the self into components—not unlike Freud's similar differentiations into ego, superego, and id. Mead proposed that we acquire a sense of self through putting ourselves in the place of others—taking their role towards us—and responding to our self as if it were an object. Inherent in this process, according to Mead, are two self components, the "me" and the "I". By and large, the me is that part of the self that the role-taking process makes evident. It is the distillation of the responses of others to us as we call up those responses to us as an object.

The I, on the other hand, is *our* response to the responses of others to us, that is, to the me. In very rough terms, the me parallels Freud's superego, while the I shares something of both the id—in the form of impulse—and the ego, in the form of integrated response.

Herbert Blumer (1969), the doyen of recent symbolic interactionism, took these notions very far indeed. For him, and for many who follow in his path, all of social life results from these processes whereby actors confront situations involving others, indicate to themselves possible responses the others might make to their proactive moves, and respond to these with evaluations and choices. A key guide to choice is the meaning of the acts of both self and others. Meaning in the Meadian pragmatist–symbolic interactionist tradition can be understood as the response that a stimulus evokes. The meaning of "chair" is the physical response of sitting. The meaning of shouting "Fire!" in a crowded theater is the speedy rising and seeking exit of the audience. For Blumer, meanings govern, as the individual calls up the possible responses of others. The meanings, of course, pertain to the goals and interests of the self.

One possible reason for psychologists' reluctance to examine the structures of mind and self more deeply is that, at least in one extreme Blumerian version, symbolic interactionism turns its back on conventional models of science. Significantly, it scoffs at the possibility of predicting how mind and self will fare in the process of role-taking and self-indicating of meaning, or what evaluations and final choices will be made. Hence, for this group no science of mind or society is possible. Of course, the subject matter of what it takes for granted—the constructing and indicating processes of mind and self—are fundamental grounds for psychological analysis. Regrettably, no psychologists have joined with the symbolic interactionist sociologists to acquire a complete description of how Mead's process works.

As a consequence of the antiscience approach of many of the symbolic interactionist school, there is virtually no cumulative body of findings nor is there any theory to aggregate those findings into empirical generalizations (Lofland, 1970). There is only faith in the process by which mind and self operate. Lest this be scoffed at, this faith has indeed moved a mountain. It is at the core of a larger movement that prevails in sociology, anthropology, literary criticism, and feminist theory that is generally known as social constructionism. This view holds mainly that no social arrangements or forms of individual conduct are "natural" or inevitable, but are determined by social fiat. Thus there are no privileged stances from which to observe or analyze the world. Conventional science claims the right to describe the world, but it is merely one among many forms of discourse about the world and there is no justification for choosing it over others. The current poststructuralist mode of deconstructionism is emblematic of the social constructionist mode. In this approach, the world is the equivalent of a text, and each viewer, or reader, composes it differently. Lest this seems to be a program of solipsism, the social constructionists point out that the meanings that individuals examine in the texts of the world are socially derived. Thus, instead of anarchy there is some order but an unpredictable one. Individuals are constantly composing and recomposing the world from the menu of choices that society offers. They are also sometimes—though admittedly rarely—inventing the world, as the unpredictable "I" redistributes old elements into new shapes.

Although the social constructionist approach might not be thought to apply to emotions, it fits neatly with one of the main psychological paradigms for emotions, namely, the cognition–emotion approach. Perhaps at present the dominant view in psychology, it has afforded the symbolic interactionists who study emotions a nearly perfect accommodation to at least one aspect of psychological thinking on emotions, namely, the cognitive position of Schachter and Singer (1962). While at least some psychologists were turning away from it (see Marshall & Zimbardo, 1979; Maslach, 1979; Cotton, 1981; Reisenzein, 1983), social constructionist sociologists were flocking to it (eg Shott, 1979; Gordon, 1981; Hochschild, 1983b; Coulter, 1986). Although they would ordinarily have had little interest in physiological aspects of emotion—it is simply too distant an analytical plane from the normative and cognitive—they welcomed Schachter and Singer's (1962) classic work of physiological scholarship enthusiastically. Schachter and Singer presumably showed that emotion is formed in joining a cognition—any cognition—to physiological arousal. Since the arousal was supposedly physiologically identical for any emotion, the true differentia specifica for emotions was to be found in cognition. Berscheid and Walster (1974) suggested that even so grisly a scene as a hanging could evoke arousal that might subsequently transmogrify into love in the right cognitive conditions. This meant that culture and cognitive processes control emotion, and that specific emotions do not simply flow from specific situations, as the social structural sociologists maintain. And some sharp battles have taken place over this issue among sociologists of emotion (Kemper, 1980, 1981, 1983; Shott, 1979, 1980; Hochschild, 1983a; Hunsaker, 1983), although an accommodation between the two positions has been suggested (Kemper, 1987b).

One of the most elaborate symbolic interactionist perspectives on emotion is presented by Hochschild (1979, 1983b). In her view, situations or "frames" give rise to emotions in what might be called a natural way. But social intervention takes over quickly. Hochschild postulates the existence of "feeling rules", often unarticulated yet somehow known—feel happy at parties, sad at funerals, etc.—that are like heat-seeking missiles for experienced emotions. In the early stages of the emotional process, the emotion and the putatively applicable rule are subjected to a congruency test. Although this mainly tends to happen out of awareness, it is likely that when there is discrepancy the result becomes conscious. A feeling rule that disagrees with a feeling is in the position to overrule the feeling. There then proceeds either "surface" or "deep" acting to bring the emotion into better alignment with the rule. Surface acting would be to assume some of the elements of the emotion, for example to smile, if that is what is required by the feeling rule. The idea is that such surface acts sometimes elicit the other elements of an authentic emotion. Thoits (1990) reviewed data that suggest that such surface display of emotion can ramify for the more interior cognitive and physiological aspects. Deep acting, by contrast, is the assumpton of a stance that actually produces the desired emotion. For example, if one is feeling sad when social norms say that one should be happy, one may think of a ground for happiness which may then make one feel happy. Deep acting, as Hochschild acknowledged, owes something to Stanislavski's (1948/1965) method for actors, in which performers build an emotion for stage presentation by evoking it in themselves.

For Hochschild (1983b), emotion results from a discrepancy between what we perceive and what we expected; thus, as Freud proposed, it has a "signal" function. Emotion announces "our relation to the world" (p. 219). But this relation is not complete until the emotion is given full cognitive status through the attachment of a name which derives from the culture. Thus culture directs how we feel and how we name what we feel. Ordinarily the process of perception and selection of cultural emotional options takes place out of awareness, but it depends on five categories of perceptual focus. These are: motivation (what I want); possession (what I have); value (what I approve); agency (who caused it); and self-agent relations. Together these form a perceptual template for generating emotions. For example, shame is constructed of the five perceptions: I want to do right; I have done wrong; I disapprove; I am the cause of the event; and, the audience of the event is better than I am. Given the management perspective, emotion is not fixed or frozen for Hochschild, and certainly not in any sense determined by biological factors that are immutable. Indeed, biology itself is managed in the management of emotions. To see how this is done, we must look at the work of Thoits.

Thoits (1985, 1990) has taken Hochschild's themes of emotion management systematically further. She views emotions as complexes of situational cues, physiological changes, expressive gestures, and an emotion label. These are systemically interconnected, so that a change in one inaugurates a change in the others. Thoits proposed that when discrepancies occur between emotion and feeling rule, they can be handled through either behavioral or cognitive application to any of the four elements of emotion: situation, physiology, expression, and label. For example, one can withdraw from a group in which unwanted emotions arise (behavior–situation); or one can exercise or take drugs to change one's visceral feelings (behavior–physiology); or one can redefine one's context so that its implication for emotion changes (cognitive–situation); and so on.

As a precondition for the management of emotions, Thoits required the notion of emotional deviance first proposed by Hochschild (1979, 1983b). This is the experience of emotions that are contrary to what is prescribed in the given situation, thus requiring management. For example, the bride who is glum, the mourner who is cheerful, might feel about their feelings that they need some rectification to bring them into line with normative expectations for their occasion. Thoits proposed four social conditions that might dispose one to emotional deviance: multiple-role occupancy; subcultural marginality; role transitions; and rigid rules governing ongoing roles or ceremonial occasions.

Multiple-role problems can induce deviant emotions, for example the father who becomes jealous over his wife's attention to their newborn child, thus violating the prescription for his feeling the happy father. Subcultural marginality signifies the person who has an identity that may conflict with the identity imputed to him or her by the dominant culture; emotional deviance may occur when the two cultures impose different rules, for example a gay person who must cope with deviant feelings of attraction to a same-sex person in a heterosexual context. Role transitions, such as becoming divorced, becoming a step-parent, or becoming a physician can foster emotional deviance because of either uncertain role expectations or cultural ambiguity as to what the role requires emotionally. Finally, ongoing roles may be subject to rigidly delimited feelings—the new spouse must feel loving—while reality simply evokes other emotions; or ceremonial occasions closely specify the appropriate feelings, allowing little room for variability or lack of wholeheartedness of feeling.

Thoits pointed out that deviance includes not only contranormative emotions, but also emotion that is too intense, too prolonged, or is directed at the wrong target. Yet, from a sociological perspective, even deviant emotions, if experienced by a sufficiently large number of persons, may become legitimate and normative. Social protest movements are composed of emotional deviants. They feel intensely and differently about matters that the remainder of the community accepts with equanimity or in a conventional way. The antiwar movement during the Vietnam period is an example of how deviant emotions came to be more widely and effectively shared. Instead of managing their emotions, the protesters converted others to their emotional point of view.

Denzin (1984, 1985, 1990) represents a somewhat different departure in the cultural and social constructionist school from that of Hochschild and Thoits. He derives from a tradition with roots in phenomenological philosophy as detailed by Heidegger and Merleau-Ponty, among others. One of its foremost tenets is that unlike infrahuman forms, which may be best described by behavioral principles, humans can judge their judgments, and, further, judge that they judge their judgments, and so on. That this can be done, and sometimes is done for a few steps along the infinite path, demonstrates for Denzin the importance of the self-indicating faculty as elaborated by Blumer (1969) described above. This further entails the idea of emotion as "lived experience". This means that the analyst must get at the way human actors experience emotion in all of its specificity, including sensible feelings (eg pain or hunger), feelings of the lived body (eg sorrow, fear, anger), intentional value feelings (that is, the intention to have a feeling and having it), and moral feelings of the self (how one feels about oneself as a moral being).

Finally, what Denzin calls emotional practices actually produce the full complement of the four feeling elements (sensible feelings, etc). The practices can be whatever action produces feeling (eg working, making love, cooking, exercising, etc). The critical thing for Denzin is that emotional practices are gender-specific and governed by ideologies that determine the general patterns of stratification in a given society. To obtain an understanding of the way these influences operate in the field of emotions, Denzin (1990) has examined cultural products such as films, television programs and the like to extract from them the implicit messages of gender-based emotional socialization that they convey. In the style of structuralist and poststructuralist literary criticism, Denzin regards culture as a text, and his interest is in the emotional subtext that is prevalent in what for many in his tradition is a "postmodernist" age.

Yet another thrust in the social constructionist approach to emotions is provided by the work of Gordon (1981, 1990). He contended that emotions *per se* are elemental, biological, and, shortly after childhood, of relatively little consequence. This is because social construction takes place, so that cues and signals of, let us say, anger are transformed into culturally meaningful "sentiments" such as resentment, righteous indignation, etc, and are thus removed from the biologically rooted emotion. Similar cultural transformations convert all emotions into sentiments and it is these that individuals both experience and express. Since sentiments are socially formed, they can also be abandoned or invented.

The principal exponent of this view is Norbert Elias (1978a,b), who in a series of works on the evolution of manners has shown how what might be called the "emotions of the alimentary canal" (Kemper, 1981) slowly evolved as part of the relations between aristocrats and the emerging bourgeoisie. The nobility was distinguished from lower orders not only by its power and status, but also by its practices. Among these were different ways of treating the daily chores and occasions of dining, self-cleansing, executing toilet functions, and so forth. The superior status of the nobility was marked by their culturally endorsed superior manner of conducting these activities. For a long time, the nobility was not threatened by imitation from lower estates in society. But the emergence of a new class of relatively well-off tradesmen and craftsmen who sought to differentiate themselves in turn from the mass, from whom they had elevated themselves, led to their aping the manners of their social superiors. Thus the aristocratic monopoly on desirable manners was lost. But, as Elias pointed out, they moved to other domains of refinement of feelings and experience, again out of the reach for a while of the bourgeoisie.

Taking Elias' work as a model, Gordon (1981, 1990; Cancian & Gordon, 1988) has looked at the transformations in the cultural emphasis on the feeling rules about love; his conclusion is that sentiments are always subject to a historical process that adjusts them to the social demands and requirements of a particular pattern of social organization. They are thus not fixed in the way emotions, somewhat biologically conceived, might be.

Although symbolic interactionism has been mainly employed to undermine the idea of fixity in the domain of emotional response, Shott (1979) and

Scheff (1988) have also employed it to show how certain emotions that involve the symbolic interaction process underlie social stability and order. That there is pattern and predictability in social life, rather than chaos and randomness, poses one of the long-standing problems in sociological analysis. Certainly, it is not a matter of biology, since it can be observed that social order is expressed differently in different cultures, and there is no evidence of Lamarckian transmission of culture. Thus, social order is implanted through a cultural process. The reverse side of social order is social control, namely, that society manages somehow to instill in individuals a propensity to comply with required social forms, and that deviance from these forms, though greater in some periods than in others, is actually quite limited. How is this accomplished?

There are two main answers to the question, and both of them turn on emotion. First, social order may be imposed by dominant and powerful groups. Their tactic is to evoke fear about non-conformity. Although it has been argued that such regimes cannot be stable (Parsons, 1951), in the short run at least they have remarkable sticking power. Decades or centuries may elapse before a feared form of government is overthrown. The second ground for social order is some form of acceptance of the existing pattern of things. And here sociologists have split somewhat on what is accepted. On the one hand, social order can flow from belief in the validity of the social norms. One pays one's taxes, serves in the armed forces, does not write a crooked balance sheet, surrenders one's seat on the bus to a frailer person, and so on, because the rules are deemed good and it is morally right to abide by them. A second view, which is becoming increasingly prominent, is that underlying social order is an emotional order. Without an emotional basis, social order would not be possible.

Attacking the question from a symbolic interactionist perspective, Shott (1979) proposed a set of "role-taking emotions" that are central to social control: guilt, shame, embarrassment, pride, and vanity. Each of these involves the central symbolic interactionist mechanism of putting oneself in the place, or taking the role, of the other person and thereby evoking his or her perspective. The result of such role-taking can be an emotion directed towards the self, because it evokes in the self the judgment that others are making about the self. Guilt involves the self- and (presumed) other-judgment of "moral inadequacy". Shame entails the self- and (presumed) other-rejection of an "idealized self-image". Embarrassment arises from the realization that others view one's self-presentation as "inept". The difference between shame and embarrassment is that the latter refers to failure to perform adequately in a situational identity while the former is assumed to affect a more comprehensive sense of self. Pride comes from placing oneself in the position of others and regarding oneself with approbation; vanity is a reduced form of this, in that one is not sure of others' approval.

These emotions (with perhaps the exception of vanity) operate on the individual with homeostatic effects. Given that guilt, shame, and embarrassment are unpleasant, and that pride is pleasant, the individual is moved to reduce the incidence of the unpleasant and increment the incidence of the pleasant. How is this done? Obviously, one avoids the unpleasant emotions by avoiding conduct that would earn the disapprobation of others. One gains pleasant emotions by engaging in conduct of which others approve. In general, the emotions gear one in to the moral requirements of others who are themselves governed by the same set of pre- and proscriptions for social conduct.

Shott suggested that the role-taking emotions are, overall, an inexpensive way for society to obtain social order, since they make each person his or her own guardian. Although no-one other than oneself is privy to one's emotional barometer, it is sufficient to make one a policeman over one's conduct so that the emotional tone of one's life remains, on balance, more pleasant than painful. This makes each individual an agent of social control through self-control. Where self-control fails, the prospects of social order are not entirely dim, for the emotions that ensue—guilt, shame, or embarrassment—motivate reparative action to rebalance both the social order and others', ergo one's own, opinion of oneself. Thus, guilt and shame have been shown to increase compensatory altruism towards others, and embarrassment has been shown to evoke compensatory supererogation or attainment as a way of reequilibrating the judgments of others about the self so as to return to a positive balance.

Finally, Shott proposed a role-taking emotion that is not reflexive in that it does not pertain to a judgment of the self. This is empathy, which allows one to feel what the other person in the situation is feeling, or what one would likely feel if one were in the place of the other person. Empathy makes any emotion accessible vicariously. Where the emotion reveals the other to be in a socially vulnerable place, one has the embodied sense of the need that other has for social rescue, and the likelihood of engaging in that rescue is enhanced. Thus empathy allows for the evocation of solidarity with others and the preservation of social order through protective behaviors that take up the slack when others are unable to act suitably on their own behalf.

Scheff (1988) was also concerned with social order, but he focused on shame and pride as the *ne plus ultra* emotions in this regard. Taking the symbolic interactionist perspective too, he relied on Charles Horton Cooley's (1922/1964, p. 184) famous looking glass metaphor: "Each to each a looking glass, reflects the other that doth pass". Cooley asserted that pride and shame were the emotional engines for getting individuals to conform to the requirements of their fellow members in society. As a result, Scheff proposed that individuals are continuously in a state of either pride or shame, but he then posed the question as to why, if these emotions are so important, so little evidence of them is seen. Indeed, he argued that in modern societies both shame and pride often arouse a sense of shame. Thus shame is probably the dominant emotion of social control.

Scheff suggested that shame is a recursive emotion. That is, once present, it has a tendency to evoke more shame, or even anger, over the fact that one is ashamed. This can lead to a spiral of emotion about emotion about emotion . . . that leads both to an inability to escape the emotion and a tendency to hide it from others—a frequent response when coping with shame. This hiddenness, proposed as a defining feature of shame, ties in with the work of Helen Block Lewis (1971), whose intensive analysis of psychotherapy protocols revealed two types of "unacknowledged" shame: overt, undifferentiated shame and bypassed shame. The former was manifested by painful feelings and self-derogation (I am stupid, foolish, feckless, incompetent, and the like). Often this was accompanied by stammering, unnecessary word repetition, averted gaze, declining audibility of speech. Both the verbal, paralinguistic and proxemic forms are means of hiding the self from the evaluating lens of others.

Bypassed shame, on the other hand, led to covert symptoms, such as obsessive focusing on the episode that evoked the inadequate response as if the replay could retrieve the lost status. Thought and speech were hyperactive, actually preventing one from participating with others in the natural rhythm of conversational flow. Both types of shame shared the common characteristic of low visibility.

Through an analysis of the details of Asch's (1956) famous experiment on conformity to group pressure, Scheff concluded that subjects in that experiment who yielded and adopted the erroneous judgments of the group were experiencing strong symptoms of either overt or bypassed shame, thus demonstrating the power of shame as the emotional foundation of social control. Even those who were able to remain independent of group pressure experienced shame, but were, unlike the yielders, able to acknowledge it. Scheff suggested that self-esteem may be a mediating variable in such conformity processes. Those with sufficiently high self-esteem can acknowledge their uncomfortable feeling and thus discharge it.

This formulation, involving the notion of catharsis, ties in with Scheff's (1979) earlier work on the problem of discharged emotions. Scheff proposed that catharsis of these residual emotions can only occur in properly "distanced" settings. Here Scheff took a cue from the concept of "aesthetic distance" proposed by Bullough (1912) in his analysis of drama. According to Bullough, an audience can experience a dramatic presentation in various ways according to its emotional distance from what appears on stage. Too little distance involves the audience so deeply that it forgets it is merely watching a play and wants to mount the stage in defense of the hero. Too great distance leaves the audience uninvolved, indifferent to whatever murder or mayhem may be happening on stage. Optimum, or aesthetic, distance, like the last of Goldilocks' porridge bowls and beds, is "just right", providing a suitable level of emotional arousal and thus leading to the purgation of pity and terror which, according to Aristotle (1947, p. 631), was the aim of serious drama.

In a similar vein, Scheff proposed that troublesome residual emotions may also be purged in social settings where there is optimum distance. To do this, he suggested, requires that the expressive emotional content be retrieved (for example crying, trembling, sweating), but in a context in which the individual can be both participant and observer of his or her own emotional display. When these conditions for emotional aesthetic distance are met, catharsis occurs. This is signaled by an anomalous emotional outcome: even though the residual emotion may be unpleasant, discharging is not unpleasant, and there is a succeeding state of clarity of thought, relaxation, renewed energy or exhilaration. Although the catharsis paradigm is somewhat different from the social control paradigm, the two are linked in that unacknowledged shame which is not discharged often leads to spirals of emotion (eg anger over shame over fear) that incapacitate individuals in their social interactions, resulting sometimes in violent outbursts that break though all the bonds of social control.

A final niche within the cultural approach to the social construction of emotions is the sociology of knowledge. One of the most powerful models of sociological analysis, stemming mainly from the work of Marx (Marx & Engels, 1846/1947), Durkheim (1915/1965), and Mannheim (1936), the sociology of knowledge poses all issues not so much directly as in terms of the knowledge that is socially available about them, and examines the conditions and consequences of the knowledge itself. It seeks to understand how knowledge serves to establish or maintain social organization. Some current sociological approaches to emotion fit within the knowledge framework, thus providing yet another source of social understanding of emotions.

McCarthy (1989) stringently dissociated emotions from the body, though she acknowledged the functional relationship between the two (p 56). What is important about emotion is that, like mind and self, it is emergent from social interaction, and this is related to the forms of knowledge that are available in the given social context. In the current age, emotion knowledge has been appropriated by and institutionalized in a set of occupatic ˜al roles—counselors, therapists, psychologists, sociologists, and the like—whose work is to create and disseminate emotion knowledge. These practitioners afford us emotional options and enhance our "literacy in [their] language" (p. 64). This means that on the large cultural scale, the emotions of our times must differ from the emotions of previous periods because ours is an age with different forms and degrees of knowledge about emotions. Indeed, within a society different groups are seen to experience themselves and their time through the emotions that are available to them. McCarthy illustrated this historically grounded point about emotions through reference to the notion of "bourgeois anxiety" (which we can contrast with Calvinist anxiety, as discussed above). As presented by Gay (1984), in the nineteenth century, the ascendant and often triumphant middle class had nonetheless its sleepless nights as it pondered the brooding power of the still unsatisfied masses below it and the contempt of the aristocrats who hovered above. This anxiety was a guiding emotional theme in their interpretation of social life and themselves. It determined the patterns of commerce and work as well as the aspirations and practices of domestic life.

In a different sociology of knowledge approach, Perinbanayagam (1989) regarded emotions as vocabularies that are used to define situations and the actions to be taken in them. Of course, vocabularies are cultural products that are shared and transmitted as knowledge, and mastery over our emotions is a function of the availability of "linguistic instruments" that enable us to detect and delineate gradations and nuances of feeling. Releasing emotions into action is also somewhat akin to assembling the words that compose a sentence that will express an interest of the self. But the form the sentence takes follows a social template whose meaning is more or less clear. For example, in the case of anger, violence need not ensue. But the translation of anger into violence is assisted when social knowledge provides a model for it. In particular, according to Perinbanayagam, the state, which is the legitimate possessor of the means of violence, expresses its "anger" through violence.

The reliance of the cultural approach to emotions on mental structures, susceptible to socialization and variable according to historical conditions of change, directly conflicts with at least some elements of the social structural position. The latter relies more on universal situational determinants of emotion, and on some biological mechanisms that articulate with the situation–emotion nexus. Kemper (1987b) has attempted to reconcile some of the opposing views through a syncretic analysis, focusing on the issue of primary and secondary emotions.

Kemper proposed that a large body of cross-cultural, phylogenetic, autonomic, social relational, and classificatory evidence leads to a model of four primary emotions: fear, anger, sadness, and joy (or normal variants of these). Since there are additional emotions, the question is what is their source? Kemper proposed that emotions beyond the primaries may arise from a specific pattern of socialization in which a social definition and label are applied to a situation in which one of the primaries is being felt. For example, pride may be derived from socialization to the idea of self-regard for accomplishment in a context of joy. Shame may result from socialization to the idea of self-rejection in a context of anger. And guilt may derive from socialization to the idea of self-rejection for what is defined as morally wrong action in the context of fear. The primary emotion contexts are regarded as important since they provide the autonomic, ergo specifically emotional, underpinnings of the secondary emotions. The cultural components, such as situational definitions and emotional labels, are considered important since they help the person differentiate and specify the feeling to particular social and behavior contexts.

I will conclude now with two final topics to complete the spectrum of diverse approaches to emotions by sociologists.

Biosocial models

Sociologists have generally paid little attention to the biology of emotions, with some notable exceptions. The less important of these comprises the culturally oriented sociologists of emotion who sought support for their position in the putative findings of Schachter and Singer (1962), as discussed above.

Their interest was in no way substantive, since it does not build towards, nor make a sociological contribution to, any biologically relevant theory of emotions. The more important exception is found in works that actively pursue a biosocial theory of emotions, for example Hammond (1990) and Kemper (1978).

In recent years, sociologists and anthropologists (but, strangely, not biologists) have had to contend with an intellectual assault from sociobiology (Wilson, 1975; Lumsden & Wilson, 1981). The main thrust from that quarter is that a good deal of social practice, including social hierarchy, sex-role differentiation, and intergroup aggression, is genetically, not socially, provenanced. Since these are main topics in sociological analysis and in sociological understanding of how societies are organized and what some of their main processes are, little that is independent of genetic determination remains. Although the sociobiological argument has been subjected to severe criticism (not the least of which is that there is no evidence for it; see Kaye, 1986), it remains a formidable challenge to sociologists. Indeed, the recent spectacular advances in molecular biology forebode an effort to reduce a good deal of the human behavioral repertory to the operation of proteins and enzymes according to a genetic code.

Sociologist Michael Hammond (1990) has challenged some parts of the sociobiological argument from the unusual perspective of emotions. It is important, he asserts, that unlike infrahuman forms, humans have only scant direction from "instincts". How we shall act and what we shall do is in the state of the "to be determined", rather than genetically programmed. However, although humans do not have instincts, they do have emotions, and Hammond's fundamental assumption is that humans have an inherent need or desire for what he calls "affective maximization". This is simply a state of satisfaction of positive emotional goals, for example security, ease, pleasure. Since humans are fundamentally social animals, affective maximization is mainly sought with other humans. The presence of such a motive sets up certain problems, mainly how to achieve it in an efficient manner. Hammond proposed that certain social arrangements are more likely to lead to affective maximization than others, and that there is likely to be a bent towards these. He argued that this is somewhat like the operation of the neurochemistry of opiates. Some chemicals work as opiates because their structure mimics the structure of naturally occurring chemicals in the brain, thus producing a positive feeling when taken. Similarly, some social arrangements are more likely to unlock the neurological key to affective maximization than others. Thus, these arrangements are likely to emerge.

Hammond postulated that one approach to affective maximization would be for individuals to sample all opportunities for their affective maximization potential. This would mean that every occasion of possible satisfaction would need to be investigated. Elaborated over a whole social group, this would mean that all would be seeking to discover the most satisfying emotional experiences from among all others. This would be a highly inefficient system, beggaring the ability to perform other needed behaviors in the service of personal and group survival.

In consequence, Hammond suggested, a plausible alternative might emerge. One way to make the search for affective maximization efficient would be to differentiate the cast of characters, so to speak, from among whom affective maximization might be sought. One might differentiate according to such criteria as age, or sex, or membership in the group, and so forth. These are especially likely categories of differentiation because they are low in information demand. One can easily identify individuals by means of them, in contrast with such criteria as moral goodness, aesthetic sensibility, religiosity, and the like. Thus, the previously undifferentiated world is now divided into categories, and one may now sample from among categories rather than from the undifferentiated mass of individuals. Hammond supposed that this did indeed happen in human groups, and had something to do with the human tendency to form categories (cf Rosch, 1978).

But even this system can be improved, and the way to do it, according to Hammond, is to rank the categories in terms of preference, that is, which categories are more likely to provide satisfaction and which categories are to be preferred. This creates hierarchical social differentiation, or a system of group ranking. As in George Orwell's *Animal Farm*, some groups are now "more equal" than others. This is what we ordinarily refer to as stratification.

While this need for efficiency in the attainment of affective maximization prevails in groups of all sizes, in small groups the information problem is relatively manageable and the need for a rigid stratification is less intense. But as a group grows larger, the information problem becomes crushing and stratification takes on a more definite character. Preferences are now more rigidly ranked. Concomitantly, larger groups also tend to develop on the basis of more productive technologies, and this leads to the accumulation of levels of wealth that small groups are unlikely to attain. This inevitably gets drawn into the stratification system of preferences, so that the rank orders of both wealth and desirability for affective maximization become linked in a single pyramid of "more and less".

Obviously, many are excluded from the upper reaches of desirability both regarding wealth and as candidates for affective maximization. Here, Hammond suggests, is a matrix for the emergence of a cultural innovation that compensates the deprived and provides them with hope for at least ultimate attainment of high levels of affective gratification. This is the differentiation of time itself into a ranked order of present and hereafter. If affective maximization is not possible in life, it can be adumbrated as a fulfilment in one's afterlife.

By contrast with sociobiologists' reliance on specific genetic bases for a variety of human social patterns, Hammond has essentially postulated a single more embracing point of origin for a number of important social institutions, namely, a need for strong emotional gratification. Social forms develop so as to provide reliable, efficient means to optimize satisfaction of the need.

Kemper (1978, 1987b) takes a quite different approach to the sociological nexus with the biological, one that is somewhat close to the concerns of at least some psychologists. By means of the power–status model of social relations, he proposes a number of emotions that appear to result from power–status interaction outcomes. These emotions are also related to certain neurophysiological and autonomic structures and processes. The main work connecting these biological substrates to emotion was done by physiologist Ernst Gellhorn (1967, 1968) and psychiatrist Daniel Funkenstein (1956). The latter found that the autonomic responses that are associated with anger are those instituted by the neurotransmitter norepinephrine (NE), while the autonomic responses that accompany fear are those instituted by the neurotransmitter epinephrine (E). These relationships have also been found in the work of a number of other investigators (Elmadjian, Hope & Lamson, 1958; Graham, Cohen & Schmavonian, 1967; Kadish, 1983). The significance of this for a biosocial theory of emotions is that if E is the neurotransmitter of the fear response, by extension it is also connected with power, the social relation of fear. Similarly, if NE is the neurotransmitter of anger, by extension it is also connected with status (withdrawal), the social relation of anger. Thus there may be good reason to posit an architectonic structure of social relations, emotions, and autonomic processes that are in parallel and together constitute the fundamental elements of the emotional matrix. What is of great interest is that fear and anger, the two emotions for which distinct neurotransmitter evidence has been obtained, are the classical flight/fight responses, fundamental survival behaviors that have important phylogenetic continuity. Tying in the power and status dimensions at this point locks the biological, the emotional, and the social relational into a single biosocial model of emotions. (Lest it seem untoward to omit positive emotions from the model, it can be speculated that acetylcholine (ACh), the neurotransmitter of the parasympathetic nervous system, which has been associated with satisfying, consumatory responses (Gellhorn, 1967), is the transmitter of satisfying emotions and the social relations that produce them, namely, adequate power and relatively high status.)

Emotions in the micropolitics of interaction

From the beginning, sociologists have sought to understand how social arrangements and transactions produce specific emotions. Also from relatively early on, sociologists have examined the way emotions contribute to social organization. More recently, they have addressed questions of how emotions function in microsocial contexts, interpersonally. Emotions can not only be felt, they can be used as interaction tools to gain or to prevent oneself from losing power and status in relations with others. Following Goffman, Candace Clark (1990) has referred to one's location in a social relational structure as one's "place". Place is the summary of one's privileges, priorities and powers *vis-à-vis* others. It entails location in a hierarchy, and the higher one's place, the more comfortable, secure, and pleased one is likely to be. Changes of place are the most emotionally intense occasions, and substantial amounts of interaction are devoted to gaining, regaining, or maintaining one's place in relation to others. According to Clark, emotions are political weapons in the ongoing struggles over place in microinteraction.

First, one can douse others in negative emotions: disdain, contempt, disgust, anger, exasperation, and so forth. To be successful as a place manoeuver, the other must feel a corresponding emotion: shame, humiliation, guilt, embarrassment, and the like. Or, the other may become awed or fearful, thus unable to act on his or her own behalf. The result is a favorable placement for the one who has launched the negative emotions or a displacement of the one towards whom the emotions were directed.

A second tactic is to express positive emotions towards others: admiration, respect, love. These are often effective in battles over place because they frequently gain others' acceptance and approval. Especially if the others are of high status, to be highly regarded by them is to be elevated in one's own place, perhaps even to the status of equal. Is this not what love is capable of doing? Of course, the positive regard of the place-seeker may simply be flattery, insincere and calculating. Astonishingly, it often works, especially if well hidden and carefully dramatized as authentic.

A third strategy is to manipulate the other's emotional arousal. Showdowns over place often go to the one who can remain cool and unaroused. This enables one to conduct the struggle in a more calculating manner, but it also wins the approval of the audience if there is one. Western social norms for arousal display in public contests lean strongly in favor of emotional coolness, "grace under pressure", as it is sometimes called. Those who lose their head, as the expression goes, are rarely winners, nor are they regarded as deserving to win. Thus, the use of emotion to rattle and upset another while remaining cool oneself is a time-honored tactic in struggles over place. Fear and "blind" anger are two emotions that are most likely to unhinge the other person's good judgment. But evoking contempt for self in another is an equally effective tactic. This is a frequent plot device in melodrama, where the hero deliberately appears to be less adequate than he is, thus evoking contempt from his opponent, but with the purpose of causing the opponent to drop his guard.

A fourth tactic in the micropolitics of place is to create a feeling of obligation in others. To the degree that another has been cozened by this tactic, one is safe to assume that the other will respond as one wishes. Frequently, it requires only reminding the other of the social norms that govern the relations between self and other. In some instances, it means actually giving something of value so that the other will feel indebted. Virginity has often been dedicated to this tactic of gaining place. (We do not actually know the success rate.)

Finally, paradoxically, one can gain place by being sympathetic with the woes of another, especially when the other has not asked for sympathy. A sympathetic stance towards another is usually possible only from a position of superiority.

That position is created to a small degree whenever one expresses sympathy. Its most telling effect on relative place is when a nominal inferior expresses sympathy for a nominal superior. This reverse flow of affect elevates the inferior to a higher place than that of the superior.

CONCLUSION

Although the main effort in the recent sociological study of emotions began barely a decade and a half ago, it exhibits a perhaps startling range and diversity. In this it reflects the breadth of modern sociology, which is marked by a multiplicity of paradigmatic facets and approaches. Notwithstanding this close embrace by sociologists of emotion of their home discipline, many of the problems they address share common ground with psychology or are on contiguous ground. I would like here to point out some of these areas in which a mutual concern may be fruitful.

A socio-psychophysiological theory of emotions

Perhaps the broadest possible ground for cooperation between psychologists and sociologists lies in the pursuit of a socio-psychophysiological theory of emotions. This theory would take into account not only the nether (body) and upper (social) anchors of emotion, but would seek also the important connections between them. Theoretically, there must be some link between the biology and the sociology of emotion, otherwise emotions that are responses to social environmental stimuli would have no solid organismic substrate. The body must in some way cooperate with society and, of course, society with the body.

Sociologists and psychologists both have much to learn about the possible and proper ways of sharing their common subject, the person. This is a real, as opposed to merely boundary problem between disciplines. By examining the interaction between body and society, psychologists and sociologists can better shape their own studies. We can imagine, for example, stringent impositions and control by society of the body, through overwork, undernourishment, gross sexual denial, and so on. Each of these ways of regulating the body imposes a contra-organismic constraint for which a price must be paid, first by the body but ultimately by the social order that has overregulated its constituent biological entities. The body also may claim a disproportionate share through slothful self-indulgence, excessive appetite, sexual exhaustion, and so on. These drain society of its social energy to accomplish collective goals that override the personal.

Sociologists and psychologists of emotion are closest to these kinds of issues. Cooperation to explore the limits of the demands of body and society and the consequences of different mixes of these would seem to be a natural basis for progress for both disciplines. Students of emotion who model their theories with the strictures of both body and society in mind will not only learn a good deal about the "other" perspective but will necessarily gain insight into their own. There is already some work towards such an overarching socio-psychophysiological frame of understanding for emotions in sociology, and a great deal of progress might be realized quickly if this problem were addressed explicitly by psychologists.

Cognition and emotion

Perhaps the dominant paradigm in the psychology of emotions is the cognition–emotion approach, and, as indicated above, a substantial body of sociologists of emotions are also disposed to this view. However, there is a "black hole" in the analytic plane where we remain perhaps unnecessarily ignorant. Sociologists who take the cognitive (cultural) perspective stop short of specifying the cognitive processes that produce specific emotions, except in the most general symbolic interactionist terms. This is probably sensible from a jurisdictional perspective, since sociologists are disciplinarily not competent about cognitive processes. But the same does not hold true for psychologists, for whom the nuts and bolts of cognitive processes are (or ought to be) stock in trade. This is not to say that immaculate theories are available, but rather that the tools for theory-building are, as well as the natural interest in using them.

I noted above the odd crossover on this issue between sociologists and psychologists in reference to one of the main orienting theories in the field, namely that provided by G. H. Mead. At the least, Mead provided a heuristic framework for beginning the analysis of how cognitive processes contribute to emotions. In the Meadian tradition, Blumer spoke of self-indicating processes, by which the relevance for the self of the meaning conferred on objects is obtained through how this meaning is reflected back to the self from the reactions of others. It seems logical to suppose that a close examination of the self-indicating process—for example the range of possible meanings, the range of possible reactions, the interplay between the two—would yield a significant return in the understanding of emotion via the cognitive route. Setting the problem within a sociological model of interaction, Collins (1989) has proposed some hypotheses about the kind of cognitive content that might be most prevalent in the self-indicating process. It is a first step towards linking cognitive processes with social behavior and deserves a more complete exploration by cognitively oriented psychologists whose territory is also the emotions.

Affect control theory

Astonishingly, since its origins are in the impression formation work of Gollub (Gollub, 1968; Gollub & Rossman, 1973), affect control theory (ACT) has not attracted the kind of interest from psychologists that might be expected. Indubitably, Heise (1979, 1989) has the most methodologically rigorous program of all sociologists, with the added attraction of its mathematical precision.

This ought to have some appeal for those psychologists who may scoff at some of the softer approaches that are prevalent in sociology. The suppleness of ACT is one of its particular strengths. Any theoretically framed combination of actors, behavior, objects, and emotions can be investigated with an attractive precision. Fundamental too is the theory's predictive aspect. Using the cultural meanings of its constituent terms, and combinations of terms, as the raw materials, ACT is, if nothing else, a simulation program par excellence. It can formulate both emotional outcomes of situations and situational outcomes of emotions in a manner that is more efficient than any other presently available in either sociology or psychology.

Social relations and emotions

One of the most direct contributions of the sociological approach to a psychological understanding of emotions is the social structural model. Fundamentally, it suggests what content of social cognition might produce which emotions. In the cultural approach, the initial social cognition is open to subsequent modification through the self-indicating process and through the process by which evaluations are themselves subject to evaluation, as Blumer suggested. But the social structural model proposes the emotion directly from social relations as the individual perceives these. In some versions of the model, there is less room for interpretation. For example, Collins takes social position as publicly specified, that is, whether one gives commands or obeys them. On the other hand, Kemper's approach allows for some interpretation of what the operative power and status conditions are. Thus, regardless of actual social position, the individual responds emotionally to the felt sense of the social relations. These may violate the conventional relational conditions associated with social position. Thus, an individual whose social position involves giving orders may not feel confident, assured and energetic, as Collins suggests, if the order-giver senses that others are indifferent to his power, or are prepared to resist it. In the extreme instance, the patriot who submits to torture unto death frustrates the intentions of his or her captor, who is in the order-giving position. However the source of the social relations may be conceived, sociologists have provided systematic models of the emotion-relevant social cognitions.

Psychotherapy and the emotions of our time

Psychologists have certainly not looked as deeply at the historical contexts of emotions as have sociologists. This is due mainly to the professional division of labor in which topics become apportioned to disciplines in a manner that becomes convention. Yet famous exemplars have successfully violated the norms here. Freud is most prominent in his breadth of concern, from neurology to philosophical anthropology, from what is the body to what is man (literally)?

In the domain of emotions, while psychologists have mainly stuck close to the body and the person in an *a*historical manner, sociologists have much more freely examined the emotions of the time, and of people involved in real social structures with real consequences for their lives: flight attendants and others, mainly women, in service industries (Hochschild, 1983b); men and women in modern two-career marriages (Hochschild, 1989); order-givers and order-takers in work settings (Collins, 1975, 1990); men and women in the context of their gender and social class memberships (Denzin, 1990); individuals of a certain historical time (McCarthy, 1989).

The emotions of these concrete individuals are the stuff of daily lives—at work, in love, in the community—and they are also the emotions that lead to the real joys and real despairs that accompany being alive. When work relations sour because of new conceptions and ideologies of both managerial and subordinate roles; when the clash of the new and old gender politics causes disruption in marriage; when the extension of civil rights to previously excluded groups—minorities, women, the handicapped, homosexuals, hospital patients, consumers, children, and so on—is not yet assimilated by dominant social groups, all these are loci of intense emotions. These are the emotions that are brought most prominently to the attention of counselors and psychotherapists. Most often the individuals themselves do not process their feelings in terms of social and historical transformations and upheavals, or of changes in culture that have intersected their biography. But therapists and those in helping professions must be cognizant of the sociological and historical contexts of emotions, lest they err in their diagnoses and prescriptions, as psychiatrists often did in treating discontented or depressed women patients before the rise of the women's movement in recent decades. The sociological approach, insofar as it examines the emotions of real people in real historical time, offers not only a general understanding of the time, but also a baseline against which to evaluate what emotions in what contexts are normal, deviant, or pathological. In this way, psychotherapists must necessarily depend on the results obtained by sociologists of emotions.

REFERENCES

Allport, G. (1968). *The Person in Psychology: Selected Essays*. Boston: Beacon.

Aristotle (1947). *Introduction to Aristotle*, R. McKeon (Ed.). New York: Modern Library.

Arnold M. (1960). *Emotion and Personality*, Vols 1 & 2. New York: Columbia University Press.

Asch, S. (1956). Studies of independence and conformity: 1. A minority of one against a unanimous majority. *Psychological Monographs*, **70**, 1–70.

Averett, C. & Heise, D. R. (1988). Modified social identities: Amalgamations, attributions, and emotions. In L. Smith-Lovin & D. R. Heise (Eds), *Analyzing Social Interaction: Advances in Affect Control Theory*. New York: Gordon & Breach, pp. 103–122.

Averill, J. R. (1974). An analysis of psychophysical symbolism and its influence on theories of emotion. *Journal for the Theory of Behavior*, **4**, 147–190.

Averill, J. R. (1980). A constructivist view of emotions. In R. Plutchik & H. Kellerman (Eds), *Emotion: Theory, Research, and Experience*, Vol. 1. New York: Academic Press, pp. 305–339.

Berscheid, E. & Walster, E. H. (1974). A little bit about love. In L. Huston (Ed.), *Foundations of Interpersonal Attraction*. New York: Academic Press, pp. 356–382.

Blauner, R. (1964). *Alienation and Freedom: The Factory Worker and his Industry*. Chicago: University of Chicago Press.

Blumer, H. (1969). *Symbolic Interaction*. Englewood Cliffs, NJ: Prentice-Hall.

Bullough, E. (1912). Psychic distance in art and as an aesthetic principle. *British Journal of Psychology*, **5**, 669–679.

Campbell, D. T. (1970). Natural selection as an epistemological model. In R. Narroll & R. Cohen (Eds), *A Handbook of Method in Cultural Anthropology*. New York: Natural History Press.

Cancian, F. M. & Gordon, S. L. (1988). Changing emotion norms in marriage: Love and anger in US women's magazines since 1900. *Gender and Society*, **2**, 308–342.

Clark, C. (1990). Emotions and micropolitics in everyday life: Some patterns and paradoxes of place. In T. D. Kemper (Ed.), *Research Agendas in the Sociology of Emotions*. Albany: State University of New York Press, pp. 305–333.

Collins, R. (1971). Functional and conflict theories of educational stratification. *American Sociological Review*, **36**, 1002–1119.

Collins, R. (1974). Reassessments of sociological history: The empirical validity of the conflict tradition. *Theory and Society*, **1**, 147–178.

Collins, R. (1975). *Conflict Sociology*. New York: Academic Press.

Collins, R. (1981). On the microfoundations of macrosociology. *American Journal of Sociology*, **86**, 984–1014.

Collins, R. (1989). Toward a neo-Meadian sociology of mind. *Symbolic Interaction*, **12**, 1–32.

Collins, R. (1990). Stratification, emotional energy, and the transient emotions. In T. D. Kemper (Ed.), *Research Agendas in the Sociology of Emotions*. Albany: State University of New York Press, pp. 27–57.

Colomy, P. & Barchas, P. R. (1984). Social roles and hemispheric laterality. In P. R. Barchas & S. Mendoza (Eds), *Social Cohesion: Essays Toward a Sociophysiological Perspective*. Westport, Conn.: Greenwood.

Cookson, P. W., Jr & Persell, C. H. (1985). *Preparing for Power: America's Elite Boarding Schools*. New York: Basic.

Cooley, C. H. (1922/1964). *Human Nature and the Social Order*. New York: Schocken.

Cotton, J. L. (1981). A review of research on Schachter's theory of emotion and the misattribution of arousal. *European Journal of Social Psychology*, **11**, 365–397.

Coulter, J. (1986). Affect and social context. In R. Harre (Ed.), *The Social Construction of Emotion*. Oxford: Blackwell, pp. 120–134.

Denzin, N. (1978). *The Research Act*. New York: McGraw-Hill.

Denzin, N. (1984). *On Understanding Emotion*. San Francisco: Jossey-Bass.

Denzin, N. (1985). Emotion as lived experience. *Symbolic Interaction*, **8**, 223–240.

Denzin, N. (1987). *The Alcoholic Self*. Newbury Park, Cal.: Sage.

Denzin, N. (1990). On understanding emotion: The interpretive–cultural agenda. In T. D. Kemper (Ed.), *Research Agendas in the Sociology of Emotions*. Albany: State University of New York Press, pp. 27–57.

Durkheim, E. (1915/1965). *The Elementary Forms of the Religious Life*, translated by J. W. Swain, New York: Free Press.

Ekman, P. (1982). What are the similarities and differences in facial behavior across cultures? In P. Ekman (Ed.), *Emotion in the Human Face*. Cambridge: Cambridge University Press, pp. 128–143.

Ekman, P., Friesen, W. V. & Ellsworth, P. (1972). *Emotion in the Human Face: Guidelines for Research and an Integration of Findings*. New York: Pergamon.

Elias, N. (1978a). *The Civilizing Process*. New York: Urizen Books.

Elias, N. (1978b). *The History of Manners*. New York: Urizen Books.

Elmadjian, F., Hope, J. M. & Lamson, E. T. (1958). Excretion of epinephrine and norepinephrine under stress. In G. Pincus (Ed.), *Recent Progress in Hormone Research*. New York: Academic Press, pp. 513–545.

Engels, F. (1845/1958). *The Condition of the Working Class in England*, translated and edited by W. O. Henderson & W. H. Chaloner. Oxford: Blackwell.

Evans, B. (1968). *Dictionary of Quotations*. New York: Delacorte.

Franks, D. D. (1989). Power and role-taking: A social behaviorist's synthesis of Kemper's power and status model. In D. D. Franks & E. D. McCarthy (Eds), *The Sociology of Emotions: Original Essays and Research Papers*. Greenwich, Conn.: JAI, pp. 153–178.

Freud, S. (1917/1957). The taboo of virginity: A contribution to the psychology of love III. In J. Strachey (Ed.), *The Standard Edition of the Complete Psychological Works of Sigmund Freud*, Vol. 11. London: Hogarth, pp. 191–208.

Freud, S. (1930). *Civilization and its Discontents*. New York: Hogarth.

Funkenstein, D. (1955). The physiology of fear and anger. *Scientific American*, **192**, 74–80.

Gay, P. (1984). *The Bourgeois Experience Victoria to Freud: Education of the Senses*. New York: Oxford.

Gellhorn, E. (1967). *Principles of Autonomic-Somatic Integrations: Physiological Basis and Psychological and Clinical Implications*. Minneapolis: University of Minnesota Press.

Gellhorn, E. (1968). Attempt at a synthesis: Contribution to a theory of emotion. In E. Gellhorn (Ed.), *Biological Foundations of Emotion: Research and Commentary*. Glenview, Ill.: Scott, Foresman, pp. 144–153.

Goffman, E. (1959). *The Presentation of Self in Everyday Life*. New York: Doubleday.

Goffman, E. (1967). *Interaction Ritual*. Garden City, NY: Doubleday.

Goffman, E. (1981). *Forms of Talk*. Philadelphia: University of Pennsylvania Press.

Gollub, H. (1968). Impression formation and word combination in sentences. *Journal of Personality and Social Psychology*, **10**, 341–353.

Gollub, H. & Rossman, B. B. (1973). Judgments of an actor's "power and ability to influence others". *Journal of Personality and Social Psychology*, **19**, 391–406.

Gordon, S. L. (1981). The sociology of sentiments and emotions. In M. Rosenberg & R. S. Turner (Eds), *Social Psychology: Sociological Perspectives*. New York: Basic Books, pp. 562–592.

Gordon, S. L. (1990). Social structural effects on emotions. In T. D. Kemper (Ed.), *Research Agendas in the Sociology of Emotions*. Albany: State University of New York Press, pp. 145–179.

Graham, L. A., Cohen, S. I. & Shmavonian, B. M. (1967). Some methodological approaches to the psychophysiological correlates of behavior. In L. Levi (Ed.), *Emotional Stress: Physiological and Psychological Reactions. I. Medical, Industrial, and Military Applications*. New York: Elsevier.

Hammond, M. (1990). Affective maximization: A new macro-theory in the sociology of emotion. In T. D. Kemper (Ed.), *Research Agendas in the Sociology of Emotions*. Albany: State University of New York Press, pp. 27–57.

Heise, D. (1969). Some methodological issues in semantic differential research. *Psychological Bulletin*, **72**, 406–422.

Heise, D. R. (1979). *Understanding Events: Affect and the Construction of Social Action*. New York: Cambridge University Press.

Heise, D. R. (1988). Affect control theory: Concepts and models. In L. Smith-Lovin & D. R. Heise (Eds), *Analyzing Social Interaction: Advances in Affect Control Theory*. New York: Gordon & Breach, pp. 1–34.

Heise, D. R. (1989). Effects of emotion displays on social identification. *Social Psychology Quarterly*, **52**, 10–21.

Henley, N. M. (1977). *Body Politics: Sex, Power, and Non-Verbal Communication*. Englewood Cliffs, NJ: Prentice-Hall.

Hochschild, A. R. (1979). Emotion work, feeling rules, and social structure. *American Journal of Sociology*, **85**, 551–575.

Hochschild, A. R. (1983a). Comment on Kemper's "social constructionist and positivist approaches to the sociology of emotions". *American Journal of Sociology*, **89**, 432–434.

Hochschild, A. R. (1983b). *The Managed Heart: Commercialization of Human Feeling*. Berkeley: University of California Press.

Hochschild, A. R. (1989). *The Second Shift*. New York: Viking.

Hunsaker, D. (1983). Comment on Kemper. *American Journal of Sociology*, **89**, 434–440.

Kadish, W. (1983). Personality traits and the norepinephrine to epinephrine ratio. Senior doctoral thesis, Department of Psychiatry, Yale University School of Medicine.

Kaye, Howard L. (1986). *The Social Meaning of Modern Biology: From Social Darwinism to Sociobiology*. New Haven: Yale University Press.

Kemper, T. D. (1973). The fundamental dimensions of social relationship: A theoretical statement. *Acta Sociologica*, **16**, 41–58.

Kemper, T. D. (1978). *A Social Interactional Theory of Emotions*. New York: Wiley.

Kemper, T. D. (1980). Sociology, physiology, and emotions: Comment on Shott. *American Journal of Sociology*, **85**, 1418–1423.

Kemper, T. D. (1981). Social constructionist and positivist approaches to the sociology of emotions. *American Journal of Sociology*, **87**, 336–62.

Kemper, T. D. (1983). Reply to Hochschild and Hunsaker. *American Journal of Sociology*, **89**, 440–443.

Kemper, T. D. (1987a). A Manichaean approach to the social construction of emotions. *Cognition and Emotion*, **1**, 353–365.

Kemper, T. D. (1987b). How many emotions are there? Wedding the social and the autonomic components. *American Journal of Sociology*, **93**, 263–289.

Kemper, T. D. (1990a). Themes and variations in the sociology of emotions. In T. D. Kemper (Ed.), *Research Agendas in the Sociology of Emotions*. Albany: State University of New York Press, pp 27–57.

Kemper, T. D. (1990b). Social relations and emotions: A structural approach. In T. D. Kemper (Ed.), *Research Agendas in the Sociology of Emotions*. Albany: State University of New York Press, pp. 207–237.

Kemper, T. D. & Birenbaum, A. (1987). *Sine ira ac studio?* Emotional nexi in Weber's ideal-typical conception of organizations. Presented at annual meetings of the American Sociological Association, Chicago.

Kemper, T. D. & Collins, R. (1990). Dimensions of microinteraction. *American Journal of Sociology*, **96**, 32–68.

Lazarus, R. S. (1984). On the primacy of cognition. *American Psychologist*, **39**, 124–129.

Lazarus, R. S., Averill, J. & Opton, E. M., Jr (1970). Toward a cognitive theory of emotions. In M. Arnold (Ed.), *Feelings and Emotions*. New York: Academic Press.

Lerner, H. (1977). *Anger and Oppression in Women*. Topeka, Kan.: Menninger Foundation.

Lewis, H. B. (1971) *Shame and Guilt in Neurosis*. New York: Wiley.

Licamele, W. & Goldberg, R. L. (1988). Tourette syndrome. *American Family Physician*, **37**, 115–119.

Lofland, J. (1970). Interactionist imagery and analytic interruptus. In T. Shibutani (Ed.), *Human Nature and Collective Behavior: Papers in Honor of Herbert Blumer.* Englewood Cliffs, NJ: Prentice-Hall.

Lumsden, C. & Wilson, E. O. (1981). *Genes, Mind, and Culture: The Coevolutionary Process.* Cambridge, Mass: Harvard University Press.

Lutz, C. (1981). The domain of emotion words on Ifaluk. *American Ethnologist,* **9,** 113–128.

Mandler, G. (1975). *Mind and Emotion.* New York: Wiley.

Mannheim, K. (1936). *Ideology and Utopia.* London: International Library of Psychology, Philosophy, and Scientific Method.

Marshall, G. D. & Zimbardo, P. G. (1979). Affective consequences of inadequately explained physiological arousal. *Journal of Personality & Social Psychology,* **37,** 970–988.

Marx, K. (1842–44/1971). *The Early Texts.* Edited by D. McLellan. Oxford: Blackwell.

Marx, K. & Engels, F. (1846/1947). *The German Ideology.* New York: International Publishers.

Marx, K. & Engels, F. (1848/1959). The communist manifesto. In L. Feuer (Ed.), *Marx and Engels: Basic Writings on Politics and Philosophy.* Garden City, NY: Doubleday, pp. 1–41.

Maslach, C. (1979). Negative emotional biasing of unexplained arousal. *Journal of Personality and Social Psychology,* **37,** 953–969.

McCarthy, E. D. (1989). Emotions are social things: An essay in the sociology of emotions. In D. D. Franks & E. D. McCarthy (Eds), *The Sociology of Emotions: Original Essays and Research Papers,* Greenwich, Conn.: JAI Press, pp. 51–72.

Mead, G. H. (1934). *Mind, Self, and Society.* Chicago: University of Chicago Press.

Mills, C. W. (1956). *The Power Elite.* New York: Oxford University Press.

Osgood, C. H., May, W. H. & Miron, M. S. (1975). *Cross-Cultural Universals of Affective Meaning.* Urbana. Ill.: University of Illinois Press.

Osgood, C. H., Suci, G. C. & Tannenbaum, P. H. (1957). *The Measurement of Meaning.* Urbana: University of Illinois Press.

Parsons, T. (1951). *The Social System.* Glencoe, Ill.: Free Press.

Pelto, P. J. (1970). *Anthropological Research: The Structure.* New York: Harper & Row.

Perinbanayagam, R. S. (1989). Signifying emotions. In D. D. Franks & E. D. McCarthy (Eds), *The Sociology of Emotions: Original Essays and Research Papers.* Greenwich, Conn.: JAI Press, pp. 73–92.

Piaget, J. (1948). *The Moral Development of the Child.* Glencoe, Ill.: Free Press.

Piaget, J. (1977). *The Development of Thought.* New York: Viking.

Pike, K. L. (1967). *Language in Relation to a Unified Theory of Structure of Human Behavior,* 2nd edn. The Hague: Mouton.

Plutchik, R. & Kellerman, H. (1980). *Emotion: Theory, Research, and Experience,* Vol. 1. New York: Academic Press.

Plutchik, R. & Kellerman, H. (1983). *Emotion: Emotions in Early Development,* Vol. 2. New York: Academic Press.

Plutchik, R. & Kellerman, H. (1985). *Emotion: Biological Foundation of Emotion,* Vol. 3. New York: Academic Press.

Poster, M. (1978) *A Critical Theory of the Family.* New York: Seabury.

Reisenzein, R. (1983). The Schachter theory of emotion: Two decades later. *Psychological Bulletin,* **94,** 239–264.

Rosch, E. (1978). Principles of categorization. In E. Rosch & B. B. Lloyd (Eds), *Cognition and Categorization,* Hillsdale, NJ: Erlbaum, pp. 27–48.

Schachter, S. & Singer, J. L. (1962). Cognitive, social, and physiological determinants of emotional state. *Psychological Review,* **69,** 379–399.

Scheff, T. J. (1979). *Catharsis in Healing, Ritual, and Drama*. Berkeley: University of California Press.

Scheff, T. J. (1987). The shame/rage spiral: Case study of an interminable quarrel. In H. B. Lewis (Ed.), *The Role of Shame in Symptom Formation*. Hillsdale, NJ: Erlbaum, pp. 109–150.

Scheff, T. J. (1988). Shame and conformity: The deference–emotion system. *American Sociological Review*, **53**, 395–406.

Seeman, M. (1959). On the meaning of alienation. *American Sociological Review*, **24**, 783–791.

Shott, Susan. (1979). Emotion and social life: A symbolic interactionist analysis. *American Journal of Sociology*, **84**, 1317–1334.

Shott, S. (1980). Reply to Kemper. *American Journal of Sociology*, **85**, 1423–1426.

Smith-Lovin, L. (1988). Impressions from events. In L. Smith-Lovin & D. R. Heise (Eds), *Analyzing Social Interaction: Advances in Affect Control Theory*. New York: Gordon & Breach, pp. 35–70.

Smith-Lovin, L. (1990). Emotion as the confirmation and disconfirmation of identity: An affect control model. In T. D. Kemper (Ed.), *Research Agendas in the Sociology of Emotions*. Albany: State University of New York Press, pp. 238–270.

Smith-Lovin, L. & Heise, D. R. (1988). (Eds). *Analyzing Social Interaction: Advances in Affect Control Theory*. New York: Gordon & Breach.

Stanislavski, C. (1948/1965). *An Actor Prepares*. Translated by E. R. Hapgood. New York: Theatre Arts Books.

Thoits, P. A. (1984). Coping, social support and psychological outcomes: The central role of emotion. In P. Shaver (Ed.), *Review of Personality and Social Psychology*, Vol. 5. Beverley Hills: Sage, pp. 219–238.

Thoits, P. A. (1985). Self-labeling processes in mental illness: The role of emotional deviance. *American Sociological Review*, **91**, 221–249.

Thoits, P. A. (1989). The sociology of emotions. *Annual Review of Sociology*, **15**, 317–342.

Thoits, P. A. (1990). Emotional deviance: Research agendas. In T. D. Kemper (Ed.), *Research Agendas in the Sociology of Emotions*. Albany: State University of New York Press, pp. 180–203.

Thomas, W. I. & Thomas, D. S. (1926). *The Child in America*. New York: Knopf.

Turner, R. H. (1976). The real self: From institution to impulse. *American Journal of Sociology*, **81**, 989–1016.

Ure, A. (1835/1967). *The Philosophy of Manufactures*. New York: Kelly.

US Congress. Senate Committee on Labor and Public Welfare (1972). *Worker Alienation*. Washington, DC: US Government Printing Office.

Weber, M. (1904–05/1958). *The Protestant Ethic and the Spirit of Capitalism*. Translated by T. Parsons. New York: Scribner's.

Weber, M. (1922/1968). *Economy and Society*. New York: Bedminster.

White, M. (1955). *The Age of Analysis*. New York: New American Library.

Wilson, E. O. (1975). *Sociobiology: The New Synthesis*. Cambridge, Mass: Harvard University Press.

Wittgenstein, L. (1981). *Zettel*, G. E. M. Anscombe & G. H. von Wright (Eds). Translated by G. E. M. Anscombe. Oxford: Blackwell.

Zajonc, R. B. (1965). Social facilitation. *Science*, **149**, 269–274.

Author Index

Phillips, A. G.   85, 91
Piaget, J.   104, 131, 132, 136, 304
Pike, K. L.   325
Pike, K. M.   235
Pinel, J. P. S.   79
Pittenger, J. B.   115
Platman, S. R.   55
Plutchik, R.   8, 51, 52, 53, 55, 60,
   146, 204, 269, 279, 304
Poeck, K.   91
Poincare, H.   277
Porch, B.   125
Poster, M.   305
Pott, C. B.   80
Potts, R.   231
Prange, A. J.   89

Rachman, S.   208
Randall, J. I.   67
Reardon, K.   132, 133
Redmond, D. E., Jr   80
Reis, D. J.   65, 111
Reisenzein, R.   328
Renfrew, J. W.   83
Reynalds, R.   275
Richards, R.   275
Rime, B.   196
Rincky, C. M.   233
Ritchie, J.   235
Roberts, V. J.   80, 91
Rodgers, R. J.   67
Rodman, P. S.   45
Romatowski, J. A.   233
Rompre, P. P.   84, 85
Ronning, R. R.   275
Rosaldo, M.   227, 269
Rosemann, I.   144, 150, 151, 156,
   310
Rosenman, R. H.   254, 255
Rosenthal, R.   122
Ross, S.   17, 29
Rossi, J., III   73, 84
Rossmann, B. B.   320, 342
Rotter, G. S.   234
Rotter, N. G.   234
Rusell, J. A.   52, 53, 146, 189, 296
Russell, B.   101, 106
Ryle, G.   189, 221, 272

Saarni, C.   234, 240
Sabatelli, R.   123

Sabini, J.   20
Sacks, D. S.   79, 80, 81, 91
Sadella, E. K.   45
Sagar, S. M.   87
Sahley, T. L.   73, 78
Sakabara, T.   253
Sakaguchi, A.   65, 111
Samuels, A.   45
Sandler, G.   80
Sandvik, E.   237
Sato, K.   149
Scaife, M.   40
Schachter, S.   101, 153, 260, 328,
   336
Schaefer, E. S.   55
Schaffer, M. A.   253
Scheff, J. J.   324, 332, 333, 334
Scheier, M. F.   256
Scheler, M.   213
Scherer, K. R.   6, 42, 144, 148, 149,
   152, 153, 154, 156, 158, 187, 191,
   195, 199
Schlosberg, H.   146
Schmavonian, B. M.   339
Schmitt, P.   80
Scholz, J.   19, 20
Schoner, G.   19, 20
Schottstaedt, W. W.   252
Schulman, G. A.   232
Schultz, S. C.   85
Schuster, M. M.   252
Schwartz, G. E.   257
Scott, J. P.   73, 78
Seeger, T. F.   68
Seeman, M.   305
Seligman, M.   150
Seyle, H.   251, 260
Shaffer, D. R.   211
Shand, A. F.   207, 214
Shannon, C. E.   127
Sharp, F. R.   87
Sharp, L. K.   259
Shaver, P.   189
Shaw, R. E.   115
Shekelle, R. B.   257
Shelton, S. E.   73
Shields, S. A.   232, 286
Shiller, V.   17, 18
Shimanoff, S. B.   238
Shott, S.   324, 328, 331, 332
Siegel, A.   80, 83
Silk, J. B.   45
Silverman, A. J.   111

Subject Index